"Lohfink always impresses with the detailed care with which he delves into significant biblical texts. This extensive probe into seventy major 'words' of Jesus in the synoptic gospels will keep the reader thinking but also praying for a good long time. These 'important words' as Lohfink reads them both inform and challenge our own discipleship. If we take up or renew our acceptance of Jesus' daily invitation, 'Come, follow me,' Lohfink spells out the consequences with a most satisfying blend of theological depth and spiritual wisdom."

— Genevieve Glen, OSB, author of
Sauntering through Scripture and *By Lamplight*

"Gerhard Lohfink has graced us with many books that have helped us to see the New Testament in a refreshingly new way. In *The Most Important Words of Jesus*, he explains seventy of Jesus's sayings that deal with his mission and its meaning for contemporary life. Those familiar with Lohfink's writings will not be disappointed. Those who have not read his works will be amazed. This is a sure resource for those who preach the gospel and for those who seek to be nourished by it."

— Frank J. Matera, Professor Emeritus,
The Catholic University of America

Gerhard Lohfink

The Most Important Words of Jesus

Translated by

Linda M. Maloney

LITURGICAL PRESS
Collegeville, Minnesota

www.litpress.org

Cover illustration by Br. Martin Erspamer, OSB, a monk of Saint Meinrad Archabbey, Indiana. Used with permission.

Scripture quotations are based on the author's German translation from the original Greek.

1 2 3 4 5 6 7 8 9

Library of Congress Cataloging-in-Publication Data

Names: Lohfink, Gerhard, 1934– author. | Maloney, Linda M., translator.
Title: The most important words of Jesus / Gerhard Lohfink ; translated by Linda M. Maloney.
Other titles: Wichtigsten Worte Jesu. English
Description: Collegeville, Minnesota : Liturgical Press Academic, [2023] | "Originally published as Die wichtigsten Worte Jesu by Gerhard Lohfink, 2022 Verlag Herder GmbH, Freiburg im Breisgau." | Includes bibliographical references and index. | Summary: "Based on the research of many biblical scholars, this is a book about Jesus' most important "sayings," or "logia." It explores the power and beauty as well as the seriousness of these central sayings of Jesus, helping readers understand what Jesus was really talking about in these "sharply-honed" words"— Provided by publisher.
Identifiers: LCCN 2022054412 (print) | LCCN 2022054413 (ebook) | ISBN 9780814668504 (hardcover) | ISBN 9780814668511 (epub) | ISBN 9780814668511 (pdf) | ISBN 9780814668528 (pdf)
Subjects: LCSH: Jesus Christ—Words.
Classification: LCC BT306 .L58513 2023 (print) | LCC BT306 (ebook) | DDC 232.9/54—dc23/eng/20230224
LC record available at https://lccn.loc.gov/2022054412
LC ebook record available at https://lccn.loc.gov/2022054413

When Christ died he did not leave documents but disciples.

That society is not Christian in which no one sins, but one in which many do penance.

The church is not here to accommodate Christianity to the world, not even to accommodate the world to Christianity; instead, its task is to preserve within the world a counter-world.

Nicolás Gómez Dávila

Sources: Nicolás Gómez Dávila, *Es genügt, dass die Schönheit unseren Überdruss streift . . . Aphorisms* (Stuttgart, 2010), 111; *Scholia to an Implicit Text* (Colombia, 2013).

Contents

Part Three: A Disciple's Existence

Part Four: Living in Light of the Reign of God

Part Five: Jesus' Exalted Claim

Part Six: Israel's Crisis

Part Seven: In View of Death

Preface

The parables of Jesus stand out boldly within the rich traditional material of the four Gospels. They were easy to retell. But besides the parables there are a large number of brief, succinct sayings that, thanks to their clear structure and pictorial character, were unforgettably implanted in the minds of Jesus' disciples.

In 2021 I published a book on *The Forty Parables of Jesus*.[1] As I was writing it I began to think that there really needed to be a book in similar format about Jesus' sayings. The word *logia* for the sayings of the Lord has long since found a home in the church's language. Biblical scholars later adopted this early church expression and made it a special term for brief, self-contained sayings of Jesus, even though in Greek a *logion* was originally an oracular saying, and Jesus did not utter oracles; he disclosed the true situation of the people of God, preached the presence of the reign of God, and gathered people for the eschatological Israel. Even so, the word *logion* (plural *logia*) has been with us for a long time and should be retained.

What follows, then, is a book about Jesus' most important "sayings" or *logia*. In this book, too, I gratefully refer to the researches of many biblical scholars. Technical terms will not be lacking, but they should not be in the foreground. My wish, above all else, is to place before my readers' eyes the power and beauty as well as the seriousness of central sayings of Jesus. Naturally I also want to open to them the truth of what Jesus was really talking about in these sharply honed words.

Gerhard Lohfink
February 2022

[1] Gerhard Lohfink, *The Forty Parables of Jesus*, trans. Linda M. Maloney (Collegeville, MN: Liturgical Press, 2021).

Opening Remarks

1. I spoke in the preface of Jesus' words, sayings, or *logia*. That was somewhat vague. In reality we encounter the Lord's words in very different forms. There are pithy one-liners such as:

> *The Son of Man is lord even of the sabbath.* (Mark 2:28)

Or there are two-liners with the following structure:

> *Why do you see the speck in your neighbor's eye, but do not notice the log in your own eye?* (Matt 7:3)

In this second case we can see right away from the double "eye" that the two lines have a parallel structure—and yet they are *antithetically* parallel, for first there is the eye of the fellow believer and then one's own eye, and first there is a speck and then a log. So what we have is a skillfully structured "antithetical parallelism." We will come across this stylistic figure again and again in Jesus' speech. Still, not all Jesus' sayings are one-liners or two-liners. There are also multi-liners such as:

> *When you are offering your gift at the altar, if you remember that your brother or sister has something against you, leave your gift there before the altar and go; first be reconciled to your brother or sister, and then come and offer your gift.* (Matt 5:23-24)

This multi-liner, however, is by no means just a row of sentences. It is artfully structured as a "concentric" series—and according to a scheme in which each line is governed by a central idea:

A[1] — your gift
B[1] — your brother or sister
C[1] — your gift
B[2] — your brother or sister
A[2] — your gift

In this way the middle item (C) is emphasized as the center of the whole figure. The result is a pointed statement: *Better to leave your sacrifice unoffered (than to sacrifice without being reconciled)*! This example shows that even in longer sayings Jesus had command of the technique of well-crafted language and he knew how to shape what he wanted to say in a variety of forms.

2. Obviously in this one book we cannot interpret every *logion* that might be considered an authentic word of the Lord. I was forced to make a selection. First I had a preliminary list of about 150 sayings that I then reduced to 70. You may well understand how hard it was for me to eliminate 80 sayings of the Lord, and yet the process made tangible something that I had been carrying around with me without knowing it: namely, how incomparably great is the number of words of the Lord that have been reliably handed down to us.

3. Because the first three Gospels have a great deal of traditional material in common, many words of the Lord have been handed on in several of them, and often in differing versions. In part those are variant traditions; in part they are the result of redaction by the authors of the Gospels. Obviously I have, in such cases, always chosen the evangelist who probably comes closest to the *original* form of the Jesus-saying in question.

However, it is not the purpose of this book to give a detailed reconstruction of the oldest form (*ipsissima forma*) of the Jesus-sayings dealt with here and then to use the reconstructions as a textual basis. A text marked with a vertical bar is normally a "canonical" text from the first three Gospels and not a reconstruction. I am not excluding the possibility, however, that in my interpretation I will again and again inquire about the original form and intention of the individual sayings.

4. There were certainly sayings of the Lord that were easy to understand all by themselves and therefore could be handed on without any introduction or context—for example, this antithetical parallelism:

> *It is easier for a camel to go through the eye of a needle than for someone who is rich to enter the heavenly reign.* (Matt 19:24)

But then throughout the Gospels there is a practice of combining a number of *logia* in a single context. Where it seemed reasonable I have addressed the current context of individual *logia*, but I have not hesitated to treat words of the Lord *in isolation* when they are now embedded in a narrative or constitute the conclusion to a narrative introduction that is constructed wholly with regard to that *logion*. In literary criticism an incisive word that is thus prepared for by means of a very succinct introduction is called an *apophthegm*. Since I will occasionally use that concept in what follows, here is an example from classical antiquity:

> *When a garrulous barber asked him, "How shall I cut your hair?" he said, "In silence."*[1]

5. At this point I need to refer to another scholarly term. Matthew and Luke often take up traditions they found in Mark's Gospel, but both of them also draw on a probably written source made up primarily of Jesus-*logia*. New Testament scholars refer to it as the "Sayings Source" and abbreviate it as "Q" (for German *Quelle* = "source"). In this book I will consistently use the term "Sayings Source." Unfortunately, the traditions contained in the Sayings Source can only be hypothetically deduced from the common material in Luke and Matthew—and then only when the tradition in question is missing from Mark, or when it appears in Luke and Matthew in a significantly different form from that in Mark. Biblical scholars even discuss whether there were different versions of the Sayings Source and whether Matthew and Luke had separate versions. When it seems necessary or reasonable I will indicate the background of a saying of the Lord in the Sayings Source.

6. When "*par*" or "//" appear in this book between two biblical passages they represent parallel traditions for a Jesus saying now found in Matthew and Luke (and perhaps also in Mark). For example: (Matt 5:3 *par* Luke 6:20) or (Matt 12:39 // Mark 8:12 // Luke 11:29).

7. A table on p. 339 shows the liturgical location of the Jesus-sayings discussed as they occur in the gospel readings for the Sundays of the church year.

Gerhard Lohfink

[1] For this text see Plutarch, *Regum et imperatorum apophthegmata* 177A. The anecdote is about the Macedonian King Archelaos I (413–399 BCE).

Abbreviations

BBET	Beiträge zur biblischen Exegese und Theologie
BDAG	Danker, Frederick W., Walter Bauer, William F. Arndt, and F. Wilbur Gingrich. *Greek-English Lexicon of the New Testament and Other Early Christian Literature*. 3rd ed. Chicago: University of Chicago Press, 2000.
Bib	*Biblica*
BTS	Biblisch-Theologische Studien
BZ	*Biblische Zeitschrift*
CwH	Calwer Hefte
EKK	Evangelisch-katholischer Kommentar
FAT	Forschungen zum Alten Testament
FB	Forschung zur Bibel
FS	*Festschrift*
GSTR	Gießener Schriften zur Theologie und Religionspädagogik des Fachbereichs Evangelische Theologie und Katholische Theologie und deren Didaktik der Justus-Liebig Universität.
HThKNT	Herders Theologischer Kommentar zum Neuen Testament
HTR	*Harvard Theological Review*
JSHRZ	Jüdische Schriften aus hellenistisch-römischer Zeit
KEK	Kritisch-exegetischer Kommentar über das Neue Testament (Meyer-Kommentar)
LTK	*Lexicon für Theologie und Kirche*
NTD	Das Neue Testament Deutsch
NTL	New Testament Library

NTS	*New Testament Studies*
ÖTK	Ökumenischer Taschenbuch-Kommentar
RNT	Regensburger Neues Testament
SBAB	Stuttgarter biblische Aufsatzbände
SBS	Stuttgarter Bibelstudien
SHAW.PH	Sitzungen der heidelberger Akademie der Wissenschaften. Philosophisch-Historische Klasse
SNTSU.A	*Studien zum Neuen Testament und seiner Umwelt/A*
TBei	*Theologische Beiträge*
TDNT	*Theological Dictionary of the New Testament*. Edited by Gerhard Kittel and Gerhard Friedrich. Translated by Geoffrey W. Bromiley. 10 vols. Grand Rapids: Eerdmans, 1964–.
TDOT	*Theological Dictionary of the Old Testament*. Edited by G. Johannes Botterweck, Helmer Ringgren, and Heinz-Josef Fabry. Translated by John W. Stott, Geoffrey W. Bromiley, David E. Green, and Douglas W. Stott. 17 vols. Grand Rapids: Eerdmans, 1977–2021.
TRE	*Theologische Realenzyklopädie*
TTZ	*Trierer theologische Zeitschrift*
UTB	Uni-Taschenbücher
WUNT	Wissenschaftliche Untersuchungen zum Neuen Testament
ZAW	*Zeitschrift für die alttestamentliche Wissenschaft*
ZNW	*Zeitschrift für die neutestamentliche Wissenschaft und die Kunde der* älteren *Kirche*

Part One

The Coming of the Reign of God

The first part of this book is about the *Event*, the *Coming* (*Ereignis*)—we might say the *Happening*—of the reign of God. The word is deliberately chosen. By no means is this only about the *idea* of the reign of God. When Jesus not only preaches the reign of God but announces it—when he calls his disciples blessed because they see what prophets and kings have desired to see and have not seen—when he announces to the poor the overturning of all existing conditions—when he speaks of the new wine that cannot be poured into old wineskins—in short, when everything that will be spoken of in this first section comes to pass, that is an *Event*, a *Happening* that cannot be comprehended in a simple definition or in a word.

Even so, we have to talk about the *idea* of the reign of God. This once, by way of exception, I will permit myself a few word-statistics because even a dry statistical summary can make clear, in its own way, what happened when Jesus appeared in Israel. So here I will offer a table of the usage of the concept "reign/kingdom of God" (or "kingdom of heaven") in the individual New Testament books:

Matt	37	Eph	1	Heb	–
Mark	14	Phil	–	James	–
Luke	32	Col	1	1 Pet	–
John	2	1 Thess	–	2 Pet	–
Acts	6	2 Thess	1	1 John	–
Romans	1	1 Tim	–	2 John	–
1 Cor	4	2 Tim	–	3 John	–
2 Cor	–	Titus	–	Jude	–
Gal	1	Phlm	–	Rev	1

The table shows that in the New Testament letters the idea of the reign of God clearly withdraws into the background. It occurs only occasionally in the Pauline letters and is almost completely absent from the remaining body of letters. Something similar is true for the Gospel of John and, incidentally, for the "Apostolic Fathers." The only exception among the latter is the *Shepherd of Hermas* (written in Rome, ca. 150 CE)—and that is because the document makes several uses of the phrase "enter into the reign of God." For the early literature of Judaism the case is the same; the idea of the "reign of God" is familiar, and it appears especially in prayers, but in comparison to its occurrence in the first three Gospels it is relatively rare.

In contrast, we have to say that there is a positive *eruption* of the idea in the Synoptic Gospels. Obviously we could further refine the above statistics by striking all the occurrences in the first three Gospels that can be traced to the Evangelists' redaction, but that would make no essential difference. Even then the statistics would show that the idea of the reign of God was simply central to Jesus' preaching—but not only as an *idea*. The focus, rather, was on the *fact*, and it will constantly occupy our attention in this book.

Some New Testament scholars, especially Hans Conzelmann in his *Theology of the New Testament*, thought that for Jesus the preaching of the coming of the reign of God on the one hand and the teaching about God and ethics on the other stood alongside one another but were relatively unconnected.[1] Thus, for example, the command to love one's neighbor was not eschatologically based but came from the theology of creation. A closer analysis of Jesus' words, however, leads us to contradict Conzelmann's basic supposition. In this book we will repeatedly come across the reign of God—including in the teaching about God and in Jesus' ethics. The coming of the reign of God shaped all of Jesus' thoughts and actions. In essence it is already questionable to talk about a "doctrine of God" and an "ethics" in Jesus' teaching. Such conceptual distinctions make sense in theological tractates, but they are unsuited to any analysis of Jesus' proclamation.

[1] Hans Conzelmann, *An Outline of the Theology of the New Testament*, trans. John Bowden, NTL (London: SCM, 1969), 100–125.

1. The Proclamation of the Reign of God (Mark 1:15)

It would be worthwhile, for once, to ask each of the four Gospels separately what are the first words that Jesus speaks "directly," in the first person. In Mark they are found in two extraordinarily compact theological statements:

> The time is fulfilled, and the reign of God has come near. [Therefore:] repent, and believe in [this] gospel! (Mark 1:15)

Are those two sentences nothing but a later summarizing of Jesus' preaching by the author of the Gospel of Mark?—a kind of recapitulation? Many commentators think so. Rudolf Bultmann went even farther: in his *History of the Synoptic Tradition* he asserted that what we find here is "a quite secondary formulation made under the influence of a specifically Christian terminology," and thus "a summary of the Christian message of salvation." As far as "specifically Christian terminology" is concerned, he points to the expression "believe in the gospel."[2]

Was Bultmann right? Obviously "belief," "gospel," and "repentance" were essential elements of early Christian preaching, but that tells us nothing: "the reign of God has come near" was by no means central to the earliest Christian proclamation of the gospel. That spoke of Jesus Christ and—as we have just seen—scarcely mentioned the reign of God any longer. When Paul speaks of the "gospel of God" he does not mean the good news of the reign of God but the gospel of the death and resurrection of Jesus Christ (cf. Rom 1:1-4; 1 Cor 15:1-5).

In the same way, within the New Testament the concept of repentance/renewal never appears in immediate connection with the idea of the reign of God except in the Synoptic Gospels, and the expression "believe in the gospel" does not occur in that wording anywhere except in Mark 1:15 and nowhere else in the New Testament.[3] Here

[2] Rudolf Bultmann, *The History of the Synoptic Tradition*, trans. John Marsh (New York: Harper & Row, 1963), 118, 127.

[3] There is only an *indirect reflection* of the formula "believe in the gospel" in Mark 16:15-16; Acts 8:12; 15:7; Rom 1:16; 10:16; 2 Thess 1:8, but there is a partial reflection of Mark 1:15 (or the tradition behind it) in those passages. This is obvious especially

again, then, we are by no means looking at a "formula" of early Christian preaching. Consequently Mark 1:15 can scarcely be a subsequent insertion of Christian preaching language into that of Jesus. The movement is in the opposite direction. Jesus' genuine speech influenced the later language of preaching. Therefore Mark 1:15 may very well go back to Jesus himself.

There is also a much weightier reason to say this: we know from Mark 6:7-13 and Matthew 10:5-15 that at some point Jesus sent out twelve of his disciples to various locales in Galilee (or throughout Israel?). In their number (twelve) he made them a living symbol of his true goal: gathering the people of the Twelve Tribes as the eschatological community of God, in light of the approaching reign of God. The Twelve were the symbolic center as well as the instrument of this gathering movement. They were to proclaim the reign of God in the villages and small towns (Matt 10:7; Luke 10:9, 11). To put it another way: they were to "announce" it. Therefore it was necessary to speak of the reign of God in the *form* of an announcement as well.

But how could the disciples formulate that announcement? A proclamation of things about to happen immediately must be made up of brief, compact sentences—that is, it must have a form such as a herald needs in order to be able to convey it in a loud voice. Jesus could not simply leave it to his disciples to formulate such statements. They had to be true. They had to be accurate. They had to be simple and yet bold, striking, and also easy to remember. But that is precisely the case with Mark 1:15. Jesus himself shaped such sentences; he himself used them, and the Twelve memorized them.[4] Therefore Mark 1:15 could—at least in its basics—represent the wording of the proclamation Jesus entrusted to the Twelve. In that case our text would have a clear *Sitz im Leben* (location in place and time)—namely, the public appearance of disciples sent out by Jesus. The brief statements

---

in Luke (and, in dependence on Luke, in the canonical ending of Mark): Luke—countering the theology of Gnosis—wants to show that the earthly Jesus' proclamation of the reign of God continued after Easter in direct succession to Jesus' preaching.

[4] So also Martin Hengel and Anna Maria Schwemer, *Jesus and Judaism*, trans. Wayne Coppins (Waco, TX: Baylor University Press, 2019), 375: "The message of the inbreaking of the reign of God that is proclaimed by those sent out is nothing other than Jesus' message. In our opinion their very sending presumes the first shaping—indeed, so that they could convey *his* message through a memorization—of core parts of Jesus' preaching."

with their verbs placed first for emphasis fit that scenario, as does their content. What, then, is the substance of this proclamation? What does it say?

First of all, it says that the time has been fulfilled. "Time" (*kairos*) here means the appropriate time in the history between God and God's people. What Israel had awaited, longed for, prayed for, and hoped for over the centuries, what had been affirmed and promised for them—*that* is now coming to pass. Time has reached its goal. It is "fulfilled," and therefore the turning point has arrived. The time of fulfillment, the end time, is now present.

The proclamation speaks of what is about to come as the "reign of God." The Greek is *basileia tou theou*. The word *basileia* can be translated "kingship," "royal rule," "kingdom," or simply "rule" or "sovereignty" or "realm." But for Jesus *basileia* originally meant a dynamic event; only secondarily is it a realm or "kingdom." Therefore in interpreting the texts in this book I will speak much more frequently about the "reign of God" than the "realm" or "kingdom" of God.

Matthew mainly uses the expression "realm/kingdom of heaven" rather than "realm/kingdom of God." It means the same thing; "heaven" is just a reverent substitution for "God." But because even today Matthew's "kingdom of heaven" has the fatal consequence that Christians constantly equate the "kingdom of heaven" with "heaven," thus suppressing the *present aspect* of Jesus' message about the reign of God, in speaking of Matthean texts I will always use the phrase "heavenly reign."

I will also avoid the translations "kingship" or "kingdom." Nowadays we are rather dubious about kings and their rule. Often kings are only puppets or symbolic figures; the real power of the state lies in other hands. Or they are autocrats who pretend to be benefactors but really are exploiters of their people (cf. Luke 22:25).

Ancient Israel already had the same reservations. When it came to be (during the so-called period of the "judges," ca. 1200–1020 BCE) the people wanted nothing to do with a "state" of Israel—and therefore with a king. They detested such things as the divine kingship of the Egyptian pharaohs and likewise the systems of control exercised by the city-kings of Canaan. The desire was to establish a free confederation of tribes, deliberately differentiated from those kinds of governing structures, an association in which freedom, equality, and sisterhood/brotherhood ruled. On the whole the people of God had bad experiences of the kingdom that eventually came into being out of necessity (cf. 1 Sam 8).

Nevertheless, the period of the kings that was so brutally ended by the expansionist politics of Assyria and Babylon left one thing in its wake: a longing for an ideal royal rule in which, thanks to the charism of a true king, justice, freedom, and peace might bloom at last. Psalm 72 paints that longing in shining colors.

Even so, Israel knew that achieving such a rule, one under which society would be transformed and creation itself would be renewed, is beyond human ability. Therefore they hoped either for the true king given by God (namely, the "Anointed One," the Messiah) or else the royal rule of God.

In the time of Jesus the "kingship of God" or "reign of God" was a long-established idea. In Psalm 145 the pious are called upon to proclaim this royal reign of God without ceasing. In the middle of the Psalm we read:

> *They shall speak of the glory of your kingdom,*
> *and tell of your power,*
> *to make known to all people your mighty deeds*
> *and the glorious splendor of your kingdom.* (Ps 145:11-12)

Thus Jesus could presuppose the idea of God's *basileia*; he did not introduce it. Still, the following is important to note: in the Old Testament and in early Judaism people did not talk only about the "eternal" reign of God that has always sustained and governed the world. The more oppressive Israel's political situation became, the more people longed for a mighty revelation of that reign in the world. In that sense the reign of God was still something in the future.

Precisely here we can see what is so overpoweringly new about the proclamation that came through Jesus, for which he also sent out his disciples: this very reign of God is now entering into history. It has "come near." It is close at hand. It will transform Israel and, through Israel, the whole world.

Later on we will observe, as we examine other sayings of Jesus, that his speaking of the "nearness" of the reign of God conceals an elementary tension. On the one hand the reign of God is not yet present. It must be implored. Jesus tells his disciples to pray "your kingdom come!" (Matt 6:10 // Luke 11:2). On the other hand God's reign is already a present reality. It can be seen, heard, grasped—

namely, by looking at Jesus, at what he says and does. Many of the sayings of Jesus I will discuss in this book will again and again bring that reality before our eyes. In Mark 1:15 this tension between present and imminent future is expressed in the phrase "is at hand."

The first part of this proclamation thus speaks about an event that changes everything. The turn of the ages is here. The reign of God that Israel longs for is happening now and from now on. God bestows on the world *God's kind* of "sovereignty": justice, peace, salvation, restoration of creation—and all of it in incomprehensible fullness. That is the first statement; it is the message. But this awesome reality demands consequences, marked stylistically by the imperative that is asyndetically linked to the statements: "repent and believe in this gospel!" In light of God's forthcoming action, the people of God cannot go on living as before.

Jesus takes the call to repentance from Israel's prophets (Isa 31:6; Jer 3:14; Ezek 18:32; Zech 1:4, etc.) and above all from the last great prophet, John the Baptizer (Matt 3:8 // Luke 3:8; Mark 1:4). But, differently from the Baptizer's proclamation, the reason for repentance is no longer the imminent judgment; instead it is something profoundly joyful and exhilarating: the reign of God.

The proclamation describes the nearness of the reign of God as "good news," more precisely "gospel." Where does that idea come from? It was common enough in the Greek world, and it appears also in the Old Testament (2 Kgs 18:22, 25 LXX). Among other things it described the news of victory brought by a messenger. The idea played a particular role in the Roman imperial cult: news about the emperor, especially the inauguration of his rule, was called gospel (= joyful news). Still, the New Testament concept of "gospel" has a particular, even unique echo that comes from an entirely different direction. Its background lies in Isaiah 52:7 (cf. Isa 61:1):

> *How lovely upon the mountains are the steps of the messenger who announces peace, who brings good news, who announces salvation, who says to Zion, "Your God reigns."*

This text from Isaiah is fundamental to an understanding of Mark 1:15 because it combines immediately prior stages of the two concepts "reign of God" and "gospel." The meaning is: now the definitive royal rule of God is revealed in that Israel is being rescued from its forsakenness and drawn into salvation. Evidently Jesus saw himself as the messenger of joy described in this text. Jesus proclaims the peace and salvation it portrays. He preaches: the time Isaiah spoke about is now at hand. God is accomplishing that saving rule in the world. This is the "good news," the "gospel." Jesus himself established this specific echo of the word "gospel" on the basis of Isaiah 52:7—and that is the only reason why the word could play such a prominent role later, in the earliest Christian preaching.

So the gospel demands repentance, but still more: it requires faith. Here the Old Testament idea of faith lies in the background (cf., e.g., Gen 15:6 or Exod 14:31). In the Old Testament "faith" or "belief" does not refer to *general truths of faith* but to God's concrete *promises* or divine *action in history*. Thus the reign of God is not simply present and observable, like the weather or any other kind of event. The reign of God must be *believed*—because it comes precisely inasmuch as it is believed. And it demands repentance because it intends to change the world.

Certainly what is so fascinating about all that is that this repentance is not a moral requirement, some action that is simply demanded of human beings. Rather, repentance ("turning back") is already anticipated by God's liberating action. Repentance and faith are a *response* to what precedes them: human beings may see the joy of the reign of God, experience it directly, taste it—and therefore faith and repentance are not just debt but desire. There is no contradiction in saying that the reign of God is experienced as joy and yet must be believed: *faith* and *experience* are inextricably bound up together.

It may be that we can start to sense all that is contained in these two statements of Jesus' fundamental proclamation. Jesus composes it powerfully and compactly in two lines. What joy it would have been to be present when the Twelve, as Jesus' co-workers—sent out two by two (Mark 6:7)—shouted those two statements in the marketplaces, or when Jesus himself spoke them to his audiences, perhaps as the beginning or the end and summary of a longer discourse!

But we can be present, after all. We hear these statements in the Liturgy of the Word as "gospel." They are still being proclaimed. Every Sunday. In our midst.

2. The Least Is Greater Than the Greatest (Luke 7:28)

In Luke 7:24-27 *par* Matthew 11:7-10 we find a short speech in which Jesus praises John the Baptizer before assemblies of the people—but no, Jesus not only praises him. He bears witness to him and thus sets him above everything a prophet in Israel could be. This speech, which Luke and Matthew took from the Sayings Source (Q), is artistically shaped and contains some ironic undertones that we must not overlook when Jesus is speaking, because they are characteristic of a good many Jesus-sayings.

> *"What did you go out into the wilderness to look at? A reed shaken by the wind? What then did you go out to see? Someone dressed in soft robes? Look, those who put on fine clothing and live in luxury are in royal palaces. What then did you go out to see? A prophet? Yes, I tell you, and more than a prophet. This is the one about whom it is written,*[5] *"See, I am sending my messenger ahead of you, who will prepare your way before you."* (Luke 7:24-27)

Reeds that grew along the lower course of the Jordan river could reach a height of fifteen feet or more. Immediately beyond the girdle of reeds was barren land. It was in such a region, more or less directly east of Jericho, that John baptized. We might paraphrase the first rhetorical question as: "you certainly didn't go to the Jordan just to see reeds." That would take the word "reeds" literally.

But there is another possibility. We could also understand "reeds" metaphorically. In that case Jesus would be alluding to the local ruler, Herod Antipas. In Jesus' day he had begun building the city of Tiberias on the western bank of Lake Gennesaret. Around the year 20 CE he had coins minted in honor of the founding of his new capital city, with a reed on the face.[6] In antiquity a reed symbolized a city on a river or a large lake. There was another good reason why Herod chose a plant motif rather than his own head: images of people or animals were forbidden in Israel. So the reed replaced an image of Herod, but Jesus could have given that reed on Herod's coins another meaning, an ironic one.[7] He could have made the reed symbolize the dodgy and slippery character of Herod the tetrarch: "You probably didn't

[5] Behind this text lies a whole fabric of Scripture citations: especially Mal 3:1 (+ Exod 23:20). Before the final judgment a messenger of God will appear. In Mal 3:23-24 that messenger is interpreted as the returning prophet Elijah.

[6] For Herod Antipas's coinage, especially the coins he had minted to mark the foundation of Tiberias, cf. Marius Reiser, "Numismatik und Neues Testament," *Bib* 81 (2000): 457–88, at 469–70.

[7] The following hypothesis comes from Gerd Theissen, *The Gospels in Context: Social and Political History in the Synoptic Tradition*, trans. Linda M. Maloney (Minneapolis: Fortress Press, 1998), 26–42.

go out to the desert for the sake of this minor ruler who himself is a shaky reed."

Jesus' second rhetorical question shows that this interpretation of the reed motif could be accurate. Suddenly he is talking about people wearing luxurious clothes. There were such people in the desert as well, since the powerful people among the Jews liked to build fortresses containing richly adorned palaces in remote places. Think only of the fortress of Machaerus on the eastern side of the Dead Sea.

But even if Jesus was not making ironic allusion to Herod Antipas here, he was most certainly saying that a bendable reed and soft garments contrast sharply with the Baptizer, who wore a garment of scratchy camel's hair (Mark 1:6) and showed himself to be anything but a wavering reed—for example, when he publicly criticized Herod Antipas for his marriage to Herodias, the wife of his half-brother Simon Boethus, a marriage forbidden by Torah (Mark 6:17-18). That unbending firmness cost him his life (Mark 6:27).

But in this passage all that is only preparation for the third question, the real one: "You didn't go out to see a reed, or courtiers in expensive garments—did you perhaps think to see a prophet?"

The people who were drawn to the Jordan did, in fact, want to see a prophet. But Jesus says that what they had seen was "far more than a prophet!" For the Jewish mind he is not only elevating the Baptizer to a high place but to an absolutely exceptional position—and precisely that prepares us for the climax of the whole composition, namely, the Jesus-saying that is our focus here:

> I tell you, among those born of women no one is greater than John, yet the least in the reign of God is greater than he. (Luke 7:28)

This incisive two-liner constitutes the effective finale of our text passage and consequently could have been part of it from the beginning—or it could have been handed down separately. It is coherent in itself and is strictly defined. We have already seen that Jesus very often summarized his preaching in sentences or clauses that are *antithetically* related. Here, in this saying, the "greater" in the first line are contrasted with the "least" in the second, and that contrast serves to reveal a paradox: "even the least in the reign of God is greater than the Baptizer, who stands above all." Sharp contrasts and paradoxical formulations of the sort are typical of Jesus' language.

But what does this Jesus-word really intend to say? It must have been spoken in a situation in which Jesus was talking about the Baptizer. Such situations are easy to imagine, because John the Baptizer was a figure in Israel who unsettled people. Everyone was talking about him and trying to evaluate him. Jesus, too, must have been asked about his opinion of the Baptizer. That is the starting point.

Evidently Jesus took advantage of such an opening to say something fundamental about the reign of God. The Baptizer was already close to it. He was the one who paved the way for it and he stood on its threshold. That was his greatness and the thing that made him different from all the prophets before him. Thus Jesus, by first pointing to the greatness of the Baptizer, can shed light on the radical newness of the reign of God. Everything that has gone before, even the figure of the Baptizer, remains far behind what is happening now.

It would not make sense to question this Jesus-saying analogously to Matthew 18:1 by asking who, then, is "the least in the heavenly reign," to inquire about whether there were "lesser" and "greater" and even "the greatest" in it. That would miss the rhetoric of the contrast. Likewise, the question of what share the Baptizer himself has in the reign of God is completely irrelevant here. This Jesus-saying is solely about the sharp distinction between the reign of God and everything that preceded it.

It is equally improper to read the "reign of God" here as representing the *church*. The reign of God that Jesus proclaims is not simply equivalent to the church. Likewise, here Jesus is not talking about the *perfected form* of the reign of God to which many will "come from east and west and recline at table with Abraham, Isaac, and Jacob in the heavenly reign" (Matt 8:11). No, this word of Jesus is about the reign of God that is now being proclaimed in Israel, that is already coming, that distinguishes itself by its newness and because of whose fascination people are letting themselves be gathered around Jesus to form the eschatological Israel, the anticipation and narthex of the reign of God. This saying is about the greatness and glory of the reign of God that puts everything else in the shade.

3. Blessed Are Those Who See What You See (Luke 10:23-24)

Jesus' words about the Baptizer already indicated how the reign of God surpasses everything that has gone before and puts it in the shade. Luke 20:23-24 // Matthew 13:16-17 (from the Sayings Source) takes up the same theme, but here Jesus does not compare the new thing with the figure of the Baptizer. Instead, he speaks of the longing of the prophets and kings of Israel, and yet another aspect enters the picture: the reign of God is not only coming, not only pressing in on us—it is already present.

> Blessed are the eyes that see what you see!
> For I tell you:
> Many prophets and kings desired to see what you see
> but did not see it,
> and to hear what you hear but did not hear it.

Looking at this saying, we can see right away how carefully it is structured. But the people around Jesus did not read it; they heard it. Sayings that people hear have to be all the more carefully structured or else they will not be quickly understood. Above all: the listeners will not be able to remember them easily. A significant number of the hearers in those days could not read at all, but they were all the more alert to the structures of language, much more than we are. They listened more closely and grasped series, parallelisms, antitheses, alliterations, rhythms, and metric structures far faster than we can.

Our saying begins with a beatitude: "Happy, blessed are the eyes that see what you see!" Thus it is not simply: "blessed are all who see what you see!" Instead, it is the *eyes* of those who see that are called blessed. We immediately recall the compliment a woman from a crowd offered Jesus:

> *Blessed the womb that bore you and the breasts that nursed you!* (Luke 11:27)

In speaking of Jesus' mother she is calling Jesus blessed as well—and the mother herself is blessed when her womb is blessed. The situation here is similar: *eyes* are called blessed, but they represent the whole person. Such stylistic means were popular in antiquity, and especially in the ancient Near East. Jesus himself uses them repeatedly.

The blessing of the eyes that see is linked to a sharp contrast: here Jesus' current hearers—there the prophets and kings of Israel. The one group sees; the other group *wanted* to see, but they neither saw nor heard.

In Matthew's version of our saying we read not "wanted to see" but "longed to see" (Matt 13:17). That is still sharper, and Jesus could have said it that way. It was the fervent desire of the prophets that they themselves might behold the salvation they were authorized to proclaim in God's name, but it was not permitted them. Likewise, the good kings in Israel—such as King Josiah (2 Kgs 22–23)—deeply desired to establish in Israel a just society under the rule of the one, only God. They worked for it with all their strength. They did not achieve it. It was not given them.

Jesus formulates all that in an antithetical parallelism: some see; others are not allowed to see. He pairs "seeing" and "hearing." The ear and the eye are among the most important human sense organs, and even in the Old Testament they were often associated (Ps 94:9; Isa 6:9; Jer 5:21, etc.).

Still, we should note that in the context of Jewish expectation of the future time of salvation the texts speak mainly of "seeing." Thus in the Psalms of Solomon (a Jewish collection of psalms from the second half of the first century BCE) those are called blessed who at some time in the future, under the saving rule of the "Anointed One," the Messiah, will be permitted to "see" the wonders of the messianic age:

> *Blessed shall they be that shall live in those days,*
> *and shall see the goodness of the Lord*
> *which He shall perform for the generation that is to come,*
> *under the rod of chastening of the Lord's anointed.* (PsSol 18:6-7; cf. 17:44)

Certainly the question arises: why, in such texts from early Judaism, are the benefits of salvation *seen*? Today we would speak of "experiencing" them. In this context "seeing" is evidently biblical language that rests on a formula in the book of Deuteronomy, which says frequently that the spoiled, constantly grumbling Exodus generation will "not see" the land promised to their ancestors (Deut 1:35). Only Caleb and his descendants will "see" it, that is, live in it (Deut 1:36). Moses begs God to be allowed to "see" it in that sense (Deut 3:25), but God does not permit him to do so. He is only allowed to *look over* the promised land from a distant peak (Deut 3:27; 32:52; 34:4). Of course, the "land" here represents the promises of salvation, and to "see" them means to live in and taste those things. Thus the case of Moses makes clear the ways in which one can play with that word.

So Jesus is referring to biblical language here. For him the future time of salvation is already present, has dawned, is "seen." But for him "hearing" the time of salvation goes with "seeing" it. The reign of God is not only present in his healings of the sick but also in his words, for mere "seeing" has to be interpreted. In itself it is ambiguous; the interpretation, and thus the real making-present, happens in the word. Fundamentally, the necessity not only to see but also to hear points to the hiddenness of the reign of God. It is not simply there. It has to be believed and grasped.

Thus we finally arrive at the question: to whom is Jesus really addressing this beatitude? The people, or his disciples? In itself it could be spoken to a crowd that is listening to Jesus; they could be called blessed on account of what they are now experiencing. But in both Matthew (13:10) and Luke the saying is clearly directed at the disciples. Luke even emphasizes that Jesus spoke these words "privately" to his disciples (10:23), and that evidently is correct as far as the original *Sitz im Leben* is concerned. Why?

This is not just about seeing and hearing in the purely physical sense. Concretely: one could directly experience one of Jesus' healing miracles and still be against him. This is evident from the healing of the lame man in Mark 2:1-12. In Luke 10:24 the terminology shifts from "beholding" to "seeing." This signals that it is about perceiving in a deeper sense: not only seeing the outside of the new thing but *grasping* it and *understanding* it. It is about "eyes that see" and "ears that hear."

It is about the disciples' perception at depth. What do they see? Jesus' healings. And what do they hear? The gospel that Jesus preaches. Whoever has eyes to see and ears to hear can recognize in both those things the unheard-of event that is now taking place.

All that is contained in this saying—but there is still more. Jesus not only speaks in general terms of the fulfillment of all longings and all promises. He is also speaking here about himself, for it is *he* who proclaims the Good News, and it is *he* who heals the sick. But he does not say that directly; he uses veiled language. The self-statement about Jesus that is *hidden* in the text can best be recognized if we imagine how Jesus could have spoken, but did not. He does not say:

Blessed are the eyes that see me!
For I tell you:

Many prophets and kings desired to see me but did not,
and to hear me but did not.

In the language used by the Gospel of John, Jesus can and must speak with that kind of directness because there it is a question of putting his mission and ministry into words theologically. That takes place on a level of theological interpretation. The historical Jesus did not talk that way; he spoke indirectly. He says: "Blessed are the eyes that see what you see!" That is in itself unheard-of, and it is adequately interpreted in the "I speeches" of the Fourth Gospel. But Jesus himself, the one who walked the roads of Galilee with dusty feet, only pointed to it. He speaks—although only when it is about his secret, his mystery—in veiled, self-concealing language.

We will often come across this "implicit Christology" hidden in Jesus' words (and in his actions). Jesus does not put himself on display and say: "Look here: it is I." He does not shove his way forward. He does not polish his "profile." It is precisely this self-deprecation that is typical of him; it can even serve as a criterion for the genuineness of a Jesus-saying.

Does this beatitude apply to us? May we see things that, apart from Jesus, cannot be seen or heard?—that are not even perceived by those who do not believe in him? I think we may. We have the great joy of being able to recognize the truth: truth about people, about ourselves, about the world and its future. And we have a share in the salvation already given: being able to live in peace with God, to be "the Body of Christ," to sense the bliss of the Holy Spirit. However, the experience of salvation and redemption must *not* be restricted to knowing truths or to inner experience. *Redemption must be visible*: in ourselves, in the shaping of our environment, in the way we speak with one another and live with one another. Jesus, at any rate, stood fast on this fundamental principle of Judaism.

4. The Miracles of the Time of Salvation (Luke 7:22-23)

Luke 7:18-23 *par* Matthew 11:2-6 (derived from the Sayings Source) tells of how John the Baptizer sent messengers to Jesus with the question: "Are you the 'one who is to come,' or are we to wait for another?" Jesus sends the messengers back with this answer:

> Go and tell John
> what you have seen and heard:
> The blind receive their sight,
> the lame walk,
> the lepers are cleansed,
> the deaf hear, the dead are raised,
> the poor have good news brought to them
> and blessed is the one who takes no offense at me. (Luke 7:22-23)

Are you the Coming One? Many New Testament scholars have queried whether the Baptizer could possibly have asked such a question, for the "Coming One" he had announced is to baptize no longer with water, as he himself does, but *with storm and fire.*

In the Gospels this proclamation by the Baptizer has become a baptism "with the Holy Spirit" (Mark 1:8) or "with the Holy Spirit and fire" (Matt 3:11 // Luke 3:16), but that is already post-Easter language, in which the Baptizer's preaching is supposed to point already to Christ and be entirely about him. What John originally preached is hard to reconstruct: the Greek word *pneuma* and its Semitic equivalents mean not only "spirit" but also "storm" or "wind." If we leave out "Holy," the Baptizer quite obviously spoke about a Coming One who is to baptize Israel "with storm and with fire," in other words, "with a firestorm."

Those who had to experience the burning of whole inner cities in the night bombings of the Second World War know from experience what a firestorm is. The enormous heat, as it rose, sucked air from all sides into the center of the gigantic fire. The draft and the corresponding storm could be so strong that they tore people off their feet. The same is true of major forest fires.

It is precisely this phenomenon that underlies the Baptizer's metaphorical language: immediately after him there will come One who will baptize Israel no longer gently and protectively in water, as he does, but in a firestorm—as a fiery judge who knows mercy no longer but will extirpate all sinfulness in the people of God (Matt 3:10 // Luke 3:9) or burn it like chaff (Matt 3:12 // Luke 3:17). Once we are clear about these metaphorical connections we may, of course, ask whether the Baptizer could conceivably connect the merciful, healing Jesus even remotely with the terrifying figure of his fiery judge. That is: could he even ask, "are you the dreadful judge I have proclaimed?"

So the questions of critical exegetes about whether one may really connect Jesus' words describing rescue and liberation ("the blind see, the lame walk . . .") with the Baptizer's question are justified. On the other hand, we know much too little about the fiery judge to whom the Baptizer referred. For example, there is dispute over whether he was thinking of *God* as the judge thus pictured or of one *sent by God*. We also know far too little about the real relationship between the Baptizer and Jesus to be able to declare the former's question historically impossible.

Therefore we should not separate the formally coherent speech of Jesus, pointing to the signs of salvation that are now evident, from the Baptizer's inquiry. John's question about Jesus' real identity is certainly possible historically. Who can exclude the possibility that the Baptizer or his disciples were profoundly disturbed by Jesus' arrival—especially since the Baptizer has announced the *Coming One* as now *arriving*: the fiery judge has already laid the axe to the trees of Israel's planting (Matt 3:10 // Luke 3:9). That is: he is already estimating where he will strike. Also, he is standing on the threshing floor and has the shovel in his hand so that he can separate the grain from the chaff (Matt 3:12 // Luke 3:17). The chaff blows away in the wind and the straw will be burned. That Jesus—metaphorically—does not work with axe and fire but instead promises salvation and is already bringing it about: that was the profound uncertainty that may have lain behind the Baptizer's question.

Most certainly, we cannot deny that Jesus pronounced the significant reference to what is now to be seen and heard. There are a number of reasons to trust the authenticity of this more and more weighty six-part series leading to the conclusion.

First: the individual lines in this series, with its concluding beatitude, are as brief as they possibly can be. They are baldly stated and yet rhythmic in shape—and for that very reason they are impressive. We find other such succinct series in Jesus' speech elsewhere (cf., e.g., Matt 10:8).

Moreover: in these six lines Jesus refers back to the book of Isaiah. For the blind, see Isaiah 29:18; for the lame, Isaiah 35:6; for the deaf, Isaiah 35:5; for the dead, Isaiah 26:19; for the poor, Isaiah 61.1. But Jesus does not just list five passages from Isaiah. What we have before us is not merely a stilted collection of citations. Jesus uses the book of Isaiah very freely, and precisely that sovereign use of biblical texts is characteristic of him. The texts to which he alludes all, without exception, speak of a coming time of salvation that will fundamentally change everything. When Jesus brings the keywords in Isaiah into play for all the downtrodden in the people of God he is saying: This time of salvation has come. It is already beginning.

In his *New Testament Theology*, Joachim Jeremias rightly pointed out that in Israel at that time the lame, blind, lepers, and childless were as good as dead.[8] They were thought to be living already in the realm of the underworld, that is, in the place of death. But if now the blind, deaf, lame, and lepers are made whole, then everything has changed. Then the revolutionary New Thing that Jesus promises in many other sayings also—it is already beginning.

Also in this connection we should note that the sixth part of the series speaks not of Jesus' miracles but of his proclamation. Here again, as we already saw, the book of Isaiah (namely, Isa 61:1) is in the background. It may not be unimportant that this last member before the concluding beatitude points to Jesus' *preaching*. Does Jesus want to emphasize here that what is crucial is not the external appearance of the miracles but the "word" that interprets what is thrilling about the miracles and reveals their true meaning?

Yet another observation speaks in favor of the historical genuineness of our text: Jesus does not directly answer the Baptizer's question. He says neither "Yes, I am the one who is to come, the one you have preached," nor "I am the Messiah," nor "I am the Son of Man (the Human One)." Instead, he says: "Listen to what people tell you about what is happening now in Israel, what is to be seen and heard at this hour. Take note of that, and evaluate it. That must be enough for you."

This indirect, measured language that calls others to a free decision and therefore does not coerce is characteristic of Jesus—at any rate, whenever it is about himself. Certainly, if we listen more closely, this brief series of statements betrays an incomprehensible awareness of sovereignty. This culminates in the conclusion of the series: "blessed is anyone who takes no offense at me." Immediately before this, as we saw, there was reference to Isaiah 61:1, where the text says:

[8] Joachim Jeremias, *New Testament Theology: The Proclamation of Jesus*, trans. John Bowden (New York: Scribner, 1971), 104.

> *The spirit of the Lord* G*OD* *is upon me,*
> *because the* L*ORD* *has anointed me;*
> *he has sent me to bring good news to the oppressed,*
> *to bind up the brokenhearted. . . .*

Among the writings found at Qumran, 4Q 521 has become especially important. In this text, written between 100 and 80 BCE, Isaiah 61:1 is applied to the Messiah because of the word "anointed." Thus at that time it was possible, and even likely, that Isaiah 61:1-9 would be interpreted as speaking of the Messiah and the Messiah's time. When Jesus referred to Isaiah 61:1 precisely in the closing line of his speech he could only have meant to say that he understood himself as the messianic messenger of joy in Isaiah. But Jesus does not say that directly. The Baptizer himself is called to reflect on it. It may be that he will then realize who Jesus is, and he will see that his own images of the fiery judge are not really adequate for describing the mystery of the figure of the "One who is to come."

5. Expelling the Demons (Luke 11:20)

The fact that Jesus expelled demons cannot be doubted, because the Gospels tell stories of Jesus' expulsion of demons in a great many different places: in Mark 1:21-28; 5:1-20; 7:24-30; 9:14-29; Matthew 9:32-33, and in the corresponding Synoptic parallels. Still, what is more important than the stories is the argument between Jesus and his opponents. The latter assert that "He casts out demons by Beelzebul, the ruler of the demons" (Luke 11:14-23 // Matt 12:22-30; cf. Mark 3:22-26). This hostile accusation proves the historicity of Jesus' exorcisms more clearly than all the narrative accounts. Evidently Jesus' therapeutic success was so striking that even his opponents could not deny it. They had no choice but to distort it and to declare Jesus himself demonized and in cahoots with the supreme leader of all demons (Mark 3:22).

In their confrontation Jesus counters his opponents primarily with the statement: "If Satan's kingdom were so chaotic that the demons were fighting among themselves, it would have fallen long since." He adds: "If I cast out the demons with the aid of the ruler of all demons, by whom do your sons cast them out?" That is: "When you argue that way you not only discredit me but your own exorcists as well, since one could have the same suspicion about them." This somewhat ironic argument is followed immediately by the Jesus-saying that concerns us here:

> If it is by the finger of God that I cast out the demons, then the reign of God has come to you. (Luke 11:20 // Matt 12:28)

The link between this statement and what went before it is immediately obvious: it is not with the help of the *head of all demons* that Jesus drives out demons, but with the aid of *God*. It is not *Satan*'s rule that shows itself in Jesus' works, but the sovereignty of *God*. "In my exorcisms," Jesus says, "the reign of God has already come to you." That is: it is not only near; it has "arrived," it "has come to you," indeed, it "has come upon you." All that lies behind the Greek *ephthasen eph' hymas*. There is no other saying of Jesus that speaks as clearly about the arrival of the reign of God as this one does.

Another thing is striking about this two-liner from the Sayings Source: Jesus does not speak in the abstract. He does not say that he drives out the demons with God's "help." No, he expels them with the "finger" of God.[9] That is a clear allusion to Exodus 8:17-19,[10] where Aaron uses God's staff to transform the dust of Egypt into horseflies. Here the Pharaoh's magicians fail; they can no longer keep up. They have to acknowledge: "this is the finger of God." In this way, with a tiny reminder, Jesus brings the complex liberation theology of the Exodus narrative into play: as once God led Israel out of Egypt with outstretched arm, so now he himself, with the power of God, is freeing Israel from the rule of the demons—and his opponents are as baffled as was Pharaoh of old. As with many other passages in the Gospels, so also here we see that Jesus knew his Bible and how to apply its language. The natural way in which he does it—here with an allusion whose terseness is unsurpassable—speaks in favor of the authenticity of Luke 11:20.

Still another indicator also favors authenticity: Jesus' *Sitz im Leben* (life situation) is palpable in this two-liner. There are many other occasions when Jesus is heaped with slurs and accusations: he is said

[9] The Sayings Source had "by the finger of God." Matthew replaced that with "by the spirit of God" (cf. Matt 12:28 with Luke 11:20).

[10] Numbering in English translations.

to be "a glutton and a drunkard, a friend of tax collectors and sinners" (Luke 7:34 // Matt 11:19). Another accusation is added here: he is acting in league with the Devil. Jesus defends himself powerfully and cleverly against such charges, which are intended to strip him of any and all authority. As so often happens, he turns the accusation around and makes it part of his preaching; he does so by tying his exorcisms directly to the arrival of the reign of God.

This linking of demon-expulsion and the reign of God—we know of nothing comparable to it in any of the Jewish exorcists we have heard of. The author Flavius Josephus (*Antiquities* 8.2.5) tells of how he himself was present when a Jewish exorcist named Eleazar freed a man from demonic possession:

> *He put a ring that had a root of one of those sorts mentioned by Solomon to the nostrils of the demoniac, after which he drew out the demon through his nostrils.*

This Eleazar also addressed the possessed man in incantations supposedly composed by Solomon and adjured the demon in Solomon's name. In Mark 9:38-40 we learn that a Jewish exorcist used the name "Jesus" to drive out demons, to the irritation of Jesus' disciples. Evidently it was crucial to an exorcism that a powerful name be spoken.

It was completely different with Jesus. He did not work with magical practices as Eleazar did. He used no magic roots or abracadabra. Nor did he call on a powerful name. He commands the demons (Mark 1:25; 9:25) as God rebukes the opposing powers (Isa 17:13; Zech 3:2). But above all, the context of his reference, the framework of his healings and exorcisms, is always and only the reign of God that is now arriving in Israel.

It is clear from the example of the unknown exorcist in Mark 9:38-40 and from the case Josephus narrates that exorcists and exorcisms were rather common in Israel and elsewhere at that time. In particular there were evidently a lot of people who were considered "possessed" or who thought they themselves were captive to demons. To put it bluntly: demon-possession was an ordinary phenomenon. How can we explain that?

The basic structure of the phenomenon of possession, the nature of which is really quite complex, can be described this way: a person is no longer in possession of herself or himself, feels controlled and driven. Such a person feels helplessly delivered over to a strange power or powers. These external powers that rob the person of a "self" are then objectified as "demons" who come and go.

What is crucial is that this "social construct" was generally acknowledged in particular eras and specific cultures. When someone was attacked by unexplained illness, and especially when that person went out of control, she or he was thought to be possessed by a demon.

Because this social construct was generally accepted, a person could—unconsciously, of course—"enter into" it. This was true for the sick, the handicapped, the socially oppressed, people in hopeless situations—in short, all those socially stigmatized. All such people could "sink into" the role of a possessed person (or be assigned that role by others). The marginalized in society, or those who were utterly despairing, thus had access—without knowing what was happening—to a means by which they could express their need in terms of a publicly accepted syndrome of sickness. Thus they "grabbed" attention, caused people to do something for them, and were "treated"—by an exorcist, of course.

We have the right and, in fact, the duty to ask ourselves today what was the basis of the phenomenon of possession then (and later): medically, socio-medically, and psychologically. Moreover, we will not hesitate to regard the actions of exorcists in those times as a pre-professional kind of psychotherapy. Still, we must not fall into the error of saying, on the basis of such knowledge, that belief in demons at that time (and later) was nothing but fantasy and imagination. If we do that we will not appreciate the profound need that lies behind all the phenomena of possession. This is about people who suffer under inhuman compulsions, who have lost their freedom and even their very selves.

How did they get into these situations of unfreedom and compulsion? Sometimes it was their own fault, but much more often it was the result of the egoism, thoughtlessness, lies, heartlessness, and mechanisms of oppression that characterized the societies in which they lived. Violence and oppression not only happen again and again; they are embedded in society as disastrous circumstances, as "potentials" for evil. It is precisely in this context that the New Testament speaks quite correctly of "powers and authorities" (1 Cor 15:24; Eph 6:11-12). Every thinking person knows that these powers and authorities for evil exist, that they consolidate themselves to form a "potential," a context for evil that poisons history everywhere in the world. They really exist: the demons of power, rivalry, greed, lies, deliberate deception, and division that fix themselves within society and leave their fearful traces in the forms of mental and physical illnesses.

And it is precisely the weak, the marginalized, the sensitive people within society who are handed over to those powers. It can happen that the chaos and guilt, the obsessions and false convictions of whole generations become physically concentrated in such people and run riot.

Jesus must have possessed a profound power to bring such need to light, to employ a vocabulary that took the misery of affected persons seriously, to stand up against the underlying evil, and to heal the disempowered. He thus demonstrated that he was the stronger one (Luke 11:21-22) who could not be deterred by the wounds that evil can inflict.

It would be naïve to think that we can simply leave Jesus' exorcisms behind us as a time-conditioned phenomenon. After all, they are *his* confrontations with the power of evil and everything in the world that is inimical to God. It is true that we ourselves have to confront the demons of society in a different way, but the measure of what we do must remain Jesus himself: he who could not allow God's good creation, and above all the human beings within it, to be spoiled and destroyed by the power of evil.

6. The Fall of the Adversary (Luke 10:18)

The evangelist Mark reports the sending out and return of the twelve disciples (Mark 6:7, 30) whom Jesus had chosen as symbol of the eschatological gathering and sanctifying of Israel (Mark 3:13-19). Those twelve were sent to expel demons (Mark 6:7) and to heal the sick (Mark 6:13). This sending, in Mark, is accompanied by a relatively brief "instruction for mission" (Mark 6:8-11). Luke knew those texts from his copy of Mark's Gospel, but he also knew a much longer mission instruction from the Sayings Source. Evidently he concluded that there were two different missions and therefore he tells also of a later sending of *seventy-two* disciples (Luke 10:1-20). He then linked the instruction from the Sayings Source with this second mission (cf. Luke 10:2-16). When the "seventy-two" in Luke's depiction return and joyfully report that even the demons had to obey them, Jesus tells them:

> I watched Satan fall from heaven like a flash of lightning. (Luke 10:18)

At first glance this extremely compact statement of Jesus' own experience seems to fit quite well here. Then Jesus would be telling his disciples: "When the demons had to obey *you*, *I* beheld the heavenly disempowerment of Satan." But because Luke created the framework of the "mission and return of the seventy-two" it is questionable whether we should locate the vision account in Luke 10:18 historically in connection with the return of the disciples (that is, the Twelve).

Certainly that redaction-critical problem should not prevent us from taking seriously (both historically and theologically) this account of Jesus' vision, which, incidentally, is also reflected in John 12:31. After all, we have reports of other visions by Jesus—namely, at his baptism (Mark 1:10-11) and during his testing in the wilderness (Matt 4:1-11 // Luke 4:1-13). We should not conclude, from the vantage point of our rationalistically shaped horizon of experience, empty of visions as it is, that things were the same at all times and in all cultures. At any rate, the content of this vision fits extremely well within a basic experience Jesus had again and again: his healings and exorcisms showed him that the reign of God is breaking in and the rule of Satan is ending (cf. esp. Luke 11:20-22).

Obviously the expression "vision" can simply be a literary form an author uses in order to shape a narrative and give it emphasis. But the vision as a literary form would not exist if there were no real visions. Countless instances, especially from the lives of the saints, could be listed here. Paul, for example, attests to his visions quite directly (cf. 2 Cor 12:1-5). Of course, one may simply deny that he and many other people—in other religions as well—have had such visions, but that would be nothing but primitive cultural imperialism, which makes one's own experiences—or, better, one's lack of them—the standard and judge of all earlier cultures.

But let us just consider visions among the people of God! Obviously, here as elsewhere, every vision incorporates a multitude of impressions, images, imaginative forms, and learned elements that are stored in the visionary's unconscious. That is especially clear in Luke 10:18: Jesus' brief account of his vision presupposes, as a matter of course, that Satan was in the heavens; otherwise he could not fall from there. What ideas are in the background here?

Probably the clearest image comes from the beginning of the book of Job. There we can read how the "heavenly beings" are gathered with God. One member of the group is the Satan, who has just come back from traveling throughout the world (Job 1:6-7). So we are to picture something like a heavenly "council meeting" whose members bear the honorary title "sons of God." Satan now joins this divine privy council and questions God's assessment of the pious and God-fearing Job. God then gives him the power to test Job's righteousness with terrible blows. Satan here is clearly a member of the heavenly council who serve as God's advisers and carry out God's commissions—but who also profoundly question God's knowledge. Still, the Satan here is not yet an embodiment of evil as such.

It is different with Psalm 82. True, there is no Satan here, but we again encounter the idea of a heavenly council, and the gathered council is suddenly transformed into a court judging its own members. God tells these "children of the Most High" (Ps 82:6) that they are constantly abusing their offices. Instead of helping the poor and oppressed, the needy and suffering on earth, they are on the side of the oppressors. Hence God now deprives them of their office and they are toppled, just as princes fall (Ps 82:7). It is an uncanny psalm. It means to say: God is a God who is concerned for righteousness, who stands wholly on the side of the disenfranchised and the victims of violence. And here we have it: the "fall" of the corrupt members of God's council—of the false "gods."

The fall of a false, self-appointed god is depicted from a completely different perspective in Isaiah 14:4-21. Here it is the city of Babylon, but that city is an archetype of anti-God concentration of power. An ironic "threnody" tells how Babylon sought to raise itself to the heavens, even to the stars—only to be thrust down:

How you are fallen from heaven,
O Day Star, son of Dawn!
How you are cut down to the ground,
you who laid the nations low!
You said in your heart,
"I will ascend to heaven;
I will raise my throne
above the stars of God;
I will sit on the mount of assembly
on the heights of Zaphon;

I will ascend to the tops of the clouds,
I will make myself like the Most High."
But you are brought down to Sheol,
to the depths of the Pit. (Isa 14:12-15)

Texts of this kind, which Jesus obviously knew, must have taken concrete shape in him as he saw the fall of Satan in a vision. Of course, that is far from fully explaining the vision in Luke 10:18. Its real roots were in the direct experience of his exorcisms in which he found that he is the "stronger one" who can disarm and despoil the "strong" (Luke 11:21-22)—but he is the only one who can do it because now the reign of God is happening, by God's power, through him.

To that extent it was altogether appropriate for Luke to locate the vision we are considering here in connection with Jesus' and his disciples' expulsions of demons. And obviously neither the images from Jesus' unconscious mind nor his own experiences with demons exclude the possibility that in this vision God was revealing truth to him. In a "genuine" vision God "acts" and at the same time the human being "acts" through the power of imagination. Here again we find one of the basic principles of the doctrine of grace: God's action does not suppress that of human beings but sets it free.

7. Blessed Are You Poor! (Luke 6:20-21)

We have seen that Psalm 82 intends to describe the true nature of God as One who will not tolerate the denial of rights to the poor and oppressed. This God has no patience for a divine council that refuses to perform the duties of its office: to support the poor by securing their rights. Therefore this council is cast out, and God acts directly on behalf of the poor. Psalm 82 is not a myth; it uses mythical images from Israel's religious environment to make a deeply considered statement about the gods of this world and the true God.

Thus Psalm 82 wants to say that now God takes personal charge of the poor, no longer leaving them at the mercy of the powerful who are supposed to do it. We can certainly call this a dramatic event, one that runs throughout history. It began when God brought the oppressed Israelites out of Egypt, and it now comes to its climax in Jesus. God's intervention on behalf of the poor is at the innermost core of Jesus' proclamation and practice of the reign of God. That is also the place of the "beatitude" for the poor that will be our subject here.

We must always keep focus on the truth that Jesus does not call the poor "blessed" because their hunger and sorrow *as such* have some value; he does so because now God's intervention is beginning and now it is precisely the *hopeless* who will experience God's salvation. We must also keep in mind that Jesus not only calls the poor "blessed" because they will soon be helped. No, in calling the poor blessed he is calling for salvation. The reign of God that is now coming will overturn everything. Nothing will remain as it is, and that begins already when he says, "Blessed are you poor!" So "blessed are you poor" has nothing to do with a mystique of poverty. It is the proclamation of a revolution.

The announcement of this radical overturning of all relationships stands at the beginning of the programmatic discourse whose Matthean version is called the "Sermon on the Mount" and in Luke is dubbed the "Sermon on the Plain" (Matt 5:1–7:29; Luke 6:20–7:1). Luke has the oldest form of this blessing of the poor, laid out in three brief statements that are clearly connected with one another.[11] The second and third statements interpret the first:

> *Blessed are you who are poor, for yours is the reign of God.*
> *Blessed are you who are hungry now, for you will be filled.*
> *Blessed are you who weep now, for you will laugh.* (Luke 6:20-21)

To whom do these beatitudes apply? For Luke, clearly they are for Jesus' disciples because Luke 6:20-21 is introduced by the statement: "Then he [Jesus] looked up at his disciples and said . . ." and after the blessing of the poor, the hungry, and the sorrowful he continues, "Blessed are you when people hate you, and when they exclude you, revile you, and defame you on account of the Son of Man" (Luke 6:22-23). That can only refer to Jesus' disciples.

The case is similar in Matthew. The whole Sermon on the Mount is addressed to the disciples (Matt 5:1), but they represent the beginning of the Israel to be called anew. This is clear from the careful

[11] The question whether these three beatitudes were originally in the third or second person—that is, in the form found in Matthew or that in Luke—is difficult to answer. There are good grounds for both. Beatitudes in the Bible, as such, are usually in the third person; Luke could have changed them to second. But we must also keep in mind that Jesus played freely with language forms.

description of the larger crowd around the disciples: they come from all Israel (Matt 4:25–5:1).

But did Jesus himself address the beatitude for the poor to his disciples? Probably not! We have already seen that for Jesus, Isaiah 61:1 joins Isaiah 52:7 as a kind of key text. Jesus saw himself as the messenger of joy from Isaiah 61:1, who proclaimed his message of joy to the "poor," "prisoners," "captives," the "brokenhearted," the "despairing," the "derided," and the "maimed" in Israel. Isaiah 61 is about the whole people of God, "those who mourn in Zion," for in the post-exilic situation the state of the people of God was certainly characterized by widespread poverty. Not only was there poverty among the people on the lowest rung of society's ladder, who were really as poor as beggars. There were many other forms of poverty as well—such as the situation of the sick, the persecuted, and those robbed of their freedom.

But here we must face the crucial question. I have already said that the revolution in which the poor will really be helped, at last, is already beginning. It begins when Jesus calls them "blessed," and it begins with everything Jesus then does. But how should we picture that?

Jewish apocalypticists of the first century CE, as they present themselves in 4 Ezra or the Syrian Apocalypse of Baruch—if we could ask them—would have said: Yes, there will be rescue for the poor, but no longer in this eon. This present world of tribulation, sorrow, and injustice that has become subject to the power of Evil must first be destroyed. It is unable to fulfill God's promises (4 Ezra [= 2 Esdras] 4:27). It must be consumed by fire. But that will be the hour in which a new eon is born (4 Ezra 7:26-44)—a world of justice and peace, of blessing and eternal joy. Only then, when the old world has vanished, will the poor (insofar as they were pious) receive recompense for their misery.[12]

In all likelihood many Christians answer the question of "when" in much the same way, because apocalyptic dualism has eaten its way deeply into Christian thinking. A lot of Christians probably think: in this world there is no way to eliminate the suffering of the poor and the brutal power-games of the mighty. They keep coming back; in fact,

[12] It is true that a detail of older messianic eschatology is inserted in 4 Ezra (12:32-34). Nevertheless, the doctrine of two eons dominates. The messianic era is limited to four hundred years; then the Messiah must die (4 Ezra 7:28-29).

as history goes on they get more and more horrible. A complete change in relationships will have to happen beyond this world. Only then can true freedom come to be; only then will we receive genuine heavenly consolation; only then will true salvation bloom.

Jesus thinks differently. He is no apocalypticist such as was, for example, the author of 4 Ezra. For him the fulfillment of the prophets' promises does not begin only in a new, different, absolutely otherworldly world. Incidentally, in this Jesus stands firmly on the ground of Torah, which is at pains to eliminate the crisis of the poor *now*. The book of Deuteronomy in particular is intended to educate the people into a society of sisters and brothers shaped by God in which, for example, all debts are forgiven every seven years (Deut 15:1-4) and at the same time all the enslaved are granted freedom (Deut 15:12-18). Even one's personal enemies must be aided when they need help (Deut 22:1-4). The solidarity that exists within the family must be extended to all Israel. It is true that the book of Deuteronomy is thoroughly aware of the helplessness and neediness of human beings. It admits: "There should, however, be no one in need among you" (Deut 15:4).

Here the lawgiving in this book within the Old Testament becomes one of the most concrete *proposals* for the new society that is unconditionally given with Jesus' proclamation of the reign of God: the reign of God begins now, and not only somewhere beyond. And where God reigns, the violent rule of some people over others that casts the weak again and again into poverty, hunger, and misery must cease. The poor will be helped *now*; the hungry will be filled *now*; the sorrowing will be comforted *now*.

Obviously Jesus knows that it is with the reign of God as with a field of wheat that has many enemies (Mark 4:1-9). Even so, the seed that has fallen on good ground grows and cannot be stopped until it achieves an abundant harvest. Jesus knows just as well that the tiny mustard seed will become a world-tree (Matt 13:31-32) and a small portion of sourdough will ultimately raise a huge quantity of dough (Luke 13:20-21). For him, then, the "perfected form" of the reign of God exists. Still, there is a "before" in which the perfection is already growing. To put it another way: as far as the present is concerned there is an "already" and a "not yet." Anyone who no longer believes in that dialectic, with its "already," does not believe in what Jesus proclaimed.

Jesus himself lived the "already." He healed the sick, cleansed the lepers, sought out sinners, visited the outcasts. And he is convinced that the sparks he is casting, like an arsonist, over the land with his preaching (Luke 12:49) will set things in motion. The revolution is already beginning in the crowd of his disciples. Where else are the statements of that unbelievably radical *ethos* that will later be collected in Jesus' "Sermon on the Mount" supposed to end up?

In the third and fourth parts of this book we will see in detail what is so radical about this *ethos*. One thing is certain: where the *ethos* of the Sermon on the Mount is lived—as it reveals the central meaning of the social order given at Sinai (Matt 5:17)—there are no more poor people; there cannot possibly be. Of course this cannot be programmatic for a civil government, but it can be for a discipleship that aims to be yeast for the people of God—and for that people of God in turn to be yeast for the world. To that extent Matthew and Luke were right after all when they directed the blessing of the poor at the *disciples*. Moreover, the church has always seen this aspect of Jesus' reign-of-God message. From the beginning it has cared for the poor, the sick, and others in need of help. It has erected an extensive system of education and has bought the freedom of prisoners. All that can only be mentioned in passing here. A history of Christian *caritas* would fill whole books.

8. New Wine in New Wineskins (Mark 2:21-22)

Some forms of speech are typical of Jesus. These include the antithetical parallelism, the form used in so many parables, but also the so-called "double-image sayings" and "double strophes" that make the same statement with the aid of two different fields of imagery. We find such a double-image saying in Mark 2:21-22 (cf. Matt 9:16-17; Luke 5:36-38):

> No one sews a piece of new [or: unshrunk] cloth on an old cloak.
> Otherwise, the patch pulls away from it, the new from the old,
> and a worse tear is made.
> And no one puts new wine into old wineskins.
> Otherwise, the wine will burst the skins,
> and the wine is lost, and so are the skins.
> New wine [belongs] in fresh wineskins.

We can see right away that the two images are structured with strict symmetry. Each begins with something no experienced and reasonable person would ever do (first statement). Anyone who does so deserves the consequences in both cases (second and third statements). A final statement is added after the second in the series, finishing off the whole: "New wine in new wineskins!"

Quite a few exegetes are irritated by the question of precisely what the two images are meant to convey. They are especially annoyed by the first. Doesn't it say that the new may not be combined with the old, since otherwise the old will be destroyed? In the end, doesn't the image favor the old?

But that makes no sense. The intent, rather, is that new things cannot be combined with old ones; they are incompatible. But clearly the positive value belongs to the new. We can see this from the simple fact that the old garment already has a rip in it. But if anyone is still doubtful, the addition to the second image teaches definitively that "new wine belongs in new wineskins."

Thus the double metaphor is carefully constructed. It was easy to remember. It makes an impression because it says the same thing with the aid of two different fields of imagery. Still, there is a deliberate intensification: in the first image the tear in the already damaged garment gets bigger, while the patch remains whole and can still be used elsewhere. But in the second image both things are lost: the wineskins are ruined and the wine has been spilled.

Probably Jesus used such double images, or emphatic single images, to recapitulate things he had already spoken about at length. In that case such *logia* served as summaries at the end of a longer speech. Otherwise he might begin a discourse with such a *logion*. In that case the listeners would have been on tenterhooks, waiting to find out what would come next. So also with us: we are excited to learn what this double image really means to say. But first we have to consider the "unshrunk patch" and the "wineskins," because that is all unfamiliar to us. Nobody in our households shrinks (fulls) cloth, and we no longer preserve wine in wineskins.

It was different then. The work of the household included spinning, weaving, and fulling. Woolen cloth was dampened and then pressed, trodden, and beaten until the fibers were "fulled" (felted), producing a thicker and more valuable "cloth." "Unfulled" cloth, of course, makes no sense in this context since it was the process of fulling that rendered the material properly solid. If the focus here were on the fulling process Jesus would have been better advised to speak of a "fulled" cloth, since a firm, soft, fulled cloth would be the proper contrast to the ripped garment. Therefore in our text "unfulled" must simply mean "not yet prepared," "fresh from the loom," hence "new." Thus the translation "new" is justified; in fact, it is the correct one.

The relationship to the "wineskins" is similar: normally, in the ancient world, wine was poured into *amphorae*, large clay vessels that narrowed toward the bottom and had two curved handles, easy to grasp. The wineskins to which Jesus here refers are tanned goat- or sheepskins whose openings were tied shut. They were also used for storage, but primarily for transporting wine on pack animals. Old wineskins were softened and crumbly; they could no longer endure the fermentation or the transportation of the wine. They split. "New wine" is wine that has not yet completed its fermentation and thus is still busily processing.

Enough said about the two fields of imagery we have to deal with here. But what did Jesus want to say with this double image? The words "old" and "new" are key. Four times—and if we include "unfulled," five times—we read the provocative word "new." Clearly it has a positive meaning for Jesus. That seems obvious to us, since we almost always think of the "new" as the "better" thing. Better to install a *new* heating system that lowers energy costs than to go on using the old one. When it is time to buy a smartphone we wait for the newest model with its expanded features. And we would rather buy the famous nineteenth-century Russian novel we have waited so long to read in the much-praised new translation than the first one, with its somewhat archaic language. Although we can also think of old things that were better than the new, the word "new" simply has a fresh, vivid, promising echo.

Still, our favoring of the new is anything but a matter of course. In previous cultures thinking usually ran in the other direction. The old was tested and had proved itself good. The new, on the other hand, was regarded as untested and thus dangerous. Jesus Sirach, the great Hebrew wisdom teacher from the second century BCE, uses the example of an old friend to illustrate that. With an old friend you know where you are; with a new friend, not so much. She or he might prove unpleasant and annoying. The wisdom teacher even uses a "rule for wine" to illustrate that:

Do not abandon old friends,
for new ones cannot equal them.
A new friend is like new wine;
when it has aged, you can drink it with pleasure. (Sir 9:10)

So we should not simply attribute our obsession with the new to previous cultures. In that sense Jesus' double image has something daring—indeed, revolutionary—about it. To a degree it anticipates the language of later revolutionaries who wanted to change everything. In the twentieth century they talked about a "new attitude," the "new human being," a "new society," a "new age." Regrettably, they flagrantly misused their favorite word "new." The "new thing" that came was, in fact, the worst kind of terror.

Nevertheless: we should not water down Jesus' fighting spirit, his awareness of the new, his uncompromising stance. Think only of his saying, "Let the dead bury their own dead!" or, "If your hand causes you to stumble, cut it off!"

Our double image is radical because it refuses any mixing of old and new. We can only apply it to the reign of God. What is now coming creates a new situation in Israel, one that demands a new attitude. It is impossible any longer to hold to the usual, the familiar, the comfortable rituals, and no one may seek to burden the new thing with ossified traditions. "New wine belongs in new wineskins!"

What that means in detail, certainly, must be tested in individual cases. In parts 3 and 4 we will be dealing almost exclusively with Jesus-sayings that show what Jesus meant by this "new."

We must absolutely not fall into one particular trap: that of thinking that Jesus had dismissed the Torah given at Sinai and put something new in its place. Jesus did not abolish the Torah. If he had done so, he would have abandoned Israel. No, with an unbelievable assurance he distilled the Torah to its core; he removed the ambiguity from divergent statements in it; he radicalized Torah, and in doing all that he revealed its innermost meaning. He did not abolish it. He interpreted it with sovereign authority.

9. Fasting at a Wedding? (Mark 2:19)

"No one," Jesus says, "sews a new piece of cloth on a torn garment. And no one fills young wine that is still fermenting into a crumbly wineskin. No reasonable person would do that." A few verses before this, Mark gives us something that no one, I mean *no one*, would ever do:

> The bridegroom's companions cannot fast while the bridegroom is with them, can they? (Mark 2:19)

I have given a somewhat free translation of part of this saying. The Greek speaks not of the "bridegroom's companions" and certainly not of the whole company of wedding guests, but of the "sons of the bridal chamber." That is a Semitism. "Child" (or "son") here obviously does not mean a fleshly child but, as so often in the ancient Near East, it expresses belonging. A "son of the bow" is an arrow (Job 41:20), and the "children of misery" are the miserable (Prov 31:5).

The "sons of the bridal chamber" are the friends and companions of the bridegroom, who obviously are invited to the wedding and play an important role in it. They help to organize the event, perform stories and songs, and so help to make the seven days of the wedding feast a genuine festival. It is beyond imagining that they would not feast and drink with the bridegroom, but instead would fast.

Clearly, Jesus could only have said such a thing if there were a concrete occasion for it, and it must have had something to do with fasting. Therefore we may suppose that the occasion the Gospel of Mark gives was really the historical moment in which Jesus spoke these words. Mark 2:18 reads:

> *Now John's disciples and the Pharisees were accustomed to fast [that is, they regularly kept their fastdays]; and people came and said to him [Jesus], "Why do John's disciples and the disciples of the Pharisees fast, but your disciples do not fast?"*

The question was justified. Fasting meant that on two days out of the week one would eat nothing (and probably drink nothing) until sundown (cf. Luke 18:12). That was hard, and it earned respect for those fasting. If this great healer, teacher, and prophet everyone was talking about did not fast, and his disciples did not fast either, but instead they all dined with sinners and questionable characters—well, there had to be critical questions about it.

Evidently at some point Jesus had answered such a question by saying: "But we are celebrating a *wedding feast*. How can we fast?"

That answer contains a claim that can only be recognized against its biblical background. In that context it had to mean: Now the time of salvation promised by the prophets has begun, the time when Israel's fastdays will become "days of joy and gladness" (Zech 8:19). Now the wedding feast of God with Israel (Hos 2:18, 21-22), the festival of the reign of God, has begun. Now that ultimate wedding feast and time of joy for "Daughter Zion" has come, the one of which Isaiah 62:4-5 says:

> *You shall no more be termed Forsaken,*
> *and your land shall no more be termed Desolate;*
> *but you shall be called My Delight Is in Her,*
> *and your land Married;*
> *for the Lord delights in you,*
> *and your land shall be married.*
> *For as a young man marries a young woman,*
> *so shall your builder marry you,*
> *and as the bridegroom rejoices over the bride,*
> *so shall your God rejoice over you.*

To go on keeping fastdays would, in fact, pervert this time of rejoicing given by God. It would no longer be a happy time. It would mean refusing to accept what God is now preparing for God's people, but despising it instead. Indeed, probably Jesus says a great deal more with this radical statement. Can't we also sense in it the assertion that he himself is the bridegroom—as is directly formulated later in Revelation 19:6-9? But Jesus did not say that, and so we may have here another of the many instances in which he only hints at his most profound secret and does not drag it into the light.

10. The "Violent" in the Reign of God (Matt 11:12-13)

All the sayings of Jesus that have been studied in this book, to this point, have spoken directly or indirectly about the reign of God that is already coming to be, and thus they have treated the core of Jesus' message: the turn of the ages is here. The reign of God is advancing with power. It is already so close that it can be proclaimed, announced. More than that: it is already visible. Unlike the kings and prophets who had only been hoped for, this is something one can see, for the miracles of the reign of God are already happening in the midst of

Israel. The demons of society must give way, and Satan's power is visibly shaken. The poor, the hungry, and the sorrowing are not only congratulated because new *hope* is entering their lives now. No, the alteration of all relationships is already promised to them. The coming of the reign of God brings a genuine revolution with it. Even the least in the reign of God is greater than John the Baptizer, the greatest of all humans. The time of salvation announced by the prophets is breaking in like a wedding feast. Therefore now everything is new, and it can no longer be confused with the old. Still, the reign of God now dawning is no magic kingdom to which one suddenly awakens. It calls for faith; it demands profound repentance; it requires passion. The reign of God makes Israel a battlefield.

The struggle that is being carried out there for the sake of the reign of God is the subject of the so-called "assailant saying" transmitted to us in Matthew 11:12-13 *par* Luke 16:16—in two very different versions. The basis of both may have been the Sayings Source. It seems that Matthew's version is closer in its wording to Q and to Jesus. There is dispute, however, over how the Greek text there should be translated. The verb in the first clause of the assailant saying can be read as passive, and that affects the subsequent clause. Then the saying would read:

From the days of John the Baptizer until now
the [heavenly reign] has suffered violence,
and the violent take them [the people] by force.

If we translate it this way, Jesus' saying is a bitter lament: "Everything I am doing will be destroyed by my opponents. And so it was with the Baptizer. He was killed. Violence is being done to the reign of God, and the violent are snatching it from the people who want to share in it." However, we could also translate the verb in the first clause of Matthew's version as medial/intransitive. Then we would have:

From the days of John the Baptizer until now
the [heavenly reign] is breaking its way by force,
and the violent are snatching it for themselves.

In that case the assailant saying would not be a lament, but the very opposite. It would be a shout of victory. The reign of God is coming with power, and that powerful action of God is matched by all the people who now, with the utmost effort and the greatest determination, are doing everything in order to have a share in the reign of God.

Which of those two translations matches what Jesus himself wanted to say? Interpreters are utterly divided here. The assailant saying has been a battlefield for a long time. There are very few sayings of Jesus that have been so disputed in New Testament exegesis, and for such a long time. In interpreting it, though, we should also consider the Lukan version. It reads:

> *The law and the prophets [were in effect] until John came;*
> *since then the good news of the reign of God is proclaimed,*
> *and everyone tries to enter it by force.*

For two reasons this Lukan variant takes us farther. First of all, here the time of the Law and the prophets (including John the Baptizer) is distinguished from the time of the reign of God. That matches the clear separation in Luke 7:28: "the least in the reign of God is greater than John, who was the greatest of all human beings." Then what is said here about the effect of the coming of God's reign has a positive meaning: everyone is trying to get in. That is at least a hint that the Matthean version could also be meant as positive. Thus there is a good deal in favor of the idea that the assailant saying originally read:

> The Law and the prophets were until John.
> From then on the reign of God is breaking its way with violence,
> and violent people are seizing it for themselves.

Here, then, I have chosen as my basic text not one from the Gospels, but a reconstruction. That is necessary for once, by way of exception, because of the difficulty at hand. The Matthean version, because of its metaphor of violence, would be preferred over that of Luke because it is the more difficult. The author of Luke's Gospel has already interpreted and smoothed it. On the other hand Luke, with his clear distinction between the time of the reign of God and the time of the Law and the prophets, is much closer to Jesus' proclamation, which announces something radically new.

Could Jesus really have formulated the idea that the reign of God is being raped (or utterly constrained) and that perpetrators of violence will rob humanity of it? It is true that Jesus was affected and thwarted by the nuisance efforts of his opponents—but he had shown their hostilities for what they were. Could he really have said that they were in a position to rape and defile the reign of God? That is hard to imagine, and it would be altogether unbiblical. God does not accept violation—from anybody. Not even from the worst of enemies. But the case is entirely different with the statement that the reign of God is now breaking its way with violence, is conquering, is gaining space everywhere in Israel. Such a statement fits excellently within Jesus' proclamation of the reign of God, a proclamation that is sure of victory.

We may not argue against this positive interpretation of the assailant saying that it is not really a possible reading in terms of Greek semantics: the verb *biazō* (use violence, oppress) has an entirely negative significance, and so does the noun *biastēs* (perpetrator of violence). That is selectively true of the negative meanings of *biazō* and *biastēs*, but it is futile because this argumentation overlooks what is so characteristic of Jesus: he constantly takes the liberty of playing on conventional ideas, images, and even text types. He makes use of purely negative ideas in order to make a positive statement and thus to lead his hearers to the essential point.

One typical example of such freewheeling use of language is Jesus' response to the calumny spread by his opponents about his celibate status. They whispered that he was probably a eunuch, a castrated male. Jesus counters: indeed, there are "eunuchs who have made themselves eunuchs for the sake of the reign of God" (cf. Matt 19:12). That is, there are people who deliberately remain unmarried for the sake of the reign of God.

There are further examples of similar figures of speech, especially in Jesus' parables. Think only of the parable of the talents (Matt 25:14-30) in which the third subordinate buries his capital in order to keep safe what has been entrusted to him, while the first two double their capital with risky speculations or even through sketchy dealings. They act exactly like their chief, who "reaps where he did not sow" (Matt 25:26). Or consider the parable of the dishonest manager who is threatened with dismissal because of his embezzlement and proceeds to secure his future by means of criminal manipulations (Luke 16:1-8).

Jesus tells, in such cases, of "immoral heroes,"[13] but it is precisely through such figures that he emphasizes his point. No one can delay

[13] I owe this syntagm to the important book by Tim Schramm and Kathrin Löwenstein, *Unmoralische Helden. Anstößige Gleichnisse Jesu* (Göttingen: Vandenhoeck & Ruprecht, 1986).

or deter the reign of God, for it is God's own work. But access to it belongs only to those who risk everything and so put their existence on the line. The reign of God needs "violent" people like that. Essentially, just a glance at the metaphors of violence in Matthew 5:29-30 should have sufficed to lay the dispute over the assailant saying to rest. There we read:

> *If your right eye causes you to sin—*
> *tear it out and throw it away!*
> *It is better for you to lose one of your members*
> *than for your whole body to be thrown into hell.*
>
> *And if your right hand causes you to sin,*
> *cut it off and throw it away!*
> *It is better for you to lose one of your members*
> *than for your whole body to go into hell.*

Here Jesus, with shocking harshness and implacability, demands acting violently toward oneself in order not to lose one's own life—we may add: in order to preserve it for the reign of God. In Matthew 5:29-30 and in many similarly radical sayings of Jesus we are very close to the assailant saying. In this positive sense Jesus' disciples were also "violent" people. We will speak about them in the next two parts of this book.

Part Two

The Mission of the Twelve

We spoke in part 1 of this book about the mission of the Twelve and their task of announcing the reign of God in Israel. We also saw that, historically, the mission of the Seventy-Two in Luke 10:1-20 derived from Luke's misunderstanding and simply reflects the mission of the Twelve (chap. 6). At least in the Gospels of Mark and Luke those missions mark an important *caesura*: now the themes of discipleship and emulation of Jesus take center stage.

It therefore makes sense for us now to devote more detailed attention to the mission of the Twelve, because there are quite a few sayings of Jesus that are connected to it—primarily those associated with his "instructions for mission."

There is a difficulty here, however. Quite a few New Testament scholars have long denied that Jesus ever sent out his disciples in this way. Rudolf Bultmann, for example, in his *History of the Synoptic Tradition*, describes the whole instruction for mission in Mark 6:8-11 *par* Matthew 10:5-16 *par* Luke 10:2-12 as "development of the primitive Christian idea of Mission" as if that were something simply taken for granted. For him it is the post-Easter community of the Risen (or Exalted) One that is speaking.[1]

Frequently there is reference in this connection to the itinerant apostles like those attested in the *Didachē*, an early Christian community order probably from the first half of the second century CE. In *Didachē* 11.3-12 there are rules for how local Christian communities should deal with such itinerant apostles, who—especially in Syria—went from village to village preaching the gospel. Scholars studying the *Didachē* surmise that at a very early time such itinerant apostles summarized their own way of life and rules for preaching in the form of a brief mission instruction and attributed it to the time of Jesus' activity. It is said that the Sayings Source as well as Mark 6:7-11 can show us the outlines of these self-created rules for the behavior of itinerant missionaries.

[1] Rudolf Bultmann, *History of the Synoptic Tradition* (see part 1, n. 2 above), 145n1.

There certainly can be no question that these later itinerant apostles or prophets existed and that they found themselves reflected in the mission instructions of the Sayings Source. More: they helped to shape that text-complex. Their intention was to carry on what Jesus had begun, though under changed circumstances. But they wanted to *continue* what had preceded them: the itinerant lives of Jesus and his disciples.

Consider just the *first part* of the mission discourse in the Sayings Source. Today it is usually reconstructed (from a comparison of Luke 10:2-12 and Matt 10:5-16, with minor variants) as follows—with Luke furnishing the real basis of the reconstruction:

> *He [Jesus] said to his disciples: The harvest is plentiful, but the laborers are few; therefore ask the Lord of the harvest to send out laborers into his harvest!*
>
> *Go! See, I am sending you out like lambs into the midst of wolves.*
>
> *Carry no purse, no bag for provisions, no sandals, no staff; and greet no one on the road!*
>
> *When you enter a house, first say, "Peace to this house!" If anyone there is a "son of peace," your peace will rest on that person; but if not, it will return to you. Remain in the same house, eating and drinking whatever is there, for the laborer deserves to be paid! Do not move about from house to house!*
>
> *Whenever you enter a town and its people welcome you, eat what is set before you! Cure the sick who are there, and say to them, "The reign of God has come near to you!" But when you enter a town and they do not welcome you, leave that town and shake off its dust from your feet! I tell you, on that day it will be more tolerable for Sodom than for that town.*

First of all, we notice that the "equipment rule" at the beginning of this text is shockingly radical. Jesus' messengers must not have any money with them, and no food for the journey; they must walk barefoot and may not even carry a staff (Matt 10:9-10 // Luke 10:4). As a comparison with the parallel account in Mark 6:8-9 shows, these instructions were softened at some point: now at least sandals and a staff were allowed. The later concessions show very clearly that the equipment rule was not invented after Easter but goes back to Jesus' own radicality.

We also notice that if we consider this mission instruction purely in itself we do not yet find in it the christological titles that were part of the post-Easter proclamation: neither "Christ" nor "Son of God."

There is only a very subtle, implicit Christology such as what characterized Jesus until the event at Caesarea Philippi (Mark 8:27-30). What is altogether in the foreground is the coming of the reign of God. That also speaks against a post-Easter invention of the mission.

Furthermore: behind the whole mission instruction is the conviction that there is no more time left. The reign of God must be proclaimed *now*, one must act *now*, every household and every place must decide *now*. Thus the motif of the harvest in Matthew 9:37-38 *par* Luke 10:2; therefore the command not to greet anyone in Luke 10:4; therefore the proclamation of the nearness of the reign of God in Matthew 10:7 *par* Luke 10:9. Certainly all that fits also with the church's eschatology in the first decades after Easter, but first and foremost it was part of Jesus' own preaching, which stands entirely within eschatological portents.

Finally: as we will see in more detail, the sending on mission consists almost entirely of a sequence of provocative sign-actions. The establishment of the Twelve was itself a deliberate sign-action. After all, it was a very long time since there had been a structure of twelve tribes, but Jesus, by choosing twelve men from among his disciples, not only manifested his intention to gather all of Israel but *constituted* eschatological Israel in a real-symbol. The mission itself was also a provocative sign, as was the lack of equipment (and thereby the absolute defenselessness of the Twelve) and the shaking off of the dust in places that rejected the messengers' preaching. Sign-actions of that sort, however, were especially characteristic of Jesus.

All this shows that the choice of the Twelve, their mission, and an associated "instruction for mission" belong to the time of the historical Jesus. Nowadays the majority of biblical scholars are of the same opinion. Jesus did, in fact, demonstratively "choose" a group of twelve disciples (Mark 3:14). He sent them out two by two (Mark 6:7), probably in the rural parts of Galilee, and he gave them instructions for their mission (Mark 6:8-11; Luke 10:3-12), including the matter of equipment (Mark 6:8-9; Luke 10:4). This obviously does not exclude the possibility that later experiences of mission further influenced the texts. That is fairly certain as regards "do not move about from house to house!" (Luke 10:7). But on the whole we are here present with Jesus himself and hear words that in their brevity, pictorial language, and radicality are quite typical of him. No later itinerant missionary would have dared to impose on fellow apostles in the name of Jesus the command—so profoundly impolite in the ancient Near East—"Greet no one on the way!"

11. Like Lambs in the Midst of Wolves (Luke 10:3)

Probably the mission instruction began in the Sayings Source with the lines:

> *The harvest is plentiful,*
> *but the laborers are few;*
> *therefore ask the Lord of the harvest*
> *to send out laborers into his harvest.* (Matt 9:37-38 // Luke 10:2)

In fact it is improbable that this saying originated in the context of the disciples' mission because those who were sent at that time were the Twelve, and that number has high symbolic value. Given its reference to the people of the twelve tribes, it could not signify a greater number. Thus Jesus would not have said this in the context of the sending but on another occasion.

Even so, it is very apt for illuminating the situation in which a mission was in order. The saying presupposes a certain period of Jesus' activity. It is no longer the time of beginnings, the time of sowing, of Jesus' first experiences as he began to appear in public. Harvest time in southern regions calls for a large workforce to be set in motion from one day to the next; otherwise the grain on the stock or the grapes on the vine may be ruined. So Jesus sees the crisis; the time is short. The harvest must be gathered. Therefore he speaks, like a good manager, about the meager number of workers. Such considerations are important because in this chapter I am addressing these words of Jesus, which follow immediately:

> See, I am sending you out like sheep into the midst of wolves. (Matt 10:16 // Luke 10:3)

Who are these wolves? Since the mission of the Twelve is solely to the people of the twelve tribes, the reference can only be to people in Israel—people who oppose Jesus' preaching there because his behavior is a profound irritant for them. They attack not only him but also his disciples. That, however, assumes that Jesus' work has been going on for some time.

Given these indicators, it seems that historically the mission of the Twelve cannot be located at the very beginning of Jesus' public activity. None of the Synoptic authors do so: not Mark, not Matthew, not Luke. When Jesus tells the twelve disciples that he is sending them like lambs into the midst of devouring wolves there must already have been an opposition forming.

The image of a pack of wolves tearing defenseless lambs to pieces is horrifying, but Joachim Jeremias[2] rightly pointed out that we should not think of organized persecution here. This is about individual actions: slanders (Matt 10:25), defamation (Luke 6:22 // Matt 5:11), denial of shelter and hospitality (Luke 10:10 // Matt 10:14). Those of us who live in cities housing millions of people or in thickly settled regions can scarcely imagine how important hospitality was in the ancient Near East and how painful its refusal could be.

Moreover, there is much in favor of the idea that this image is not primarily about the viciousness of the wolves but rather the defenselessness of the lambs, since it is precisely that lack of protection that Jesus demands in what follows. The Twelve are not to wear shoes on their feet: thus they could not run away over Palestine's stony ground. They are not to carry a staff and thus will not be in a position to defend against attackers. Indeed, they are not to defend themselves. To borrow a saying from the Sermon on the Mount, they should rather allow themselves to be struck in the face (Matt 5:39), and they are to accept being driven out of places that refuse to receive them.

In the time of salvation that is coming, as announced in the book of Isaiah, wolf and lamb will together enjoy hospitality, and the leopard will lie down with the kid (Isa 11:6; cf. 65:25). Jesus knows that this situation, which is essentially a miracle, has not yet been achieved in Israel. When lambs set out on the road they will very quickly be encircled by a pack of wolves. Jesus sees the situation in the world with critical sobriety.

That in no way means that he doubted the prophecy of the book of Isaiah, because he demands of his disciples precisely what Isaiah depicts: that among them wolves and lambs should live together. He knows that even among his disciples, as in any human community, there are wolves and lambs. For that reason they must first make the

[2] Joachim Jeremias, *New Testament Theology: The Proclamation of Jesus* (see part 1, n. 8 above), 240.

promises of Isaiah a reality among themselves. Certainly Jesus does not use the image of wolves and lambs as a model for community but rather that of enslaved service (Mark 10:43-44). The disciples are to serve one another like slaves, and therefore none may desire to be greater—that is, more powerful—than any other. On the contrary: whoever wants to be first must be last of all (Mark 9:35; Luke 22:26).

The sibling community of wolf and lamb must therefore begin with the disciples themselves. Only then will Israel allow itself to be transformed and, through Israel, the nations of the world. The defenselessness of the Twelve should display something about their faith that the promises of Isaiah 11 are already being fulfilled—and, moreover, that they hope their own vulnerability will drain the aggressiveness from their opponents. To that extent their refusal of all means of security is, in fact, a provocative sign-action.

12. Take Nothing for Your Journey! (Luke 9:3)

The Twelve's lack of any kind of security is evident not only from the absence of sandals and staff. They are also to take no money in their belts and no provision sack with bread and other foodstuffs. In Mark 6:9—and, drawing on Mark, in Matthew 10:10 // Luke 9:3—they are even forbidden to carry a change of clothes. All the clothing they have should be just what they are wearing. In Luke 9:3 this equipment rule (here combining Mark 6:8-9 and the Sayings Source) is:

> Take nothing for your journey,
> no staff, nor bag, nor bread, nor money—
> not even an extra tunic! (Luke 9:3)

So the Twelve are not to take any money with them. That means, for one thing, that they are not to have even a penny for difficult situations that may befall them! Above all, however, it means that they are never to accept payment for healing the sick and certainly not for their preaching (Matt 10:8).

We should not imagine the staff as some kind of thin stick; it would have been a fairly stout piece of wood with which one could defend oneself against people and animals and kill poisonous snakes, for example. But Jesus denies the disciples even this minimal form of defense.

The most severe command was probably to wear no sandals. In the world of that time no one went barefoot except those who were mourning the dead—or poor beggars who did not even *have* sandals—or, of course, children. As I said before, not having shoes made swift flight impossible, and the danger of being bitten by a snake was all the greater as well. We have to keep all that in mind if we are to grasp what Jesus was demanding of his disciples with this equipment rule.

Certainly the more important question is: what was the purpose of the rule? I once took the trouble to review the interpretations of the "equipment rule" in all the commentaries on the Synoptic Gospels I could lay my hands on. They spoke of being without property, without means, poverty, having modest needs, being undemanding, being carefree, doing without, vulnerability, defenselessness, lack of protection, peaceableness. Most frequent by far was the word "poverty."

Still, that very word makes clear how problematic all these words are unless we add that they must be applied in every respect to the particular situation of the now-appearing reign of God. Poverty is not a value in itself. In Luke 6:20-21 the poor are only called blessed because in the reign of God they will be delivered from their misery, and a "woe" is only spoken over the rich in Luke 6:24 (cf. Mark 10:25) because fixation on their riches makes it impossible for them to enter the reign of God.

The poverty or, better, the lack of means on the part of the Twelve must thus have something to do with surrender to their duty of proclamation. Because they are without means they are freer and more flexible. They are not burdened with the everyday cares of securing their existence. But their lack of means has still further effect: it creates a more profound connection to all those they visit. The families and localities that receive them also care for them. In turn, the messengers of the reign of God care for the families and places in which they are received: they promise them the peace of the time of salvation. We will have more to say about this mutuality in chapter 14.

In summary: keywords like "poverty," "lack of possessions," "absence of means," and "renunciation" are only correct in the context of the mission if exegesis makes it clear that they are inseparable from a particular system of reference: they are connected with the proclamation of the reign of God. Hence words like "undemanding" and "having modest needs" are misleading. They were part of the self-concept of itinerant Cynic philosophers and have nothing—nothing at all—to do with Jesus' equipment rule.

The keywords "vulnerability," "defenselessness," and "peaceableness" form a group in themselves. They have the advantage of being clearly connected to the demands of the equipment rule. Having no staff in one's hand means being unprotected and unable to defend oneself. Forbidding someone to carry a staff presupposes, of course, that Jesus' disciples do not carry a dagger or short sword either. No question of that! Likewise, someone who is barefoot is not only unable to flee but also cannot fight. So in this context we should not just speak of defenselessness but of something more: *nonviolence.*

Oddly enough, this keyword does not appear in connection with the equipment rule anywhere in the German commentaries I found—even though in the Old Testament nonviolence is a clear mark of the time of salvation. Think only of Isaiah 2:4—the swords that will be turned into plowshares—and of the messianic king in Zechariah 9:9-10 who disarms the city of Jerusalem.

Obviously there are also calls for violence at many places in the Old Testament: for example, as a threat of counter-violence in order to limit the tide of violence (thus, e.g., Gen 4:15) or to obtain recompense (thus, e.g., Isa 35:4). But especially in the Prophets there is also a clear line of reference to absolute nonviolence. Jesus adopted that line of tradition with marvelous clarity and made nonviolence an essential characteristic of the eschatological people of God. Thus it would be very odd if his demand for absolute nonviolence did not play a role especially in the case of the messengers of peace he sends to the people of God. We will, however, speak more fully about the theme of nonviolence in Jesus' preaching at a later point (see chap. 36).

The absence of the keyword "nonviolence" in the commentaries accessible to me was matched by a lack of reference to "Zealots." In almost all cases the sparse equipment of the itinerant Cynic philosophers is compared to that of Jesus' messengers. Unlike Jesus' disciples, those itinerant philosophers had, at a minimum, a mantle, a staff, and a sack for provisions containing at least a little bread. The commentaries emphasize the much more extreme lack of possessions on the part of Jesus' disciples—almost as if the equipment rule were a deliberate confrontation with the competing image of itinerant pagan preachers.

As far as Galilee is concerned, a contrast with the Zealots would come much closer to the reality. They, after all, were armed, and they sought not peace but war with the Roman occupying power—primarily because of the tax that had to be paid to the Romans. While the Zealots appealed to the reign of God, for them it meant primarily overcoming Roman rule and freedom for the land given by God.

The activities of those Jewish freedom fighters did not begin in connection with the uprising in the years between 66 and 70; they had come much earlier with Judas the Galilean, when Judea was made a Roman province in 6 CE.[3] Characteristic of the Zealots was their employment of guerrilla tactics and thereby their unashamed use of violence. Thus it is hard to imagine that the signs of radical nonviolence Jesus demands of his messengers would have had nothing to do with a sharp distancing from the Zealots.

In any case, Jesus wanted by all means to prevent his messengers from being mistaken for freedom fighters stirring up trouble. Therefore they had to differ from the "warriors for God" of that period to the utmost extent, including external details. Evidently Jesus saw clearly how fundamentally the Zealot ideology of violence contradicted the message of the book of Isaiah about the nonviolent Servant Israel (Isa 50:6; 53:7). His image of eschatological Israel was completely different from that of the Zealots. The destruction of Jerusalem in the year 70 CE by the Romans and the brutal struggles between different groups within Judaism inside the already-besieged capital city would have validated his stance.

13. Greet No One on the Way! (Luke 10:4)

In the Sayings Source the command not to greet anyone came immediately after the equipment rule discussed above (chap. 12). We have it only from Luke 10:4; it is absent from Matthew. He probably omitted it because he could not understand it or because he thought, at least, that his readers would not. At first glance the command not to greet anyone presents itself as apparently without reference or commentary:

> Greet no one on the way!

[3] The fact that Josephus says scarcely anything about the Zealots in the period between the appearance of Judas the Galilean in 6 CE and the death of King Agrippa I in the year 44 CE is occasioned by his own interests and should by no means lead us to suppose that there were no Zealots during the time of Jesus' activity.

In the Sayings Source, however, this remarkable prohibition was followed immediately by:

> *But when you enter a house, first say: "Peace be to this house." If anyone there shares in that peace* [lit.: is a son of peace], *let your peace abide on that one* (reconstructed from Luke 10:5-6 // Matt 10:12-13).

Thus a solemn *shalom* was to be spoken on the houses—evidently the greeting of peace that was not permitted on the road. The order not to greet and the instruction for greeting are mutually related. From the text of the Sayings Source we see that the direction not to greet is in fact to be understood as a temporary withholding of greeting until the moment for greeting/blessing arrives; it is really all about that greeting. The real salutation by Jesus' messengers takes place in the houses or in the squares of the local towns—in the place where those messengers proclaim the reign of God.

As far as this link between sayings is concerned, a number of questions remain open because in the Near East the refusal of a greeting was (and still is today) not only a base rudeness but could be seen as a hostile gesture. Hence the prohibition against greeting deserves further investigation. What could Jesus have meant by that order?

Ambrose of Milan (339–397) offered two reasons for it in his commentary on the Gospel of Luke. *First*: Jesus' messengers should not let themselves be delayed. They had to hasten to their goal. *Second*: Failure to greet pointed to their complete dedication to their commission to preach. Both reasons are plausible, especially the reference to eschatological urgency.

Still, the question remains: why would a brief greeting on the part of Jesus' messengers have been an impediment to haste or to their concentration on their duty? To answer that we need to consider that in the Near East, in whose cultural history large portions of the Bible are embedded, greetings were much more strongly ritualized than they are with us, and they usually lasted much longer. The British scholar Wilfred Thesiger, who between 1946 and 1950 traveled through the Roub-al-Khali desert in southern Arabia, speaks of an encounter in the Arabian desert:

> The riders had now come quite near. . . . There were seven of them, all of them Rashid. We formed up in line to receive them. They halted their camels thirty yards away, couched them by tapping them on their

> necks with their sticks, got up, and came towards us. . . . When they were a few yards away Mahsin, whom I identified by his lame leg, called out "Salam alaikum," and we answered together, "Alaikum as Salam." Then one behind the other they passed along our line, greeting each of us with the triple nose-kiss, nose touching nose on the right side, left side, and again on the right. Then they formed up facing us. Tamtaim said to me, "Ask their news"; but I answered, "No, you do it. You are the oldest." Tamtaim called out, "Your news?" Mahsin answered: "The news is good." Again Tamtaim asked, "Is anyone dead? Is anyone gone?" Back came the immediate answer: "No! Don't say such a thing!" Question and answer were as invariable as the responses in the Litany. No matter what had really happened, they never changed. They might have fought with raiders; lost half their number and still not been able to bury them; their camels might have been looted, any affliction might have befallen them—starvation, drought, or sickness, and still at this first formal questioning they would answer, "The news is good."[4]

Thesiger continues by describing how, after the first, formal part of the greeting had been completed, carpets were spread on the desert sands and coffee was prepared. Then a bowl of dates was passed to each of the guests, and coffee in the order of their esteem. Only after that were all seated, and now, at last, all sorts of news was exchanged for hours on end.

We note how ritualized it all is. These people take their time and enjoy long conversations. Certainly the news they exchange is, at least in part, vital. What springs have water at this time? Where has it recently rained, so that green fodder for the camels may be found there? Above all: were any groups of hostile tribesmen encountered on the way?

Obviously Palestine is not Southern Arabia, and yet there, too, an encounter with familiar or unfamiliar travelers had much greater significance than it has for us. Here, too, there were rituals of greeting, news was exchanged, new relationships were formed or old ones deepened. And here, too, "greeting each other" could require a lot of time.

In 2 Kings 4:29 Gehazi, Elisha's servant, is ordered to go as quickly as he can to the dead child of the Shunamite woman and lay Elisha's

[4] Wilfred Thesiger, *Arabian Sands* (London: Penguin, 1991), 101–2.

staff on his face. That "as quickly as possible" is expressed in the words "if you meet anyone, give no greeting!" But does that command really mean that Gehazi must not even shout out a *shalom* to someone approaching him? Isn't it really an order not to engage in time-consuming conversation?

In that light it seems questionable whether Jesus forbade his messengers even a brief greeting, and whether the word "greet" does not instead refer to ritual greetings and long interchanges. In Acts 18:22 and 21:7 the word for "greet" that Luke uses in this gospel passage is not a verbal exchange but a short visit. There "greet a community" is shorthand for "make a brief visit to the community." So in any case the word "greet" has a somewhat elastic meaning.

Bernhard Lang proposed the thesis that in forbidding greetings Jesus was ordering them not to visit their relatives while they were on mission.[5] That would be similar to "greeting" in Acts 18:22; 21:7. We have to consider that possibility also, because visits to family would have taken up time. Probably none of the Twelve would then have been able to avoid listening to all kinds of news about each individual family, with associated commentary, and it would have taken them far away from their proclamation of the urgently approaching reign of God.

Basically, we are facing a problem here that appears at other places in the Gospels as well: what we have received is often only a brief saying of Jesus, but he must have explained such sayings to his disciples and given reasons for them, and we no longer have those explanations. The same is true in this case. So we have to reconstruct what it could have meant.

Still, we need to keep in mind that, as mentioned in the introduction to this second section, the very sending of the disciples reveals a whole succession of sign-actions. The very fact that Jesus "created" the Twelve (Mark 3:14)—that he chose them from among a larger number of disciples and constituted them as a group—was clearly a sign-action. The same is true of their being sent out two by two; in that way they show that they are witnesses, in accordance with the biblical rule for testimony (Deut 17:6; 19:15), and indeed witnesses to the now-inbreaking reign of God. Their minimal equipment also

[5] Bernhard Lang, "Grußverbot oder Besuchsverbot? Eine sozialgeschichtliche Deutung von Lk 10:4b," *BZ* 26 (1982): 75–79.

has a sign-character; it signals their nonviolence. Most certainly a sign-action occurs when they shake the dust from their feet because a place has not received them and has rejected their eschatological message (Luke 10:10-11 // Matt 10:14). The dust-shaking gesture signifies: You are like unclean pagan land. We dare not have anything at all to do with you when the coming judgment strikes you.

The inhabitants of a Jewish community who witnessed that demonstration of shaking-the-dust-from-the-feet would have seen it as a severe provocation. Should we assume that "not-greeting" would also have been a deliberate provocation[6] since it said: "We have no time. We are on more important business—now is not the time for exchanging everyday news because the really new thing that changes everything, the reign of God, is dawning?"

If that was the sense of the command not to give greetings, then the people passing by who were not greeted would also have needed to be able to recognize what the haste of Jesus' disciples meant. Did the disciples shout to the passersby? Or did the word about who these barefoot, unarmed people traveling from place to place were, and what they were saying, get around very quickly in the villages and towns of Galilee and neighboring districts?

Unfortunately we do not know any of that, and so I would like to leave open the question whether Jesus' command not to greet was also a deliberate and provocative sign-action. What I find to be certain is that, *first*, Jesus' prohibition of greeting is authentic; *second*, that it was intended to keep attention directed solely to the nearness of the reign of God; and therefore, *third*, that it forbids the disciples at least to exchange the usual news and banalities. Doesn't the gospel of the reign of God also prohibit all kinds of gossip about other people and all needless words (Matt 12:36)?

14. When You Enter a House (Luke 10:5-12)

Continuing our examination of the so-called instructions for mission, we find that the "equipment rule" is followed by instructions for exactly what is to be proclaimed, closely bound up with "rules

[6] That is the carefully-grounded thesis of Iris Bosold, *Pazifismus und prophetische Provokation. Das Grußverbot Lk 10,4b und sein historischer Kontext*, SBS 90 (Stuttgart: Katholisches Bibelwerk, 1978).

for lodging." In Luke 10:5-12 (as we have seen, here Luke generally follows the Sayings Source) these instructions are found in two pieces of text. First Jesus' messengers are told how to behave in the *houses* they enter:

> Whatever house you enter, first say, "Peace to this house!" And if anyone is there who shares in peace, your peace will rest on that person; but if not, it will return to you. Remain in the same house, eating and drinking whatever they provide, for the laborer deserves to be paid. Do not move about from house to house. (Luke 10:5-7)

This is followed by instructions for how to act in a *city* or *town*:

> Whenever you enter a town and its people welcome you, eat what is set before you; cure the sick who are there, and say to them, "The reign of God has come near to you." But whenever you enter a town and they do not welcome you, go out into its streets and say, "Even the dust of your town that clings to our feet, we wipe off in protest against you. Yet know this: the reign of God has come near." I tell you, on that day it will be more tolerable for Sodom than for that town. (Luke 10:8-12)

When we compare these two sections of the text we see right away that they have a lot in common:

- entering the house or the town
- greeting of peace/announcement of the reign of God
- eating whatever is offered
- the possibility of rejection in the houses or towns.

Essentially the instructions for behavior, first in the houses and then in the towns, are a broadly constructed parallelism. An additional element in the second part is the statement about healing the sick, shaking off the dust, and the reference to the city of Sodom. Of course the dust-gesture and the comparison with Sodom do not fit the "house" theme, so they are absent there, but they also constitute an effective closing to the whole. All that favors the supposition that what we have here are not two different instructions that were subsequently put together—one for "how to behave in houses" and one for "how to behave in towns." Rather, what we have here is a composition in which everything was connected from the very beginning, and elements of one part explain elements in the other part.

This insight into the compositional intent of Luke 10:5-12 is important for the interpretation—and above all for a right understanding of the greeting of peace in the houses, since at first glance it seems odd that the reign of God is not proclaimed in the houses, but only a "peace" is spoken. But if the two sections of text are deliberately placed in parallel it is clear that the peace that is given to the whole family (represented by the *paterfamilias*) is nothing other than the peace-bringing blessing of the reign of God—and the reign of God proclaimed in the squares of the towns is the eschatological time of peace that will change everything.

If a household rejects Jesus' messengers, then of course the reign of God cannot happen there. Peace cannot enter, and it withdraws together with the messengers. Thus it was conditioned on the reception of the messengers and—we may well say—on eating with them. (Incidentally: that Jesus' messengers are to eat whatever is set before them could mean that they should not worry about whether the food is really *kosher*, what is permitted by the Jewish food laws).

The second parallel passage also clarifies that the peace of the reign of God is not only a peace of the soul. It is all-encompassing salvation: even the sick are healed. A comparison with the corresponding texts in Mark 6:7 (// Luke 9:1; Matt 10:8) shows that this command to heal also includes driving out demons. The Twelve are to do everything that Jesus himself does. They come not only *on orders from* Jesus but *as his representatives*; they come *in his stead*. When they come it is as if he himself came. And they come not only into the towns but into the houses as well. The two sections of text belong together; they give mutual clarification and augment one another.

So much for the structure and meaning of our text! What about the historical reality the text describes? Why does the mission instruction, with its rules for where to dwell, speak not only of towns but also of houses? Would it not have sufficed for Jesus simply to tell the Twelve to proclaim the reign of God in the squares of the cities and towns? Why do the houses play an equal role?

The answer, in the first place, is quite simple: Jesus' messengers must have something to eat, they have to quench their burning thirst, and they need shelter for the night. Hence the role of the houses! We may imagine that Jesus' missionaries first sought out the centers of the towns and shouted out the news of the reign of God. The decision whether that town was open to their preaching would be made very quickly. If Jesus' messengers encountered hostility they left the town. If they were received hospitably they quickly found someone who was prepared to house and feed them.

What I am describing here, of course, would scarcely apply to real cities or large towns. This is about villages in Galilee where people lived close together, knew each other, and it made sense to say, "If a town receives you . . ." A historical map of lower Galilee in Jesus' time reveals some fifty villages and small settlements in addition to the real cities or towns of Sepphoris, Magdala, and Tiberias.[7] Our text takes place solely in those villages and settlements. It only makes sense there.

"Houses," however, have another significance. The fact that Jesus puts so much emphasis on them is presumably connected with the fact that houses had a special meaning for him as brief rest stops or bases for his work. In the latter case we may think especially of Simon Peter's house in Capernaum (Mark 1:21, 29); among the former would be, for example, the house of Martha and Mary (Luke 10:38), the home of the toll collector Zacchaeus in Jericho (Luke 19:5), or the house of the unknown person in whose upper story Jesus celebrated his last Passover meal with the Twelve (Mark 14:12-16). Jesus must again and again have experienced what houses meant for his itinerant life in Galilee and his travel to Jerusalem. Probably it was often in the houses that the selective preaching in the marketplaces became intensive teaching, that mere spectators became believers, that those who at first were only curious became followers of Jesus.

It is true that relatively few of those who received Jesus' message left their families and traveled throughout the land with Jesus in his restless wandering. But the families in which Jesus or his disciples lodged were changed by it. They became more available, more open, no longer concentrated on themselves (Luke 19:8). Houses mean fami-

[7] Cf. Willibald Bösen, *Galiläa als Lebensraum und Wirkungsfeld Jesu. Eine zeitgeschichtliche und theologische Untersuchung* (Freiburg: Herder, 1985), 59; David A. Fiensy and James Riley Strange, eds., *Galilee in the Late Second Temple and Mishnaic Periods*, 2 vols. (Minneapolis: Fortress Press, 2015), contains detailed maps as well as studies on Galilean history, village life, economics, and archaeology.

lies, people who previously had nothing to do with each other and now developed relationships. At last they had something that profoundly connected them. So, in the midst of Israel—at first still invisibly and yet unstoppably—the new thing God was planning began to grow. It was out of the disciples who traveled with Jesus through Israel, out of those who sympathized with the Jesus movement, and out of the families who received Jesus and his disciples, openly and full of expectation, that, after Easter, the first communities arose.

Those post-Easter itinerant missionaries we know of from the *Didachē*, who had no fixed abode but moved from community to community, were, most certainly, extremely important for the transmission of all the radical words of Jesus that called disciples to leave their families. Such Jesus-sayings reflected what those missionaries themselves were living. That is by no means to say that they were the *only tradents* of Jesus' words, and they were most certainly not *creative inventors* of all Jesus-sayings that are demanding and are critical of families.

After all, the cornucopia of Jesus-*logia* transmitted to us by no means consists only of sayings that presume a radical-itinerant *ethos*. Consider only the *logia* that underlie the antitheses in the Sermon on the Mount. Second, even Jesus-sayings addressed to the twelve missionaries or specifically meant for the circle of Jesus' disciples could bear fruit for adherents tied to house and village. Think just of the Our Father, originally a prayer only for disciples. Its fourth petition presupposes the precarious situation of the disciples (see the next chapter). Nevertheless, the Our Father very quickly became a prayer for firmly settled Christians as well.

In any case, after Easter the "houses" quickly acquired great significance, for the first Christian communities gathered in houses (Acts 2:46; 12:12; Rom 16:5; Col 4:15; Phlm 2). Where else? That is why the communities were so accessible and inviting. There, in their domestic closeness, people could struggle for unanimity, trust one another, care for one another, bear one another's burdens, receive, and transmit—handing on even radical words of Jesus.[8]

[8] For this role of the early Christian houses cf. especially the excursus "Urchristliche Hausgemeinden" in Peter Stuhlmacher, *Der Brief an Philemon*, EKK 18, 2nd ed. (Düsseldorf: Benziger; Neukirchen-Vluyn: Neukirchener Verlag, 1981), 70–75, esp. 74.

It would thus be a serious methodological error to conclude from the significance of the later house communities and the itinerant missionaries traveling between them that the mission discourse simply retrojected the situation of the church at a much later time into that of Jesus. The case is exactly the opposite: it was precisely because the "houses" played such an important role for Jesus himself and the mission of his followers that, after Easter, believing households from Jesus' time could form the first Christian communities. And obviously the people in those household communities were interested in preserving and handing on the traditions of Jesus.

15. Bread for the Day to Come (Matt 6:11)

The Gospels contain a whole series of texts that are not part of the "mission instruction" and yet are closely connected to the mission of the Twelve and, in general, to the unstable wandering life of Jesus and his disciples. One of those texts is the "bread petition" in the Our Father. The "official" English version of the petition is:

> *Give us this day our daily bread!*

That corresponds to the standard translations of the fourth petition of the Our Father in many other languages, and above all that of the Latin liturgy: *Panem nostrum quotidianum da nobis hodie!* But that familiar version, in that form, does not exist in the New Testament. How did that happen? Within the New Testament we have the Our Father only in the Gospels of Matthew and Luke (Matt 6:9-13 // Luke 11:2-4), but its wording varies between the two at many points—and those include the bread petition. Compare:

Matthew 6:11	*Our . . . bread give us today!*
Luke 11:3	*Our . . . bread give us daily!*

The official versions of the bread petition seek to iron out the difference between Matthew and Luke by simply combining them. But besides the problem with this posterior harmonizing, there is another: it is the Greek adjective *epiousios*, which falls precisely at the point where I have inserted ellipses. *Epiousios* appears nowhere in ancient literature outside the Our Father. Its meaning has to be deduced.

In all probability *epiousios* goes back to the Greek verb *epienai* = "be coming, follow." Acts speaks several times of the "coming (day)," using *epienai* (Acts 7:26; 16:11; 20:15; 21:18). If *epiousios* is derived from *epienai*, the meaning must be that the bread is requested for the day to come, the next day. But then how would we reconstruct the bread petition as a whole? Should we follow Luke or Matthew?

Better Matthew! It is true that he offers a version of the Our Father that contains a number of expansions: for example, the third petition ("thy will be done") and part of the final petition ("but deliver us from the Evil One"). But in the petitions that are common to both Matthew and Luke, Matthew is closer to the original wording. Therefore the preferable translation is:

> Give us today our bread for the day to come!

When we look at that we can see immediately why none of the usual versions of the Our Father translates it that way. Who could understand it? "Give us today our *daily* bread!" is much more accessible, and yet the translation of Matthew 6:11 we have chosen puts us directly in the situation in which the Our Father was first prayed, because it is precisely the situation described in the preceding chapters:

Jesus' disciples are on the road. They are carrying nothing: no spare robe, no staff, no money, no sack for provisions, no bread. So they are utterly dependent on places that will receive them and houses they can visit for the night. What they need from them is above all a lot to drink in order to quench their thirst and an adequate meal to restore their strength. That is precisely what the word "bread" means here: not just the then-common flatbread but necessary food and drink—in short, everything a person needs in order not to succumb.

Of course, this peculiar "today for the day to come" creates difficulties. The disciples need a meal on this very day, this evening. Why not just say "give us our bread for this evening!" But that difficulty dissolves as soon as we realize that, in the Jewish view, the coming day does not begin at midnight, and certainly not on the following morning, but the evening before—as soon as the sun has set. (We know that the Sabbath begins on Friday evening.) The bread petition in the Our Father thus means: give us this evening the bread for the new day to come—that is, the (most important) meal we need for every day.

We can see especially in the bread petition how precisely the Our Father suits the situation of those missionary disciples who, by Jesus' command, are not to have anything with them, not even "a buttered roll" for the journey. Obviously, though, the bread petition also fits the disciples who travel with Jesus through the land. They, too, need hospitality in the evening, a larger meal, a place to spend the night.

Thus the bread petition is altogether concrete and sharply situated. We can understand that for centuries its interpreters avoided that placement. They interpreted the bread as "heavenly bread" or in terms of the coming eschatological meal in the reign of God. Or they read it in terms of the daily reception of the Eucharist. Likewise, in our time of globalization many preachers, despite Luke 11:1-2, do not want to accept that the Our Father is a disciples' prayer. It has to have worldwide significance and apply to all people! Thus the bread petition becomes a kind of "bread for the world." Even serious Bible scholars try to avoid the specific situation of disciples and situate the bread petition in the lives of Galilean day-laborers who are to pray to God that they will be hired in the early morning and so be able to earn their bread, that is, their life-sustenance for the coming day.

But those are all escape nets. Either they spiritualize the bread petition unbearably or they expand it so much that nothing remains of the disciples' situation. Obviously that is all well-meant: the bread petition should be contemporary. But we can only achieve an appropriate updating of the Our Father if we start with its original meaning, and there the bread petition is about Jesus' disciples (and not the bread petition alone). It is about the fact that they abandon all security. They are to beg their heavenly Father, in profound trust, that they may always receive what they need, just for this one day. They can be as carefree as the "birds of the air" and the "lilies of the field" (Matt 6:25-34). And they need not think about the day to come, for Jesus must have smiled as he jokingly said to his fearful disciples, so hesitant in the face of their mission:

> Do not worry about tomorrow,
> for tomorrow will bring worries of its own! (Matt 6:34)

But this is not just about Jesus' disciples. It is equally about those who offer them hospitality. It is precisely because now, everywhere in Israel, the peace-producing companionship that will be crucial for the new thing that is part of the inbreaking reign of God develops wherever there are people who receive Jesus' disciples, eat with them, and offer them a bed. The disciples who have left their own families in order to follow Jesus need the help of the "houses"—that is, other families—so that they can work with dedication and without worry. The other families, in turn, need the help of Jesus and his disciples so that they can believe in the coming of God's reign.

The true current significance of the bread petition in the Our Father lies in this mutual being-for-others. We only have to look away from ourselves and think of our Christian sisters and brothers in China, North Korea, Iran, Iraq, Syria, Somalia, Sudan, or Egypt. There the people who believe in the gospel of Jesus are often isolated or in great danger, and for that very reason they depend on each other. They have to rely on mutual aid from house to house and the exchange of help between the preachers and the believing families. The differences between disciples and people, between "devoted" and "less devoted" Christians have long since become fluid in those countries. There emerges quite clearly what is meant by a discipleship that sustains itself also under persecution and discrimination.

Christians will soon live in similar situations in many other countries—not because they are persecuted everywhere but because they will have to exist in an environment in which Christianity, and certainly Jesus' gospel, have become absolutely foreign and, essentially, a matter of sheer indifference. Then the Christians will have to distinguish themselves much more firmly from their environment than they do now, not only in the strength of their faith but also in their *way of life*. Here is the real "now-ness" of the Our Father and especially its bread petition. Obviously the church must be an advocate for all the hungry of the world. But still more important are solidary communities who live according to the measure of the reign of God—as an example for the world. Only then will the suffering and hungry of the world really receive enduring help.

16. Whoever Listens to You Listens to Me (Luke 10:16)

In the Sayings Source the mission discourse must have ended with a Jesus-saying that constituted a powerful conclusion:

> Whoever listens to you listens to me,
> and whoever rejects you rejects me,
> and whoever rejects me rejects the one who sent me.

This three-liner—like so many other Jesus-*logia*—is artistically structured: the first two lines constitute a parallelism while the second and third lines, taken together, establish a "synthetic parallelism," that is, one in which the second line further develops the first. The whole three-liner, however, delivers a so-called "stepwise" or "climactic parallelism," because the three members establish a climax, an intensification:

Disciples → Jesus → God

However, it is disputed whether the Matthean parallel may offer the more original version. It is more simply structured and with "welcomes" it seems to fit better with Jesus' messengers' search for accommodations than does "listens" in Luke 10:16:

Whoever welcomes you, welcomes me.
And whoever welcomes me welcomes the one who sent me. (Matt 10:40)

Certainly this better fit could point precisely to Matthean redaction. The same is true of the simpler form of Matthew 10:40. Matthew could have used Mark 9:37: "Whoever welcomes one such child in my name welcomes me, and whoever welcomes me welcomes not me but the one who sent me." On the other hand we should consider that we find the version in Matthew 10:40 in John 13:20 also:

Amen, amen, I tell you:
Whoever receives one whom I send receives me; and whoever receives me receives the one who sent me.

All these versions show that we have here a Jesus-saying that was extremely important to even the earliest communities. It was transmitted in several forms. It could be varied to apply to new situations. I consider Luke 10:16 the more original version of the *logion*.

But even if it were not so, the mission discourse here reaches a climax and (at least in the Sayings Source) its conclusion, and that conclusion now opens itself clearly—more clearly than everything in the mission discourse before it—to Christology. "Whoever listens to those sent by Jesus hears Jesus himself, and whoever rejects them rejects Jesus, and whoever rejects Jesus rejects God." In the Matthean variant: "Whoever welcomes Jesus' missionaries welcomes Jesus himself, and whoever welcomes Jesus welcomes God."

The background of those formulations is the Jewish law regarding messengers: "A person's messenger is [considered] like him-/herself" (*m.Ber.* 5.5). That is: the one sent represents the sender, comes with the sender's authority, is fully representative and even makes the sender present. That is true, in the first place, of the Twelve, whom Jesus has formally sent out. But it is equally true of Jesus, who was sent by God, represents God, and makes God present. He speaks and acts in God's stead. Whoever hears him, hears God. Whoever welcomes him, welcomes God. This is an implicit Christology—and it comes from the lips of Jesus himself. It is not yet a developed Christology that makes use of eminent titles of majesty such as Messiah or Son of God. It is a Christology that, like the veiling words about the Human One (see chap. 52), is fully restrained—and yet this implicit Christology contains everything the theologians of the early church would subsequently think and develop.

What is fascinating about this conclusion to the mission discourse, however, is not only its Christology. The stepwise parallelism of Luke 10:16 conceals a large portion of ecclesiology. More precisely: it contains the foundation for a doctrine of church offices. The Twelve are sent by Jesus, and that is not accidental or just on the surface; they entirely represent him. They not only act on his orders but in place of him; they make him present. We can see that from the fact that they are permitted, and even required, to do everything Jesus does: proclaim the reign of God, offer peace, heal the sick, drive out demons. "Jesus confers his power upon the apostles and thereby makes their office strictly parallel to his own mission."[9]

After Easter, office in the church would develop on the basis of that sending of the Twelve by Jesus. It would be true of that office as was already true for the Twelve that it is not an empowerment by humans, by human power, resources, efforts; it is empowerment by Jesus Christ and thus by God. It is not, certainly, that "power" is given in the sense our society understands, but power that is simultaneously weakness. The Twelve are sent like lambs in the midst of wolves, without means and without armament, completely dependent on the help of people who receive them into their homes at night.

This high empowerment that in truth is also defenseless weakness belongs, of course, not only to the Twelve. It is true of all disciples Jesus chooses. That will be the subject of part 3 of this book.

[9] Joseph Ratzinger, *Called to Communion: Understanding the Church Today* (San Francisco: Ignatius Press, 1996), 113.

Part Three

A Disciple's Existence

The theme of part 2 of this book was Jesus' sending of the Twelve. But beyond the group of the Twelve there must have been a larger circle of disciples; after all, the creation of the Twelve (Mark 3:14) suggests that Jesus was able to select them from an existing group of disciples. In fact, all four Gospels indicate that there were many of them.

In Matthew's version it seems as if "disciples" and "the Twelve" are identical. Matthew speaks sometimes of the "twelve disciples" (Matt 10:1; 11:1; 20:17; cf. 28:16). Did he mean to restrict the group of disciples to the Twelve only? That is unlikely, because in that case the words of the Risen One, "make disciples of all nations" (Matt 28:19), would say "make all peoples some kind of disciples of the Twelve."

The matter is absolutely clear in Mark. In 2:13-14 he tells how Jesus calls the toll collector Levi to be a disciple. Thereupon Levi throws a party at his house and invites a crowd of friends and acquaintances. In this context we read:

> *And as he sat at dinner in Levi's house, many tax collectors and sinners were also sitting with Jesus and his disciples—for there were many who followed him.* (Mark 2:15)

This little note makes it clear how Mark imagines the situation: there is already a broader circle of disciples from among whom the Twelve will soon be chosen (Mark 3:13-15).

Our question receives an even clearer answer from Luke, who gives a vivid description of the installation of the Twelve: Jesus gathered all his disciples around him and chose twelve from among them; these he called "apostles" (Luke 6:13). That is immediately followed, in Luke, by the so-called Sermon on the Plain, and the audience for it is carefully arranged by Luke: Jesus is surrounded by the newly constituted group of the Twelve, together with the "great crowd" of other disciples—and finally, in a still wider circle, the multitude of people (Luke 6:17-20). Luke thus clearly reckons with a larger number of disciples.

And then there is John's Gospel! Here it is especially clear how and to what extent the boundaries of the group of disciples were fluid. The number of the Twelve, of course, is fixed (John 6:67–71), but the number of disciples shifts. The Fourth Gospel tells how, one day, a large group of disciples became offended at Jesus and abandoned him (John 6:60–66).

We are fortunate to have the names of a number of individuals who were not part of the Twelve but probably belonged to the wider circle of disciples: Nathanael (John 21:2), Cleopas (Luke 24:18), Joseph Barsabbas (Acts 1:23), and Matthias, who took Judas Iscariot's place in the circle of the Twelve (Acts 1:23, 26). We also have, from Mark 15:40-41, the names of the following women disciples: Mary Magdalene, Mary the mother of James the younger and of Joses, and Salome. It is explicitly said of these women that they "followed" Jesus during his Galilean activity and "served" him (Mark 15:41).

There is another list of women (probably assembled by Luke himself) in Luke 8:2-3. Here again, Mary Magdalene is first; her name is followed by those of Johanna the wife of Chuza (one of Herod Agrippa's officials), and finally a Susanna of whom we hear nothing further other than that she, like Mary Magdalene and Johanna, had been healed by Jesus. Luke avoids the word "follow" here but takes up "serve"[1] from Mark 15:41 and clarifies it: "out of their resources." Does Luke mean to say that these women were unable to follow Jesus as the male disciples did, but served according to their means or opportunity? There is little point in speculating about the question. What is crucial is that Jesus' disciples included women. That was remarkable in the circumstances of the time, and it was anything but a matter of course. Evidently in this Jesus deliberately transgressed the social structures of his time.

Let me add a brief remark on the word "disciple," which I have used routinely over quite a few pages. It appears often in the Gospels, always representing the Greek *mathētēs*. We could translate *mathētēs* as "student," but the concept is broader. At that time a *mathētēs* was someone who was educated by another—hence the term would apply to every pupil and student in a philosopher's circle. In Latin the New Testament *mathētēs* was translated *discipulus* (= student, pupil), and in English

[1] The word for "service," in both cases, is *διακονία*. —Trans.

translations of the Bible as "disciple." In Hebrew the word corresponding to *mathētēs* was *talmid*. *Talmidim* were the students of rabbis.

And here, precisely, lies the problem. We must absolutely not equate those who followed Jesus with the rabbis' students.[2] What Jesus demanded of his followers had nothing at all to do with rabbinic schooling. The rabbis' students chose their own teacher, whereas it was exactly the reverse with Jesus' followers. Rabbinic students were bound to *stabilitas loci*, that is, an orderly educational process, always in the same place; Jesus' students traveled with their master throughout the land in a precarious, itinerant fashion. The rabbis' students studied Scripture; they came to their teacher to "learn Torah." For Jesus and his disciples it was all about full commitment to what was happening now, with the arrival of the reign of God. So Jesus says in Luke 14:26: "Whoever comes to me and does not hate father and mother, wife and children, brothers and sisters, yes, and even life itself, cannot be my disciple." In using the word "disciple" Jesus may be adopting the terminology of rabbinic study, but he then changes it provocatively to mean a radical demand to surrender all family ties (cf. chaps. 18, 21, and 23). He demands that not only of the Twelve but of all his disciples.

So much for the existence of a broader circle of disciples around the Twelve! In part 3 we will discuss only *logia* that could apply to all disciples, female and male, and not simply to the group of the Twelve.

17. Foxes Have Holes (Luke 9:57-58)

Jesus' pilgrimage to Jerusalem for his last paschal feast begins, in Luke's version, with a solemn introduction couched in biblical style: "When the days drew near for him to be taken up" (Luke 9:51). From that point onward Luke includes episodes as often as possible that serve to visualize Jesus' journey to Jerusalem. One of the first is the encounter with a man who says to Jesus, "I will follow you wherever you go" (Luke 9:57). Jesus answers him:

[2] For what follows see esp. Martin Hengel, *Nachfolge und Charisma*, in his series *Jesus und die Evangelien*, Kleine Schriften 5, ed. Claus-Jürgen Thornton, WUNT 21 (Tübingen: Mohr Siebeck, 2007), chap. 3, 40–138. This work of Martin Hengel's on Luke 9:59–60 // Matthew 8:21-22ff. is fundamental for the question of "discipleship" of Jesus.

> Foxes have holes,
> and birds of the air have dwelling places;
> but the Son of Man [= Human One] has nowhere to lay his head.
> (Luke 9:58 // Matt 8:20)

Jesus' response is found in the Sayings Source, so Luke and Matthew have it in common, but Matthew introduces it differently from Luke. In Matthew it is a scribe who comes forward—and in the First Gospel this occurs in a much earlier phase of Jesus' activity—and says, "Teacher, I will follow you wherever you go" (Matt 8:19). Jesus answers in exactly the same words as in the scene shaped by Luke.

As far as the form is concerned, both Matthew and Luke use what is called an "apophthegm." Both Matthew 8:19 and Luke 9:57 clearly illustrate how the narrative introduction could be varied. Quite often it was formulated by the particular evangelist or at least accommodated to the intent of the narrative, but frequently the *logion* at the heart of it all remained the same. It was a word of the Lord, carefully preserved and handed on.

The same is true here! Jesus' disciples must have memorized the three-line composition with the foxes first, the birds second, and the Son of Man (the returning world-judge) third; it is unforgettable. But it was not only the unusual combination of *foxes – birds – world-judge* that stamped it on their memory. The *holes* of the foxes and the *nests* of the birds also match the peculiar sequence—and then comes the unexpected crash: the Human One, the highest of all "living things," does not even possess what the animals have. In the great vision in Daniel (Dan 7:1-14) the "one like a human being" is also found at the end of a sequence of animals (lion, bear, leopard, beast, Human One). In Daniel these animals embody the great world empires, yet the Human One is placed above all of them. All the great empires must serve that One. But here, in this sequence, the "Son of Man" is far inferior to the other figures in the comparison.

Nearly every translation of this *logion* speaks of the birds' "nests."[3] In the context that is more or less right: birds build nests. But here we

[3] One exception is Michael Wolter, *Das Lukasevangelium* (Tübingen: Mohr Siebeck, 2008), 371. [English: *The Gospel According to Luke*, 2 vols., trans. Wayne Coppins and Christoph Heilig (Waco, TX: Baylor University Press, 2016), 2:49–50.] Wolter translates the word as "Unterkünfte" [quarters, lodgings]. His correct but unusual translation

find in the Greek not the usual word for "nest," as, for example, in Psalms 83:4b and 103:17a (LXX). Instead, the word here is *kataskēnōsis*. In the Septuagint (LXX), the Greek Old Testament, *kataskēnōsis* is used exclusively for God's dwelling in the Jerusalem temple (1 Chr 28:2; Tob 1:4; 2 Macc 14:35; Wis 9:8; Ezek 37:27). How do we explain that? Was Jesus speaking here, jokingly, of the wondrous "dwellings" of the birds, equal to a dwelling in the temple?

If so, we would again have here a witness to Jesus' humor—even in serious situations. In that case Jesus would, in the sense of this *logion*, be saying that "the Human One has nothing at all: neither the dark holes of the foxes nor the bright and wondrous dwellings of the birds." It could be that with the "dwellings" of the birds Jesus was thinking of Psalm 84:1-4,[4] which speaks of the "dwelling place" of God in the temple (v. 1) and the "swallow's nest" in which she "may lay her young" close to "the altars of God" (v. 3). If this were the correct interpretation the three-line composition would step up from the homes of the foxes to the much brighter dwellings of the birds in the temple area, closer to God, and then the fall would be that much greater. In any case the word *kataskēnōsis* here is very, very striking.

Obviously what Jesus says here is not a *lament* at his own situation of wandering and lack of a dwelling; it is a sharp *warning* to his conversation partner: "If you want to follow me, think hard about what you are asking!" Jesus speaks of his own homelessness only so that this person may really consider what such discipleship means.

Jesus is talking about hard realities here: his own family want to confine him at home because his brothers think he is crazy—and so he has to separate from his family (Mark 3:20-21, 31-35). It is his mission to proclaim the coming of the reign of God everywhere in Galilee, and then later in the capital city—and for that reason he is unsettled and lacks a fixed abode. It could easily happen that, contrary to all Near Eastern rules for the reception of guests, he cannot even find shelter for the night—and then he has nowhere to lay his head. Luke

---

caused me to research the subject further. (Translator's note: the unusual usage is not reflected in the published English translation.)

[4] For the following reading of Ps 84:1-4 cf. Erich Zenger in Frank-Lothar Hossfeld and Erich Zenger, *Psalms 2*, trans. Linda M. Maloney, Hermeneia (Minneapolis: Fortress Press, 2005), 348–58, esp. 358.

had described such a situation immediately before this: Jesus and his disciples were not received in a Samaritan village (Luke 9:52-56).

Now I have spoken, together with all exegetes, about Jesus' homelessness and that of his disciples. Jesus talks of it in this *logion* quite realistically and with no cosmetic cover. But at the same time we could think here about Jesus' unmarried state and the fact that his disciples had to leave their wives, children, and houses to follow Jesus.

"The Human One has nowhere to lay his head." Doesn't a spouse creep into our thoughts here, almost unnoticed—the spouse whom the man may embrace, in whose love he can breathe, in whose understanding he can rest, indeed, on whom he can rest his head? Jesus had none of that. Why not? Was it because he was a shy, inhibited man? or because he rejected the body's pleasures, or sexual pleasure in particular? or because of rigorism or fanaticism? No! For Jesus there was only one reason for his own celibacy as for his disciples' temporary separation from their wives: the reign of God, which must be proclaimed *now*.

But here we must reflect that the homelessness of which Jesus speaks in our *logion* is much more than a rational choice, that is, a temporary refusal of house and home for the sake of greater mobility. It is about the reign of God—and in the sense that Jesus' homelessness makes visible that other home that should reveal itself already in the "new family" of many sisters and brothers. For the reign of God demands a people of God in which all join their lives together. It calls for a new community, a new way of being together.

18. Let the Dead Bury Their Own Dead! (Luke 9:59-60)

In the Gospels of both Luke and Matthew the short narrative that in Luke 9:57-58 culminates in "the foxes have holes . . ." is followed by a similar apophthegm, also from the Sayings Source (cf. Matt 8:21-22). In Luke's version it reads:

> To another he said, "Follow me." But he said, "Lord, first let me go and bury my father." But he said to him: "Let the dead bury their own dead; but as for you, go and proclaim the reign of God!" (Luke 9:59-60)

The crucial sentence, "Let the dead bury their own dead," is the same in Matthew and Luke and must have read that way in the Sayings Source. By contrast, the two evangelists have framed the apophthegm differently: in Matthew a "disciple" approaches Jesus and asks that he first be allowed to bury his father. Only then does Jesus say: "follow me, and let the dead bury their own dead." That sequence is somewhat awkward. Luke places "follow me!" at the beginning, but adds at the end, "but as for you, go and proclaim the reign of God!" That concluding command is missing in Matthew and may well be a Lukan expansion that fits the situation very well. Of course, we need not concern ourselves with the exact wording of the original frame: what is crucial is the central *logion*. Still, from the beginning it must have been told as occurring within some situation.[5]

Obviously this *logion* is about a concrete occurrence. It does not state a general norm. And yet: what Jesus says here is not only uncompromising: it is shocking, and it applies to everyone who dares to follow Jesus. It is true that we do not know whether the father of the one whom Jesus summons to follow him has just died, or if he is on his deathbed, or if he is only in decline. But that does not matter because in any case what Jesus calls for in this saying contradicts a demand of Torah, namely, the Fourth Commandment.

For centuries the Fourth Commandment was interpreted by Christians as being about young children. They should be good and obey their parents. In reality the commandment was addressed to adults. They were to care for their aged parents when they could no longer look after themselves. They should obtain justice for them when they were in peril and, in the end, give them decent burial.[6]

The weight of the Fourth Commandment in that concrete form is obvious when we understand that in those times care for the aged was not provided by public institutions, as it is with us, but was solely the responsibility of adult sons. We should also keep in mind what a *ritually proper* burial signified for people in that world. In Judaism the burial of the dead was at that time, and still is, the most important of all "good works," and when an occupying power refused burial

[5] Cf. Martin Hengel, *Nachfolge und Charisma* (see n. 2 above), 45.

[6] Cf. esp. Rainer Albertz, "Hintergrund und Bedeutung des Elterngebots im Dekalog," *ZAW* 90 (1978): 348–74.

to someone executed, that was one of the most horrible "added punishments" there could be.

Thus when in our text someone who was deeply moved by Jesus or had even been called to follow him asks to be allowed first to bury his "father" and Jesus forbids him to be with his aged parent as he is dying, or even to bury him, that was the sharpest possible blow against piety and custom, indeed, directly against Torah itself. The reason Jesus gives for this severe offense is the urgency of discipleship—and obviously that discipleship is directly connected to the nearness of the reign of God. "Preaching the reign of God is now more important than the Fourth Commandment and more urgent than all family ties," Jesus says.

"Let the dead bury their own dead!"—no one who has heard those words can ever forget them. "The dead . . . dead" is keenly calculated rhetoric. Everyone knows that the dead cannot bury the dead, because they are themselves dead. So this evidently means that those who are *spiritually dead* should handle burials—people who do not receive Jesus' message, who have not comprehended what this hour has brought.

That, at any rate, is how this text is often interpreted, and that interpretation can appeal to the fact that other passages in the New Testament speak of the "spiritually dead" (cf., e.g., 1 Tim 5:6 or 1 John 3:14). But it is possible that what Jesus says here is more demanding. Could he have meant,[7] "Now it is all about the reign of God; now it is about life in a new world. Who cares about the dead then? *Let the dead—that is, those who have died—bury themselves in their own company*"? That would have been extreme irony. Jesus would be making no distinction at all between those who are *really* dead and those who are *spiritually* dead. For him there would be no either/or: living in the realm of the dead or in that of life, namely, in the now-inbreaking reign of God.

One way or the other! This saying of Jesus is shocking, and for a Jew in Jesus' time it must have been far more scandalous than it is for us because the pious burial of the dead was, indeed, the highest duty, a supreme command, more important than many other matters.

[7] For what follows cf. esp. Ulrich Luz, *Matthew 8–20*, trans. James E. Crouch, Hermeneia (Minneapolis: Fortress Press, 2001), 18–19, with reference to Carl Friedrich August Fritzsche, *Evangelium Matthaei* (Leipzig: Fleischer, 1826), 323.

But we ourselves only have to imagine that our own parent lies dying and we dare not even take time to visit or to attend the funeral.

In saying this did Jesus make himself superior to God's commandments? No, but he interprets them with majesty and sovereignty—as if he himself were the lawgiver. The scribes collected and compared biblical passages in order to interpret what Torah says, down to the tiniest detail. They battled over every letter. Not so with Jesus! He speaks and acts, truly, as if he stood in place of God.[8] But we will examine Jesus' sovereign claims more fully in part 5.

19. Whoever Puts a Hand to the Plow (Luke 9:61-62)

Luke appended a third apophthegm to the two about the foxes and the dead—which, as we saw, were drawn from the Sayings Source. Like the two preceding it, this one speaks of the unconditionality—indeed, the recklessness—that is required of everyone who wants to follow Jesus. This third apophthegm is Lukan special material:

> Another said, "I will follow you, Lord; but let me first say farewell to those at my home." Jesus said to him, "No one who puts a hand to the plow and looks back is fit for the reign of God." (Luke 9:61-62)

This text clearly has an Old Testament background. The First Book of Kings tells how the prophet Elijah calls a disciple. The Old Testament call story is also about departure from one's family—and there too the motif of plowing plays a role:

> *So [Elijah] set out from there, and found Elisha son of Shaphat, who was plowing. There were twelve yoke of oxen ahead of him, and he was with the twelfth. Elijah passed by him and threw his mantle over him. He left the oxen, ran after Elijah, and said, "Let me kiss my father and my mother, and then I will follow you." Then Elijah said to him, "Go back again; for what have I done to you?" He returned from following him, took the yoke of oxen, and slaughtered them; using the equipment from the oxen, he boiled their flesh, and gave it to the people, and they ate. Then he set out and followed Elijah, and became his servant.* (1 Kgs 19:19-21)

[8] Here I am referencing Ernst Fuchs's expression in *Studies of the Historical Jesus*, trans. Andrew Scobie (London: SCM, 1964), 20–22.

This text depicts Elisha as the son of a wealthy landowner: his fields can be plowed with twelve yoke of oxen at the same time! Elijah calls him by throwing his mantle over him, thus claiming Elisha for God's cause. Elisha realizes immediately what that means for him: breaking with his former calling, leaving his family, living an uncertain life, discipleship. The rest of the story then only describes how the wealthy heir leaves family and profession behind him.

The parallel with Jesus' story is found primarily in the fact that Elisha also asks permission to take leave of his parents. He knows, then, that he is no longer his own master but is Elijah's servant. Elijah allows him to go home and take his leave; this rather difficult text can scarcely be read any other way. By saying "what have I done to you?" he permits him full freedom. One who is called must be absolutely free to choose to follow.

It appears, however, that this very permission makes Elijah aware of what has happened to him. The text evidently means to say that he does not return home at all but instead improvises a farewell feast for his servants in the field. At any rate, he uses the wooden yokes of one pair of oxen to make the fire—a vivid sign that God's cause allows for no delay and that he is abandoning his previous occupation.

It would be wrong to suppose that Luke 9:61-62 is a post-Easter text, simply made up by clever storytellers in the community in imitation of the Elijah-Elisha story. Jesus knew the biblical texts too. When speaking of someone just called as "first taking leave" he must immediately have thought of the story from Kings. The fact that it also spoke of plowing may have led him to the statement that no one who is plowing can look back: otherwise the furrows will be crooked. Jesus' own initial calling (to carpentry) could also have played a role here: a builder cannot afford to set up crooked walls or let them deviate from the vertical.

If we take the Old Testament and New Testament stories together, the result is a disturbing image of biblical theology of vocation: it first reveals the necessity of the "immediacy" of discipleship but also that the new thing God has begun in the world with Israel can only be handed on from person to person. There is no automatic transfer of faith to the next generation. Calling and charism must be given face to face. Elisha had to feel Elijah's mantle on his body.

But the two narratives show still more: namely, the importance of the nonprofessional. By himself Elisha would probably never have thought of becoming a prophet. He had other things in mind: his parents' business, commerce, family. Probably that is just why he was called. God needs more than learned officials; God also needs seasoned nonprofessionals, people who are in a position to direct servants driving twelve spans. And it is no accident that Jesus sought out people like Peter and Andrew, James and John, who understood their work as fishers or, like Levi the tax collector, could add and subtract.

The two stories also show that no one can call herself or himself. Calling must come through others. When someone declares himself or herself to be called, it can be a dangerous mistake. Such miscalculations are balanced by the ancient experience of the People of God: people need to hear from other people that God is calling them.

Luke 9:61-62 appears at first to be almost inhuman. As in other sayings, so also here Jesus reveals a positively shocking clarity and unconditional firmness. While Elijah allowed his disciple to take leave of his family, Jesus no longer does. He demands "recklessness" in the literal sense and keeping one's eyes to the front: whoever looks back is useless for the reign of God. But those who have understood and followed these words of the Lord, even from a distance and with all the fears and shortcomings that bind us—these know and will never forget the freedom and joy into which Jesus' unconditional calling leads.

20. Jesus' Single Life (Matt 19:12)

We spoke briefly about Jesus' celibacy in chapter 17, but it is worthwhile pursuing the subject further because when Jesus demands that his disciples put their families last (see chap. 21) it is obviously related to his own unmarried state. There is a four-part *logion* that can take us a step further here: namely, Matthew 19:12, which is preceded by a conflict with Pharisees about divorce that Matthew took from Mark 10:2-12 and updated at certain points. He then appended the Jesus-saying that is our subject here, with his own introduction. Given our primarily historical perspective, we need not concern ourselves with this context. The saying itself reads:

> There are eunuchs who have been so from birth,
> and there are eunuchs who have been made eunuchs by others,
> and there are eunuchs who have made themselves eunuchs for the sake of the heavenly reign.
> Let anyone accept this who can! (Matt 19:12)

The skillful structuring of this three-line saying, plus a final challenge, is immediately obvious. Three kinds of eunuchs are named in succession: The first line speaks of men with defects we would today call genital abnormalities. The second line is about those who are castrated. Jesus' listeners must have been on tenterhooks to know what the third line would be, because (as with jokes) the third part often had a surprising twist. Here it is the reference to men who have castrated themselves—something that would be a horror to Jewish ears. Thus it is only the exaggerated third line that reveals Jesus' intent: self-castration is being used in a transferred sense to speak of celibacy—a *self-chosen* celibacy for the sake of the reign of God. The three-liner is extended and concluded by the challenge: "Let anyone accept this who can!"

The whole *logion* is shaped to be so offensive that this alone favors its authenticity. Ultimately, Jesus *apparently* describes himself as a *castratus*. He could talk that outrageously. Still, he probably would have avoided *this type* of challenge if it had not been forced upon him. That is, there is much in favor of the idea that the occasion for Matthew 19:12 was discrimination against Jesus by his opponents.[9] Apparently, in order to destroy his reputation, people had accused Jesus of being not only a glutton, a drunkard, and possessed by the devil, but also a eunuch.

It is characteristic of Jesus that, in the face of that calumny, he did not keep silent or simply deny it; rather, he took it up, turned it around, and so brought to light the real reason why he was not married: the reign of God. It is likewise characteristic of him that he does not say "*I* am unmarried for the sake of the reign of God." Jesus prefers to make such statements about himself indirectly: His answer begins, "*There are eunuchs*." It could also be that some of his disciples were included as well. They would have been similarly accused, because they had left their families and from then on they were on the road with Jesus in Galilee.

All that favors the authenticity of Matthew 19:12. Jesus' unmarried state must have been a much greater offense than we can imagine. The rabbis, appealing to Genesis 1:28 ("be fruitful and multiply!"), regarded the production of children as a commandment. Rabbi Eliezer

[9] Thus esp. Josef Blinzler, "Εἰσὶν εὐνοῦχοι," *ZNW* 48 (1957): 254–70.

ben Hyrcanus (ca. 90 CE) would later say "Anyone who does not engage in the propagation of the race is as though he sheds blood" (*Yeb.* 63b), and Rabbi Eleazar ben Pedat would write "Any man who has no wife is no proper man; for it is said, 'Male and female created He them and called their name Adam'" (*Yeb.* 62b-63a).

What is crucial in our context is that here Jesus connects his own celibacy and the separation of his disciples from their families directly with the reign of God. He asserts that there is such a thing as a free decision not to marry for the sake of the reign of God. Not everyone, he says, can understand that: "Let anyone accept this who can!" But those who accept it have understood something essential about the reign of God.

Although Jesus speaks altogether drastically here, he remains discreet. Still, those who want to hear can hear: his unmarried state was not blind fate and most certainly not accidental, nor was it a marginal phenomenon in his individual life history. It was part of his absolute submission to the reign of God. Celibacy was at the center of Jesus' person. From that point of view we can, in turn, understand more deeply why Jesus could also demand of others that they abandon their families, interrupt their marriage relationship, and let go of all ties to house, business, and home.

21. Without Concern for One's Own Family (Luke 14:26)

The *logion* to be discussed here is one of Jesus' offensive sayings that seem to open an unbridgeable chasm between "family" and "discipleship." Matthew and Luke found it in the Sayings Source, but each made changes in both form and content. Here, first of all, is Luke's wording:

> Whoever comes to me and does not hate father and mother, wife and children, brothers and sisters, yes, and even life itself, cannot be my disciple. (Luke 14:26)

In Matthew the same *logion* reads:

> *Whoever loves father or mother more than me is not worthy of me;*
> *and whoever loves son or daughter more than me is not worthy of me.*
> (Matt 10:37)

How did these two different versions come about? Luke may have added "wife," "brothers," and "sisters" in order to present as full a family panorama as possible. He may also have inserted "even life itself" from Mark 8:35. It refers to one's beloved "I" with all its wishes and dreams. Those who want to follow Jesus have to surrender even that last stronghold. On the other hand, the keyword "hate" was certainly part of this *logion* from the outset. Luke retained it.

Matthew, on the other hand, replaced "hate father and mother" with "whoever loves father and mother more than me." Did he want to soften Jesus' harshness? He may, however, have retained the original, simple sequence "father and mother" / "son and daughter."[10] One could argue about whether the parallelism in Matthew's version, which seems almost too smooth, was original or was created by Matthew. If we think it is original, the *logion* may have read this way in the Sayings Source (conceding the fact that the reconstruction remains uncertain):

> Whoever does not hate father and mother cannot be my disciple.
> Whoever does not hate son and daughter cannot be my disciple.

The real difficulty in this saying of the Lord is obviously the verb "hate." Why such language? Why a concept that apparently stands in direct opposition to the biblical love commandment? A look at the Old Testament is helpful here. There we find the opposition between "loving" and "hating" quite frequently, and every biblical scholar knows that, at least in some of these instances, the meaning of the words does not simply equate with our "loving" and "hating." In many cases we should, instead, translate along the lines of "prefer/disadvantage" or "love/avoid." Let me take just one example. In Deuteronomy 21:15-17 the subject is the inheritance right of the first-born son. Here the legal prescription of the Deuteronomic law code is as follows:

> If a man has two wives,
> one of them loved and the other disliked,
> and if both the loved and the disliked have borne him sons . . .

[10] Thus the Sayings Source (cf. Matt 10:37) originally spoke only of parents and children, not of wives. Their absence is noticeable. Could it be because our *logion* comes to us *by way of the Sayings Source* and in the phase during which the Sayings Source was being handed on—that is, after Easter—when the apostles again had their wives with them, as we know Simon Peter did (1 Cor 9:5)?

The text then adds that the man must respect the rights of the *firstborn* son, even if the firstborn is the son of the woman he "hates." Here "hate" quite obviously does not simply mean what we normally understand as "hatred," namely, a purely emotional state. The meaning is, rather, something like "have less regard for," "disadvantage," "neglect," thus the opposite of "prefer" or "favor." Other texts point in the same direction.

It is against this background that we should interpret Luke 14:26. It in no way means that those who follow Jesus should cultivate feelings of hatred toward their families. Instead, the idea is that one must set aside one's own family in favor of discipleship, in the sense that one becomes completely free for the task at hand. Matthew would have intended to make that clear with his own intervention in the text.

Still, we must not read these semantic explanations as a softening or watering-down of what is said. The word "hate,"[11] even when it is understood in the sense described here, is still extraordinarily severe—as much as when Jesus says, "If your hand causes you to stumble, cut it off!" (Mark 9:43).

What Jesus demands here is justified only because it is about the reign of God, or more precisely because it is about complete self-surrender to the proclamation of the reign of God. In that case it may be that one's family must be less important. It may then be that one's wife, together with her children, must return to her parents' house (something that was stigmatized).[12]

Well then, must one's own family be totally and definitively dismissed in this way? No! It must happen only if its members oppose the calling of one of them to be a disciple, as described immediately before this *logion* in Matthew 10:34-36, drawing on Micah 7:6: son against father, daughter against mother, daughter-in-law against mother-in-law.

But if the family behaves differently, if it is in harmony with the one who leaves in order to follow Jesus or even supports that discipleship, we have a completely different situation. Then the old family even becomes an important part of the new—namely, the "new family" that is now subject to the reign of God. John 19:25-27 depicts that very event.

[11] NRSV softens to "dislike."

[12] Cf. Joachim Jeremias, *New Testament Theology* (see part 1, n. 8 above), 224.

22. Already a Hundredfold (Mark 10:29-30)

At the end of the preceding chapter we spoke of the "new family" that comes into being, subject to the reign of God. The concept has its direct antecedent in Jesus' own life. We need only read Mark 3:20-21, 31-35. Jesus is in a house, surrounded by a crowd of people who are listening to him. His relatives show up to "restrain him," that is, to take him home by force. Evidently his public behavior had offended them. Those with authority in the family are convinced that he "has gone out of his mind." But it seems that they want to avoid pushing their way through the crowd to get to Jesus, so they ask that he come outside. When Jesus is told that his brothers and mother are asking about him he does not go out; rather, he distances himself from his own family in positively juridical form by saying: "Who are my mother and my brothers?" He turns to the crowd around him and—again using juridical language—creates a "new family" with the words,

> *Here are my mother and my brothers!*
> *Whoever does the will of God is my brother and sister and mother.* (Mark 3:34-35)

Thus the meaning of "new family" does not originate in the experiences of the young communities that formed after Easter.

These preliminary remarks were necessary for understanding the following Jesus-saying and to help us locate it correctly. We have it from Mark:

> Amen, I tell you:
> there is no one who has left house or brothers or sisters or mother or father or children or fields, for my sake and for the sake of the good news, who will not receive a hundredfold [in return], now in this age: houses, brothers and sisters, mothers and children, and fields, [although] with persecutions—and in the age to come eternal life. (Mark 10:29-30)

In the form in which we have it this Jesus-saying has already been reworked from a post-Easter perspective by the addition of "for the sake of the good news/gospel" and "with persecutions." It is possible that the schema of two eons or "ages" in Jewish apocalyptic ("this age" . . . "the age to come") was also inserted after the fact, since in the two-age schema the real fulfillment of the promises is realized only in the "age to come" and not yet in this time of suffering and sorrow. For Jesus, in contrast, the time of fulfillment is already beginning, and that is precisely what our text is saying. The new family, with its many sisters and brothers, has already begun as a sign that the reign of God is now coming to be. If Jesus actually used *concepts* from the two-age model here, he corrected the model himself. If we take all that into account, though a concluding future match for "in this age" cannot be excluded with certainty, the original Jesus-saying could have read:

> *Amen, I tell you:*
> *There is no one who has left house, brothers, sisters, mother, father, children, or fields for my sake who will not receive [in return] a hundredfold:*
> *[already] in this age: houses, brothers, sisters, mothers, children, and fields.*

The listings in this parallelism are here significantly longer than in the *logion* in Luke 14:26 we previously studied. As a result the situation it describes emerges all the more pointedly: brothers and sisters are blood relatives, the clan into which a person of that time was bound in a way that would be nearly unbearable to us today, but that in return was also a reliable support and protection. Father and mother: behind this is the ancient order of the patriarchal family. Children: they were one of the greatest joys of the people in Israel, their pride and their security in old age. Above all, they are the bearers of the Promise. And fields: they represent Israel's portion in the holy inheritance given by God. Behind "fields" we must see the idea of the "Land" that was of the highest importance for every believing Jew.

Jesus' disciples have left all that behind: their houses, their fields, their clan, their parents, their children—not, of course, for the sake of abandoning them all, not because leaving them was something valuable in itself. It was for the sake of Jesus, who represents the already-inbreaking new life in the reign of God. So much for the first part of the parallelism.

Then, in the second part, comes the unexpected thing, the thing that is crucial for our text: Jesus promises and affirms with the utmost certainty (after all, the whole parallelism is headed by a solemn "Amen") that those who dare to give up everything and follow Jesus will find a new family in which, paradoxically, there will again be brothers and sisters, mothers and children. But that will not be at some vague time in the future; it will happen now! Already, in this very hour, the disciples of Jesus receive everything they have abandoned—a hundredfold! They have left their families, but in the group of disciples they have new sisters and brothers. They have left their parental home, but in the houses everywhere that receive them with hospitality they have new mothers. They have left their children, but people are constantly coming to them, filled with the new thing. They have left their fields, but in their place they find a solid and sustaining community as a "new land."

All that is not just a promise; for Jesus it is already palpable reality. At that time, and still today, that was and is hard to believe. The worthy Roman Catholic New Testament scholar Josef Schmid, whom I greatly respect, wrote in his commentary on Mark's Gospel:[13]

> *The hundredfold replacement for the earthly goods that have been sacrificed cannot mean a hundredfold of the goods that are named, but only something that is a hundred times as much, i.e., worth infinitely more, namely, communion with God. The hundredfold reward is therefore not to be understood as earthly, but rather heavenly, and the usual interpretation in terms of the consolation and help and strengthening the disciples find, in the midst of persecutions . . . in the "family" of the Christian community, is therefore unsatisfying.*

I can understand that skepticism. Christian congregations and communities all too often fail to present an image of belonging-together such as Jesus promises here—and yet all that does exist. Those who have experienced it know what Jesus means to say here.

It has surely become clear that the *logion* of the "hundredfold" goes far beyond the saying in Luke 14:26 we previously discussed. To assert that Mark 10:29-30 is only a variant on Luke 14:26 that developed in the swift-flowing stream of tradition[14] is to miss the points of the two *logia*. Luke 14:26 speaks of the *fundamental condition* of discipleship; Mark 10:29-30 of the *reward*. Those are two different things, and they probably derive from different situations.

[13] Josef Schmid, *Das Evangelium nach Markus*, RNT 2, 3rd ed. (Regensburg: Pustet, 1954), 197. [English: *The Gospel According to Mark*, trans. Kevin Condon (Staten Island, NY: Alba House, 1968).]

[14] Thus, e.g., Walter Schmithals, *Das Evangelium nach Markus 2. Kapitel 9,2–16,18*, ÖTK 2/2 (Gütersloh: Gütersloher Verlagshaus Mohn, 1979), 458–59.

Unfortunately, in the jungle of discussion about the tradition history and literary backgrounds of the two *logia* the fact that Mark 10:29-30 contains explosive theological and cultural-historical material often fades into the background. The father, who is still mentioned in the first clause, is missing from the second. The second part of the clearly constructed parallelism leaves him out.

Obviously that is no mistake. In the new family that now exists in light of the reign of God there will be no more "fathers." They are all too symbolic of a false form of power and rule. Don't misunderstand me here. Fathers there will and must be in the biological sense, and most certainly fathers in the sense of the parable of the lost son (Luke 15:11-32). But there will be no more fathers who decide and control everything, who rule ruthlessly and subject everything around them to themselves, including their wives and children—that is to say, fathers representing all the shady sides of patriarchalism. That kind of father, our *logion* says casually, can no longer exist in the reign of God and the new community of life that is now beginning in it. In the next chapter we will pursue the subject of "fathers" more extensively.

23. Only One Is Your Father (Matt 23:9)

There is another very important saying of Jesus on the subject of "fathers." It is found in Matthew 23:9:

> Call no one your father on earth, for you have one Father—the one in heaven.

Who is being addressed here? Matthew has built into his overall composition a section directed at the scribes and Pharisees (Matt 23:1-39) that represents a kind of catechesis for teachers and leaders in the Christian community. This excursus links to the assertion (Matt 23:7) that the scribes like to be addressed as "Rabbi" (literally: "my great one"), and it then says in deliberate opposition:

But you are not to be called rabbi,
for you have one teacher, and you are all students [lit.: brothers].
And call no one your father on earth,
for you have one Father—the one in heaven.
Nor are you to be called instructors,
for you have one instructor, the Christ.

> *The greatest among you will be your servant.*
> *All who exalt themselves will be humbled,*
> *and all who humble themselves will be exalted.* (Matt 23:8-12)

Clearly we are hearing words directly formulated by Jesus, at least in part (e.g., in the last two sayings), while in other parts the formulation comes from later tradition or from Matthew himself (e.g., the third saying in which the title of majesty, "Christ," appears). It is also clear that problems of the early church are being addressed here. The temptation to enjoy distinction in the form of titles of honor evidently began quite early. Matthew takes an extraordinarily hard position against such thirst for titles. He denies church officials not only honorable titles like "Father" but even functional designations like "Teacher."

How did Matthew get so sensitive to a situation that, unfortunately, the church has not become more sensible about to this day? He could only have received the impetus from Jesus. It is true that the excursus in Matthew 23:8-12 is partly redactional (especially in the first and third sayings), but the spirit of Jesus emerges from every line. In our context we are only concerned with the second saying. It not only reveals the spirit of Jesus; here the historical Jesus himself is speaking.

Here, as the context shows, Matthew understood the word "father" as a title of honor just like "rabbi" and "teacher." In the Christian communities—Matthew means to say—no one may lay claim to the title "father." In this way he actualizes the underlying words of Jesus and applies them to his purpose. Jesus, naturally, had spoken not about leading figures in the community but instead about the physical fathers of his disciples. Matthew 23:9 is part of the radical *ethos* of discipleship we discussed in the previous chapter. What did the saying mean originally?

The disciples who traveled with Jesus through Galilee had left their families, and with them also their natural fathers—and with the natural father also his care for them, resting on a long life experience, that had sustained them. In this situation, which had to make the disciples profoundly uneasy, Jesus points them to their true Father, namely, God, who has now taken the place of their earthly fathers. In their new situation they need not—indeed, they must not—call anyone "father" other than their Father in heaven. They must, therefore, break with their natural father; indeed, they have already done so. From now on the Father in heaven will care for them. If we take the saying in Matthew 23:9 out of the context in which it now stands we can quite correctly read it anew as follows:

> *Call no one your father on earth any longer,*
> *for only one is [from now on] your Father: the one in heaven.*

With these reflections I have tried to determine the original *Sitz im Leben* for a Jesus-saying that we have received in Matthew's Gospel in a new catechetical situation. The semantics and grammar do not offer the least obstacle.[15] Even the Greek version in Matthew can be understood in the sense given here as soon as the saying is extracted from its current context.

Moreover, a whole series of other texts supports this original meaning of Matthew 23:9: for example, those about freedom from care that Matthew has worked into the Sermon on the Mount (Matt 6:25-34 // Luke 12:22-31). There Jesus urges his disciples to abandon all care about food and clothing because, after all, *their heavenly Father* cares for them.

Likewise, the apophthegm (cryptic maxim) about the one who first wants to go home and bury his father, who has it said to him, "let the dead bury their own dead" (Luke 9:59-60), belongs in this same context: those who follow Jesus must detach themselves from their natural fathers. But above all, the Our Father enters the picture here (Matt 6:9-13 // Luke 11:2-4); it is purely a prayer for disciples addressed to the *abba* in heaven and, in its fourth petition, asking only for bread for the day to come. God will take care of it.

Thus Matthew 23:9 in its post-Easter sense must be interpreted against the background of its original meaning. For those who are baptized into Jesus Christ, God has become Father: so much so that they may no longer use "father" as a polite address for anyone else.

24. Whoever among You Wants to Be First (Mark 10:43-44)

The *logion* that is our subject here is multiply attested in the Gospels. Moreover, it is narratively developed in the parable about the work of an enslaved person (Luke 17:7-10). Besides the Matthean

[15] There is absolutely no syntactical problem: *humōn* goes with *patera*. *Patera* has been displaced, however, because of the rhetorical form of *hyperbaton* (transposition), which places the emphasis on *patera*.

parallels in 20:26-27 and 23:11, it appears in three different lines of tradition: namely, in Mark 9:35; 10:43-44 and in Luke 22:26. Evidently this saying of Jesus struck an ecclesial nerve from the very start. We can argue about which of the three lines of tradition comes closest to the original version. I have chosen Mark 10:43-44:

> Whoever wishes to become great among you must be your servant, and whoever wishes to be first among you must be slave of all.

What Jesus says here is more than merely a "principle of modesty."[16] Such a definition in no way does justice to this saying. It is loaded with dynamite. It talks about a different kind of society. That is what we most need to speak about. But first: just as one can argue about which is the oldest line of tradition, we can also dispute the situation in which Jesus might have spoken these words. The Gospels offer three different possibilities:

1. The Twelve have been talking "on the way," apparently among themselves, about which of them was the "greatest." Jesus instructs them on that subject with Mark 9:35.
2. A dispute arises among the Twelve at the Last Supper about "which of them was the greatest." Jesus instructs them with Luke 22:26.
3. James and John ask Jesus for seats next to him in the coming reign of God—one on his right and the other on his left (Mark 10:37). When the other ten hear about it they are angry at the two. Jesus instructs them with Mark 10:43-44.

A location at the Last Supper is the least plausible. Here, evidently, Luke wanted to contrast Jesus' surrender of his life with the behavior of the Twelve. The petition from the sons of Zebedee for places next to Jesus in the coming reign of God is a more persuasive possibility. So let us consider this location for the present.

It is clear that this is not just about seats of honor. James and John evidently imagine the approaching reign of God in terms of the contemporary systems of sovereignty, with everything that went with

[16] Thus, *inter alia*, Rudolf Pesch, *Das Markusevangelium* 2, HThKNT 2 (Freiburg: Herder, 1977), 103, 154.

them. They want to occupy the highest offices in the ruling hierarchy alongside Jesus.

Jesus cuttingly rejects this dreamscape—or should we say this career-fixation? He replaces the high office they desire with its direct opposite: first the servants at table who carry away the remains of the meal (the upper crust at the time just dropped them on the floor during their banquets), then the slaves, who had no rights and whose lives were entirely in the hands of their masters. Thus an intensification is built into the parallelism: from "servant" to "slave." But when the "greatest" and the "first" in the reign of God are equated with "slaves," that is more than a call for enduring modesty. This is about an alternative social project that turns everything on its head. That this is not a false interpretation is evident from the Jesus-saying that immediately precedes this one in Mark 10:42-43 (// Luke 22:25-26):

> *You know that among the Gentiles those whom they recognize as their rulers lord it over them, and their great ones are tyrants over them. But it is not so among you.*

Note the categorical formulation:[17] "but it *is* not so among you." That is: "it can and must not be so with you." This contrast-saying looks directly at the type of lordship that was common at the time, as exercised, for example, by Herod the Great. In the Lukan parallel it is still more obvious, for Luke speaks of rulers who let themselves be called "benefactors." Many Hellenistic rulers not only bore the official title *euergetēs* (= benefactor); it appeared on quite a few inscriptions honoring them. It was a vital element of the reputation of powerful Hellenistic and Roman rulers that they practiced demonstrative largesse: building stadiums and baths, endowing festal games, distributing food. That was the customary way of cultivating one's image. At the same time the people were squeezed dry, and everyone who might even possibly be a rival was done away with.

Still, the familiar contrast built into our *logion* essentially applies to any state, for every government is a hierarchical system built on propaganda and especially on violence. Even a government of laws has need of force in order to limit the chaos that always threatens. In

[17] For what follows cf. Marius Reiser, "Ethik und Anthropologie in der Spruchweisheit Jesu," *TTZ* 126 (2017): 58–82, at 70.

that case we are talking about a legitimate system of governance built on law and justice—but nevertheless on violence. The state monopoly of violence (and this is an important and welcome advance) has replaced the rule of the iron fist.

But in our *logion* Jesus proposes a world in strict contrast to all that. Obviously there is "rule" or "governance" in it, for a society without laws, without order, without offices is impossible. It could not stand. But here "rule" is something completely different. It is pure service that dare no longer support itself on propaganda, power, and violence. This kind of rule is powerless. It cannot fight for or compel anything for itself. It can only ask for understanding, and it can only attest, bear witness, and serve. Therefore it must reckon at every turn with being misjudged, insulted, despised, or eliminated.

It is anything but an accident that our *logion* culminates in the one about the Son of Man who will "give his life a ransom for many" (Mark 10:45), and that Luke positions it at the Last Supper in light of Jesus' death. In Mark 10:43-44 Jesus proposes what is, in its deep structure, the image of an alternative society, one that contrasts with the state.[18] It presupposes the state; it knows how bitterly necessary it is. It does not despise it. But it knows that all legally limited violence requires subsocieties, even antisocieties, that live without violence.

The church is thus subject to an enormous demand, for a system of organization that reverses all other systems built on power in favor of pure service for others and rejects every kind of violence has been unconditionally given it by Jesus Christ. Often, and ever and ever again, following Jesus, it has lived up to that demand. Yet just as often, or even much more frequently, it has fallen victim to the temptation to become a state in itself (church-state), or to take possession of the ruling structures of the state for its own ends, or to forge an intimate connection to the state (state-church). Or—still more ominous—people in the church have pretended to powerlessness and simultaneously exercised a sublime "spiritual" terror, worse than physical misuses of power.

Even so, what Mark 10:43-44 intends has been irrevocably given to the church. In every celebration of the Eucharist, with every read-

[18] This alternative society contrasts with the state but also, obviously, with all pre-state societies, which are themselves built on deterrence—for example, through the institution of blood vengeance.

ing of the Gospel, in the liturgical chant "O Lamb of God," but above all in the image of the Crucified One who hangs, powerless, on the cross, it is set before its (our) eyes.

25. Taking Up One's Cross (Luke 14:27 // Matt 10:38)

A post-Easter disciple's existence includes not just having the cross of Jesus Christ constantly before one's eyes. Jesus says it in much more radical terms. Disciples must not only look at the cross but seize it and lay it on their shoulders. That, at any rate, is the formulation of the reconstructed version of the Sayings Source that I will here (by way of exception) again take as the basic text:[19]

> Whoever does not carry the cross and follow me cannot be my disciple. (Luke 14:27 // Matt 10:38)

It is easy to understand why people often deny that Jesus said those words. The expression "carry the cross" or "take up the cross" in the transferred sense of accepting all that is difficult and painful does not appear to be attested anywhere in antiquity or in Judaism in this direct and succinct form. Should we not therefore suppose that the formulation of this statement already referred to Jesus' death by crucifixion?

Of course, such a critique must entertain the question: was Jesus dependent on existing metaphors? We must not forget how inventive he was, how clever in his use of language, not only in his parables but also in his sayings. The camel that more easily passes through a needle's eye than a rich person into the reign of God; the log in the eye; "cut off one's own hand" or "tear out one's own eye"—none of these creative expressions lay ready to hand. He himself put these sometimes humorous, sometimes incredibly violent images into words. He was capable of such things.

[19] The *logion* of bearing the cross is well-attested: once in the reconstructed version from the Sayings Source I have chosen here, represented by Luke 14:27 // Matt 10:38, and also in Mark 8:34 // Matt 16:24 // Luke 9:23. Crucial to the reconstruction is the probably-more-original "taking up" the cross attested by Matt 10:38 and the Markan version.

Besides, the image of "taking the cross" (Matt 10:38) or "bearing the cross" (Luke 14:27) did not have to be invented. Again and again, throughout the Roman Empire and even in Palestine, rebels were crucified by Roman soldiers. For example: during the unrest that followed the death of Herod the Great (4 BCE), P. Quinctilius Varus, the imperial legate in Syria, had two thousand rebellious Jews crucified near Jerusalem.

Every one of Jesus' hearers could have witnessed crucifixions or heard them described. The person being executed did not carry the whole cross, only the *patibulum*, the crosspiece. That was heavy enough. The procession to the site of execution was itself something deliberately staged by the occupying power. Still worse, then, was the nailing to the crosspiece and the hours-long sinking and then pulling oneself back up on the nails in order to breathe.

Jesus uses that scenario of horror to show what it means to join in his cause. Those who follow him must reckon with false accusations, calumnies, fanatic opposition, and severe suffering.

Quite naturally, after Easter the image of bearing a cross was inextricably linked to the real death of Jesus on the cross. It became a fundamental metaphor for discipleship of Jesus. But initially it was Jesus himself who chose the metaphor, with the deliberate intent that hearers should recoil from it. Jesus wants to warn against following him, because those who do so must act in complete freedom and should first consider carefully. Moreover, the parallel to our *logion* in the line of tradition attested by Mark presents a no less horrifying picture:

> *If any want to become my followers, let them deny themselves and take up their cross and follow me.* (Mark 8:34 // Matt 16:24; Luke 9:23)

Here the image of "taking up one's cross" is linked to the expression "deny themselves." What does that mean, denying oneself? What is it saying? The Greek *aparneomai* basically means "say no" and "refuse." Other meanings are "reject someone" and "break with someone." In our case it evidently means "say no to oneself," "break with oneself."

Therefore those who want to follow Jesus to the point of what is meant by "discipleship" must abandon their own beloved "I." They may no longer cling to themselves, their own ideas, desires, life plans, and comfort zones. They have to "free themselves from themselves" and hand over their lives. Thus we again arrive at precisely what "take up one's cross" meant, and the question arises whether Mark's line of tradition might not also lead us to an authentic saying of Jesus.

Still, however one reads the tradition criticism, one thing is certain: Jesus' saying that those who want to follow him must take up their crosses does not refer to the many everyday "crosses" daily annoyances, tedious details, the unending unpleasantnesses and embarrassments of life. It does not even mean persistent illnesses and, ultimately, the death we all must die. First and fundamentally it means surrender of one's own life for God's cause, for what Jesus lived and preached. Only when one has fully accepted that fundamental decision do life's troubles, small and great, become an integral part of discipleship.

26. Those Who Lose Their Life Will Save It (Mark 8:35)

In the sequence of Mark 8:34-38 the saying about "taking up one's cross" is followed immediately by the one about losing and saving one's own life.[20] Did Jesus say this only about the calling of disciples, or does it apply to the whole nation? Does it belong to the *ethos* of discipleship (and thus here in part 3) or to the *ethos* that touches everyone in Israel (and thus in part 4 of this book)? The decision is not easy. But because in the Gospels Mark 8:35 follows immediately after the saying about "taking up one's cross,"[21] it needs to be addressed also in this section and at this point. By way of exception I will exclude a redactional addition by the Evangelist. "For the sake of the gospel" is certainly a Markan addition.[22] What remains is as follows:

> . . . those who want to save their life will lose it,
> and those who lose their life for my sake . . . will save it.

[20] The direct parallels to Mark 8:35 are Matt 16:25 // Luke 9:24. The parallels from the Sayings Source are Matt 10:39 // Luke 17:33; cf. also John 12:25. The *logion* discussed in this chapter is thus received in a variety of versions.

[21] Except in Luke 17:33.

[22] Cf. Mark 10:29 and the parallels from the Sayings Source, Matt 10:39 // Luke 17:33.

We see right away that this two-liner is also artfully arranged. It is not only an antithetical parallelism; the verbs form a chiasm (a cross-shaped sequence):

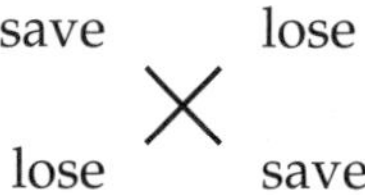

Moreover, the *logion* creates a paradox: who can lose life and thereby save it? The paradox gets bigger when we look at the traditional translations, which, beginning with Martin Luther, have fixated on "lose." But there is another possibility.[23] The underlying Greek word *apollumi* also means—in fact, its basic meaning is—"tear down," "destroy." If we suppose that was the basic meaning of Mark 8:35, the *logion* reads:

> *Those who want to save their life will destroy it.*
> *Those who for my sake destroy their life will save it.*

In that case Jesus' saying is even more drastic because it places a keener emphasis on the demand that disciples themselves destroy their old life for Jesus' sake—which precisely matches the radicality we already encountered in the saying just described above. Jesus' disciples leave father, spouse, children, and everything they own. They put it all behind them: everything on which their life has been based, everything they have built up for themselves. This tearing-oneself-away from everything is an active event, and it is a tearing-down of the previous construction of their lives. The disciples actually level to the ground the whole of their old life—and precisely in doing it they save their life. Nothing is lost. They receive everything back a hundredfold. The paradox is the same as when the translation is "lose," but the suggested alternative is so much better defined and so strongly reflects Jesus' skillful use of language.

[23] Cf. the translation by Fridolin Stier, *Das Neue Testament* (Munich: Kösel; Düsseldorf: Patmos, 1989), 98–99. It is well known that Fridolin Stier constantly strove for a correct rendition of the text, often against the broad current of translational tradition. His phrase "zugrunde richten" means literally "tear down," i.e., "destroy."

It could be that the background of this word of the Lord is a fixed form that is frequently attested in antiquity.[24] According to that pattern, field commanders who make one last speech immediately before battle say to their soldiers: "Those who put their whole lives into it and support their fellow fighters will be saved, but any coward who flees will lose his life, because no one will help him."

If the motif of such a "general's speech" has slipped into Jesus' saying we have another sign that Jesus was educated and knew more about the world than many people give him credit for. But quite apart from that, Mark 8:35 reflects the unconditional nature and radicality of Jesus' own life—the same unconditional stance he demands of his disciples.

Now, at the end of this chapter, I am again inclined to think that Jesus demands this same radicality of all of us. Mark 8:35 and its parallels do not refer solely to the martyrs' surrender of their lives, although even that extreme confession of Jesus may, in some instances, be demanded of every Christian and certainly echoes in this word of the Lord. Normally, though, it is about something else: all people, including devout Christians, are constantly working to "save" their own projected desires, their private models and life plans, and above all their social standing. But precisely these rescue actions endanger one's life or even bring it down—namely, the *true* life offered to each of us if we exist under the reign of God.

Of all the radical Jesus-sayings in the Gospels, probably none of them so clearly judges current tendencies in Christianity as Mark 8:35 does, for in the present time Christians have to listen, all too often, to the exact opposite of what is said in this word of the Lord. Today they are told, in ever-new variations like an endless loop, such things as "Be fully within yourself!" "Be in harmony with yourself!" "Be one with yourself!" "Trust yourself!" "Trust the power of your own depths!" "Listen to your heart's dreams!" "Discover the riches of your life!" "Be kind to yourself!" "Don't hurt yourself!" "Say an unconditional 'yes' to yourself!" "Finally forgive yourself!" "Determine your own life!" I did not invent a single one of those sayings. I took every one of them from the new Christian esoteric "devotional literature." But they do not whisper to us only in advice-literature and trivial magazine articles.

[24] See the usage as early as Homer, *Iliad* 5.529–32; 15.561–64. Further examples are in Michael Wolter, *The Gospel According to Luke* (see n. 3 above), 1:387–88.

They don't only come from the lips of self-help advisers and psychologists. They have found voice for a long time in catecheses and sermons. And yet what Jesus demands of those who want to belong to him is not self-love but self-surrender.

27. When the Salt Loses Its Savor (Luke 14:34-35)

We have received the saying about salt not only in a Markan version (Mark 9:50). It was also in the Sayings Source (cf. the commonalities between Luke 14:34-35 and Matt 5:13 against Mark). In this case the Sayings Source has a more original version than that of Mark. Luke 14:34-35 is to be preferred for reconstructing its wording. There this *logion* reads:

> Salt is good;
> but if salt has lost its taste[25]—
> how can its saltiness be restored?
> It is fit neither for the soil nor for the manure pile;
> they throw it away.

This text sounds odd in our ears because it comes from a world in which salt was a much-desired and often quite expensive article. Obviously, as with us, salt was used for seasoning and for the preservation of food. But it was also employed for cleaning, for softening pelts, for cosmetic and medical purposes. Newborns were rubbed with salt (Ezek 16:4). Salt was indispensable. Hence our text says at the very beginning, "Salt is good."

But how can salt lose its "saltiness"? For the pure table salt we use nowadays that is impossible. Sodium chloride (NaCl) remains sodium chloride. But at that time there was no such thing as completely pure salt—not in Palestine, at any rate. There, for centuries, salt was derived primarily from the Dead Sea, whose water was channeled into flat beds to dry. In the course of the drying process a great number of other ingredients could be isolated from the desired salt, but not completely. Traces of calcium sulfate and other chemical impuri-

[25] I will not enter further into the much-discussed problem of translating the Greek word *mōrainō* [foolish, tasteless, etc.] here. See, on the one hand, Joachim Jeremias, *The Parables of Jesus*, trans. S. H. Hooke (New York: Scribners, 1955), 125, and, on the other hand, Michael Wolter, *The Gospel According to Luke* (see n. 3 above), 2:227.

ties remained in the salt. If it was kept in damp conditions in the house or elsewhere it could then happen that the salt would—at least in part—dissolve out, and so the taste of the impurities could become stronger; it could happen that the salt would become completely unpalatable.

Another problem in our text lies in "how can [its] saltiness be restored?" (Or, more literally, "with what can [it] be flavored?"). We could leave out the "it" or "its," so that the meaning would be: "if you no longer have any good salt, what will you use for seasoning?" But the next line makes that interpretation impossible. The subject can only be the salt (which, incidentally, is how Mark 9:50 interprets it). So Jesus means to say: "What will you use to salt your salt when it has become unsalty?" That kind of pointed talk is typical of him.

One more problem is the "soil." Evidently the presumption is that at that time most of the household garbage could be used to fertilize the fields. In ancient Roman instruction books for farming, for example the work of Columella (d. ca. 70 CE), there are long discussions of proper fertilization.[26] Here, then, we have to translate the Greek *gē* (earth) with "soil" or "ground." Obviously the spoiled salt could not be put on the dung heap or on the field. It had to be disposed of somewhere else.

Another question posed by our text is often overlooked—and with it we arrive at the real interpretation: to whom was this "salt saying" addressed? Was it only for the disciples or also for the crowds, some of whom even ran after him? If it is addressed to all, then this saying was a sharp warning to Israel. In that case the people of God were being seen in their role in relation to the nations. Israel was to be a blessing for the whole world (Gen 12:3) and a "light to the nations" (Isa 42:6). But if it does not accept its calling because it wants to be like the other nations, then its salt has become saltless—and it will be trodden under foot like discarded salt (Matt 5:13). In that case the salt saying would be taking up John the Baptizer's judgment speech, which had just as keenly called Israel into question (Matt 3:9).

The saying could also be addressed, however, to Jesus' disciples. In that case it was about their duty toward Israel. Through their very existence the disciples were the eschatological salt for Israel. If that salt loses its power to witness, it is useless; it will even become

[26] Columella, in his twelve-volume work *Rei rusticae libri* (here at 2.5.9.15), speaks at length of the production, storage, and proper application of manure.

offensive. It will no longer be needed and will be cast out (Luke 14:35). It is of no use even as fertilizer; it pollutes the "Land."

If we consider the contexts in Mark (9:31, 35), Matthew (5:1-13), and Luke, either the disciples are the addressees or else the people are placed face to face with the requirements of discipleship (Luke 14:25, 33). It would probably have been the same for Jesus as well. Jesus wanted to make it clear to those who had left everything and followed him: "You must never abandon your real duty, which is to gather Israel for the reign of God; and you must live according to the ways of the reign of God. Otherwise you are superfluous, even a mischief." As a matter of fact, the two possible addressees are not a strict either/or. They are closely connected: the disciples are, for Jesus, the essence and center of growth of the eschatological Israel—and that eschatological Israel does not exist for itself; it was chosen for the sake of the world.

28. The Millstone around the Neck (Luke 17:1-2)

The saying about the millstone is also doubly transmitted: first by Mark, with the wording:

> *If any of you put a stumbling block before one of these little ones who believe in me,*
> *it would be better for you if a great millstone were hung around your neck and you were thrown into the sea.* (Mark 9:42)

The second version is in the Sayings Source, but the complete *logion* there is available to us in this case only through Luke.[27] There the same Jesus-saying reads:

> Occasions for stumbling are bound to come,
> but woe to anyone by whom they come! You would be better off if a millstone were hung around your neck and you were thrown into the sea than if you cause one of these little ones to stumble. (Luke 17:1-2)

If we see how this saying of Jesus is situated in each context it is obvious that he addresses it to his disciples (cf. Mark 9:35, 38 and Luke

[27] Matthew 18:6 follows the Markan text with minor stylistic changes, but by means of the *logion* about the *skandala*, which he places immediately after this one, Matthew shows that he knew the corresponding text in the Sayings Source.

17:1). As regards the genre, then, we are in the milieu of "instruction for disciples." Strictly speaking, it would have to have been about a crisis, or crises, among the disciples that seemed so dreadful to Jesus that he responded with the *logion* about the millstone. But that is pretty improbable. Still less likely is that what we have here is a post-Easter construct by the community in reaction to internal scandals. Who in the early church would have formulated such a drastic saying? We must therefore assume that this is a saying of Jesus addressed directly to his opponents, although after Easter it could be employed for situations within the communities (temptations to abandon the faith).

Which of the two versions is closer to the original? The Markan text is simple and easily understood. The crucial point, namely, causing "little ones" to stumble, is stated directly in the first line and in the form of a generalized statement. Literally: "Whoever causes one of these little ones to fall."

In contrast, the version in the Sayings Source has a brief introduction that makes a kind of rhetorical concession we could paraphrase as: "As things stand there is no getting around the fact that people are caused to stumble." The "woe" is then a transition; only after it does the subject become more concrete, so that we can almost envision a real instance. Thus in the *logion* about the millstone the Sayings Source speaks more rhetorically and in more refined language, and so is closer to the concrete conversation. We can easily imagine that Jesus spoke in just that way when addressing his opponents. Therefore I have chosen Luke 17:1-2, with the Sayings Source in the background, as the more original version. Obviously, that remains a hypothesis. One could just as easily choose the Markan text.

Both versions present translation problems. First, there is the noun *skandalon* in Luke and the verb *skandalizō* in Mark. A *skandalon* was originally the trigger mechanism in a trap that was transferred in biblical language to mean the push that caused one to fall—especially as temptation to a fall from faith. Since the Authorized ("King James") Version, English Bibles have commonly used the word "offense" for *skandalon*. The New Revised Standard Version has "put a stumbling block" for *skandalizō* and "occasions for stumbling" for the plural *skandala*. The latter feels awkward, but it is closest to the original image and more precise than the vague "offense."

Mark speaks literally of a "donkey's millstone," while Luke simply says "millstone." Here Mark is closer. The reference is to the upper part of a stone mill standing on a flat place. That part moved horizontally on its base and was turned by a donkey. Only the upper stone was a "hundredweight," that is, heavy.

What is crucial, however, is that the "little ones" were *not* children. It is true that the scene in which Jesus places a child before the disciples is found fairly close to this text (cf. Mark 9:33-37); in Matthew it stands immediately before it (Matt 18:1-5). But it would be wrong to conclude from this that our *logion*—at least in its original meaning—is to be interpreted as being about leading children astray. As Matthew 10:42 shows, the "little ones" are Jesus' disciples (or, rather, the disciples as transparent for later members of the communities). After all, it was not the priests, the learned scholars, the professional interpreters of Scripture whom Jesus was able to gather. They were more likely to be his opponents. It was the ordinary people, the insignificant, the uneducated, and also those discriminated against, the sinners and the sick, who hoped in Jesus and put their faith in his message about the coming of the reign of God (cf. also Matt 11:25 // Luke 10:21).

In our case the saying is applied especially to Jesus' disciples. They, too, are no religious "specialists," and therefore they were scarcely acquainted with arguments drawn from Sacred Scripture. Evidently Jesus' opponents not only sought repeatedly to discriminate against *Jesus* but had approached his *disciples* in an effort to undermine their faith in Jesus. It was against that background that this saying belonged.

It presents a dreadful image. We have to imagine how a person tied to such a massive stone would be dropped into the "Sea of Galilee," that is, Lake Gennesaret. Pagan practices of execution by drowning were forbidden in Israel. They were especially offensive to Jews because in such cases the person executed could not be buried. Thus Jesus not only chooses the image of a gruesome and dishonorable execution but makes it still worse by specifying the heavy weight of the millstone. Visitors to Israel can still view ancient donkey-powered mills near Lake Gennesaret with their upper and lower stones and be profoundly disturbed.

Still, the whole thing is made even more extreme by the expression "you would be better off." This is a free but accurate rendition.[28] Mark has a slightly different literal formulation than Luke uses: "for that one it would be better if . . . ."

[28] From the *Neue Genfer Übersetzung* (New Geneva Translation).

Meanwhile, impelled by translation problems, we have long since arrived at the question. For Jesus the attempt by his Bible-skilled opponents to destroy his disciples' faith in him must have seemed a direct attack on God's action. He must have thrown the saying about the millstone angrily in their faces—not directly naming God's coming judgment on his opponents but meaning it when he said "if one of you cause one of my disciples to break with me and, for that, you were to be tied to a millstone and thrown into the lake, that would be an easy fate compared to what really threatens the tempter."[29]

For Jesus to have spoken that way, how important for God's cause must his disciples have been to him! And how precious to him, evidently, were all the miserable and insignificant people who placed all their hope in the message of the closeness of the reign of God!

29. A Cup of Cold Water (Matt 10:42)

That Jesus' disciples were extremely important to him is evident not only from the saying about the millstone but also from the one about a cup of cool water. We find it in Mark 9:41, but the parallel in Matthew is probably not simply a reworking of Mark's text. It may go back to a separate line of tradition that was available to Matthew, and his version seems to be older. Hence it will be the basis for the interpretation here:

> . . . if anyone gives even a cup of cold water to one of these little ones because he is my disciple—
> Amen, I tell you, he will not lose his reward. (Matt 10:42)

Matthew has placed this *logion* effectively, at the end of the great mission discourse to the "twelve disciples." Of course it does not fit well in an instruction for the disciples; the addressees are not they, but other persons. Mark places the text after the *apophthegm* about the unfamiliar miracle-worker (Mark 9:38-39), and it does not fit there either. We can see from this that what we have here is a *logion* that originally circulated independently and for which the Evangelists had to find a place. But they rightly saw that the "little ones" are Jesus' disciples—and with that we come to what the *logion* means to say.

[29] For this paraphrase cf. Julius Schniewind, *Das Evangelium nach Markus*, NTD 1 (Göttingen: Vandenhoeck & Ruprecht, 1963), 132.

It was simply the custom to offer passing travelers a drink of water; that was one of the rules of Near Eastern hospitality. Israel's wisdom literature expanded it to command giving drink even to one's enemy:

> *If your enemies are hungry, give them bread to eat;*
> *and if they are thirsty, give them water to drink.* (Prov 25:21)

It was thus a matter of course to offer a drink of water to a stranger. What is unique here is that the refreshment is to be given to someone *as a disciple of Jesus*. With that the whole thing shifts to a different level—one that, for God, is crucial because, besides Jesus himself, Jesus' disciples are those most engaged in the transformation of the world that is now taking place through the coming of the reign of God. Everyone who comes to the aid of Jesus and his disciples, even with fresh water, is for that very reason promised a higher reward.

Matthew, toward the end of his Gospel, will take up the basic idea of our *logion* again—in the discourse about the return of the Son of Man (Matt 25:31-46), who will say to the blessed on the right:

> *I was hungry*
> *and you gave me food.*
> *I was thirsty*
> *and you gave me something to drink.*
> *I was a stranger*
> *and you welcomed me.*
> *I was naked*
> *and you gave me clothing.*
> *I was sick*
> *and you took care of me.*
> *I was in prison*
> *and you visited me.*

And a little later Jesus, as the world's judge, speaks to these very people who have helped his disciples and himself as well:

> *Amen, I tell you,*
> *just as you did it to one of the least of these who are my sisters and brothers,*
> *you did it to me.* (Matt 25:40)

Nowadays this text is interpreted in countless sermons, catecheses, and speeches as if it were about all the suffering, all the hungry, all the miserable of this earth. They are "the least among Jesus' sisters and brothers." That kind of interpretation corresponds fully to our current mentality, or more precisely to our modern humanism. It expresses our longing for an undogmatic and practical Christianity, but it also matches our openness to the *ethos* of other religions: no matter what religion and worldview a person professes, one helps one's fellow human beings in distress—and is therefore justified.

But Matthew was thinking of something else. For him the "least" in Jesus' family are not the many poor and suffering of the world; they are the disciples Jesus has sent out, who are hungry at nightfall, have no roof over their heads, are in need, are often rejected and persecuted. Matthew had depicted all that at length in the great mission discourse in 9:35–11:1. The disciples who are sent out are not welcomed everywhere (10:14). They fall prey to "wolves" (10:16) and are handed over to councils (10:17), drummed out of the synagogues (10:17), brought before governors and kings (10:18), betrayed by their own kin (10:21), and hated by everyone (10:22).

Who, then, are the "least . . . of my sisters and brothers" in Matthew 25:31-46? What was Matthew's focus when he was writing the Gospel, some time after 70 CE? I think he saw it this way:[30] When the day of the world's judgment comes, the gospel will already have been preached among all the Gentile peoples (Matt 24:14; 28:19). Thus the Gentiles will have had in their midst witnesses to Christian faith who came to them poor and harassed, often persecuted and needy; they will also have had Christian communities among them who gave witness to Jesus Christ by their existence. For the Gentiles the criterion at the world's judgment will be how they have behaved toward the messengers of Christian faith and toward Christian communities. If they have helped them, even if only with fresh water (cf. Matt 10:42), they have thereby aided Jesus' cause and have a share in the reign of God. If they have not helped them they do not belong to the reign of God; they will be judged.

Thus in Matthew 25 the Son of Man, the Human One, identifies in a positively offensive way with his disciples, his followers, his communities. As much as Christ is on the side of all the poor, for him the

[30] For what follows see the longer discussion in Gerhard Lohfink, *Im Ringen um die Vernunft. Reden über Israel, die Kirche und die Europäische Aufklärung* (Freiburg: Herder, 2016), 478–94.

most important thing in the whole world is the existence of his people, because it is only through this people that the poor of the earth can really be helped in the long run.

Although this interpretation is emerging more and more clearly in current exegesis, it is alienating to many. Joachim Gnilka wrote in his commentary on Matthew:[31]

> *This point of view [sounds] neither very Christian nor very Matthean: the Christians as the privileged of this earth!*

In the context of the whole Bible an interpretation focused on Jesus' persecuted disciples is not at all unusual. Moreover, it is quite Matthean: Israel, or the church, is God's instrument for the salvation of the world, and whoever comes to the aid of Jesus' disciples helps Jesus also (Matt 10:40-42).

Moreover, we must insist that not *everything* was demanded of the Gentiles who came into contact with Christians. What was asked of them was, in the first place, that they treat Christians as fellow human beings. Often a cup of water would suffice. A great deal more was demanded of the Christians: not just a cup of water but their whole existence, their whole life, a clear confession of Christ. And obviously the disciples are also subject to the Son of Man's judgment. This is in no way about a "privileged" Christianity.[32]

So we come to the end of part 3. What Jesus demands of his disciples has become especially clear in this part. They are to leave everything: father and mother, spouse and children, houses and fields. But Jesus goes even further: he also calls those who want to follow him to abandon all their previous plans for their lives and even the vital interests associated with maintaining them—all for the sake of the reign of God. As we have seen, this demand from Jesus culminates in the statement:

[31] Joachim Gnilka, *Das Matthäusevangelium* 2, HThKNT 1.2 (Freiburg: Herder, 1988), 375.

[32] Roman Catholic Lectionary: Thirteenth Sunday in Ordinary Time, Year A; *Revised Common Lectionary* Proper 8A (Pentecost 5).

> *. . . those who want to save their life will lose it,*
> *and those who lose their life for my sake . . . will save it.* (Mark 8:35)

At least at that point the question almost necessarily arises: for such self-surrender to be possible wasn't it necessary to have an apocalyptic view of the end time, something that had emerged among certain groups in Israel long before Jesus and had become widespread throughout Israel since the preaching of John the Baptizer? Was it not true that for Jesus, too, the end of the old world, the end of time and history, had arrived?

In the preceding chapters I have consistently avoided the phrase "end of the world," replacing it with words like revolution, overturning, and transformation of the world. Still more: I have deliberately excluded the idea of "imminent expectation," convinced as I am that the concept may be understood wrongly, and indeed that it does not do justice to Jesus' eschatology. Was that, perhaps, a mistake?

Are not Jesus' demands, after all, associated with an extremely imminent expectation of the end? Isn't it easier to abandon everything if the end of the world is going to arrive in a few weeks or months? Did not the Baptizer also draw the masses to himself at the Jordan with his language about fiery judgment? And is it not possible that Jesus sent out the Twelve with the message about the violent inbreaking of the reign of God and did not expect them to return? Wouldn't that really make it possible to understand the haste he demanded of them?—a haste that even forbade them to engage in customary greetings?

Those sorts of questions are understandable, and they have been asked repeatedly since the eschatological urgency of Jesus' preaching was rediscovered in the nineteenth century. But they do not address what Jesus meant by the "nearness" or "approach" of the reign of God.

Certainly Jesus knew, and said as clearly as possible, that there is no more time—but that is connected to the coming of the *reign of God* and not with an *approaching end of the world*. The question, indeed, is *how* the reign of God comes. With violence? As a cosmic catastrophe? As an apocalyptic end of history? Or is it in the way that a tiny amount of sourdough leavens a huge quantity of flour (Luke 13:20-21)?

Still more: Jesus knew, as no one else ever has, who God is. For him God is not a "higher being" resting in perfection and self-sufficiency. God is not "self-contained"; God goes outside God's self and leaves self behind, as every true lover does. God created the world so it might have a share in God and be filled with God's love. We have to say these things in a very human way because we have no other: God is "waiting," since the beginning of creation, to be able to enter the world. God is by nature the *One Who Comes*. Certainly we may pose the critical question why God did not enter the world much sooner, if God is really the *One Who Comes*. Why, then, so late?

What "delayed" God's coming was the resistance of history or—better said—the "costs of freedom." God desires no force, no fetters, no love that has to submit. God can only will creation in such a way that it encounters God in full freedom. Therefore the slow progress of evolution, the slow dawning of spirit in the human; therefore the awkward human attempts to sense the divine, but also the developing distortions of who God is and, finally, the possibility of skepticism and even hostility to God.

Only and at last in Jesus, who is *pure openness*, and in a long history leading to him, one that began with Abraham, could God enter this world irrevocably, unsullied and unseparated. Therefore, with Jesus, the reign of God is present—and yet at the same time it is not present because the world's resistance, indifference, and unbelief continue. Indeed, they not only continue but harden themselves.

Precisely for this reason the reign of God is "already" and "not yet." Precisely for this reason Jesus had to say, "If it is by the finger of God that I cast out the demons, then the reign of God has come to you" (Luke 11:20)—but at the same time "The reign of God has come *near*" (Mark 1:15). Moreover, he had to say, "The reign of God is [already] among you" (Luke 17:21), and still teach his disciples to pray "your kingdom *come*" (Luke 11:2).

Jesus stands within this blessed and simultaneously oppressive tension, and so do his disciples, and so does the church. In any case the linking of "already" and "not yet," of the already given *presence of the reign* and the "not yet" of the consummation means that there is no time left. Those who have grasped that they are standing "between times" can no longer say "my repentance can wait." It cannot wait. Now, in this hour, one must act. And it is not only about the individual; it is about the whole world. Humanity is bordering on self-destruction.

Therefore the idea of imminent expectation is extremely misleading. It is usually understood to mean that, after a long stretch of time, the goal is finally near. But that falls short of the concept of what Jesus announces. In Jesus the goal has already been reached because, in Jesus, God is already in the world, and with Jesus the reign of God is here also.

So the time is already fulfilled, and simultaneously it is intensifying in a way we cannot sense. The love already present is calling for a response. The reign of God wants to be received—simply because it is present. In any case, no one can any longer make excuses because the end is not yet. The invitees have already been summoned: "Look, I have prepared my dinner, my oxen and my fat calves have been slaughtered, and everything is ready; come to the wedding banquet!" (Matt 22:4).

Part Four

Living in Light of the Reign of God

In the previous parts of the book we have dealt again and again with the question: to whom was a particular word of the Lord really addressed? The question proved not to be an idle one because it often helped us to discern the content of a saying more precisely. The authors of the Gospels, too, constantly tried to name the addressees of Jesus' words or whole discourses. We regularly—in Luke's Gospel, for example—come across remarks such as:

> *Then he looked up at his disciples and said . . .* (Luke 6:20)
> *After Jesus had finished all his sayings in the hearing of the people . . .* (Luke 7:1)
> *Then he said to them all . . .* (Luke 9:23)
> *Then turning to the disciples, Jesus said to them privately . . .* (Luke 10:23)
> *When the crowds were increasing, he began to say . . .* (Luke 11:29)
> *Then he took the twelve aside and said to them . . .* (Luke 18:31)

Such notes by no means functioned only to establish a continuing flow of the narrative. More than that, the Evangelists wanted to show clearly for whom a particular word or discourse of Jesus was intended. After all, it makes a difference whether a saying is directed to someone wanting to become a disciple, to Jesus' enemies, to the Twelve in connection with their mission, to all disciples, or to the whole of Israel.

It is occasionally asserted or silently assumed that, beyond such considerations, Jesus' preaching was for all people, that is, the whole world. But that overlooks a fundamental difference that is true of the whole Bible: of course it is always about the world. But God's way of reaching all the nations of the world is through the descendants of Abraham: the people Israel. And Jesus' way of reaching all of Israel was the Twelve, as disciples.

Therefore with regard to nearly every Jesus-saying I have asked who, in the Evangelists' minds, were the addressees in each case—and then I have inquired further: who were Jesus' own addressees? In part 2 and part 3 we spoke of *logia* addressed to the Twelve or to all the disciples—or else to people who wanted to follow Jesus.

In contrast, part 4 will deal with *logia* in which Jesus had all Israel in view. Many of them are in the Sermon on the Mount (Matt 5:1–7:29) or, correspondingly, in the Sermon on the Plain (Luke 6:20-49). Both evangelists are drawing here on the "programmatic discourse" in the Sayings Source.

It is Matthew in particular who places the greatest emphasis on the fact that, while all Jesus' disciples are gathered around him during the Sermon on the Mount (Matt 5:2), there are also crowds of people from all parts of the land of Israel, present and past,[1] namely, "Galilee, the Decapolis, Jerusalem, Judea, and . . . beyond the Jordan" (Matt 4:25). Matthew wants to illustrate that the Sermon on the Mount is obviously addressed to Jesus' disciples, but beyond them to representatives of all Israel. The eschatological people of God to whom Jesus speaks, whom he heals (Matt 4:24), and whom he wants to make holy (Matt 5:48) is already visible in this great assembly.

What I have just described is, first of all, Matthew's theology and what he wants to depict. But for Jesus, too, it is all about God's will to bring Israel together and sanctify it in order to make it a light for the nations (Matt 5:14). Everything Jesus does has this true, eschatological Israel in mind—an Israel in which the social order of the reign of God will be lived. Certainly Jesus never called for a political-revolutionary change in Jewish society, but the repentance he demands as a consequence of his message about the reign of God is meant to inaugurate within the people of God a movement in comparison with which the usual kinds of revolution are utterly toothless.

Part 4 of this book is about that revolution: for example, Jesus' demand for absolute nonviolence (chap. 36). That nonviolence is by no means simply a matter of an inner attitude: it is about concrete praxis. Nor is it merely something for individuals: it demands people who act in common to live nonviolence seriously. Nonviolence, just like love of enemies or the refusal to dominate others, can be carried out only in a nexus of social reality—more precisely, in a fabric of mutual aid. Jesus' appeal for nonviolence, love of enemies, and refusal to dominate thus implies the perspective of an alternative society in contrast to the state since every state is based on violence, either *legitimate* or *illegitimate*.

[1] For a full defense of this thesis see Gerhard Lohfink, *Wem gilt die Bergpredigt? Beiträge zu einer christlichen Ethik* (Freiburg: Herder, 1988), 15–38 and 199–209.

When we speak in what follows about rejection of violence, reconciliation, love of enemies, the sacredness of marriage, purity, absolute truthfulness, confident prayer, and rejection of riches it will never be simply about personal sanctification. It is always at the same time about the eschatological sanctification of the people of God as a social reality—and thereby about changing the world.

30. If You Are Angry with a Brother or Sister (Matt 5:21-22)

Within the Sermon on the Mount the six so-called antitheses (Matt 5:21-48) form a positively sensational section. In this chapter I will deal with the first antithesis. It reads:

> You have heard that it was said to those of ancient times,
> "You shall not murder:"
> and "whoever murders shall be liable to [the] judgment."
> But I say to you:
> if you are [even] angry with a brother or sister,
> you will be liable to [the] judgment;
> and if you insult [say *raka* to] a brother or sister,
> you will be liable to the council [Sanhedrin];
> and if you say, "You fool,"
> you will be liable to the hell of fire. (Matt 5:21-22)

This text has caused myriad headaches for interpreters from the outset. To try to understand it, let us take the parts in order. The "thesis" of the text is:

> *You have heard that it was said to those of ancient times:*
> *"You shall not murder"*
> *and: "Whoever murders shall be liable to [the] judgment."*

This is all quite clear. "Those of ancient times" are the wilderness generation who had received the Torah at Sinai. At that time "it was said to them." The passive construction is used here to avoid the word "God." The meaning is thus that, in the proclamation of the Torah at Sinai, God had told Israel, "You shall not murder." This is a literal quotation of the commandment against murder in Exodus 20:13 // Deuteronomy 5:17, with the addition of "and whoever murders shall be liable to [the] judgment." There is no further discussion of what happens to the murderer in court, because it is a matter of course. Anyone who murders another person will be punished by death (cf., e.g., Lev 24:17). It is not unimportant to note that the "you" in the Ten Commandments does not refer directly to individual Israelites but to Israel as a whole—and, within that whole, obviously to the individual members as well.

That is the thesis! Jesus only calls to mind what was a matter of course for all Jews. They "have heard it"—namely, in their synagogues when the Torah was read. Then, in sharp contrast, comes the antithesis:

> *But I say to you:*
> *if you are [even] angry with a brother or sister*
> *you will be liable to [the] judgment.*

This "but I say to you" is frightening. If God was being quoted before, this "But I . . ." can only mean: "I am now speaking with the same authority God had when speaking then. I am speaking for God." And what does Jesus say? What does he proclaim with the same authority God formerly used at Sinai? He says: animosity toward one's brother or sister—that is, toward one's fellow believers within the people of God—is the same as murder. As the murderer is brought to court and then punished with death, so anyone who is only angry with a sister or brother in faith will come to judgment and be punished with death.

The verb form "be angry with" does not have a precise meaning in English, just as the noun "anger" covers a range of emotions. There is "righteous anger" and even "holy anger." In this case anger bleeds over into outrage and disgust—for example, at severe injustice or inhuman behavior. In such cases the anger can be combined with the unconditional will to change such relationships for the better. The New Testament can also tell of that kind of anger on Jesus' part (cf., e.g., Mark 3:5), but there it is anger mixed with sorrow.

As the antithesis is constructed, the wrath against the brother or sister in faith can be neither righteous nor holy wrath. In addition—and this is decisive—here it must be an anger that has not yet manifested itself but is growing in one's heart and generating thoughts of hurting the other. That is, this is an anger for which no one could be brought to judgment because it is not justiciable. Otherwise the antithesis would not work, for Jesus is saying: while God has commanded that one must be taken to court for murder, I am now ordering that one must be judged even for anger in one's heart.

Every listener at that time must have clearly understood—at least after the initial shock—that while Jesus speaks here in the form of a legal pronouncement[2] he is really using the legal form only in order to uncover what it means to be embittered against one's fellow believer in one's heart. It is *like* murder.

Just such a razor-sharp play with language is characteristic for Jesus. He can float images that are scarcely imaginable, such as the log in the eye, but he can also play with modes of speech in order to provoke—or, better, to lead his hearers to insights they constantly suppress. In this case the thought is that the profound conflicts within the people of God that prevent them from being a sign for the world begin, in fact, with hatred of a brother or sister. No, they not only begin there; when hatred abides in the heart, ruin is already a reality. With that inner embitterment the murder of the sister or brother is a present reality, and so is the murder of the people of God.

So much for the first part of the antithesis! Our text continues, and the real difficulties begin with that continuation. First we have to ask ourselves: why does the text continue? The idea that a person's internal attitude can be seen as the crime of murder is as horrible as the "log in the eye" or the "hacked-off hand." There is no need to escalate further.

Still, it seems that a further escalation is intended: how else can we read the series "judgment" → "council" (the highest court in Jerusalem) → "hell of fire" than as an escalation? There must be a corresponding intensification of the invective, and initially that is the case since now there are open expressions of hostility to match the

[2] We have to make a more precise distinction here. In terms of form, the OT background of these "legal pronouncements" was a set of so-called casuistical legal decrees. They consist of a premise ("If someone does so and so . . .") and a conclusion, which is often a determination of legal consequences (" . . . that one shall be punished in such and such a way"). But the conclusion may only declare that the state of things described in the premise *deserves punishment* (declaration of guilt). There are some of those in the OT as well. Compare, for example, Lev 17:3-4c or the sequence in Num 35:16-21 (each containing also the first part of the conclusion). This distinction is important because, within the Sermon on the Mount, the conclusions in Matt 5:22, 27, 32 all fall within the second category (declaration of guilt without direct statement of legal consequences).

hidden anger. But then it gets difficult, since Greek *mōros* (= idiot, fool) seems to differ very little in its intensity from the Aramaic *raka* (instead of Heb. *reka*). Of course one could argue that we are scarcely in a position to judge the fine points and possible background of insults in that period.

Still, another difficulty remains: as we have seen, the real antithesis lies in the comparison of a murder condemned by a court to an internal aggressivity that is not justiciable because no court can prove it. But as the text continues, justiciable actions appear. Verbal injuries could certainly come before a court, and that at least weakens the sharp antithesis in verses 21-22a. Hence we may rightly ask: could it be that the extension of the antithesis with two more clauses is a later and not particularly successful expansion—either by Matthew or by Matthew's tradition? I will leave that question open. The antithesis as far as verse 22a, with its sharp contrast, is quite enough to make clear what Jesus wanted to say.

But what does Matthew 5:21-22a mean as regards Jesus' attitude toward the Law from Sinai? Did Jesus annul the Torah, or at least the Fifth Commandment of the Decalogue? Not at all! Did he replace Torah with a new law? Not that either! He let the Fifth Commandment stand as it is, but he interpreted its full depth in light of the reign of God. Among the people of God, murder begins in the heart and in the head, with a still-hidden hatred of another.

Now the crux: this explication of the roots of the Fifth Commandment begins in the Torah itself. What Jesus says is not all that new. When Cain becomes jealous of his brother Abel, when his jealousy overcomes him and his "countenance falls," God says to him:

> *Is it not so: if you do right, you may hold up your head. But if you do wrong, sin is lurking at the door; its desire is for you, but you must be its master.* (Gen 4:7)

That text also means to say that murder begins in one's head. Seen from outside, Cain has not done anything yet, but he is already prepared to murder his brother. The evil intention is at work in him; the sin threatens.

Human judges cannot judge thoughts, but before God the human being is a unity: indivisible, not analyzable. Therefore one should love God "with all your heart, with all your soul, and with all your might" (Deut 6:5). The trio of "heart, soul, might" encompasses the whole person: from the heart, the inmost part of the human, to far outside, to the place where either the sister or brother in faith is concretely aided or blood is shed.

In reality Jesus did nothing in the first antithesis of the Sermon on the Mount but set before the eyes of his audience this fundamental insight of the Torah about the indivisibility of the human being. Certainly he was being provocative and formulating his words with the utmost radicality. But his focus was precisely on the Torah from Sinai.

31. No Reconciliation, No Liturgy (Matt 5:23-24)

In composing the Sermon on the Mount, Matthew added two little textual units that expand the subject of the first antithesis: "when you are [on the way to offer] your gift at the altar" (Matt 5:23-24) and "on the way to court" (Matt 5:25-26 // Luke 12:58-59). In each case it is about immediate reconciliation. The first addition reads:

> So when you are offering your gift at the altar,
> if you remember that your brother or sister has something against you,
> leave your gift there before the altar and go;
> first be reconciled to your brother or sister,
> and then come and offer your gift! (Matt 5:23-24)

I already described the rhetorical structure of this multi-liner in the "preliminary remarks" at the beginning of this book. We saw that the text is carefully constructed around the words "gift" and "brother or sister," so that the line "leave your gift there before the altar" is the center of the saying.

A second examination reveals that this text is absolutely clear. Formally, indeed, it is an instruction or warning, but in its substructure it is a little story. Consequently, the text allows us to draw a concrete picture of the implicit narrative.

Here is someone who wants to honor God and makes a pilgrimage to the temple. We may imagine that Jesus spoke this text in Galilee. So it is about a Galilean who has been walking on dusty roads for three days. Now we see this person, having arrived in Jerusalem, bringing a private offering to the altar to hand it to the priest on duty. There is nothing said about what the offering itself is and why it is presented. That is not important as far as the point of the story is concerned. The text remains deliberately vague so that the crucial point will emerge all the more clearly.

That is the situation as presented: one that was familiar to every listener. Each of them must have been disconcerted when Jesus continued: it could be that you are about to hand over your sacrifice when you suddenly realize that, back home in your village, there is someone who has something against you. If you remember that, Jesus says, leave your gift before the altar, go back home, and be reconciled with your sister or brother in faith. Only then should you return to the temple and offer the sacrifice you want to give!

Of course that meant that the person in question would have to travel the long road four times. At a broad estimate the corresponding walks will take about two weeks. Jesus is saying to his hearers: "Nothing is more important than living in harmony with one another. For the sake of that reconciliation you have to make every necessary effort—no matter how burdensome it is. If you do not, your visit to the temple and your sacrificial gifts are meaningless." Here Jesus links directly to the prophets' critique of the cult. Amos portrays God speaking:

> *I hate, I despise your festivals, and I can no longer bear the smell of your celebrations. Even though you offer me your burnt offerings and grain offerings, I take no pleasure in your gifts; and the offerings of well-being of your fatted animals I will not look upon. Away with the noise of your songs; I will not listen to the melody of your harps. No, [among you] let justice roll down like waters, and righteousness like an ever-flowing stream.* (Amos 5:21-24)

Jesus is thinking very much in line with Amos and other prophets: if fat beasts and solemn worship services are not combined with reconciliation and social justice they are meaningless. But what is so striking is how Jesus pictures the example he uses to ground that point. He does *not* say, "If you are at the altar and realize that you have insulted or hurt your sister or brother in faith, return home immediately and beg forgiveness from the one to whom you have done the injustice." Instead, he says, "If you realize that your brother or sister has something against you . . . ."

He has not the least interest in who the guilty party may be. He deliberately leaves the question open. It would be quite possible that it was not the one offering sacrifice in the temple who was guilty in the dispute, but the one at home. Nevertheless, the one who wants to offer sacrifice has to do everything possible to achieve reconciliation. That one must interrupt every other event, even the liturgy. Things cannot be left as they are. One may *not* say: "The other started it, and the other has to take the first step if peace is to be restored. That one has to come first and apologize to me, and then we can see what happens next." Those who think that way let themselves be guided by bourgeois morality, not by the *ethos* of the reign of God.

Jesus' view of reconciliation makes the difference between mere religion and Jewish-Christian faith clear: nearly all religions feature sacrifices that are brought to the gods; so also festal seasons, pilgrimages, sanctuaries, altars, worship services, prayer, rituals, fasting, almsgiving—these are part of almost all religions, and religions are everywhere. But what is characteristic of biblical faith is that it says, with unerring sobriety: All prayers, all sacrifices, all celebrations before the face of God are evils if the worship does not produce a new community of life. In worship God reconciles with us, thus taking the initiative; consequently we must be reconciled among ourselves and so take the initiative, just as God does.

32. Adultery with the Eyes (Matt 5:27-28)

Here we come to the second antithesis within the Sermon on the Mount. This one has no parallel in Luke or Mark; Matthew is probably using special material. This antithesis has the same structure as the first one, in verses 21-22, but it is more succinctly formulated; after all, the hearers or readers still remember the first one. Hence Matthew does not need to repeat that this commandment was also given to "the ancients," that is, the desert generation at Sinai:

> You have heard that it was said,
> "You shall not commit adultery."
> But I say to you:
> Every man who looks at a woman with lust
> has [thereby] already committed adultery with her in his heart.
> (Matt 5:27-28)

The first statement (the thesis) quotes the Sixth Commandment word for word from Exodus 20:14 and Deuteronomy 5:18. Again the antithesis brings a drastic escalation. As in Matthew 5:21-22 mere hatred is equated with murder, so here a lustful glance is like adultery. This sharpening is so drastic because, according to Torah, adultery is also punishable by death (Lev 20:10).

Matthew 5:27-28 also needs some explanations. First: this is not at all about merely looking at a woman. Such rigorism, which in certain cultures has led to the requirement that women must completely cover themselves in public, was far from Jesus' mind. The reference is not to normal looking but, as the text says literally, "looking at the woman in question in order to lust after her." That is to say that the looking is consciously accompanied by sexual fantasies.

Also, this antithesis is about a married woman, as the Decalogue presupposes. Here, as there, it is also assumed that the act would be an infringement of the property rights of the woman's husband. In the ancient Near East a wife was regarded as her husband's property. For another man to commit adultery with her was a profound invasion of that property. The fact that the adulterer, if he was married, likewise broke his own marriage did not come into the picture. Precisely the way Jesus protects and hallows the institution of marriage, both here and also in his strict command that a man not divorce his own wife, goes far beyond any kind of mere property consideration, however, and gives marriage a high dignity.

Finally: as in Matthew 5:21-22, so also here we must assert that, formally, the statement in Matthew 5:28 ("every man who looks at a woman with lust has already committed adultery with her in his heart") is a legal decree. But of course Jesus does not intend to introduce a new law; rather, as in Matthew 5:21-22, he is playing with the legal form in order to provoke: a lustful glance is itself a capital crime. Jesus is deliberately intending to shock and to make people think. Again the whole human person is in view. The act by which the dignity of marriage is degraded does not happen only in a completed adulterous act. It begins long before that: in a look that undresses the woman and makes her a sexual object.

Jesus was not alone in his opinion. Apparently a similar judgment of lustful looks had been developing for a long time in Hellenistic Judaism.[3] In this matter, then, Jesus could already refer to the ethical

[3] In the *Testaments of the Twelve Patriarchs*, for example, we find the expression "whoring with the eyes" (*T.Iss.* 7.2). There the patriarch says before his death: "Except

currents of his time and his environment. What is peculiar to him is the extraordinary sharpness with which he protects marriage—with a legal decree in which he declares the lustful glance to be a crime deserving of the death penalty.

33. Divorce: A Capital Crime (Matt 5:31-32)

The third antithesis in the Sermon on the Mount is thematically linked to the second: it is about the dissolution of marriage. Here we have traditions parallel to Matthew in Luke 16:18 and Mark 10:11-12 (// Matt 19:7-9). The version in the Sermon on the Mount reads:

> It was also said,
> "Whoever divorces his wife, let him give her a certificate of divorce."
> But I say to you
> that any man who divorces his wife, except on the ground of unchastity,
> causes her to commit adultery;
> and whoever marries a divorced woman commits adultery.
> (Matt 5:31-32)

If we compare this text with the parallel traditions in Luke and Mark we see immediately that the antithesis form is absent. Matthew must have created it himself, following the pattern of the first and second antitheses. Likewise the exception that permits divorce in cases of adultery[4] was added by Matthew or the pre-Matthean tradition. Without that addition, the prohibition against divorcing a wife must once have read:

> *Anyone who divorces his wife causes her to commit adultery, and whoever marries a divorced woman commits adultery.*

---

my wife I have not known any woman. I never committed fornication by the uplifting of my eyes."

[4] The literature on this clause, which is only in Matthew, defies estimation; after all, existing Roman Catholic law on the subject contradicts it. The most serious attempt to deal with the clause is the suggestion that the Greek word *porneia* (= fornication, unchastity) should be interpreted in accordance with Acts 15:29 as illegitimate marriage within the bounds of relationship, which would make the marriage invalid from the outset. The difficulty, of course, is that Matt 5:28, just before this, was about "adultery" (*moicheuō*), and so *porneia* in Matt 5:32 would have the same meaning.

That is what Jesus would have said. The saying establishes a clear parallelism, and it breathes the radical spirit of Jesus. But what is he saying? We can only understand him if we are familiar with the divorce law in Palestinian Judaism. Divorce is permitted (with an appeal to Deut 24:1-4)—for the husband.[5] He is allowed to divorce his wife if "she does not please him because he finds something objectionable about her" (Deut 24:1). Given that very vague formulation it was relatively easy, from a strictly legal point of view, for a man to dissolve his marriage to his wife. He only had to speak the divorce formula in the presence of witnesses (cf. Hos 2:2):

> *You are no longer my wife.*
> *I am no longer your husband.*

Then he had to give her a writ of divorce. There were certain difficulties for men in the lower social classes, however, because what the woman had brought to the marriage had to be paid back.

As far as the writ of divorce was concerned, its purpose was naturally to make it possible for the wife to marry another man. However, it enabled the husband—and especially a well-to-do husband—to simply throw his wife out of the house. We have to imagine the pressure thus brought to bear on married women. No question about it: from a purely legal standpoint the wife was not treated equally with the husband.

This is clear also from other aspects of marriage law: as we have seen, if a married man had intercourse with another woman he by no means broke his own marriage; at most, if the other woman was married, he broke her husband's marriage. Not so with a married woman! If she committed adultery, she broke her own marriage. This makes it altogether clear that the wife was not regarded as a partner but as a part of her husband's property; he was free to dispose of her as if she were a thing. By committing adultery a woman damaged her husband's property; his adulterous behavior, in contrast, could at most reduce the value of what another man owned.

Only against this social background can we understand why Jesus formulates his saying about divorce entirely in terms of the husband.

[5] Divorces initiated by women are also known to have occurred in places where Judaism was more subject to Hellenistic and Roman influences. Cf. Mark 10:12.

The wife had no right, in any case, to dismiss her husband. So Jesus addresses the husband and holds up before his eyes the fact that any man who divorces his wife almost compels her to seek another husband because otherwise she has no economic basis for her existence. So with the new husband she breaks her first marriage—and her first husband is guilty because, by dismissing her, he has driven her into that situation. But the new husband also commits adultery—namely, against her first marriage, from which she had been released. To us the prohibition of divorce in its Matthean version seems extremely complicated but, against the background of the marriage law then in force in Judea-Palestine, Jesus had to formulate it that way.

Still we have not covered everything. We have to keep in mind what it meant when Jesus brusquely declared that dismissal of a wife or marriage to a divorced woman constituted adultery. As we have seen, according to Torah adultery was a crime requiring punishment—capital punishment, in fact (Lev 20:10; Deut 22:22-24). But that means that Jesus names as a capital crime something that Torah permits. That was already an infuriating insult, but when Jesus also clothes the whole in the form of a legal decree the insult is still further sharpened. What was said about the first antithesis (chap. 30) as regards arguing with a legal decree is true also here. Jesus' prohibition of divorce is a legal statement in the sense of what was outlined there. First, in the opening statement, the case is defined: "Anyone who divorces his wife . . ." or "Anyone who marries a divorced woman . . . ." The case is then declared in the following sentence to be a serious wrong, namely, initiating adultery: ". . . causes her to commit adultery" or ". . . commits adultery." In this case the sanction need not be stated because everyone knew it: adultery, if it is proven, merits the death penalty.

Thus Jesus provokes by using a legal statement. But does he really mean to make law with what he says? Certainly not! He is no more making law here than when he says "if you are angry with a brother or sister you will be liable to judgment." By using the category of "legal decree" Jesus wants to shake things up, to reveal the injustice done to the woman, to uncover the inhumanity of the then-current system of divorce. While his formulation takes on the guise of a legal decree, his intent is not to establish a new law.

So what is Jesus' attitude to Torah here? Is he destroying it? Not at all! First we must affirm that there is nowhere in Torah a separate law stating whether divorce is licit or not. Deuteronomy 24:1-4 forbids the remarriage of a husband to a divorced wife who has since married another. The procedure of divorce by means of a writ is only mentioned in passing, that is, as a presupposition for the legal problem at hand. So Jesus is not opposing a commandment or prohibition in Torah; he is condemning ancient customary law to which Torah does not object.

Moreover: in opposing this customary law Jesus appeals to the real will of God; indeed—and this is crucial—to the will of God as given in Torah itself, at the beginning. We find this in Mark 10:2-12, where Jesus refers to Genesis 1:27 and 2:24. He says:

> *From the beginning of creation, "God made them male and female." "For this reason a man shall leave his father and mother and be joined to his wife, and the two shall become one flesh." So they are no longer two, but one flesh. Therefore what God has joined together, let*[6] *no one separate.* (Mark 10:6-9)

Thus, according to Mark 10, Jesus appeals to Torah itself against a customary law that Torah presupposes. He cites the account of creation, which is part of Torah. He appeals to the profound, inseparable unity that is attributed there to both the marriage partners.

This makes it clear that with his prohibition of divorce Jesus does not contradict Torah as such; he clarifies a particular point in it. With his harsh statement, clad in legal language, he stands up for the woman who, subjected to arbitrary male decision, is degraded to the status of a thing, and he defends God's genuine will, whose original intent is concealed by being overlaid with customary law.

All that is easy to say. Have we considered the social effects of Jesus' rigorous intervention? Ulrich Luz writes, in his commentary on Matthew:[7]

> This prohibition [Luz means Jesus' forbidding a divorced woman to marry] could be devastating for the divorced woman. It is—to put it mildly—"naïve" and understandable only if one assumes that Jesus consistently proclaimed God's will on the basis of the kingdom of God

[6] The Greek here uses a negated imperative; it should be translated "shall."

[7] Ulrich Luz, *Matthew 1–7: A Commentary*, trans. Wilhelm C. Linss (Minneapolis: Augsburg, 1989), 302.

> without considering that there were in Israel despite this will of God numerous unmarried divorced women.

This text I find halfway bearable because Luz allows "that Jesus consistently proclaimed God's will on the basis of the kingdom of God." If we take that statement seriously, the now-coming reign of God is not just a lovely promise but a world-altering power. The reign of God creates for itself an eschatological Israel in which marriage is also changed, becoming a profound union of man and woman, who hold to one another in free fidelity[8]—as envisioned in Genesis 1–2.

But not only does the relationship between husband and wife thus achieve a new quality; every marriage is embedded in the community of many brothers and sisters in the "new family" in which people come to one another's aid, share burdens, and console one another in times of need. Jesus intends that married people should no longer casually separate and that when a break does occur the separated partners should find help and home.

Of course Ulrich Luz is correct when he says that at that time there were "numerous unmarried divorced women." Often they could not afford a household of their own. Many of them had to return to their parents' house or go begging or choose the path of prostitution.[9] When Jesus so firmly opposes divorce, evidently he also wants to end the circumstance that there are so many women discarded by their husbands. Is that "naïve"? It would be really "naïve" to overlook the unspeakable misery visited on children and youth by casually-ended marriages, as well as those that were entered into without the partners' intending to maintain fidelity.

One final thought: It is precisely in the case of Jesus' prohibition of divorce that Hans Conzelmann's thesis (that Jesus grounded his ethics not on the reign of God but on creation) proves too superficial. Jesus' rigorous rule that no one should initiate divorce and no man should marry a divorced woman presupposes a people of God in which persons live together *in light of the reign of God*. Without a social

[8] "In free fidelity" is a reference to a book by Rudolf Pesch, *Freie Treue. Die Christen und die Ehescheidung* (Freiburg: Herder, 1971).

[9] For the situation of divorced women in antiquity and in Judaism see Marius Reiser, "Die Neugestaltung von Ehe und Familie im frühen Christentum," *TBei* 52 (2021): 109–20.

basis of that kind not only Jesus' prohibition of divorce but his whole ethical system would be inhuman. But Conzelmann's thesis is also untenable because for Jesus there was no separation between creation and the reign of God. The coming of God's reign, in fact, means the restoration of creation. In the reign of God everyone will see what creation really means.

34. Better to Cut Off Your Hand (Mark 9:43-48)

The series of sayings about "self-mutilation" for the sake of eternal life is found in Matthew 5:29-30 and Mark 9:43, 45, 47-48 (// Matt 18:8-9), but in different contexts. Matthew must have had his own source for this text. Whether it was in the Sayings Source remains uncertain. I will choose Mark's version:

> If your hand causes you to stumble, cut it off!
> It is better for you to enter life maimed
> than to have two hands and to go to hell,
> to the unquenchable fire.
> And if your foot causes you to stumble, cut it off!
> It is better for you to enter life lame
> than to have two feet and to be thrown into hell.
> And if your eye causes you to stumble, tear it out!
> It is better for you to enter the reign of God with one eye
> than to have two eyes and be thrown into hell—
> where their worm never dies, and their fire is never quenched.
> (Mark 9:43-48)

The form here has an especially clear structure. The first line in each series ends with a command and is followed by an antithetical parallelism. The parts treat several important parts of the body: hand, foot, eye. There is also variation in the concepts of "living" and "the reign of God." What does not change is "hell," which is named three times but expanded in the third saying with a quotation from Isaiah 66:24. Just in terms of its form this is deeply impressive. No one had to make an effort to memorize such a sequence: you heard it once and never forgot it.

Besides the form, which is like three chops with an axe, there is the content. The idea of a severed hand, a hacked-off foot, and a torn-out eye is horrible. Some of Jesus' listeners probably had seen how wounded people had arms or legs amputated and the stump then cauterized to close the blood vessels, prevent the flesh from rotting, and shut out parasites. It is not hard to understand why Luke omitted this text altogether.

But Jesus could talk that way. What was he saying here? We have already encountered the metaphorical field of *skandalon* (chap. 28). Traps were set for animals, and they were either killed or captured by them. We, too, can fall into traps. They are waiting for us: our eyes draw us to them or our hands and feet get caught in them. Then we have to sacrifice parts of ourselves in order to fight our way free.

But it could be that the images Jesus proposes say even more: after all, it is our own hands, feet, eyes that tempt us to evil. Does that evil come only from outside? No, it often comes from ourselves, and then, too, we have to tear it out or cut it off. Having to give up whole parts of our lives, under certain circumstances, is a dreadful decision—but our life is at stake.

Jesus says, twice, that it is about one's life. The third time we learn that this life is nothing other than life in the reign of God—not only in what is already dawning but also in the eternal perfection of God's reign—because the ultimate hell is in contrast with it all.

So Jesus also talked about hell. He did not hesitate to call it by name, and he never talked in this context, as a new biblical commentary does, about "eschatological consequences" instead of hell. Other commentaries on the Bible do indeed dutifully quote the word, but they say nothing further about this unappetizing circumstance. It is true that the elaboration of images and threats of hell's punishments have led to long, numerous, and often positively sadistic abuses. In Germany (even in pietistic congregations) no pastor has dared for a long time now even to speak the word "hell."

But dare we be silent about that horrible possibility, if Jesus himself talked about it? Maybe we can! But only if, without using the word, we speak of what he meant by it. Then we have to talk about the seriousness of the situation in which we stand and the radicality of the decision demanded of us.

Current dogmatic theology rightly says that when speaking about hell or what it means we must always first talk about God's unconditional love and care for creation and God's clear and unmistakable will that all people should be saved (1 Tim 2:4). All Jesus' preaching is dominated by this definitive care and attention of God to the world.

The center of his message, after all, is the coming of the reign of God as joyful news and not as a threat of judgment. And Jesus not only *speaks* about the unimaginable love of God—he *lives* it also in his care for the lost, the abandoned, and those who have gone astray.

So hell represents what God does not want. That is precisely what hell is: what God does not will. Hell, as a definitive state, can exist only when a human being rejects God with everything she thinks, everything he feels, everything she or he is. But since there are so many false and misleading images of God that rational people rightly reject, we have to put it another way: hell, as a definitive state, can exist only when a human being wills not good, but evil—and wills it because it is evil. Hell can exist only where a human being wills not truth but lies—and lives them to the depths of her or his existence. Finally, it can exist only where a human being definitively says: "I am sufficient to myself. I want only myself, all alone."

If there were such a person, one who with the *fundamental decision* of his whole existence always wants only himself and no other, God must leave him to himself. God cannot rape him. Such a person would then really have only the self—and *that* is hell. We can only hope and pray that there is no such person or—better—that even in such a case God's grace will prove victorious by breaking down the self-created prison of her existence before she dies.

However, that "victorious grace" of God requires our cooperation, our hoping-with and loving-with God, not only so that human-made hells within history are driven back but so that the eternal hells cannot even begin to exist.

All the same, hell remains a dreadful possibility, given human freedom. When Jesus talks about it he wants to show us that our lives are not cheap, inconsequential games. If the reign of God and not the reign of evil is to win in the world, *everything* is demanded of us—including that in our own life-history we separate ourselves from everything that serves evil even if, metaphorically speaking, it is a hand, a foot, or an eye.

35. You Shall Not Swear At All (Matt 5:33-37)

With the same urgency and clarity as Jesus spoke about the hand, the foot, and the eye, so also he talked about the mouth, that is, about speech. He said that one day we must give account "for every careless word" (Matt 12:36-37), and that verdict about idle talk also includes swearing:

> You have heard that it was said to those of ancient times:
> "You shall not swear falsely,
> but carry out the vows you have made to the Lord."
> But I say to you: Do not swear at all!
> either by heaven, for it is the throne of God,
> or by the earth, for it is God's footstool,[10]
> or by Jerusalem, for it is the city of the great King.[11]
> And do not swear by your head,
> for you cannot make one hair white or black.
> Let your word be "Yes, Yes" or "No, No";
> anything more than this comes from the evil one. (Matt 5:33-37)

Did Jesus really talk that way? The question of the authenticity of this fourth antithesis in the Sermon on the Mount is especially enthralling. We almost have to do a little detective work here, because there is a text in the Letter of James that refers directly to Jesus' prohibition of swearing. The authorship of the Letter of James is disputed, but in any case it was written within the first century CE. It could be as old as Matthew's Gospel. If it really came from James, the Lord's brother, it would be even older. In any case the author of this very early Christian instruction orders:

> *Do not swear, either by heaven or by earth or by any other oath,*
> *but let your "Yes" be yes and your "No" be no, so that you may not fall under condemnation.* (Jas 5:12)

Comparing the two texts, we see immediately that the James text is not *antithetically* structured, as Matthew's is. There is no antithesis. And it does not say "let your word be 'Yes, Yes' or 'No, No,'" but "let your 'Yes' be yes and your 'No' be no." That is a clear difference and also much more plausible. What is offered is not a new formula; rather, Yes and No should simply mean what they mean.

[10] Cf. Isa 66:1: "Thus says the LORD: Heaven is my throne and the earth is my footstool."

[11] Cf. Ps 48:2: "Mount Zion . . . [is] the city of the great King."

Most interpreters, given these differences, have rightly drawn two conclusions: (1) Jesus' original prohibition of swearing was not antithetically structured. It was Matthew who turned it into an antithesis. (2) The Matthean "yes, yes" and "no, no" is not original. It comes from a misunderstanding of the view that was familiar to the author of James.

On the other hand the version in the Letter of James, with its listing of the oath formulas forbidden by Jesus (swearing by heaven, by earth, or any other oath), seems like the briefest possible summary of the lengthier text Matthew gives us. All the reasons (e.g., "for it is the throne of God") are omitted.

All these indicators lead us to conclude that there was a Jesuanic prohibition of swearing that was cited reliably in the Letter of James, but in a shortened form. Matthew gives us the same tradition at greater length, making it an antithesis. Also, it was probably his model text that changed its "let your yes be yes" to "yes, yes."

So much for this somewhat complicated tradition history of the command against swearing in the Sermon on the Mount. Let's get down to the thing itself! What was Jesus' purpose here? Swearing played a significant role in his world, and that was true not only in Israel but throughout antiquity in general. Still, many ancient philosophers and wise persons said that swearing was unworthy, and there were naturally such voices also in Israel (cf., e.g., Sir 23:9-11), where, above all, there was a profound unwillingness to speak the name of God—and every oath brought God into the event. Therefore here, as in other cases, the word "God" was avoided. Instead, people swore "by heaven" or "by earth" or "by the temple." Besides this, the learned teachers and scribes invented a subtle casuistry to determine when an oath formula was valid and when not. If someone swore only by the temple, that was not a valid oath, but if she or he swore by the "gold of the temple," the person in question was bound by the oath (cf. Matt 23:16-22).

Jesus rejects all these oath formulae, together with swearing itself, in the sharpest terms. For him, swearing blasphemes the name of God. It instrumentalizes God for earthly concerns when it would be fully adequate simply to speak the truth. Basically, this is about the Second Commandment: human beings must not misuse the holy name of God for their own purposes (Exod 20:7; Deut 5:11).

But something else must also have been important to Jesus where the prohibition of swearing is concerned: swearing presupposes a society in which one must constantly reckon with obfuscations, untruths, lies, and deliberate false statements. The individual is thus forced to create forms of speech for important cases, forms that signal that one is absolutely not lying. The state, in turn, has to institutionalize such forms and punish perjury. But human being-together in the reign of God must proceed on different assumptions: no longer that others might lie, but that they speak the truth.

What is presupposed here is not only a different image of society; it is also a different image of the human being. When living in the truth of the reign of God a person can be utterly simple, straightforward, and truthful—and in that way also utterly sincere. It is true of Jesus, in any case, that the splendor of truth is evident in everything he says and does.

36. Nonviolence (Matt 5:38-42)

In the Sermon on the Mount the command not to swear (fourth antithesis) is followed by the command to nonviolence (fifth antithesis). Here both Matthew (5:38-42) and Luke (6:29-30) use the Sayings Source; however, in this particular place its wording cannot be reconstructed in every detail. I have chosen Matthew's version as our basic text:

> You have heard that it was said,
> "An eye for an eye and a tooth for a tooth."
> But I say to you,
> Do not resist an evildoer!
> But if anyone strikes you on the right cheek,
> turn the other also!
> and if anyone wants to sue you and take your shirt,[12]
> give your cloak as well!
> and if anyone forces you to go one mile,
> go also the second mile.
> Give to everyone who begs from you,
> and do not refuse anyone who wants to borrow from you!

[12] Greek χιτών means "tunic, shirt" and is "a garment worn next to the skin, and by both sexes" (*BDAG* 1085). —Trans.

A comparison of this text with Luke's version shows that again in Matthew 5:38-42 the antithesis form may be secondary; that is, it should be attributed to Matthew—including the statement "Do not resist an evildoer [or: evil]." Otherwise Matthew has probably retained the original wording of the Sayings Source better than Luke. This is supported by the following observations:

1. Instead of "right cheek" Luke writes only "cheek." But as we will see, the emphasis on the *right* cheek sharpens the command.
2. Luke has eliminated the threat of judgment. That, too, is a softening: it makes the event a private quarrel about a piece of clothing.
3. Luke altogether eliminates the demand not to resist being pressed into menial service. It is unlikely that Matthew created it.
4. In the last line Luke speaks not of "lending" but of "taking away": "if anyone takes away your goods, do not ask for them again!" Evidently at this point Luke is thinking of robbery.

It is also true of Luke's version that the strict order of the sayings still visible in Matthew's version loses its rigorous logic. If we subtract the antithesis form, Matthew's text consists of four commands that move toward an anticlimax:

> No resistance to a slap in the face
> No resistance in a quarrel over one's only garment
> No resistance when forced to walk along with someone
> No resistance to annoying requests

Whereas in a climactic sequence the last element in a series (of words or sentences) represents the high point, in an anticlimax the weight lies at the very beginning—in this case on the slap in the face—and the extreme nature of that beginning is emphasized by the stepwise reduction of the violence in the statements that follow. Concretely, it looks this way in Matthew:

The end of the anticlimax speaks of lending. Somebody comes along and wants to borrow money, or maybe also food or seeds. That is obviously not unjust and most certainly not violence or pressure, but it is unpleasant. Probably Jesus' listeners imagine how the petitioner exercises "mild" moral pressure. The request for money could even be sensed as an imposition, since one was not permitted to take interest on money lent to a fellow Israelite (Deut 23:20-21; Ezek 18:8). But Jesus says: "do not refuse anyone who wants to borrow from you!"

The next-to-last sentence speaks of begging or asking. The concrete situation is not described. The listeners may be picturing beggars; anyone who can imagine how widespread and insistent begging can be in the Middle East will have a sense of what is being demanded here. Again the context implies a certain amount of pressure from the one begging; the beggar is annoying. Still, Jesus says: "Give to everyone who begs from you!"

The element of force begins on the previous level of the anticlimax. *Aggareuein* (= compel) is a *terminus technicus* for demanding service. Everything favors the idea that here we are looking at the situation of Palestine under Roman rule. The Roman cohorts assumed their right to force a Jew to accompany them as a guide or an unpaid bearer (cf. Mark 15:21). Jesus says: "If anyone forces you to go one mile, go also the second mile!"

The case before this one is even more serious. Someone is being commanded to give up her garment, forced even to the point of being sued for it. Of course, it is clear that this is happening in a milieu of poor people who own practically nothing. It may be about the seizure of something pledged as security, or it could be compensation for damages. The concrete situation is unstated. In any case this is someone who has only one gown and a single cloak. It is forbidden to seize the mantle of a fellow Jew—that law was already laid down in Exodus 22:25-26—because poor people had no other shelter from the cold of the night. It was all they had. Jesus says: Don't fight for your undergarment in court! Let it be taken from you! In fact, give up your mantle, too!

At the beginning, the apex of the whole anticlimax, we have the worst case. While to this point the subject was increasing pressure, perhaps even concealed violence, here we have an outbreak of public, brute force that at the same time is a harsh insult because it is explicitly said that the blow is struck on the *right* and not the *left* cheek. Thus it is not given with the palm of the right hand but with the back. A slap with the back of the hand was regarded in the Greco-Roman world, as also in that of Judaism, as a grave insult. Striking with the back of the hand said to the other person: "You are a weakling, a piece of defenseless dirt. You are not even worth a proper slap!" Jesus says: "Let yourself be brutally insulted! Turn your other cheek to your opponent as well!"

Thus the anticlimax descends from brutal violence that robs another of honor to an annoying request that is hard to refuse. The whole—at least in Matthew's version—is a carefully constructed composition of individual sayings that Jesus might have spoken in very different situations. In any case, each of these *logia* reflects the provocative language and radical ethos of Jesus in matters of violence or oppression. Their intent is perfectly clear. Listeners have it emphasized to them: let go of your rights! Deny yourself any revenge! Never answer violence with violence!

The demands in this text acquire a particular intensity also from the fact that they describe situations that are anything but unusual or rare. Rather, they are taken from the everyday lives of Jesus' listeners and presuppose a long scale of possibilities for hidden or public violence—from pestering to direct blows.

Obviously these demands for nonviolence—much like other commands in the Sermon on the Mount—present us with a variety of problems. When I read the words "Give to one who asks!" I always think of a scene in a supermarket: a small child had reached into a shelf that is deliberately designed to be hard to reach and brought out a whole armload of chocolate bars. He wanted them. When his mother said no, the child began to plead and then tried to put pressure on his mother by crying and shrieking. (We will suppose that the mother was familiar with the Sermon on the Mount.) Should she have followed Jesus' command: "Give to one who asks you"? Isn't she obligated, out of love for her child, to refuse the request?

Another example: On June 25, 2021, in a department store in Würzburg, Germany, a man with a knife suddenly began attacking women, leaving three dead and a number of wounded. The murder weapon was a long, sharp knife that he had asked a sales clerk to show him. He grabbed it and started stabbing; the clerk was the first of the three fatalities. Evidently she tried to defend herself at first. Should she, in line with the command "do not resist an evildoer," have bared her neck to him?

These two examples make it clear that Jesus' commands to nonviolence are impossible to apply as norms in individual cases. To put it another way: they are not parts of a casuistic catalogue. Evidently their language has another function than to serve as detailed, precise definitions for a theological ethics.

But what is that other function? The answer that such demands are not to be taken "literally" is questionable. Everything Jesus says, and everything in the Bible as a whole, is to be understood "literally." The question is only what kind of "word" or "language" are we looking at? It would seem more reasonable to say that the text is speaking in a transferred sense, "metaphorically," or "in images." But that would still be questionable.

As in many other places, Jesus talks in provocative, pointed words. That kind of language is not intended to instruct but to shake people up, open their eyes, make them think, and rip them out of their deep-rooted indifference. Still, that does not alter the fact that Jesus' goading language about nonviolence is aimed at *real* behaviors that, as such, are to be honored and that cast light on similar, model situations. Jesus actually forbids the use of violence, and he is convinced that anyone who accepts his words in the company of the people of God can go without counterviolence and revenge.

The "equipment rule" shows us how diligently we have to defend ourselves against the temptation to water down Jesus' command of nonviolence metaphorically or to use our interpretative arts to dull its edge. As we saw, Jesus forbids his messengers to take a provision sack, a change of clothing, sandals, or a staff when they are traveling through Israel proclaiming the reign of God. Going without staff or sandals leads to defenselessness and demands nonviolence; indeed, it had to be a demonstrative signal of an absolute openness to peace. Clearly, the refusal of equipment was also a provocation, but that did not change the fact that it was real. The Twelve were *not* allowed to take a staff, sandals, or a sack of provisions with them.

Recent interpretations of Jesus' rules for nonviolence frequently emphasize that this is not about pure passivity but rather an active demonstration intended to change the other person. Offering the other cheek, for example, would be a surprising reaction, disarming the opponent, intended "to overcome his malice, not himself, and bring about a peaceful understanding."[13] "That, at least, is the hope that underlies the attitude of nonviolence. It does not arise out of

[13] Thus Joachim Gnilka, *Das Matthäusevangelium* 1, HThKNT 1.1 (Freiburg: Herder, 1986), 182.

some kind of unworldly naïveté; it follows a deliberately calculated reasoning: the spiral of violence is interrupted so that the bewildered opponent is able, in light of the unexpected reaction of his victim, to change his mind. . . . The attacker should feel so exposed by the absence of the expected violent reaction that he checks himself and ceases his violent actions."[14]

All these thoughts have something right about them. If someone unresistingly hands over a tunic, adds the mantle, and stands there naked, that is a shocking gesture that really cannot leave anyone unmoved. The same is true of offering the other cheek. Within a wolfpack, for one individual to expose its throat actually functions to thwart the biting reflex of the stronger wolf. Still, it is uncertain whether such reflexes work among human beings. After all, in contrast to wolves, among us there is a long *history* of violence and an accumulating *potential* for evil. Hence demonstrative nonviolence may evoke precisely the opposite reaction: a positively sadistic paroxysm of evil.

On the whole we see that Jesus' demand for nonviolence cannot be resolved with psychological reflections on "self-stigmatization."[15] I am convinced that a major part of our difficulty with the Sermon on the Mount is due to the fact that the social context for which Jesus' commands were formulated is beyond our grasp. Jesus did not think of those demands as a general *ethos* for humanity. They were not simply for people or for society or for the individual or for the state. They were for Israel. More precisely: they were for Jesus' disciples, the beginning and center of growth for the eschatological Israel. Here is where the new thing must begin, so that eventually the whole world will be changed.

States, for example, cannot and may not institutionalize the nonviolence of the Sermon on the Mount. Without the state monopoly on violence, without police, without judges and the system for carrying out their judgments, every society would very quickly erupt in chaos

[14] Thus Eberhard Schockenhoff, *Kein Ende der Gewalt? Friedensethik für eine globalisierte Welt* (Freiburg: Herder, 2018), 469.

[15] Gerd Theissen applies this concept in an effort to explain Jesus' demand for nonviolence and, beyond that, the soteriology of the New Testament as a whole. See his *The Religion of the Earliest Churches: Creating a Symbolic World*, trans. John Bowden (Minneapolis: Fortress Press, 1999), esp. 143–45.

and anarchy. Consider for a moment, once again, the attack in Würzburg: the men who seized chairs from the restaurant and used them to cage the attacker with the knife until the police arrived acted not only bravely but correctly. They prevented more murders.

The people Jesus has in view with his command to nonviolence are those who, within the people of God and sustained by many brothers and sisters, can renounce violence and especially retaliation as a sign that illustrates how the new society of the reign of God will look. It is an alternative society, built on the principle of "for others." It rests on free decision. In that freedom Jesus preferred to renounce violence absolutely and let himself be destroyed rather than be unfaithful to his message and his mission. And his adversaries took the bait. They allowed no anti-biting reflexes to hinder them. But from his death came the church, the real place where the Sermon on the Mount must be lived.

37. Love of Enemies (Luke 6:27-28)

The key phrase "love of *enemies*," so decisive for Jesus, is absent from Mark's Gospel,[16] but in Matthew and Luke it comes impressively to the fore. Matthew, in the Sermon on the Mount, made love of enemies the conclusion and therefore the climax of his series of antitheses (Matt 5:43-48); Luke includes the commandment to love enemies twice in the second part of the Sermon on the Plain (Luke 6:27, 35). Both evangelists were able to draw this command from the Sayings Source, but they linked the *logia* that were associated there with the command "love your enemies" in different ways. I have chosen Luke's version:

> Love your enemies!
> Do good to those who hate you!
> Bless those who curse you!
> Pray for those who abuse you! (Luke 6:27-28)

Subsequently this command, which goes against all our instincts, put an extraordinary set of consequences in motion. It was recalled again

[16] It is certainly implicit in the command to love one's neighbor (Mark 12:31), as is fully clear from Lev 19:17-18. See below!

and again—first in the New Testament itself, then in the early church—and very quickly it became regarded as the essence of Jesus' message and of what "Christian" means.

As a result it was almost a matter of course that, since the advent of Humanism and the rise of strict historical research, many scholars have tried to discover whether the command to love enemies is something specific to Jesus or whether there was anything comparable elsewhere. Obviously we cannot recapitulate the history of that scholarship here. Within the purposes of this book I can only point to a few especially significant texts from the New Testament's environment.

The most important, the absolutely basic "environment" of the New Testament, is Israel. We cannot begin to speak about the commandment to love one's enemies without first taking account of the Old Testament command to love one's neighbor.[17] The central statements of that commandment are in Leviticus 19:17-18:

> *You shall not hate your sister or brother in your heart;*
> *you shall emphatically reprove those who are kin to you,*
> *so that you may not incur guilt yourself!*
> *You shall not take vengeance or bear a grudge against any of your people,*
> *You shall love your neighbor as yourself:*
> *I am the* LORD.

Our first question about this text must be: what does "neighbor" mean here? The answer is clear: "neighbor" is equated with "those who are kin to you" and "any of your people." Thus "neighbor" in this text, just like "brother or sister," can only mean a member of the people of God, the brother and sister in faith. The case is still clearer, though more subtle, if we read on and a little later, in Leviticus 19:33-34, come across the statements:

> *When an alien resides* **with you** *in your land,*
> *you shall not oppress the alien.*

[17] I am grateful that for the following reflections I was able to refer to the chapter "Love. The Ethos of the New Testament: More Sublime Than That of the Old?" in Norbert Lohfink, *Great Themes from the Old Testament*, trans. Ronald Walls (Chicago: Franciscan Herald Press, 1981), 239–54. I may also mention "What Does the Love Commandment Mean?" in *No Irrelevant Jesus: On Jesus and the Church Today*, trans. Linda M. Maloney (Collegeville, MN: Liturgical Press, 2014), 64–74.

> *The alien who resides* **with you**
> *shall be to you as the citizen among you;*
> *you shall love the alien as yourself,*
> *for you were aliens in the land of Egypt:*
> *I am the* Lord *your God.*

This text, so highly relevant in our own time, shows that love of neighbor is to apply even to foreigners who have settled in the Land.[18] What is decisive is that such a one dwells in Israel over time, or permanently. As far as love of neighbor is concerned, such a one is a part of the people. At least in the book of Deuteronomy such persons are "entitled to protection" (Deut 24:14-15), have a right to live in Israel's cities and towns (Deut 5:14), and are to have a share in the festal joy of the Feast of Weeks and the Feast of Booths (Deut 16:11, 14). It is different for passing strangers such as a foreigner on commercial business who is traveling through the land for that reason. The command of neighborly love is not valid for such a person, but the high *ethos* of hospitality applies, and that truly requires an enormous amount from the host.

All of that makes it clear that in the Old Testament the love of neighbor is not a universal love of humankind; it is for one's tribal kin, the sons and daughters of one's own people—but also for all those who dwell as aliens in the land, those to whom "with you" in Leviticus 19:33, 34 applies. It is on that basis also that "love . . . as you love yourself" is to be interpreted.

Certainly it is popular nowadays to read "yourself" as applying to the individual, one's own "I." From the pulpit in particular, and in modern therapeutic "meditation" books, we are continually encouraged to think: "First love yourself completely; then you will have the power to love your neighbor!" But that is one of the heresies typical of our present time. Such nonsense has absolutely nothing to do with the Bible. In Israel's early period, when our individualism was utterly unknown, "you yourself" meant your own family or clan. The individual owed obedience and absolute solidarity to that

[18] For the concept of the "alien" or "foreigner" cf. Georg Braulik, "Der blinde Fleck—das Gebot, den Fremden zu lieben. Zur sozialethischen Forderung von Deuteronomium 10,10," in *Menschenrechte und Gerechtigkeit als bleibende Aufgaben. Beiträge aus Religion, Theologie, Ethik, Recht und Wirtschaft. FS für Ingeborg Gabriel*, ed. Irene Klissenbauer et al. (Göttingen: Vandenhoeck & Ruprecht, 2020), 41–63.

intimate community, and it in turn owed her or him support and protection. Everyone was supposed to love one's own family and clan—though, of course, "love" did not mean some kind of romantic feelings but real, lived solidarity with one another.

It was one of the great theological accomplishments of Israel that it broke through that solidarity within one's own clan and extended it to the whole people of God, all brothers and sisters in faith (and even to foreigners in the land). Thus the commandment of love of neighbor means precisely: "You must give your neighbor, that is, everyone belonging to the people of God, the same help and devotion you would give to every individual in your own family and among your relations! You are to love everyone in Israel as your own family!" It was an admirable step within the people of God's conception of its own existence.[19] "Yourself" thus means the collective of one's own family group.

And what about love of enemies? Here it really gets exciting, because the *dissolution of the boundaries* of the old family solidarity applied not only to sisters and brothers in faith who *think as you do*, but also to your enemies within the people. The text of Leviticus 19:17-18 includes the enemy as a matter of course. After all, it says:

> *You shall not hate in your heart anyone of your kin.*

and

> *You shall not take vengeance or bear a grudge against any of your people.*

The person against whom one bears hatred in one's heart is the enemy, and the person against whom one seeks vengeance can only be an enemy. But in Israel even the enemy is a "brother" or "sister" and therefore must not be hated. Thus the commandment of love of

[19] This interpretation of Lev 19:18 assumes the usual translation, "love as you love yourself." Erasmus Gass has now suggested a different translation: "You shall not take revenge and hold grudges against the members of your people, so that you show love to your neighbor as [one shows love] to you." I cannot judge the grammatical appropriateness of this new translation, but I can point out that in effect it agrees with the interpretation I am presenting here: it is not about love for the individual "self" but about solidarity within Israel. See Erasmus Gass, "'Heilige sollt ihr werden. Denn heilig bin ich, JHWH, euer Gott.' Gott, Mensch, und Nächster in Lev 19,11-18," in his *Menschliches Handeln und Sprechen im Horizont Gottes. Aufsätze zur biblischen Theologie*, FAT 100 (Tübingen: Mohr Siebeck, 2015), 288–323, at 314.

neighbor in Leviticus 19 includes the enemy. But Torah says it still more clearly elsewhere: within the ancient "Book of the Covenant" that is incorporated in Exodus (Exod 21:1–23:33) there is an explicit command for attitudes toward an enemy:

> *When you come upon your enemy's ox or donkey going astray, you shall bring it back. When you see the donkey of one who hates you lying under its burden and you would hold back from setting it free, you must help* [your enemy] *to set it free.* (Exod 23:4-5)

Here we have two exemplary cases—presented as escalation. First case: even returning an ox or donkey costs time and is irritating to the finder. After all, one could just let the animal go on straying and so do damage to the enemy. But one dare not even want to damage her or him.

Second case: here it is about more than returning an animal; this is about working together. The two must act together to raise the animal and redistribute the heavy load—and all that has to be done hand in hand with someone who hates you or whom you yourself hate! It could be a step toward reconciliation; the word "love" does not appear here, but from the substance we can see that love, in the biblical sense, is clearly present. After all, love is not primarily a great feeling and upwelling emotion; first and foremost it is active assistance.

That is a brief version of love of neighbor in the Old Testament! Obviously, sooner or later, we have to get to the question about Jesus. Does he go even beyond all that? Does he expand it further? Does he make love of neighbor a universal, an "I embrace you all, you millions"? I don't see any basis for that in his command to love the neighbor and the enemy. Jesus holds to the commands in Leviticus 19:18 and 19:34. And—this is what is crucial—he continues to *locate the love commandments in the people of God*. The most that has changed is this: the command to love the neighbor (which, as shown, includes the command to love the enemy) is now coupled with the command to love God in Deuteronomy 6:5 and thus acquires a central position.[20] That is clear from Jesus' response to the question of the greatest commandment in

[20] It is true that already in Deut 10:12-19 the command to love God (cf. vv. 12-15) is intimately connected to the command to love strangers (10:19)—that is, love for foreigners settled in the Land and bound up in Israel's community life. And love for strangers in the Land presumes the love of neighbor commanded in Lev 19:18 as a matter of course.

Mark 12:28-34 // Matthew 22:34-40 // Luke 10:25-28. What is shown more clearly in Jesus' words, then, is the solid and unbreakable bond between love of neighbor and love of God, between Leviticus 19:18 and Deuteronomy 6:5. It is true that we cannot say the command in Leviticus 19 is somehow marginal in Torah; that is by no means the case. Still, it is significant that Jesus now clearly makes it central. Moreover, Jesus now speaks directly about "love of *enemies*."

Still, we might add the following: Jesus' version radically rejects any expectation of recompense or reparations. The text that follows makes that clear; in the Sayings Source it was already placed with the command to love neighbor and enemy. It can be reconstructed from Matthew 5:46-48 and Luke 6:32, 34, 36:

> *If you love [only] those who love you—*
> *what reward [should you expect]?*
> *Do not even the tax collectors do the same?*
> *And if you love [only] those from whom you expect a return—*
> *what reward [should you expect]?*
> *Do not the Gentiles do the same?*

Here Jesus is saying: if everything depends on mutuality, down to the last penny, on "you help me, I'll help you," or in other words "I will help you, but obviously under the clear precondition that you will help me when I need it"—thus if everything is done solely on the principle of ethical reciprocity, then the world is merciless and has no sparkle. In the community of the people of God, by contrast, there must be the grace of generosity and a complete lack of obligation, because the people of God should reflect God's own benevolence. Therefore the series of sayings cited above ends with:

> *Be merciful,*
> *just as your Father [in heaven] is merciful!* (Luke 6:36)

Jesus' contempt for every expectation of return takes us directly to the world of ancient religions, where the opposite was the case.[21]

[21] I am extremely grateful to the relevant publications of Marius Reiser for the following quotations and statements about love and hate in the ancient world. Let me refer especially to his "Love of Enemies in the Context of Antiquity," *NTS* 47 (2001): 411–27; *Der unbequeme Jesus*, BTS 122 (Neukirchen-Vluyn: Neukirchener Verlag, 2011), 98–112.

In 1989 Cambridge University Press published a book by Mary Whitlock Blundell, a professor of classical philology, with the title *Helping Friends and Harming Enemies*. In that work she shows that

> *Greek popular thought is pervaded by the assumption that one should help one's friends and harm one's enemies. These fundamental principles surface continually from Homer onwards and survive well into the Roman period.*[22]

That quotation contains the essence of the matter. Blundell speaks out of her excellent knowledge of the ancient world. She compares a multitude of texts and it appears over and over again that one should love friends, help them, lend to them. Of course, the other face of the basic principle must also rule. The Greek poet Hesiod (ca. 700 BCE) expresses it this way:

> *Love all your friends, turn to all those who turn*
> *To you. Give to a giver but forbear*
> *To give to one who doesn't give. (Hesiod, Works and Days 353–54)*[23]

What Hesiod poetically formulates here was the common view. That was the majority thinking in ancient society: it is reasonable to give only to those from whom one can receive, and it is perfectly all right to hate one's enemies. More than that: one should harm one's enemies whenever possible. Thus, for example, in Plato's dialogue *Meno*, Socrates asks what "virtue" is. Meno answers:

> *[A man] should know how to administer the state, and in the administration of it to benefit his friends and harm his enemies; and he must also be careful not to suffer harm himself.* (Plato, *Meno* 71E)

A last example: the Greek lyricist Archilochus (seventh century BCE) wrote:

> *I know how to love those*
> *who love me, and to hate my enemy*
> *and be an ant that b[ites] him.* (Frg. 23.14 [West] = *P.Oxy.* 2310)

[22] Mary Whitlock Blundell, *Helping Friends and Harming Enemies: A Study in Sophocles and Greek Ethics* (Cambridge: Cambridge University Press, 1989), 26.

[23] Translation ©Christopher Kelk. Available at https://www.poetryintranslation.com.

What Archilochus writes here is the normal, the usual, the insightful thing. Plato was one of the few to have disturbed that idea. In the very first book of his great work on the state (*Republic* 1.332A–36A), through the mouth of Socrates, he dissects the principle that it is just to do good to friends and evil to enemies, to love the righteous and hate the wicked. Likewise, in the dialogue *Crito*, again speaking as Socrates, he establishes the principle that under no circumstances may one do what is unjust. It is true that most people (!) believe it is right for one who has suffered injustice to do injustice in turn—but no, one must not return insult for insult and do further wrong, even when all that has been done to oneself (cf. Plato, *Crito* 48E–49E).

That is admirable and reflects those great philosophers in a good light. In Roman culture it was only the Stoics—especially Musonius, Seneca, Epictetus, and Marcus Aurelius—who adopted Plato's principles. Seneca (d. 65 CE) warns that one must not answer evil with evil but with good; he gives as his reason:

> *If . . . you wish to imitate the gods, then bestow benefits upon the ungrateful as well as the grateful; for the sun rises upon the wicked as well as the good, the seas are open even to pirates.* (*De beneficiis* [On Benefits] 4.26.1; cf. 7.31.1)

Seneca is very close to the Sermon on the Mount here, but that kind of thinking remains an exception in antiquity, and even the Stoics for the most part give other reasons for their aversion to hatred. For example, they consider whether it is good for human beings in any case to hate and be angry. It may be contrary to the dignity of one's own person, and it may also do damage to the soul's equanimity.

That was not stupid, but it is a universe away from Jesus' reasons. His demand for love of enemies is not advice for mental hygiene. For him, love of enemies is a consequence of the coming of the reign of God. It is a consequence of the love with which God loves the world and of God's will to lead the world out of its self-created disorder.

In no way does Jesus leave behind the Torah's principles of love for neighbor and for enemy. He thinks and lives out of his sacred scriptures, but he reads what he finds there unambiguously and brings it into an ultimate clarity. He not only interprets Torah but collects its scattered pieces. He thinks "love God" and "love neighbor" down to the bone. It is precisely on the basis of Torah that he knows who God is and therefore how the people of Israel must be.

Only in Israel? Did Jesus really stay fixated on Israel? Didn't he break through the national limits of Israel? Didn't he expand the love commandment of Leviticus 19 to apply to all people, so that the "neighbor" is everyone throughout the world?

Many Christians today hold that opinion, but precisely in doing so they misunderstand a basic principle of biblical thought. In this connection it is worthwhile to consider a widely popular current reading of the parable of the Merciful Samaritan (Luke 10:30-35). Newer commentaries on that parable regularly contain phrases like "humanitarian age," "universal human sympathy," "universal ethos of helping," "universal love of humanity"—or it is said that here Jesus has eliminated all "particular limitations" on love of neighbor.

That interpretation, however, falls short of what Jesus intends to say in the parable of the Merciful Samaritan. The very choice of the figures in the parable speaks clearly, as does most certainly the observation that we have here Jesus' only parable that is localized in the real world: "A man was going down *from Jerusalem to Jericho*" (Luke 10:30). The priest and the Levite represent the Jerusalem temple, "professionally," so to speak, and the man who is attacked represents the "laity." If he was going down to Jericho through the Wadi Qelt he was also coming from a visit to the temple, where he had prayed. The Samaritan, by contrast, represents worship of God on Mount Gerizim. YHWH was worshiped in both places, on the Temple Mount in Jerusalem and on Mount Gerizim, but—Jesus is saying—everything depends on whether this worship of the true God is matched by love of neighbor. Otherwise love of God is fragile and confused.

But the fact that Jesus chooses a Samaritan, of all people, as a counter-figure to those who worship in Jerusalem points to a further aim: Jesus wants to remind hearers that the Samaritans, despised by the Jews, were not foreigners; despite mutual hatred they also belong to the people of God (cf. the narrative in Luke 9:51-56). With the admirable figure of this Samaritan, Jesus shows how siblings *within* the people of God ought to behave toward one another. That is to say, his parable fits within the broad theme of the *gathering of Israel*. Here—and in the Bible as a whole—the point is, first of all, that at last there is a genuine solidarity within the people of God such as Leviticus 19:18, 34 or Exodus 23:4-5 demand and that is described so vividly in 2 Chronicles 28:5-15, where the Samaritans bind up the wounds of the Jews who have been badly hurt in the internecine struggle, clothe them, feed them, put them on donkeys, and bring them back to their homeland.

Jesus, just like the whole Bible, is altogether focused on Israel and, overpoweringly, on the people of God. The transformation of the world begins in a concrete place, and that place is the people God has chosen for the purpose. Only to the extent that God's alternative is lived within this people can the new thing, the different thing spread throughout the world. That spread is depicted in the Old Testament in the *topos* of the pilgrimage of nations: the peoples come to Zion to learn from Israel how nonviolence and peace can become reality in the world (cf. esp. Isa 2:1-5). For Jesus the pilgrimage of nations is a matter of course. Therefore, applied to the question just posed, it means that when love of neighbor and of enemy is lived in the eschatological people of God, then it will come to be that such a self-forgetful devotion will touch many people in the world and cause them to act the same way.

Certainly we could describe the idea of the pilgrimage of nations in an opposite way. One could say that to the extent that love of neighbor and of enemies is lived within the people of God it will spill over again and again from within to touch others who are "outside." Then for those who are "inside" every sufferer and even every person who encounters them with hostile intent will become a sister or brother. Then love of enemies will in fact happen beyond the limits of the people of God. But for that to be possible, the resources of the people of God are needed: a people of God that is not fixated on itself but is fascinated by the all-encompassing, saving will of God.

38. God Knows What You Need (Matt 6:7-8)

Prayer can free people from the tyranny of the "I"—so long as one surrenders trustingly to God's will. Or prayer can sink into a place where the human being tries to take control of God, to make God useful for one's own goals and plans. At depth, such prayer says nothing other than: "O God, please will what I will." Such perversions of prayer do not arise out of the crises of the poor, because in deep crisis people do not pray in order to control others. Rather, it is a kind of "will to power" that causes one to pray that way. It is an effort to control one's own life and even to direct God to what one considers appropriate.

Many religions have had prayers using magic, employing secret divine names or formulae meant to compel the deity to listen. And on the assumption that one's particular forms of prayer contained magical power they had to be repeated as often as possible, because that increased their magic potential. The result was long, intense prayers, endlessly repeated.

In addition, magical prayers assumed that one must speak the gods' own language.[24] Hence there were groups in antiquity that used artfully contrived words in their prayers in order to really reach the god. It had to seem like inarticulate speech to outsiders. But even where linguistic magic of that sort played no role, prayers were often long and intense so that the deity being addressed would listen and hear. Everywhere in the forecourts of ancient temples one might hear endless appeals being shouted, for even private prayers were spoken aloud.

Jesus must have known all that. After all, Hellenistic cities with pagan temples were not far away. He did not ridicule such prayer, but he referred to it in order to show his audience how wrong it is and what kind of false images of God underlie prayers of that kind. He says:

> When you are praying, do not gabble on[25] as the Gentiles do;
> for they think that they will be heard because of their many words.
> Do not be like them,
> for your Father [*Abba*] knows what you need
> before you ask him. (Matt 6:7-8)

This saying is found only in Matthew, but it fits Jesus' language and his magnificent image of God very well. Matthew places the Our Father directly after this saying. Jesus began it with the address "Abba" (= dear father). At that time children in Israel addressed their fathers with the intimate *abba*. It is probably no accident that our *logion*

[24] Cf. Hans Dieter Betz, *The Sermon on the Mount*, Hermeneia (Minneapolis: Fortress Press, 1995), 365.

[25] The Greek here is *battalogeō*. The meaning of this word, almost unattested before Matt 6:7, is disputed. Martin Luther translated it with *plappern* (babble), and many translations have followed him. (These include the NABRE. The AV, however, speaks of "vain repetitions," and the NRSV says "do not heap up empty phrases." —Trans.) It could, however, be that *battalogeō* means a kind of inarticulate, incomprehensible speech.

speaks simply of the "father." We would expect "your father in heaven" or "God, your father," and in fact important manuscripts inserted the word "God" at this point, but Jesus speaks simply of "your *abba*," the same word with which he also begins the Our Father.

That intimate and trusting address to God fits exactly with what Jesus says to his audience about prayer: "You must not try to subject God to your will. That would be a direct violation of the Second Commandment. Nor should you use a lot of words in your prayers, as if you wanted to instruct God about what you need. God already knows that. You may tell God simply, trustingly, and without many words what is on your mind—just as you talk with your human father."

The Our Father, which follows, is a perfect example of an extremely brief, trusting prayer. But if we compare Matthew's version of the Our Father (Matt 6:9-13), which is commonly used by Christians, with that of Luke (Luke 11:2-4) we see right away that the Lord's Prayer expanded as it was used in early Christian communities. It no longer begins simply "Father," but "Our Father in heaven." The third petition, "your will be done" (which is not even present in Luke's version), has also grown longer. Finally, a concluding petition has been added: "but deliver us from evil." And so that the Our Father might not be purely a prayer of petition, a final praise was attached: "For thine is the kingdom, and the power, and the glory, forever. Amen."

It appears that, despite Jesus' warning not to use many words in prayer, even in Christianity prayers had a tendency to get longer. In its earliest version the Our Father was unbelievably brief, and not simply because it was simply meant as a catechetical model for how disciples were to pray. No, it was intended as a real prayer.

Where did Jesus get his confidence that God hears the prayers of believers? More than that: how did he know that God has long since been aware of what they need, so that they do not have to expand on the subject with God? Obviously he knew it because of his unimaginable nearness to God. But that would be the ultimate answer, drawn from the depths of our faith in Jesus Christ. The *next-to-last* answer is simply: he knew it from his sacred scriptures. When he recited the psalms he prayed, with Psalm 66:16-17,

Come and hear, all you who fear God,
and I will tell what God has done for me.
I cried aloud to God—
and God was extolled with my tongue.

The one praying this psalm, who was in deep trouble, implored God—but with a profound certainty that God would hear. The image is that thanksgiving for being heard was already "under the tongue" when the petition was being recited, so that petition and thanksgiving melted together; they were almost the same prayer. Isaiah 65:24 is even clearer: it describes the coming time of salvation when wolf and lamb pasture together. Then every relationship in thc world will be healed, and the state of things between God and human will also be renewed:

> *Before they call I will answer,*
> *while they are yet speaking I will hear.*

Jesus lives in that trust (cf. Mark 11:24)—and he wants to teach the people in Israel that same trust. They may beg for the coming of God's reign, with all the joy and peace that are part of it—and they may do so without making long speeches.

But what about the by-no-means-brief prayer of the Psalms that we certainly cannot abandon? And aren't there long litanies that are quite beautiful? And do not the Catholic churches have the attractive and inviting rosary that has brought countless people profoundly close to God?

Evidently we have to make a distinction here. There is brief, inner petition, and that is all that Jesus is talking about in Matthew 6:7-8. But there is also a longer prayer that works differently: here the one praying considers the history of God with God's people, and that takes time. Or one uses a fixed set of words that is easily recited while one's innermost self is made present to God. There are even long, wordless prayers that are nothing but quiet resting in God's presence. Evidently Jesus himself often prayed in that last way, wholly within himself (Mark 1:35; 6:46) and sometimes the whole night long (Luke 6:12).

39. Stone, Not Bread? (Matt 7:9-11)

The Sermon on the Mount speaks in another place—namely, in Matthew 7:7-11—about confident prayer and the assurance of being heard. Here we have a brief, concise catechesis on prayer. The *logia* come from the Sayings Source (cf. Luke 11:9-13). I will take just the second part, using the version Matthew gives us (Matt 7:9-11). Evidently at this point Matthew has retained the wording of the Sayings Source better than Luke did:

> Is there anyone among you who, if your child asks for bread, will give a stone?
> Or if [the child] asks for a fish, will give a snake?
> If you then, who are evil, know how to give [only] good gifts to your children,
> how much more will your Father in heaven give good things to those who ask him!

Here again we are dealing with one of Jesus' many metaphors, this time a double one. Jesus speaks about "bread and stone" and "fish and snake." As usual, he speaks in very vivid imagery.

Likewise, as in many other cases, the four images draw us directly into Jesus' world. This is about bread, the principal nourishment of the poorer parts of the population. Every day the necessary quantity of wheat or barley was ground between two stones and baked into flatbreads. And it is about fish, the precious side dish from the teeming Lake Gennesaret. In those days very few people in Israel could afford meat.

So is it the case that Jesus was thinking primarily of poor families when he created this double metaphor? Of families in which even the meager food of the lowest class was not always available, so that hungry children had to beg for something to eat? That may be in the background, but it is not where the weight of the double metaphor lies. This is about the *parents*. They would never give their pleading children a stone instead of bread or a snake instead of a fish. As with the "log in the eye," Jesus pushes the images to an extreme. Still, there does not seem to be an intensification from the stone to the snake (in the sense that the poisonous serpent comes after the hard but non-poisonous stone). Instead, what it means is: first comes the stone, which no one can eat, and then a common snake that would not usually be eaten.[26]

In the Lukan version the bread and the stone are eliminated; there "fish" and "snake" come first. In the second instance the child asks for an "egg," and no parent will give a "scorpion" instead (Luke 11:12). Could it be that originally Jesus used a threefold metaphor—bread and stone, fish and snake, egg and scorpion—and that Matthew

[26] A poisonous snake does not fit the metaphor since no one would touch it. It must be a non-poisonous one such as a garter snake. I admit that this idea is hypothetical; we should not try to make images totally logical. After all, a log will not fit in anyone's eye.

omitted the egg and Luke the bread? That is very improbable. Much more likely is that a variant was created in the course of the traditioning process and that—as we have seen—it was just as clear.

Still, Jesus' sophisticated rhetoric, with its twofold metaphor, has created the basis for the goal toward which the whole is directed. What follows is a conclusion *a minori ad maius*—from the lesser to the greater: "If even *you* give only good gifts to your children, surely your heavenly Father will do the same for *his* children!"

The basic question every exegete has to ask with regard to this little catechesis on prayer from Jesus is: are we working here in the realm of Israel's "wisdom," and is Jesus speaking as a wisdom teacher? Like Jesus, the Wisdom literature loved to work with "proverbs." With the aid of such proverbs or sayings the children of upper-class parents were taught to read and write, and in the process they learned them by heart. Those sayings were timeless, reflecting many generations of experience. They were an aid to successful living: help and wisdom for life, like many of our own proverbs.

Bible scholars often say of certain Jesus-sayings that they have a *wisdom* character. If they are referring only to the *form* of the sayings, that is true in many cases, but it says far too little and can even be misleading. We have already established that Jesus could play with linguistic forms and genres. For example, he uses the form of laws, but *not* to create a law or define one more clearly; he does it to shock and disturb.

If Jesus uses the speech-forms associated with Wisdom teaching, that is far from saying that he inculcates wise rules in the way that wisdom-education did or even formulates new ones. His whole preaching speaks of a new historical situation that has never existed before and in which Israel is now living. It is an eschatological situation in which the promises are fulfilled and the eschatological Israel is being gathered. Even when Jesus makes use of Wisdom forms, their *Sitz im Leben* and their point is this urgent and acute eschatological situation. Therefore we have to ask what, against that background, Jesus' words about trustful prayer are meant to say.

First of all, they are for Jesus' disciples, who have left everything and completely reoriented their lives. They need not panic in this whirlpool they have fallen into. They will receive everything they need from the "Father" whom Jesus places before their eyes. They may ask just as children do.

Still, Jesus' words about trustful prayer are not only for the group of disciples but for all the people in Israel who count on Jesus and come to his and his disciples' aid, to the extent they are able. They, too, are entering into completely new situations. They are being ridiculed, cursed, calumniated, and "othered" (Luke 6:22). When that happens they can trust that, in spite of all their suffering, their heavenly Father will give them only "good."

In fact, in the end our text speaks almost drily, simply about the "good things" that God gives. Does it mean "good" in the most general sense? Do we have to hold the concept wide open, so that it includes everything people wish for—from health to a peaceful and comfortable life? No, it must refer to the gifts of the time of salvation, everything that the reign of God contains.

The evangelist Luke not only replaced "bread and stone" with "egg and scorpion." He also replaced "good gifts" with "Holy Spirit," writing:

> *If you then, who are evil, know how to give good gifts to your children, how much more will the heavenly Father give the Holy Spirit to those who ask him?* (Luke 11:13)

The reason for the redactional change is not, as we often read in commentaries, simply Luke's interest in the workings of the Holy Spirit. Rather, Luke wants to make it clear to his readers that the gifts Jesus speaks about in this *logion* are God's *eschatological* gifts, embodied by the Holy Spirit (Isa 32:15; 44:3; Ezek 36:27; Joel 3:1). And Luke is absolutely right. This little prayer catechesis is about praying rightly *within the new eschatological situation that is now dawning*.

The same is true of all the rest of Jesus' *logia* and parables that speak of prayer. He must have spoken amazingly often about prayers of petition; see only Mark 11:22-25; Matthew 6:5-15; 7:7-11; Luke 11:5-8; 18:1-8. This powerful emphasis on trustful prayer is always and inextricably bound up with the coming of the reign of God. The trusting prayer Jesus demands of his disciples and of all Israel corresponds precisely to the attitude people must adopt in face of the approaching reign of God, which must, in fact, make one "violent" (see chap. 10). But just so, and much more, one may allow oneself to be gifted, like a child (see chap. 46), because it is unexpected, astonishing, undeservable grace. For Jesus, then, petition and the reign of God are irrevocably linked.

40. Do Not Judge! (Matt 7:1)

We are still within the larger text of the Sermon on the Mount and have arrived at a saying of Jesus that is more urgent today than ever before. It is found in Matthew 7:1 and, with almost the same wording, in Luke 6:37. The two evangelists drew it from the Sayings Source. I will choose the version in Matthew 7:1:

> Do not judge,
> so that you may not be judged!

There is not much that needs to be said about this certainly authentic saying of Jesus. It is built on the "principle of *talion*," familiar from the Old Testament. (What you do to another will be done to you.) The passive in the second part is a so-called *passivum divinum*: that is, the word "God" is replaced with a passive form because reverence forbids the speaking of the divine name. So Matthew 7:1 says "do not judge, so that you may not be judged by God!"

Obviously that does not mean there will be no judgment on the Last Day for those who have never made themselves judges over others. Everyone must undergo God's judgment. Instead, it means "do not condemn others so that God will not condemn you in the same way—by treating you the way you treat others!" This is even clearer in a saying of Jesus that Luke has combined with "do not judge." Immediately before, in Luke 6:36, the text says:

> *Be merciful,*
> *just as [God] your Father is merciful!*

To repeat: no one can escape God's judgment. After our death the whole story of our life with all its branchings will be placed in the infinitely bright and clarifying light of God. But even in that all-penetrating judgment God remains a merciful God, because God is thus revealed in Jesus. Therefore all those who count themselves as united with Jesus must be merciful to their sisters and brothers. Certainly, if all understanding and compassion are lacking in our judgment of others we must shudder before God's judgment (cf. Matt 12:36-37). All that underlies the utterly brief, positively categorical words: "Do not judge, so that you may not be judged!" Still, many questions remain:

1. Is Jesus, in this saying, forbidding any kind of official, judicial activity in society? Certainly not! Here it is the same as with nonviolence: without a state system of justice with laws, courts, judges, and executive offices an orderly community cannot exist. Jesus' saying is for those who have chosen a life in light of the inbreaking rule of God.

2. In saying "Do not judge," does Jesus forbid any kind of official ordering within the people of God? He cannot have meant that either because, for example, it would then be impossible to make just public condemnation, within the church, of serious and ongoing misbehavior. Matthew 18:17 (excommunication); Acts 5:1-11 (Ananias and Sapphira); and 1 Corinthians 5:1-5 (incest in the community at Corinth) simply assume that such public condemnations are proper.

3. Does "do not judge" mean that individuals may not permit themselves to judge the behavior of other people? Jesus could not have meant that, either. Anyone who lives a responsible life has to make judgments about others. Parents have to judge the behavior and misbehavior of their children; teachers, the attitudes of their pupils and students; politicians, the most diverse sets of circumstances that demand they take a position. But is "judging" the same as "adjudging"?[27] No, it is not. Teachers, journalists, politicians, and people in any number of jobs and professions must not only *judge* others but, under certain circumstances, *publicly denounce* them. But it is precisely at this point that an important distinction is necessary: It is possible that we may have to pass judgment on the behavior of someone else, not only privately but publicly. That still does not mean that we must condemn the other person *as a person*. At that very point begins the destruction of humanity that has become so common in social media (and not only there).

4. But didn't Jesus himself adjudge other people? We need only think of his cutting words directed at Pharisees and scribes, or his hard judgment on the cities of Chorazin, Bethsaida, and Capernaum (see chap. 62). Answering that question demands that now we have to say something that has found an echo any number of times in this book but has not really been addressed:

[27] The German is "*beurteilen/verurteilen*." To adjudge is to condemn. —Trans.

Jesus' sovereign claim or, more precisely, the observation that Jesus speaks and acts as if he stood in place of God. We will speak of that at length in part 5. Here we can only say: we are not Jesus.

Besides, in this context we should consider a very different side of Jesus that is much weightier than all his sharp judgments. In the story in John 8:1-11, as we know, Jesus tells the woman accused of adultery: "Neither do I condemn you." That is not a stray comment or a saying that stands alone. It matches Jesus' frequently attested attitude toward tax-collectors, prostitutes, and sinners. Nevertheless, precisely this "non-judgment" again reveals Jesus' awareness of his sovereign authority from a quite different perspective. Here again he acts as one who is a pure image of God, in mercy as well.

With those four considerations we have almost advanced to pure casuistry. They could easily be expanded and refined. But precisely this entry into casuistic questions shows that what Jesus offers in his pointed sayings is not casuistry at all. He wants to make us think, to stir us up, to encourage us to a right attitude; he is not interested in constructing a systematic moral theology.

That changes nothing about the intense actuality of his prohibition. By means of modern communication our society, at present, is drifting into a situation in which every individual can wound others to an extent never before imagined, can vilify them, verbally crucify them, and destroy them. Mutual hatred and agitation, enabled by modern technology and social media, create a rage that simply could not exist in times past. Here again (and not only among the people of God) Jesus' strict command not to judge can not only frighten; it can also heal.

41. Speck and Log (Matt 7:3)

Immediately after the command not to judge, Matthew has the saying about the "speck and the log." It is also found in Luke's Sermon on the Plain (Luke 6:41), but in a different position. Both Matthew and Luke found the *logion* in the Sayings Source.[28] Its meaning is so clear that it really needs no further explanation:

[28] The *logion* in Matt 7:3 // Luke 6:41 is followed in both of them by two further sentences (Matt 7:4-5; Luke 6:42) that amplify the expression, but it is not certain in either case that the words come from Jesus.

> Why do you see the speck in your [sister's or brother's] eye,
> but do not notice the log in your own? (Matt 7:3)

As we have already shown,[29] this is an antithetical parallelism, a stylistic figure Jesus used especially often. It makes for punchy sayings, and in the present case it is sharpened still more by the personal address. Above all, however, it is strengthened by the choice of images: no one can bear even a tiny particle in an eye, but with the "log" the whole thing becomes surreal. And because Jesus speaks of looking at the eye of a *sister or brother in faith* we recoil as we comprehend what this is about: fellow members of the people of God are closer to us than others. Moreover, we see the stupidities and failings of those who are our neighbors in the faith with especially sharp eyes; we take offense, get annoyed or even angry—while we minimize our own failings, which often have quite different dimensions. For the most part, as our *logion* says, we do not even recognize them.

The extreme image of the "log in the eye" is not attested anywhere *before* Jesus;[30] it must be his own invention. Are Jesus the carpenter and his experiences somewhere in the background? Logs are used in building—and it doesn't take long before a splinter gets driven underneath a fingernail, at least. In any case we should not be surprised that crowds could listen to Jesus for hour after hour.

Some exegetes are surprised that here, as with other sayings of Jesus, there is not the least trace of his proclamation of the reign of God. Usually such words are then declared to be "wisdom sayings" and thus drained of their eschatological urgency. This question is so important that it is worth spending time on it again.

First of all: it is obvious that the coming of the reign of God was the basic theme of Jesus' discourse. But if the reign of God is his real subject, that does not mean it has to appear as the keyword in every

[29] See the "Opening Remarks" at the beginning of this book.

[30] Hermann L. Strack and Paul Billerbeck, *Kommentar zum Neuen Testament aus Talmud und Midrasch*, 9th ed. (Munich: Beck, 1997), quotes Rabbi Tarphon (ca. 100 CE): "I wonder whether there is anyone in this generation who accepts reproof, for if one says to him, 'Take the speck from between your eyes,' he will answer, 'Take the beam from between your eyes!' " (b.*Arakhin* 16b). Both Jesus and Rabbi Tarphon could have made use of a proverb that was then in circulation, or Rabbi Tarphon could have gotten it from Jesus—and that is much more likely.

logion. It suffices if the theme of a saying can be located within the eschatological preaching and above all in Jesus' actual practice.

That is clearly the case here. Jesus did not proclaim the reign of God just so that many individuals might seek to live in its light. That would be a profound misunderstanding of his work. Already in the Old Testament the subject is never just individuals. God wants to create a people in the world, and Jesus pursued that fundamental biblical theme as a matter of course. He gathered disciples around him in order to live the newness of the reign of God with them, and his group of disciples was supposed to shed its light over all Israel. Jesus' proclamation of the reign of God simply cannot be understood without that will to community, and certainly his saying that "whoever does not gather with me scatters" (Luke 11:23) is incomprehensible apart from that context.

The new togetherness, the new community that is the gift of God's reign, means, however, that one must join one's life with the lives of others—in a new way that overturns the old life utterly. It means not only *helping* one another in the common apostolic work but also *sustaining* one another and constantly *reorienting* one another toward the common goal. In other words: it demands mutual correction. It is no accident that sisterly and brotherly correction would later play such a major role in the New Testament letters to communities. Just read Romans 15:14; Galatians 6:1; 1 Thessalonians 5:14; 2 Thessalonians 3:13-15; 1 Timothy 5:19-21; 2 Timothy 4:2; Titus 1:13; 2:15. The category also, of course, contains the texts about community correction in Matthew 18:15-20 and Luke 17:3—and probably the continuation of the saying about the "speck and the log" in Matthew 7:4-5 // Luke 6:42.

In any case, "mutual correction" is a dangerous affair. If it is done without insight into one's own failures (including knowledge of one's own guilt that has already been forgiven by God), and thus without humility, correction is destructive. It then furnishes an ideal base for bossiness and hypocrisy. Jesus' drastic and positively threatening saying about the log in one's own eye, therefore, is quite directly connected with the new community in his group of disciples, with the sibling relationship of those within Israel, and above all with the coming of the reign of God. In light of what is approaching because of God's goodness, unmerited by us, there can be no more sovereign judging and adjudging of others. Mutual correction is indeed urgently needed, but those who do it must first be sure that they are conscious of the log in their own eye and are prepared to let it be removed.[31]

42. No One Can Serve Two Masters (Matt 6:24)

The next saying of Jesus also comes to us from both Matthew and Luke,[32] and in almost identical words (Matt 6:24 // Luke 16:13). We see immediately how skillfully it is shaped:

> No one can serve two masters;
> for [one] will either hate the one and love the other,
> or be devoted to the one and despise the other.
> You cannot serve God and wealth. (Matt 6:24)

The first line has the form of a proverb. It is followed by a two-line parallelism, each line containing an antithesis, and the parallelism explains the first line. The four verbs in the parallelism are arranged chiastically (in X-form):

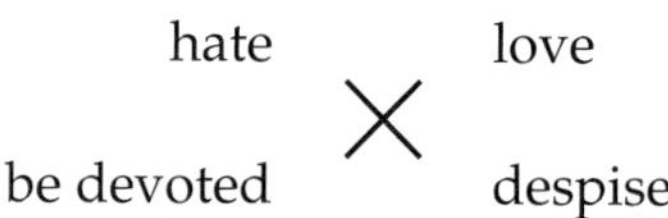

The fourth and final line permits a neutral saying in the third person that addresses the audience directly. Here again, as with so many of Jesus' sayings, it is clear that such a finely constructed text was easy to remember. Even so, the first three proverb-like lines have tempted a few interpreters to see the *logion* as merely a proverb that was tidied up into a Jesus-saying by the addition of the fourth line.

[31] Heinz Schürmann, *Das Lukasevangelium. Erster Teil*, HThKNT 3.1 (Freiburg: Herder, 1969), 371 sees the parallel in Luke 6:41-42, especially v. 42, as rejecting all correction; v. 42 is said to be ironic. "Jesus wants to steer away from a false desire to improve [others] and awaken our own willingness to do penance, not to give preconditions for correcting others." I do not perceive the supposed irony in Luke 6:42. In Matt 7:5 the corresponding passage reads, "You hypocrite, first take the log out of your own eye, and then you will see clearly to take the speck out of your neighbor's eye." The meaning is altogether clear. Against Schürmann on this point cf. also Ulrich Luz, *Matthew 1–7* (see n. 7 above), 417 and n31.

[32] Whether Matthew and Luke found the *logion* in the Sayings Source, however, is disputed.

There is no reason for such a suggestion. There are only a few subjects for which the number of Jesus' sayings is as great as for his critical challenge to wealth. Think only of the saying about the camel and the eye of the needle (Mark 10:25), or "Do not store up for yourselves treasures" (Matt 6:19), or the woes against the rich (Luke 6:24), or the parable of the rich fool (Luke 12:16-20), or the parable of the rich wastrel and poor Lazarus (Luke 16:19-31). In that context we should also think of episodes like the one about the man whom Jesus calls to follow him but who cannot separate himself from his riches and goes away sorrowful (Mark 10:17-22). Evidently Jesus often experienced what difficulty the desire for money and attachment to possessions posed to faith and discipleship. Otherwise it would be hard to explain his harsh condemnations of wealth.

Those condemnations include this saying about not being able to serve two masters: God and wealth.[33] Sharp contrasts between God and wealth are characteristic of Jesus. Where God and the reign of God are concerned there can be nothing but undivided devotion. That same "wholeness" and "undividedness" appear again and again in Jesus' instructions. It is all connected to the single-mindedness he demands in relation to God.

It is also characteristic of this kind of instruction that Jesus takes his illustrative material from the real world of his listeners. It was *their* world; they were at home in it and knew their way around. How often did an enslaved person or a servant or tenant have to serve two masters—the senior owner, for example, and likewise his son, who is different from his father but also lays claim to authority.

The word "mammon," which comes from Jesus' mother tongue and was retained in the Greek translation, also favors the authenticity of Matthew 6:24. Its basis was Aramaic *mamon*, which meant wealth, possessions, money. It is no accident that Mammon appears in the mystery plays of the late Middle Ages as an idol with demonic features who seizes complete control of people. Already in Jesus' usage there is a demonic element in the term: here there is no article attached to "mammon" and so it becomes a "personifying name."[34] For Jesus the god "Wealth" exemplifies all the powers that bind human beings

[33] Lit. "mammon," Gk. μαμωνᾶς. —Trans.

[34] Michael Wolter, *The Gospel According to Luke* (see part 3, n. 3 above), 2:271.

and thus prevent them from loving the true God *undividedly* and being capable of discipleship.

Ah, the keyword "undivided." It confronts us with a problem in which we are all entangled if we believe in God. We want both: certainly we want God; God must reign. But at the same time we want ourselves: we want to reign over our own lives. That "both" is one of the most dangerous enemies of the reign of God. We want to love God but at the same time to lead our lives as *we* picture them and as *we* think they should be. Both together, always. Yet Jesus unmistakably says—and, it goes without saying, against the background of Deuteronomy 6:5—"both" doesn't work any more. Now that the reign of God is breaking in, once and for all you can no longer serve two masters. The reign of God demands your unconditional "all."

43. Camel and Needle's Eye (Mark 10:25)

Again, with the saying about the camel and the needle's eye, Jesus calls wealth into question—ironically, of course, but also with unsurpassable clarity. The *logion* comes to us from Mark, within the continuation of the episode of the rich man who could not separate himself from his riches (Mark 10:17-31). Matthew and Luke took this episode and its continuation, together with the crucial *logion*, from their model text of Mark (Matt 19:16-30 // Luke 18:18-30). The Lord's saying is extremely brief and is structured as an antithetical parallelism:

> It is easier for a camel
> to go through the eye of a needle
> than for a rich person
> to enter the reign of God. (Mark 10:25)

That kind of talk is sheer provocation—even, on the story level, for Jesus' disciples, though they have already left everything (Mark 10:24). But what I mean here by *provocation* is primarily that Jesus is not offering *information* about how many rich people may, in fact, be saved (zero percent return). Rather, he wants to make his hearers uneasy, to "rattle" them in order to move them to turn their lives toward the reign of God. But even when we understand that this is about provocation, not information—still it remains unbearable, and it has been so through the centuries. In his book *Der unbequeme Jesus*[35] Marius Reiser writes:

> [One can] read over and over again the idea that, instead of *kamēlon*, "camel," the word was originally *kamilon*, which means "rope" or "mooring rope." But Greek has other words for "rope"; the supposed word for "mooring rope" is not found in any Greek writing. It is evidently the product of imagination, devised by Byzantine philologists in order to explain this passage.

It is true that a rope will no more pass through a needle's eye than a camel will, but at least the eye of a needle and a rope have a little more affinity than the largest animal of the Near East and the smallest opening anyone at that time could imagine.

A medieval scholar, probably an Irish monk, thought he knew better than the Byzantines with their mooring cable. He asserted that there had probably been a very small, narrow gate in the wall of Jerusalem, one that heavy-laden camels could scarcely navigate, and that gate was called "The Needle's Eye." So Jesus was saying: "It is easier for a camel with a full load to pass through that Jerusalem gate than for a wealthy person to enter the reign of God."

The purpose of these "explanations" is clear: the rich only need to reduce their load a little by giving alms; then even they can pass through the eye of the needle. Obviously such ideas are far removed from Jesus' thinking, and we have not gotten much closer even today. But there is no need to invent less harsh translations in order to bring Jesus into line. We simply don't preach about his often-offensive words and seek out only what is "acceptable" for today—above all, the "tender" Jesus.

All the same, Jesus remains inconvenient. In the present context we can see that his preaching does not explicitly address the "social function" of wealth, which would be possible and would make sense. That would mean that a rich person remains wealthy but constantly gives everything extra to alleviate society's needs. There were important theologians in ancient Israel to whom one could appeal for this model of social balance. The law code in Deuteronomy governing life in society constantly sought, by means of a variety of statutes, to

[35] Marius Reiser, *Der unbequeme Jesus* (see n. 21 above), 124–25.

eliminate the worst poverty in the land: that of orphans, widows, Levites, and foreigners. The aim was a society without poor people or, to put it more cautiously, one in which eruptions of poverty were dealt with as quickly as possible (cf., e.g., Deut 15:1-11). In that social model the propertied classes (and above all the rich) who do not close their fists in the faces of the poor have an important function.

It appears, though, that for Jesus there is really no room for this positive position for wealth. Why did he not put more emphasis on the model solutions in Deuteronomy or the rest of the Torah when he spoke against the rich? Or did he, after all—for example, when, according to Matthew 5:42, he said, "Give to everyone who begs from you, and do not refuse anyone wants to borrow from you"?

In this connection we might also point out that Jesus had quite open and unrestricted dealings with well-to-do people: He invited himself to the home of rich Zacchaeus, who then even promised in future to give half of his income to the poor (Luke 19:5, 8). He dined with toll-collectors (Mark 2:15). Independent (and therefore propertied) women supported him and his disciples out of their substance during their unstable, wandering lives (Luke 8:1-3). But all that is not so much about the social function of wealth and more that Jesus recognizes a number of stages along the way to the gathering of the people of God. Closest to him are the Twelve, and around the Twelve a larger group of disciples. But then there is also the great crowd of those who accept Jesus' message but remain tied to their homes. Beyond them there are friends, people who have been healed, sympathizers, occasional helpers, and even profiteers.[36] I would locate the rich, too, within this many-layered society of the Jesus movement: wealthy people who associated with Jesus or stood by him. They, too, are part of the assembly of the eschatological people of God, which is called to bring together all Israel, including sinners, slouches, and seekers, gathering them into the grand promises of the end of the ages.

Certainly none of that changes anything about Jesus' offensive and uncompromising condemnations of wealth. Those still resist being explained away. Are they so sharp because in Jesus' time and place wealth almost always fed on oppression and exploitation? There may be something to that, but ultimately we can understand Jesus' atti-

[36] See at length on this subject Gerhard Lohfink, *Jesus of Nazareth: What He Wanted, Who He Was*, trans. Linda M. Maloney (Collegeville, MN: Liturgical Press, 2012), 86–99.

tude on this subject only in light of the force of the onrushing reign of God.

44. What Makes People Unclean (Mark 7:15)

The saying in Mark 7:15 that will be our subject here is one of Jesus' most consequential *logia*. It has cut deep into history because it is *one* reason, though not the only one, why Christians separated themselves from the purity-Torah of the Old Testament and from many of Torah's other commands. It reads:

> There is nothing outside a person that by going in can defile,
> but the things that come out are what defile. (Mark 7:15)

Again we are faced with an antithetical parallelism in a positively textbook form and with a clarity designed to make even the simplest members of the audience prick up their ears. Mark (or Mark's tradition) located the *logion* in the following context: Pharisees and scribes from Jerusalem observe that some of Jesus' disciples do not perform the required ritual handwashing before eating, thus making their food unclean. So they ask: "Why do your disciples not live according to the tradition of the elders, but eat with defiled hands?" (Mark 7:5). That, at any rate, is how Mark presents it.

What is "the tradition of the elders" here? It is not simply the purity provisions of Torah, such as those in Leviticus 11–15 and Deuteronomy 14:3-21; 23:10-15. There we find nothing about having to wash one's hands before eating or after going to the market.[37] So it can only mean that the disciples are not keeping to the purity regulations that had developed or were beginning to develop in the Pharisees' communities. Their purpose was to extend the purity-Torah for priests to their own community and beyond it, to the whole nation.[38] It is possible that Jesus defended his disciples against such an accusation with the words found here.

[37] Of course, Lev 15:11 does not apply here.

[38] The background, for the Pharisaic community, was Exod 19:6: "you shall be for me a priestly kingdom and a holy nation." What Exod 19:6 apparently meant, however, was that Israel as a whole, by its very existence, should exercise a quasi-priestly function—namely, by mediating the will of God to the nations.

We could imagine other situations in which these words could have been spoken. Jesus often ate with people who most certainly did not hold to the Pharisees' rules for purity. Just think of his eating with toll-collectors and sinners, something mentioned fairly often (cf. Mark 2:15). Such circles would scarcely have paid any attention to ritual rules for purification. In the eyes of the Pharisees, or of people who lived according to the Pharisees' rules, Jesus made himself impure by sitting at table with such people. The saying could also come from that kind of situation. In that case it would not be a rejection in principle of the Old Testament purity laws but a way of placing the love-commandment and the proclamation of the reign of God above any kind of purity observance.

There is yet a third possibility, and I find it by far the most likely:[39] as we have seen before, there are certain gospel texts that are best explained in light of the uncertain, wandering life of Jesus and his disciples. When the disciples had been on the road all day and could feel glad in the evening to be received into a house and get something to eat they would scarcely have asked whether the meal and its preparation followed the Pharisaic purity regulations. Jesus could have legitimated such behavior with this *logion*. In favor of that is certainly the "eating and drinking whatever they provide" of the mission discourse (Luke 10:7). We might add "eating and drinking what is given to you without asking whether it is pure or not." In any case the Coptic Gospel of Thomas associated Jesus' saying about "clean and unclean" with the mission discourse (Gos. Thom. 14). If Mark 7:15 originated in Jesus' and his disciples' itinerant way of life it would not be a rejection of the Old Testament Torah of purity; it simply places the preaching of the reign of God in the context of that other law.

Certainly one must admit that Mark 7:15—taken by itself—does not point to any concrete situation; its shape is fundamental and absolute: what comes from without cannot make one impure, but only what comes out of one—namely, the evil in one's heart, which then emerges in the evil of one's actions. Hence we have to ask again: is it not true, after all, that Jesus eliminated Scripture's whole Torah of purity?

[39] See the reference to this possibility in Martin Hengel, "Jesus und die Tora," *TBei* 9 (1978): 152–72, at 164, and in Gerd Theissen and Annette Merz, *The Historical Jesus: A Comprehensive Guide*, trans. John Bowden (Minneapolis: Fortress Press, 1998), 366–67.

We can probably move forward with this difficult matter only if we compare how Jesus dealt with other statements in Torah (and their contemporary interpretation). For example, he never thought of eliminating the Sabbath commandment, but he does on occasion make it secondary when it is a question of healing someone who is sick. Obviously that happens, for Jesus, in connection with the arrival of the reign of God (Mark 3:1-6). Neither does he consider eliminating the Fourth Commandment, but when necessary he subordinates it to the demands of the reign of God (see chap. 18). And he does not think of forbidding temple sacrifices, but he can subject them to the necessary prior reconciliation (chap. 31). Similarly, we may say that Jesus did not intend to declare the Torah of purity false and outdated. In any case he orders the lepers he has cleansed to show themselves to the priests, in accordance with Leviticus 14, and to bring the required sacrifice for their cleansing (Mark 1:44).

Still, we must also add here that, before this, Jesus had touched the lepers without the least hesitation. Apparently he always acted very freely. And Mark 7:15 is really radical and strictly formulated. Is the problem unresolvable? Probably we should seek the solution in much the same way as with the forbidding of divorce. There Jesus ultimately appealed to God's will in creation: "So they are no longer two, but one flesh. Therefore what God has joined together, let no one separate" (Mark 10:6-9). When Jesus insists that nothing outside a person is unclean, but that all uncleanness comes from the wicked human heart, the creation account could also be in the background. There we read: "God saw everything that he had made, and indeed, it was very good" (Gen 1:31).

If the world and all that is in it was good at its creation, and if the coming of the reign of God restores God's original good creation and brings it to its fullest perfection, then wherever the reign of God is accepted, nothing can be unclean. Then uncleanness always and only comes from the evil that issues from humans themselves.

If Jesus thought that way he did not simply abrogate the Old Testament Torah of purity, for it is in fact one of the tools by which God is creating a holy people in the midst of the disturbed and wounded creation. Then Jesus would have brought the Torah of purity into its right light by interpreting it in terms of God's creative will. We might say he used Torah to define Torah.

Moreover, we see more and more clearly today how hasty and inadequate was the classic church solution: that the so-called "moral" norms of Torah were to be retained but all the others (the so-called "ceremonial" or "ritual" law) were declared to be abrogated *wholesale*. Why was that church solution so highly problematic?

The Torah contains extensive laws for purity (cf., e.g., Lev 11–15). These apply primarily to the house, clothing, the body, and food. Instruction is given about how people freed of skin diseases were to be declared clean. There are distinctions made between animals that are pure and those that defile. There is a listing of what types of meat may be eaten and which may not. Is that all out of date? It seems so.

Precisely in speaking of Mark 7:15, Christian theologians have said that with Jesus' distinction between "within" and "without" all external-ritual holiness is returned from a physical, pre-personal sphere to its true meaning, which is about internal, personal holiness. But one ought to be extremely careful with such formulations, because in the New Testament even the holiness that is divorced from the external and physical means decisively more than simply an inner quality of the soul or the moral person.

The whole people of God is meant to be a "holy nation" (1 Pet 2:9-10). Thus holiness always also includes the social dimension, that of community, which is inseparably tied to the person of the individual. "Holy" describes not only the individual's inner self. The conditions of life, the social structures and arrangements in the world within which the person lives and into which s/he constantly enters, must also be holy. That was precisely what the "material-ritual" purity laws of Torah were meant to bring about.

Faith in the God who led Israel out of Egypt, made them God's own people, and gave them the Land is also supposed to shape *Israel's whole life-world*. Hence from that time forward it can no longer be the case that a member of the people of God believes with tongue and heart but despises the body, lets the space in which s/he is at home fall apart, and destroys the environment. A saying of the prophet Zechariah points in precisely that direction:

> *On that day there shall be inscribed on the bells of the horses, "Holy to the* LORD*." . . . And every cooking pot in Jerusalem and Judah shall be sacred to the* LORD *of hosts.* (Zech 14:20-21)

The meaning is that a day is coming in which all Israel—not only its people, but material objects and, above all, every situation in life—will find themselves in a condition willed by God and reflecting God's sovereignty. To the extent, then, that they correspond to the will of God and are shaped by God's nearness they find their identity and support life. The intention of the Old Testament Torah of purity is not only that people be holy before God in their inner life but that faith in the holy God will shape and transform their world. As far as this aim of the Torah of purity is concerned, we are far from having attained it. The Old Testament purity laws deserve to be read and considered anew in light of their original meaning. If we can understand their inner meaning they will prevent us from exploiting the planet, destroying our environment, mixing everything together arbitrarily, and depriving things as well as human beings of their identity and symbolic power.

Perhaps we can see more clearly how concrete all that is when we consider the (probable) origin of the virus SARS-CoV-2. The virologists tell us that the virus probably did not originate in a laboratory but by inadvertent transfer from animal to human—possibly by way of the huge market for wild animals in the Chinese metropolis of Wuhan, where not only the flesh of domesticated animals but also that of snakes, rats, salamanders, toads, and various birds is for sale, together with ground bones and the dried excrement of bats (offered not as a delicacy but as medicine). We can think of many other examples of how, in the world in which we live, things and people are deprived of their identity. The consequences can be terrifying. Christian interpretation of the Old Testament Torah of purity needs to be reconsidered from that viewpoint as well.

The Old Testament scholar Frank Crüsemann has dared to say: "The identity of the biblical God is dependent upon the connection with his Torah."[40] He is right. Therefore the church can and must never abandon the Torah: *not even parts of it*. Certainly it must read and live the Torah in the spirit of Jesus—that is, in the power of the new thing that entered the world with him and out of his freedom and insight, his radicality and fear of God.

[40] Frank Crüsemann, *The Torah: Theology and History of Old Testament Law*, trans. Allen W. Mahnke (Minneapolis: Fortress Press, 1996), 366.

45. Give the Emperor What Belongs to the Emperor! (Mark 12:17)

Mark 12:13-17 presents us with a dramatic scene:[41] a delegation made up of Pharisees and Herodians[42] has been sent to Jesus "to trap him in what he says." It is true that the narrative does not specify that they have been commissioned by the council, but that is clear on the narrative level of Mark's Gospel. The listeners or readers already know it from Mark 11:18: "the chief priests and the scribes . . . kept looking for a way to kill him." It is, then, against that background that the delegation comes to Jesus and confronts him with the most acute problem that existed in Israel at that time.

Before they come to the point they pretend to flatter Jesus, saying they know he is sincere and shows deference to no one, and that he teaches "the way of God." But then comes their trick question, formulated as only a question can be when one has thought it out carefully beforehand:

> *Is it lawful to pay taxes to the emperor, or not?* (Mark 12:14)

The indirect "is it lawful" refers to God: "Does God allow . . . ?" The delegation has addressed Jesus as "teacher," one who teaches the "way of God." Having named the problem, Jesus' opponents give a short summary to emphasize the urgency of the thing. Their summary has the laconic brevity the Romans loved:

> *"Should we pay them, or should we not?"*

The trap into which they are trying to maneuver Jesus is so dangerous because the Romans, after deposing Archelaus, one of the sons of Herod the Great, had made Judea a procuratorial province and, as in every province, imposed an annual tax of one denarius per inhabitant. This head tax constantly reminded the Jews of how unfree they had become, but it also posed a religious question: if *God* was Lord and ruler of Israel, could one acknowledge the *emperor* as sovereign by paying a head tax?

[41] For what follows—especially as regards questions of the Roman denarius for the tax—I have consulted Marius Reiser's studies. Cf. his "Jesus und das Geld," *SNTSU.A* 43 (2018): 187–201, esp. 193–95.

[42] Cf. the association of the two groups in Mark 3:6.

That is the very reason why the Zealots refused to pay the imperial tax, called the people to resist, and planned a revolt. Some of the Pharisees and parts of the population were on their side. On the other hand, the priestly aristocracy in Jerusalem wanted to prevent a revolt at all costs. In their circles payment of the imperial tax was regarded as a necessity of *Realpolitik*. The Herodians took a similar view.

That is the background to our story. Either a yes or a no would create great difficulties for Jesus. After all, if he assented to the head tax he would be putting himself on the side of the council and thus indirectly supporting those powerful spiritual figures whom he had rejected by his actions in the temple shortly before this, accusing them of making God's house a den of robbers (Mark 11:17). But if Jesus says "no" to the head tax he will be putting himself on the side of the Zealots and calling for a revolt against Rome. In that case the council would indict him before the prefect, Pontius Pilate, for stirring up revolution.

The way Jesus avoids this dilemma is magnificent. He asks the delegation to show him the coin used to pay the tax. Why the coin of the tax? The money required by the Romans as payment of the tax was a silver denarius coined at Lugdunum (present-day Lyons) in Gaul, and because the issuance of silver coins was an imperial privilege it bore the image of the reigning emperor. Given the Jewish prohibition of images,[43] no Jew would normally have such a coin at hand, certainly not within the temple precincts. The only exceptions were, probably, the many pilgrims from the Diaspora attending the festivals in Jerusalem. Therefore Jesus asks that someone "bring" him a silver denarius—that is, get it from someone else, obviously the moneychangers in the temple forecourt.[44] Precisely that "bringing" shows exactly how the payment was made. In those days no Jew would carry around a coin bearing a *human image*.

[43] Images of God, human beings, and most especially rulers were a religious taboo in Israel, especially among the Zealots. The Romans respected that and the governors there avoided issuing coinages containing the imperial image, although ordinarily it would be placed on the obverse of any coin. Likewise, coins from the autonomous mints in Tyre, which were the only coinage accepted in the temple, bore no image of the emperor, though there were images of pagan gods on both sides.

[44] Jewish pilgrims came from every part of the Roman Empire and, of course, brought the greatest variety of coins with them. In order to pay the temple tax they had go to the moneychangers in the temple forecourt to exchange their coins for Tyrian tetra-drachmas.

So a silver denarius is brought. Jesus dramatically elevates it before his opponents and asks: "Whose head is this, and whose title?" We have to note the comic aspect he brings to the whole scene with that question. Obviously his opponents know what is on the coin, but they have to answer like schoolchildren: "The emperor's." And then Jesus gives them the crucial answer—just as brief and striking as their question had been:

> Give to the emperor the things that are the emperor's,
> [but] to God the things that are God's. (Mark 12:17)

The first line clearly opposes the Zealots and their refusal to pay a tax to the emperor. As we have seen, paying the tax meant using a silver denarius, and the coin becomes Jesus' "instructional material." But how? Jesus' opponents themselves have said it: the image and inscription are "the emperor's." That is: the coin belongs to the emperor—not, of course, as his private property! Rather, it is a tangible and universally circulating symbol of his authority, his rule, his power. Jesus does not question that authority; it is a simple fact that he soberly acknowledges. The next few decades will affirm Jesus' sense of reality: the Zealots' revolt against Rome will lead to nightmarish conflicts among the Zealots themselves, the death of countless people in Israel, and the destruction of Jerusalem and the temple.

Of course, Jesus does not leave it at that. He goes on. The usual translation is "*and* give to God the things that are God's."[45] But the Greek *kai* (= and) here is a *kai adversativum* and thus should be translated "but." Add to this that the parallelism—like so many other antithetical parallelisms—lays its full weight on the second line. As we have seen, the first line was directed against the Zealots and their revolutionary plans. Thus in that line Jesus seems to put himself on the side of his Sadducean opponents. But then he pauses . . . and next comes, with emphasis, his important point: "But give to God what belongs to God!" And that is a flat rejection of the leading classes in Jerusalem, who do not inquire after the living will of God but hope to silence Jesus. This rejection of his opponents in Jerusalem, which is simultaneously an uncovering of their real relationship to God, is the center of this *logion*.

[45] The only exception I have seen is *The Living Bible*. —Trans.

One often reads in newer commentaries that this saying of Jesus does not allow us to draw any conclusions about the relationship between church and state.[46] The warning is understandable because, in fact, in the course of church history Mark 12:17 has all too often been used to legitimize the then-current view of church and state—even when that relationship was altogether questionable. Nevertheless, it seems to me that the warning is off the mark. There is more behind Jesus' answer than merely a brilliant riposte to the Zealots on the one hand and the temple aristocracy on the other. At depth it is altogether about the correct social nature of the people of God.

The eschatological people of God, as Jesus desires to gather it together in light of the now-happening reign of God, must not be a theocracy such as the Zealots wish to have and seek to bring about with violence and terror—a complete melding of state power and religion. In being led out of Egypt, Israel has been delivered once and forever from the ominous social form of theocracy.

Neither may the eschatological people of God be a power like the Roman state. Jesus certainly acknowledged the necessity of state governance and the ability to keep order: hence "give the emperor what is the emperor's!" But a structure like that of the *Imperium Romanum* is built on power and violence, and the eschatological people of God must be absolutely free from violence.

The true people of God, Jesus tells his opponents, must give to God "what belongs to God." That can only be a reference to the first commandment in Deuteronomy 6:5, that Israel is to love the Lord its God with all its heart, with all its soul, and with all its strength. That love is to be lived tangibly according to Israel's Torah—as Jesus interprets it, of course. And while, as regards the social shape of the people of God, Torah proposes an image of a right society, it is *not* about a state, for the failed experiment with a state had preceded the Torah in its final biblical form. The bodies of laws in the Torah seek to shape a society that submits itself to God in free fidelity and conforms its common life entirely to God's commandments. There is no such thing as a royal power apparatus in the law-collections in Torah. Only in Deuteronomy, on the margins, does the figure of a monarch appear—but not as ruler. Instead, the monarch is part of a society

[46] Thus, e.g., Ulrich Luz, *Matthew 8–20*, trans. James E. Crouch, Hermeneia (Minneapolis: Fortress Press, 2001), 419–20; Michael Wolter, *The Gospel According to Luke* (see part 3, n. 3 above), 2:396.

marked by shared authority.[47] Moreover, the monarch must constantly have a Torah scroll at hand, make a lifelong study of it, and live as a model Israelite (Deut 17:14-20).

Jesus was not a teacher of Torah, but of course he knew it intimately and, with his own clear-sightedness, had recognized its true goal: a people chosen by God that, by a free decision and with its whole existence, seeks to love God and to make that love real in every sphere of life as "love of neighbor," that is, as solidarity with all the sisters and brothers in the people of God. Within that sphere the identity of all things and relationships in their created purpose, spoken of in the previous chapter, would appear.

Jesus did not reject the state as a force for order, but he severely disapproved of the idea that the good news of the reign of God can be served by *coopting the power* of the state, or *with the aid of the state*, or by *imitating secular political forms of governance*. That is precisely the point of Mark 12:17.

46. Like a Child (Mark 10:15)

Like the one in the previous chapter, the Jesus-saying that is our subject here is located within a narrative. It goes this way: people are bringing children to Jesus so that he may touch them, but the disciples, playing the role of Jesus' "court," rudely warn the parents to keep away. Jesus sees what is happening, refuses to cooperate, and corrects his disciples: "Let the little children come to me; do not stop them; for it is to such as these that the reign of God belongs." Then he embraces the children, lays his hands on them, and blesses them (Mark 10:13-16).

That is, in itself, a complete narrative with everything necessary: an introduction and conclusion, antagonists (namely, the disciples) and the dismissal of the antagonists. The dismissal is given in striking words that form the climax of the narrative. But those words are followed, in Mark 10:15, by a second saying of Jesus that fits with the first but has a different aim:

> Truly I tell you,
> whoever does not receive the reign of God as a little child
> will never enter it. (Mark 10:15)

[47] Cf. Norbert Lohfink, "Distribution of the Functions of Power," in his *Great Themes from the Old Testament* (see n. 17 above), 55–76.

The first Jesus-saying fits neatly within the narrative; the second also fits, but only somewhat. In the first *logion* the *children* are promised the reign of God; in the second *adults* are threatened that they will never enter the reign of God unless they behave *as a child does*.

We have already come across any number of Jesus-sayings that at first circulated independently and then had to be inserted into a narrative context by the evangelists. That is also the case here. The two "hooks" on which Mark, or his tradition, could hang the striking *logion* were "reign of God" and "child."

That observation[48] has consequences, though. Since we are seeking the original meaning of Jesus-sayings we must explain Mark 10:15 only in itself and not in terms of its current narrative context. We must most certainly not interpret it on the basis of Matthew 18:3-4, since Matthew not only chose a different narrative frame for our *logion* but also revised it.[49] In Matthew's version the disciples ask Jesus who is the greatest in the reign of God. Jesus sets a child in their midst and says:

> *Truly I tell you,*
> *unless you change and become like children,*
> *you will never enter the heavenly reign.*
> *Whoever becomes humble like this child*
> *is the greatest in the heavenly reign.* (Matt 18:3-4)

This Matthean parallel, together with its narrative frame, must not be used to grasp the original meaning of Mark 10:15.[50] In that case the puzzling "receive the reign of God like a child" would take on the meaning that the disciples must make themselves "small," like children. They must not seek to be "great." They must divest themselves of their desire to dominate.

[48] Cf. Rudolf Bultmann, *History of the Synoptic Tradition* (see part 1, n. 2 above), 32: "v. 15 [must be treated] as an originally independent dominical saying, inserted into the situation of vv. 13-16. It is certainly no use referring to Matt. 18[3] for this verse is clearly not an independent tradition, but is the Matthean form of Mk. 10[15] in another context."

[49] This, certainly, is disputed. Some exegetes consider Matt 18:3 the older version of our *logion*. The for-and-against is well summarized by Ulrich Luz, *Matthew 8–20* (see n. 46 above), 425–26.

[50] Which is what, e.g., Josef Schmid does in his *Evangelium nach Markus* (see part 3, n. 13 above), 189.

Certainly that is an important theme, one of Jesus' own (cf. only Mark 10:43-44). But this is about Mark 10:15! In speaking of "receiving the reign of God like a child" did Jesus really mean that his disciples must diminish themselves, make themselves small and humble? Do children truly make themselves small? Don't they want to grow up as fast as possible? When we encounter that, of course it is not about what the children *want* to be but what they *should* be as adults; hence in that sense the interpretation is correct, but it takes away the simplicity and directness that is characteristic of Jesus' words. No, we have to take our Jesus-saying out of all secondary interpretive contexts, consider it by itself, and ask ourselves what it originally meant. What, then, does "receiving the reign of God like a child" mean for Jesus?

In his commentary on Matthew, which in accord with the goals of the EKK series[51] always traces the history of a text's influence, Ulrich Luz assembled a long list of interpretations of Matthew 18:3 and Mark 10:15.[52] "Like children" or "like a child" has led interpreters, over the centuries, to the following conclusions among others (the list collects voices going back to the era of the church fathers):

Cited as traits of children that should be imitated are primarily innocence, gentleness, and simplicity. Besides those, it is said that children are not inquisitive, do not strive for empty glory, are not haughty, are free from malice and rivalries. They are not ambitious and do not quarrel. They are free of passions and aspirations. They are modest, not vindictive, and docilely receive instruction from their superiors.

I have shown that list to some parents among my acquaintances, all of whom have raised children. Reactions ranged from wistful smiles to loud laughter, but they all agreed that those were the opinions of people who had never in their lives had anything to do with children, or else they were teachers who wanted to say what they thought children should be.

Those voices from past centuries are really a joke. (Ulrich Luz is also critical of the list.) Children have always been curious, frequently

[51] Evangelisch-Katholischer Kommentar. The same is true of the Hermeneia series in which the English translation of Luz's commentary appears. —Trans.

[52] Luz, *Matthew 8–20*, 427–28. The "authorities" include Hilary, Origen, Basil, Luther, Zwingli, Calvin, and Goethe.

jealous, quite often quarrelsome, and always ready to fight for attention and to have their wishes granted. That was part of their makeup even before evolution. We dare not try to make it so simple to "receive the reign of God like a child."

If we want to get anywhere with this question we have to ask about the possible *Sitz im Leben* (real-life situation) of Mark 10:15. Here we are on safe historical ground: Jesus, throughout his whole public life, repeatedly had to deal with people who not only distrusted him but quickly rejected him—and not just individuals; that was true of whole groups.

There were the Pharisees and their scribes who insisted on their way of observing Torah and refused to budge. There were the Zealots, who wanted to be free of the occupying power and used violence and terror for that purpose. There was the priestly aristocracy, a hierarchy that had constructed a temple-based system of control in Jerusalem—but who interpreted and exploited the temple according to their own understanding. All those groups were solidary; they knew precisely what they were supposed to believe and just as precisely what they wanted. They did not deviate an inch from their opinions. Because they already knew everything they could only seek to get rid of Jesus; after all, they quickly discerned what he claimed to be.

By contrast, children under the age of five, unless from the beginning they have been damaged by a disordered or even wicked environment, are wonderfully open to their surroundings: they are curious and eager for knowledge. They are always wide-eyed. They absolutely insist on picking up bugs they find in the grass. They are fascinated by unfamiliar sounds; they pound their spoons on the table because it creates a new sound never heard before. They trust what their mothers and fathers tell them, because they (still) trust language itself. They are grateful for gifts and anticipate them with joy. They are full of expectation every day. But above all: they can still be surprised. They can be astonished at everything new, everything they have not yet heard, everything interesting and beautiful. We could summarize it all as simply a curious, expectant, amazed openness.

It was precisely that openness that Jesus did not find in his opponents, but he had experienced it among those who were in need: the hated toll-collectors, the despised prostitutes, the sick, the poor—and most certainly among children. Jesus must have watched children with the same curiosity and acuity he gave to women's housework, the flowers of the fields, the growth of wheat, the misery of the poor, and the allure of the rich. His parables show it at every turn. And he most certainly did not elevate children to a divine level, as did a perverse pedagogy not so long ago with its notion that children must simply be allowed to be themselves and did not need rearing. In his parable about children at play (Matt 11:16-17 // Luke 7:31-32) Jesus showed how sulky children could be and how they deliberately exclude other children.

But Jesus also knew what a miracle and promise children are. Therefore he tells us doubters, us long-since set-in-our-ways, all of us who know better and are constantly complaining: "Unless you can become as curious, amazed, grateful, and open as children you have no chance of even guessing what the reign of God is, to say nothing of having a prospect of entering it." We could also speak in very elevated and abstract terms and say that children still know what grace is, or, better: in their shining and astonished eyes we can still catch a glimpse of what grace means.

47. Seek First the Reign of God! (Luke 12:31)

Matthew and Luke got Jesus' saying about "seeking the reign of God" from the Sayings Source, where it was part of a section on "care and concern" that has been especially well preserved (cf. Matt 6:25-34 // Luke 12:22-32). Many Christians are familiar with that section as part of the Sermon on the Mount, where Matthew inserted it; it appears elsewhere in Luke. Here is Matthew's version:

> *Do not worry about your life,*
> *what you will eat or what you will drink,*
> *or about your body, what you will wear.*
> *Is not life more than food,*
> *and the body more than clothing?*
> *Look at the birds of the air;*
> *they neither sow nor reap*
> *nor gather into storerooms,*[53]
> *and yet your heavenly Father feeds them.*

[53] The Greek word here is *apothēkē*, and *apothēkē* is not only a barn but any kind of storage or storeroom. There were no barns in ancient Israel in the modern sense. For grain storage people used holes in the rocky ground under houses or nearby cliffs, or else large clay vessels that were filled from above through an opening that could

Are you not of more value than they? . . .
And why do you worry about your clothing?
Consider the lilies of the field, how they grow;
they neither toil nor spin,
yet I tell you, even Solomon in all his glory
was not clothed like one of these.
But if God so clothes the grass of the field, which is alive today
and tomorrow is thrown into the oven,
how much more you—O you of little faith?
Therefore do not worry, saying,
"What will we eat?" or "What will we drink?"
or "What will we wear?"
For it is the Gentiles who worry about all those things;
indeed, your heavenly Father knows
that you need them all. (Matt 6:25-32)

Immediately after those verses we find in Matthew, and correspondingly in Luke, the *logion* that concerns us here. The two versions read:

Strive first for the heavenly reign and its righteousness,
and all these things will be given to you as well. (Matt 6:33)

Instead, strive for God's reign,
and these things will be given to you as well. (Luke 12:31)

We can see right away that the *logion* is firmly attached to the previous section; in fact, it constitutes the climax and goal of that text. The necessities of life need no longer be named, as "all these things" or simply "these" point to them. The same is true of the Sayings Source, where the whole section in Matthew 6:25-33 // Luke 12:22-31 already constitutes a connected whole.[54] There, too, our *logion* formed the climax. That might already have been the case with Jesus. There is much in favor of the idea that the whole composition about "care" goes back to him, more or less, and that with him also everything culminated in the saying about seeking the reign of God.

---

be sealed and that had a device at the bottom through which the grain could be extracted.

[54] Both Matthew and Luke have undertaken small changes, and it is not really certain where the composition about "care" ended in the Sayings Source. Were Matt 6:34 or Luke 12:32 part of it there?

However, that is not really certain. In what follows I will assume the uncertainty and will try right away to give reasons why, in Jesus' discourse, the saying about "seeking" was not yet related to the composition about "care." At the earliest phase of its tradition our *logion* may well have been an unconnected saying circulating independently—like so many other sayings of Jesus. To begin with, in reconstructing the original wording let us simply eliminate the connections with the current context! Then the word of the Lord could have said:[55]

> Seek first the reign of God[56]—
> and everything else will be given you as well.

The question, of course, is whether there are really indications that this *logion* did not originally belong with the discourse on freedom from care. I will have to explore that at somewhat greater length.

The discourse on "care" is one of the most beautiful texts in the Gospels. It appeals to everyone from the start. How closely Jesus observed nature: the birds who collect their food, the spring flowers that bloom almost overnight on the Galilean hills after the winter rains and light up the slopes—and even the artistic architectonics of the tall grasses! There must have been a smile on Jesus' face when he spoke about the birds and the lilies, and surely he laughed when he talked about the storehouses the birds do not need. We are touched, and at first we do not even notice the problems this apparently comforting text conceals, but eventually they appear.

Aren't we being advised to live in the moment, without working? Aren't we told to lie back and relax? No, our reason tells us, that can't be what it means. The text surely does not mean that we should be goofing off. It only says we should not worry—about food or clothing or even our lives. God cares for us. But what does it mean to say we shouldn't worry? Are we not supposed to think and plan ahead? Are we being told not to provide for the future?

That, too, would be impossible for us. It would mean no thoughts about a good school for our children, one that will prepare them for

[55] This, again, is one of those rare occasions when I am using a reconstruction as my basic text.

[56] "And its righteousness" is a Matthean expansion. The concept of "righteousness" is an element of Matthean theology: cf. Matt 3:15; 5:6, 10; 6:1; 21:32.

their future calling! No food in the freezer! A nearly empty closet! And on the broader level: no economy, no industry, no science! After all, entrepreneurial initiatives, scientific projects, political activities—none of them can exist without planning and careful preparations that may extend over many years. Should we leave that to the "Gentiles"?

That, again, is impossible! We get into overwhelming difficulties in interpreting this appealing and comforting text if we do not first ask ourselves: to whom was it originally addressed? That, after all, is completely obvious: it is not spoken simply to Jewish listeners, the crowd that is always pressing around Jesus. The saying about "care" is addressed to the little group of disciples who travel with Jesus from place to place (cf. the description of the audience in Luke 12:22). It is about the situation of people who, answering Jesus' summons, have left everything—house, family, calling—and are moving with Jesus through Israel, living a dramatic itinerant life in order to proclaim the reign of God throughout the land.

I spoke previously, at length, about the situation in which they found themselves, and I pointed out that the wandering apostles were able to depend on *locally resident* adherents of Jesus—his sympathizers, friends, those who had been healed by him, helpers and supporters. It took the whole of the Jesus movement to furnish the basis for Jesus and his disciples to be able to live without cares. This, too, is where we must locate the freedom from care that Jesus speaks of in Matthew 6:25-34 // Luke 12:22-32. The disciples can be carefree and do without provisions because there will be people, again and again, who will receive them as guests in their houses. It is precisely in that way and no other that God's providence appears.

Still, the *logion* about "seeking the reign of God" can be applied to those itinerant disciples only with difficulty since, after all, they are not "seeking" it but "announcing" it. They have already left father and mother, wife and children, houses and fields to follow Jesus and shout out their message about the reign of God. Does Jesus still have to tell them to "seek first the reign of God"?

No; in fact, that command applies only to people who have not yet decided, who still entertain doubts and fears about following Jesus—those who, with some justification, ask what kind of chasms would yawn before them if they did. Jesus wants to take away their fear by telling them, "Seek first the reign of God, and everything else will be given you." The words of Matthew 6:33 // Luke 12:31 thus open themselves to a much broader circle of addressees and then, in the time of the church, to all the baptized.

This hypothesis of an originally independent *logion* may also be favored by the fact that in the overall composition the disciples who care for themselves are consistently contrasted with the image of a "father" who cares for his children. Then, at the composition's climax, the "reign of God" suddenly appears. That is certainly not incompatible with the context, but it is a different subject.

So much for the hypothesis. Now let us simply look closer at Matthew 6:33 // Luke 12:31. The beginning of the *logion* speaks of "seeking." That is a good Jesus-word, as the *logion* in Matthew 7:7 shows ("seek, and you will find"). Jesus is drawing here on Israel's wisdom literature, where the concept plays an important role; the texts speak again and again about personified Wisdom, who invites the audience to "seek her." See, for example, Proverbs 1:28; 2:4; 8:17; 14:6; Wisdom 6:12; 8:2, 18; Sirach 4:12; 6:27; 51:13, 26. Wisdom becomes the teacher of all who seek her. Still more: she has built her house and, as host, invites all to her festive banquet (Prov 9:1-6). Everyone who wants to walk in the way of God seeks to win her as companion, even as helpmeet throughout life. So in Wisdom 8:2, 16 we hear the testimony of an experienced man:[57]

> *I loved her and sought her from my youth;*
> *I desired to take her for my bride,*
> *and became enamored of her beauty.*
>
> *for companionship with her has no bitterness,*
> *and life with her has no pain,*
> *but only gladness and joy.*

When Israel's wisdom teachers speak of "Lady Wisdom," then, they do not hesitate to describe her as their beloved or as a wonderful, desirable woman. Jesus knows all those texts, but now he puts the reign of God in place of Wisdom. One must desire the reign of God as one desires a beloved spouse, seeks her, gives everything for her in order to win her. That is how one finds true life. The parable of the

[57] Supposedly Solomon.

merchant "seeking" fine pearls, who finally finds the pearl of all pearls, is also about seeking the reign of God (Matt 13:45-46). Here, of course, Jesus transposed the wisdom theology that speaks of wise living and thousand-times-tested life experiences into the uniqueness of eschatological experience. *Philo-Sophia* has become *Eschatologia*. Now is the end of time. Everyone in Israel must seek the reign of God in order to gain it, and no one may fear that anything will then be lacking. Those who really seek the reign of God and nothing else will be given everything necessary for life, over and above.

Chapter 47 concludes part 4. The theme of the section was the *ethos* of the reign of God, but not the specific *ethos* of the Twelve and all the disciples who traveled through Israel with Jesus. That was the subject of parts 2 and 3. In contrast, part 4 dealt with the *ethos* of all those who did not travel with Jesus but stayed at home or returned there: the *ethos* of the healed, the friends, the sympathizers, the occasional helpers—in short, that of all those who, after encountering Jesus, lived with him "in light of the reign of God," or of those who asked themselves whether they should follow him.

I have tried, in discussing each *logion*, to inquire after the original addressees. That, I think, is an extremely important question (and one that, alas, is often neglected by exegetes). True, there was not always a clear answer, but the question had to be asked.

In many cases a simple answer was difficult to achieve because the evangelists made nearly all the sayings of Jesus, even if they were originally addressed only to the Twelve or to the larger group of disciples, applicable to Christian communities after Easter. They were convinced that a discipleship saying once directed to the Twelve must somehow be valid also for all who would come after. We can quickly recognize this phenomenon just described, that of *transparency* or *transfer*, from the fact that in the second volume of his dual work Luke constantly describes all Christians as "disciples" (cf. esp. Acts 11:26). This finding presumes the phenomenon of transparency: to a certain degree what was once demanded in the specific situation of the disciples who were immediately present to Jesus now applies to all Christians.

That is highly significant for the Christian *ethos*. From the outset it establishes inhibitory thresholds against a two-level ethics.[58] Parts 2, 3, and 4 of this book should have shown that such a two-level ethics does not really work. To take only two examples: Jesus' saying that calls every divorce a capital crime or the one that equates every lustful glance at a woman with a capital crime of adultery demand the same radicality of married people as of those who remain unmarried for the sake of the reign of God. We could easily expand the examples. I therefore urgently beg that the succession of part 3 (disciples' existence) and part 4 (life in light of the reign of God) *not* be read as a collection of materials for an ecclesial two-level ethics.

All the so-called "orders" in the church are *ordered* to one another, need each other, augment each other, and live together in the joy as well as the seriousness of the reign of God—but they do so in their various forms, because the complexity of the real world requires many different forms of calling, and every Christian has her or his own.

[58] A "two-level" ethics usually means that there are two forms of calling in the church—either to a life completely according to the evangelical "counsels" (poverty, chastity, obedience) or to a "normal" Christian life. To exaggerate the point, it is an *ethos* for the "better" and one for the "average." Usually Matt 19:21 is called on to support this so-called two-level ethic. To the contrary cf. Gerhard Lohfink, *Jesus of Nazareth* (see n. 36 above), 86–99, esp. 98–99.

Part Five

Jesus' Exalted Claim

Part 5 of this book will speak of Jesus' claim to sovereignty. I have deliberately avoided the concept of "self-awareness," because no historian can gain access to the innermost self of a person using *her or his own* methods. One can only report and judge what presents itself in words and events.[1] Still, in the preceding chapters it has appeared, again and again, that behind a Jesus-saying or a particular action an unfathomably high consciousness of his mission may appear indirectly. Let me recall—to take just one example—the saying:

> *The bridegroom's companions cannot fast while the bridegroom is with them, can they?* (Mark 2:19)

As we saw, the primary meaning is: to keep additional fast days now would positively pervert the joyful time that is about to appear with the coming of the reign of God. It would no longer be joyful; it would mean refusing to accept what God is now giving to God's people. But probably a great deal more is hidden within Jesus' saying. Doesn't it also conceal the statement that he himself is the bridegroom? Still, Jesus did not say that directly. Here, as in many other cases, he conceals his deepest secret. He lets it be sensed but does not expand on it.

There are indeed some individual concepts or whole statements in which Jesus speaks more clearly. We will pursue those here in part 5.

48. Your Sins Are Forgiven You (Mark 2:5)

The Jesus saying we are looking at here is found in the middle of a narrative: namely, in Mark 2:1-12. Many Christians are quite familiar with this story because something altogether amazing happens in it. Jesus is in Capernaum and is "in the house"—probably the one belonging to Peter and his family (cf. Mark 1:29). A great many people have crowded in and are listening to Jesus. There are so many of

[1] Theology has not only a *theological* but also a *historical* eye, as the fundamental theologian Gottlieb Söhngen liked to say in his lectures. The reverse is also true.

them, even outside the door and in the courtyard, that there is no way for others to get inside. And then it happens: we have to imagine how the house starts to shake and rattle and how chunks fall down from the ceiling. Four men are busy breaking a hole in the flat roof in order to lower a palsied man on a pallet. The text says: "they let down the mat on which the paralytic lay" (Mark 2:4). It was obviously not a "bed"[2] with frame and mattress. In the Near East in those days the beds of the poorer people were usually only mats laid on the ground.

We can imagine how the bearers attached ropes to the four corners of such a mat, then broke open the roof and lowered the man on his pallet through the hole. It was fairly easy to make such a hole because the roofs of the houses consisted of just a few poles overlaid with branches and reeds and covered with stamped earth.[3] Jesus sees the faith of these bizarre ceiling-breakers, and when the paralyzed man finally lies at his feet he tells him (literally):

> Forgiven [you] are your sins. (Mark 2:5)

Those present must have had two things indelibly impressed on their memories: not just the dramatic break through the roof and the descent of the sick person on a mat but also that Jesus does not heal the sick man immediately; he first forgives his sins. No one who has experienced such a scene can ever forget it and will tell it again and again for a lifetime. With this part of the story and thus also with the words of Jesus that are our focus here we are on secure historical ground.

Certainly we can understand the consequential character of the story only if we know that for people in Israel at that time sickness and sin were closely connected. The relationship played an important part not only in popular belief but also in Israel's theology. A great many texts presume the link between illness and sin as a matter of course; take, for example, the beginning of Psalm 32 (vv. 1-5):

[2] Thus Luther and the AV. —Trans.

[3] In his parallel Luke changed the Markan text (cf. Luke 5:19). He portrays a more solid Greco-Roman type of house; in his version the bearers have to pull up the roof tiles.

Happy are those whose transgressions are forgiven,
and whose sin is put away!

Happy are those to whom the Lord *imputes no guilt,*
and in whose spirit there is no guile!

While I held my tongue, my bones withered away,
because of my groaning all day long.

For your hand was heavy upon me day and night;
my strength dried up as in the heat of summer.

Then I acknowledged my sin,
and I did not hide my guilt from you;

I said, "I will confess my transgressions to the Lord*."*
Then you forgave me the guilt of my sin.[4]

The symptoms described—for example, the "withering away"—are not merely images of spiritual exhaustion or the pangs of conscience; they are really about illness. We may presume something comparable in the case of the man with palsy in Mark 2:1-12. Jesus must have seen through the connection in his life; he says to him: "forgiven are your sins."

But what does that mean exactly? Is it Jesus who is freeing the lame man from his sin here? That reading does not do justice to the complexity of the statement, because the passive "forgiven are your sins" is a *passivum divinum*, a passive that serves to avoid the word "God." It should be paraphrased as: "God forgives you your sins."

Does that mean that Jesus does not really forgive the palsied man's sins but simply speaks words of consolation and encouragement to him: "You can be assured that God will certainly forgive your sins"? That would not do justice to Jesus' words either. The Greek verb-form *aphientai* that we find here is present tense expressing a unique event (aorist present). We have to read it as "*Hereby, now in this present moment* your sins are forgiven (by God)—in that I say it." Only then is it clear what is happening: *God* forgives the man his guilt but does so precisely in that Jesus tells the man so. Modern linguistics would

[4] Where the author has chosen to use a more poetic translation, that of the *Münsterschwarzacher Psalter* (as here) we will use that of the *Book of Common Prayer* (USA), with minor variations.

call what Jesus does a "performative speech-act," that is, a speech-act that changes reality.[5]

Thus Mark 2:5 says through its language structure that Jesus stands in the place of God. He does not forgive through his own authority, certainly, but God's forgiveness lies in his speaking and acting—still more, it is present in his person.

Is it any wonder that many critical interpreters have denied that Jesus spoke those words? Their reasoning is primarily that there is no other place in the Gospels where, as in Mark 2:5, Jesus explicitly announces divine forgiveness. A single, isolated instance is simply not sufficient to prove that Jesus actually declared people free from their sins.[6]

But that argument is not convincing. It is true, indeed, that the formula "forgiven you are your sins" does not reliably appear anywhere else in the Gospels. We find it otherwise only in Luke 7:48, and that instance could have been borrowed from Mark 2:5 // Luke 5:20. But notice: the formula in Mark 2:5 has a broad basis,[7] namely, in Jesus' attitude toward sinners. In Luke 7:36-50 he says of the "sinful" woman who has washed and anointed his feet, "her sins, which were many, have been forgiven; hence she has shown great love" (v. 47), even before saying to *her*, "Your sins are forgiven" (v. 48). — In the story of Jesus' visit to the chief toll collector Zacchaeus (Luke 19:1-10), who was not only regarded as a sinner but really was one (v. 8c), Jesus announces God's blessing on Zacchaeus and his whole household. — The same is true of the so-called feast of the tax collectors in Mark 2:13-17. — But above all, and this is crucial, in the parable of the lost son (Luke 15:11-32) the father forgives his son unconditionally

[5] John L. Austin (1911–1960), who first described "speech-act theory," was the author of *How to Do Things with Words*, a collection of his most important lectures at Harvard University, published posthumously in 1962. The very title of the book shows what "performative" speech means.

[6] A second argument is often added: that within Mark 2:1-12 the whole complex of forgiveness of sins, vv. 2:5b-10, is a secondary (though pre-Markan) insertion that can easily be excised from the surrounding text. One can only reply that the sequence in which Jesus first forgives the man's sins and only then frees him of his palsy is an equally plausible and even much more intriguing narrative sequence.

[7] Joachim Jeremias rightly offered a full discussion of this broader basis, which was expressed not only in Jesus' words but in his actions as well. Cf. Jeremias, *New Testament Theology* (see part 1, n. 8 above), 113–14.

(vv. 20-24). The father in the parable not only represents God; in the image of the father Jesus defends his own practice before his opponents (cf. Luke 15:2). That parable in particular reveals the same interconnection as in our *logion* in Mark 2:15 between God's actions and those of Jesus. Just as that father anticipates his son's confession of sins and—forgiving him everything—clasps him in his arms, so Jesus again and again approaches sinful people, does not judge them, and gives them God's salvation simply through his being with them. — The same is true of the parable of the lost sheep (Matt 18:12-14 // Luke 15:4-7). Here, too, Jesus speaks of God, and at the same time of himself and his relationship to sinners.[8]

Thus Mark 2:5 is only an especially powerful illustration of what Jesus did over and over again: in his speaking, in his actions, and above all in his person he made the reign of God present, and with it the fully undeserved forgiveness of sins by God. Mark 2:5 is not an erratic boulder in the Gospels but only an especially prominent outcropping of the bedrock.

49. Amen, I Tell You (Matt 8:10)

The text, "Lord, I am not worthy that you should enter under my roof, but only say the word and my soul shall be healed," recited in the Roman Catholic Church before reception of the Eucharist, comes from the story of the centurion at Capernaum (Matt 8:5-13 // Luke 7:1-10; cf. John 4:46-54). Matthew and Luke drew the narrative from the Sayings Source. It seems that Matthew shortened the text; Luke apparently has the more original version,[9] which I will follow here. What is it about?

The slave of a centurion from a foreign land[10] lies dying. The centurion has heard about Jesus and sends messengers to him to ask that he come and save his servant. Jesus starts out, and when he is not far away the centurion sends a second delegation that tells Jesus:

[8] Cf. Gerhard Lohfink, *The Forty Parables of Jesus* (see preface, n. 1), 75–77.

[9] Here let me refer to the persuasive argument of Heinz Schürmann, *Lukasevangelium. Erster Teil* (see part 4, n. 31 above), 395–96.

[10] Presumably the centurion and his soldiers were part of a group of Syrian mercenaries in the service of Herod Antipas. A centurion commanded a division of one hundred men.

> *"Lord, do not trouble yourself, for I am not worthy to have you come under my roof; therefore I did not presume to come to you. But only speak the word, and let my servant be healed. For I also am a man set under authority, with soldiers under me, and I say to one, 'Go,' and he goes, and to another, 'Come,' and he comes, and to my slave, 'Do this,' and the slave does it."* (Luke 7:6-8)

Of course, that is more than a polite gesture, for the centurion is asking for a "healing at a distance" through a simple word of command. (Normally, healers touched their subjects.) Jesus is supposed to remain at a distance and order the demon of sickness to leave the enslaved man. The reason: the centurion, out of polite concern, wants to spare Jesus, the Jew, from having to enter a Gentile's house. That all presumes, however, that the man had profound trust in Jesus and believed absolutely that he had the power to heal.

At the end of the story there is a short notice that Jesus actually did heal the mortally ill servant from a distance, but that is not the real purpose of the story. Its climax comes with Jesus' astonishment at the centurion's faith. He turns to the people following him and says:

> I tell you: not even in Israel have I found such faith. (Luke 7:9)

In Matthew, Jesus' words are given a little differently:

> Amen [= truly], I tell you, in no one in Israel have I found such faith. (Matt 8:10)

Matthew added another saying of Jesus redactionally after this one, namely, the threat about the nations who wish to sit at table with Abraham, Isaac, and Jacob in the reign of God, in contrast to the "heirs of the kingdom" (Matt 8:11-12). This makes it clear that Matthew understood the saying about the centurion's faith as criticism of Israel. It remains questionable whether Jesus thought of his saying about the faith of the centurion in those terms, since Jesus had found faith even in Israel.

As far as the introduction to the saying goes,[11] however, here we can certainly rely on Matthew since "Amen" is a Hebrew word ab-

[11] For the following treatment of the formula "Amen, I tell you," let me point especially to Joachim Jeremias, *New Testament Theology* (see n. 7 above), 35–36, and his article "Amen," in *TRE* 2 (Berlin: de Gruyter, 1978), 388–91.

solutely foreign to any Greek, and for the Greeks such foreign words were barbaric; if possible, one avoided using such words in one's own speech. It is true that in three places Luke used Jesus' formula "Amen, I tell you" as he found it in his sources.[12] But no fewer than six times he simply dropped the "Amen" from the formula,[13] and seven times he replaced it with a different word.[14] He was unwilling to continually present his readers with foreign words. Thus Matthew, with "Amen, I tell you," in any case kept the wording of the Sayings Source and probably that of Jesus as well.

The expression "Amen, I tell you" enjoys a general affirmation among scholars as a typically Jesuanic formula, one he himself created. Obviously the word "Amen" existed before Jesus in the Old Testament and Judaism, but there it is a *response*; that is, it always follows as a form of agreement, emphasis, or testimony *after* a preceding speech or text. With Jesus, in contrast, the formula *begins* a subsequent text—and that is something new.

Add to this the following observation: the formula "Amen, I tell you" appears at every level of gospel tradition—in the Sayings Source, in Mark, in Matthew's special material, in Luke's special material, and even in the Fourth Gospel—and in all of them it is reserved for Jesus, is heard only from the lips of Jesus. In the New Testament epistolary literature "Amen" appears only in its usual responsorial function and never in the way Jesus used it (cf., e.g., 1 Cor 14:16). All this shows that what we have here is a creative expression by Jesus, one that tells us something essential about him. What is that?

Evidently—and here again there is broad agreement among New Testament scholars—with Jesus, "Amen, I tell you" has replaced the prophetic messenger formula. The prophets recorded in Scripture continually announce that "the word of the Lord" has come to them and is now being conveyed to Israel through them. It is not their own words that they proclaim but the words entrusted to them by God.

[12] Cf. the Lukan parallels to Mark 10:15, 29; 13:30.

[13] Elimination of the "Amen": cf. the Lukan parallels to Mark 9:1; 12:43; 14:9, 25, and to Matt 5:18; 23:36; 24:47.

[14] A great help to me for this chapter was Marius Reiser, *Jesus and Judgment: The Eschatological Proclamation in Its Jewish Context*, trans. Linda M. Maloney (Minneapolis: Fortress Press, 1997), 197–205.

There are no such references in Jesus' words; nowhere in them do we encounter formulae such as "The LORD has spoken," or "The mouth of the LORD has spoken," or "Hear the word of the LORD," or "Thus says the LORD." Instead of these messenger formulae, which always indicate that the prophet is only a vehicle, Jesus created his own introductory formula. It characterizes what he says as being spoken on his own authority. The result is a dialectic that is difficult to describe: on the one hand Jesus speaks sovereignly in his own name and authority; on the other hand he speaks out of an ultimate immediacy to God, as we saw in his saying "hereby God forgives you your sins" in Mark 2:5.

But in closing let us return once more to the Gentile centurion. In that instance Jesus must have said: "Amen, I tell you, not even in Israel have I found such faith." Jesus is seeking believers. What should they believe in? Only that he can heal the sick? There were plenty of healers in antiquity, just as there are among us. The faith Jesus seeks in Israel is essentially greater. Jesus wants to find faith that the reign of God is now appearing—*and that it is breaking forth in what he himself says and does, in his words and his miracles*. Thus the story of the centurion reveals, not only in Jesus' "Amen, I tell you" but also in the faith he demands in light of his mission and his person, his unheard-of sense of his majesty.

50. More Than Solomon Is Here (Luke 11:31-32)

The following text comes from the Sayings Source and has been transmitted in almost identical wording by both Matthew and Luke (Matt 12:41-42 // Luke 11:31-32). Matthew, however, changed the sequence of the two "strophes," so here we will use Luke's version:

> The queen of the South will rise at the judgment
> with the people of this generation
> and condemn them,
> because she came from the ends of the earth
> to listen to the wisdom of Solomon,
> and see, something greater than Solomon is here!
> The people of Nineveh will rise up at the judgment
> with this generation
> and condemn it,
> because they repented at the proclamation of Jonah,
> and see, something greater than Jonah is here!

Again in this case let us first look at the form of our text! We are almost compelled to read it in two "strophes," because that is precisely how it is structured. Each strophe begins with the most important actor: the first with the queen of the South; the second with the people of Nineveh. Then in each case the second player is introduced: both times it is the current generation in Israel, which is condemned.

In the second part of each strophe we learn the reason for the condemnation: their behavior is contrasted with that of the queen of the South and that of the Ninevites. A clear escalation occurs between the first and second strophes: the queen of the South came to *learn from* Solomon's wisdom, but the Ninevites did much more; they *repented*. At the end of each strophe comes the cry toward which the whole is aimed: "something greater is here!"

Apart from the internal escalation the two strophes have identical structures; likewise, in each of them a historical scene is presented to the imagination. That is not only stated plainly ("at the judgment"); we see it also in that the queen of the South and the people of Nineveh "rise" from their places. Oddly enough, the two verbs have again and again been interpreted by a whole series of commentators and translators as referring to the "resurrection of the dead." But that cannot be the intention, because Luke 11:32 does not say "the people of Nineveh rise up *for the* judgment," but "they rise up *in* [i.e., *at*] the judgment." In particular, the idea of the resurrection of the dead is not at all necessary in Luke 11:31 as an interpretation of the Greek verb form *egerthēsetai*. It stands for a detail in judicial practice at that time: the judge is seated and rises only at the end of the trial to utter the judgment. During the trial the witnesses rise from their places to make their statements (cf. Mark 14:57). At the last judgment (which is what this is about) the queen of the South will arise as, so to speak, a "witness for the prosecution" and speak against the current generation in Israel. In the same way the people of Nineveh will arise to speak.

Obviously "witnesses" at a trial may not utter judgment. If they did, every decent judge would cut them off immediately. Thus here "judging" can only mean that the several witnesses will each condemn this generation (through their statements).[15] This kind of highly compact text can only use simplified language.

[15] This is a stylistic figure, as when we say "Caesar conquered Gaul." Obviously that is an enormous condensation of the real event. His legions also played a certain role.

It is thus clear from many details here how tersely, compactly, strictly, and in order—I would even say in *geometric* order—Jesus structured such texts. We already noted, in the case of the patch and the wineskin, how he does not use a single example but instead places two in sequence. We have a great many other double sayings, double metaphors, and double strophes from Jesus.[16] Here, quite rightly, we have marked a stylistic trait typical of him. These doublings also contributed to his hearers' ability to remember and internalize what he said.

What did he want to tell them with this doublet? Certainly it was spoken within the framework of a scenario of judgment on contemporary Israel at the end.[17] But obviously it is not a simple prediction of what will happen at the last judgment. Jesus' so-it-will-be sayings are meant to provoke. He wants to rip his listeners out of their false evaluation of the current situation. The fact that this is about provocation is clear from the fact that his words bring the *Gentiles*—of all people!—into the picture, and not just any Gentiles but some who appear in Sacred Scripture. The queen of the South (= the Queen of Sheba), according to 1 Kings 10:1-10, came with a great retinue to Jerusalem in order to test Solomon with probing questions, and she praises the God of Solomon when she recognizes the king's wisdom. We have to understand this against the background of 1 Kings 4:29-34,[18] where we read:

> *God gave Solomon very great wisdom, discernment, and breadth of understanding as vast as the sand on the seashore, so that Solomon's wisdom surpassed the wisdom of all the people of the east, and all the wisdom of Egypt. . . . People came from all the nations to* hear *the wisdom of Solomon; they came from all the kings of the earth who had heard of his wisdom.*

The crucial point in each case is thus that (1) the Gentiles come to Solomon to "hear." The Queen of Sheba comes and "hears" and even praises the God of Israel. (2) The prophet Jonah comes to Nineveh,

[16] Cf. the list in Reiser, *Jesus and Judgment* (see n. 14 above), 209–11 and n. 15.

[17] The expression "this generation" refers to the generation of Jesus' hearers—and with a negative accent. Jesus drew the phrase from his Bible. For the biblical findings cf. Reiser, *Jesus and Judgment*, 216–17.

[18] Hebrew 5:9-14.

the notorious metropolis,[19] and the whole city not only listens to his preaching but does penance (even the animals have to fast) and "turns from its evil ways." The whole thing is then intensified by the statement that at the final judgment God will measure the present generation of Israel against the behavior of the listening or even repentant Gentiles.

This gigantic snub directed at Jesus' contemporaries only reaches its goal, however, when Jesus says, "more than Solomon is here"; "more than Jonah is here." It is the familiar conclusion from the lesser to the greater: if the Gentiles "listened to" Solomon, and if Jonah even brought the Gentiles to "turn back," what needs to happen now in Israel? But it does not happen.

We also have to notice how Jesus speaks about himself here! He could have said "*I* am more than Solomon" and "*I* am more than Jonah," but, as so often, he takes himself out of the picture and simply says, "here is more" or "more is happening here" than with Solomon or in Nineveh. This very reticence makes Jesus believable to us. This text speaks altogether of the mystery of his person—though not with the aid of titles of honor or flashy pointings to himself.

If we listen more closely, however, Jesus in this double saying is setting himself above all of Israel's wisdom and prophecy, for "more than Solomon is here" and "more than Jonah is here" says: "I am not a wisdom teacher or a prophet." All the smart people today who assert that Jesus was a great teacher or one of Israel's great prophetic figures have this text (and many others) clearly against them. That is: they do not take seriously what Jesus is really saying. Ultimately, however, that means either that they see Jesus as a human being who vastly overestimated himself or that the early church must be responsible for the supposed "divinization" of Jesus.

51. Not Peace, but a Sword (Matt 10:34-36)

The text to be considered here also comes from the Sayings Source; still, at first glance the versions in Matthew and Luke seem to differ significantly (cf. Matt 10:34-36 // Luke 12:51-53). Apparently the two evangelists both revised the style of their model text. Still, the basic

[19] Cf. Nahum 3:1-7; Jonah 3:3.

statement is the same in both: Jesus causes division. Matthew's version reads:

> Do not think that I have come to bring peace to the [earth];
> I have come not to bring peace, but a sword.
> For I have come to set a man against his father,
> and a daughter against her mother,
> and a daughter-in-law against her mother-in-law;
> and one's foes will be members of one's own household.

Before we undertake the exegesis itself, a remark on the translation is needed: all the Bibles and commentaries I have seen translate the Greek word *gē* here as "earth."[20] "Do not think that I have come to bring peace *to the earth*." That is a correct translation because we have to suppose that both Matthew and Luke were thinking here of the whole world; this is clear from texts such as Matthew 28:19 ("make disciples of all nations") and Luke 2:14 ("peace on earth").

For Jesus—and in this book we are looking at the historical Jesus—it was different. I have to emphasize always that his focus, together with that of Sacred Scripture as a whole, was on Israel. The salvation, peace, and enlightenment God causes to happen in Israel are obviously intended to reach the whole world (motif of the pilgrimage of nations), but they have to be realized first in Israel (cf. Isa 2:5). Therefore when, as here, we are looking for the original words of Jesus the word *gē* must mean "land" (= Eretz Israel): "Do not think that I have come to bring peace to the land."[21]

The same is true for Luke 12:49: "I came to bring fire to the earth." Luke was probably thinking here of the whole world, and so again the translation "earth" may be correct. But Jesus was thinking of "setting fire" to the land, that is, in Israel (see chap. 64)—and obviously he was referring to his inflammatory proclamation of the reign of God. For Jesus it would have been completely out of the question to proclaim the reign of God outside Israel.

[20] There is a parallel problem in Matt 5:13. Should we translate "you are the salt of the earth" or "you are the salt of the land"? On this cf. Johannes Beutler, "Ihr seid das Salz des Landes (Mt 5,13)," in *Nach den Anfängen fragen. FS Gerhard Dautzenberg*, ed. Cornelius P. Mayer, Karlheinz Müller, and Gerhard Schmalenberg, GSTR 8 (Gießen: Selbstverlag des Fachbereichs, 1994), 85–94.

[21] Beyond its frequent appearance in the OT, *gē* (without further qualification) means "Palestine" at times in the Gospels as well: cf. Matt 5:5; Mark 15:33.

Conclusion: translators have to hold to what the final text and the authors of books want to say, but if their text might have revealed another dimension of meaning at an earlier stage of its composition they should at least signal it in a footnote.

So much for preliminary explanations! Now at last the real statement of our text! In the nineteenth and twentieth centuries the idea that Jesus intended to bring not peace but a sword misled any number of authors to see him as a social revolutionary or an agitator advocating violent revolution.[22] Why else would he have talked about a "sword"? But that interpretation completely misunderstood the metaphorical nature of this Jesus-saying. Here, as the context and the Lukan variant quite clearly show, "sword" represents not armed conflict but "division" (cf. Luke 12:51). That is made clear in the speech-composition—which in my opinion goes back to Jesus in its entirety—by a quotation from the book of the prophet Micah. There it occurs in the context of a description of chaos in Judea and the extirpation of the resident families. No one can trust anyone else any longer. The land is ripped apart by fear and suspicion:

> *Put no trust in a neighbor!*
> *have no confidence in a friend;*
> *guard the doors of your mouth*
> *from her who lies in your embrace;*
> *for the son thinks his father soft-headed,*
> *the daughter rises up against her mother,*
> *the daughter-in-law against her mother-in-law;*
> *one's enemies are members of one's own household.* (Mic 7:5-6)

Jesus uses this text, which reflects real conditions in the early post-exilic period in Judea, to set the current situation in Israel before the eyes of his hearers. Division and discord are everywhere! But why? Jesus sees the reason in himself. He has come forward to unite the people of God under the rule of God, and he has brought many together. He has bridged chasms. He has gathered toll-collectors and Zealots, sinners and the pious, poor beggars and the wealthy around one table. His colorful mix of disciples is a sign of this "gathering"

[22] For this literary genre see Martin Hengel, *War Jesus Revolutionär?* CwH 110 (Stuttgart: Calwer Verlag, 1970), 6–11. [English: *Was Jesus a Revolutionist?*, trans. William Klassen (Philadelphia: Fortress Press, 1971), 4–9.]

movement. Jesus has even tried to bridge the gap between Samaritans and Jews (Luke 10:30-35).

But there is a reverse side to his work in Israel: it has led to division. Jesus has encountered embittered opposition that cuts across the land and even across families. His own family tried to use force to take him home. His own relatives have said that "he has gone out of his mind" (Mark 3:20-21).

It is not only that his presence has led to separation and division; the metaphor of the sword contains still more. Jesus has not only *actually* evoked division, he has *willed* it: "I have come[23] to separate."

Thus Jesus *intended* separation.[24] He spoke of the dividing sword in the sense that he called for decisiveness, single-mindedness, clarity before God. For him the reign of God is not some nebulous something; it has clear contours. "No one can serve two masters," Jesus says (Matt 6:24). He demands of his listeners an ultimate decision for the reign of God, and that necessarily leads to divisions; in fact, it causes divisions that extend into the most intimate social relationships, into the house, the community of the extended family. Behind the composition in Matthew 10:34-36 is Jesus' experience that in stepping forth and calling for discipleship he has broken the closest human ties. He experienced that in relation to his own family, and it continued after Easter; it has not ceased to this day.

Thus the proclamation of the reign of God not only brings a time of decision. That would be saying too little. Jesus stresses that he himself is the reason why everything is coming to a head. He is the cause of the crisis. He himself tears apart the most intimate social ties. He is the one who demands decision.

Jesus would have had a variety of other ways to speak about this radical decision. He could have said: "You have to choose repentance—or not. You must decide to believe in the Good News—or choose against it. You have to adhere to the reign of God and therefore to God—or go against it." All that is present, too, in what he says.

[23] Statements with the formula "I have come" have often been regarded as post-Easter creations since they supposedly look back over an extended period of time. Cf. the counter-arguments to that thesis in Gerd Theissen and Annette Merz, *The Historical Jesus* (see part 4, n. 39 above), 524–26.

[24] In that light it seems far-fetched to regard "sword" as being about the persecutions that fall upon Jesus and his disciples: thus, e.g., Julius Schniewind, *Das Evangelium nach Matthäus*, NTD 2 (Göttingen: Vandenhoeck & Ruprecht, 1964), 135.

But beyond that Jesus dares to say: "You must decide *for me*—or *against me*." Precisely here we encounter the real irritant in his claim. We cannot avoid it: it is a claim of unconditional authority.

52. Everyone Who Acknowledges Me (Luke 12:8-9)

We have just examined particular sayings that touch on Jesus' sovereign claim: "Your sins are forgiven"—"Amen, I tell you"—"More than Solomon is here!"—"I have not come to bring peace, but a sword." There are still more along those lines, statements that give us a glimpse of Jesus' claim to sovereignty. But did Jesus go beyond that? Did he use titles of majesty that were part of the fabric of Israel's hopes for the future? The phrase "Son of Man"[25] is usually discussed in that context.[26] The first question in that regard is: did Jesus really apply that expression to himself? The second has to be: where did the concept come from and what does it mean? I cannot avoid addressing these questions before I approach Jesus' most important "Human One" sayings, namely, Luke 12:8-9 // Matthew 10:32-33.

First of all: there are serious reasons to believe that Jesus really used the idea of the "Son of Man/Human One." If we study the uses of the expression in the New Testament we find that it occurs almost exclusively in the four Gospels,[27] but there no fewer than eighty-one times—and almost always on the lips of Jesus.[28]

It is also important to note that the concept of the "Human One" appears at every level of tradition: in the Sayings Source, in Mark, in Matthew's special material, in Luke's special material, in the Gospel of John, and even in the apocryphal Gospel of Thomas.[29] If Jesus' disciples had only started to call Jesus "the 'Son of Man'" at some period after Easter, the New Testament would present us with a

[25] *Bar enosh*, lit. "son of [man = the human race]" or "the Human One." —Trans.

[26] In this chapter I am using my book *Jesus of Nazareth* (see part 4, n. 36 above), 41–44, 314–23. I have sometimes quoted the text of that book directly; at other times I have revised it.

[27] "Son of man" occurs in the NT only four times outside the Gospels; three of those citations are from the OT (Heb 2:6; Rev 1:13; 14:14). The fourth is at Acts 7:56, in the vision of Stephen.

[28] John 5:27; 12:34 are usually cited as exceptions, but even in John 12:34 the issue is what Jesus has said about the Human One.

[29] Cf. Hengel and Schwemer, *Jesus and Judaism* (see part 1, n. 4 above), 556–65.

completely different picture. Evidently the earliest Jesus-communities still knew that this was a usage that was characteristic of Jesus: it had to be left alone and could not be altered at will.[30] In short: Jesus certainly spoke of the "Son of Man/Human One." There is no doubt about it.

A problem arises, however: in the passages in which Jesus speaks of the *future* actions of the Human One (cf., e.g., Luke 17:24 or Luke 18:8) he seems to be talking about *someone else*, not about himself. Thus it is questionable whether the title "Son of Man" originally appeared in the *logia* in which he clearly speaks of himself in the *present* in those words (cf., e.g., Luke 9:58). Could it be secondary? Is it only original in the *logia* about the Human One who is *to come*? And was Jesus not referring to himself at all? Let us take the Jesus-saying that is the subject of this chapter as a test. It comes from the Sayings Source. The original version—as we will see—is Luke's. In his text it reads:

> And I tell you, everyone who acknowledges me before others,
> the Son of Man also will acknowledge before the angels of God;
> but whoever denies me before others
> will be denied before the angels of God. (Luke 12:8-9)

This double saying still plays a central role in the endless debates about the "Son of Man/Human One." Rudolf Bultmann and others concluded from the first part of the double saying that Jesus regarded the Human One as a heavenly figure distinct from himself.[31] But that was a deceptive conclusion. The shift from first to third person is by no means an indication of a change in the person referred to but is part of the style of reticent, enigmatic speech. It was long the custom for an author, in beginning a book, not to say "I" but instead "the author." The direct use of "I" was considered impolite. In fact there are things that are better said in "he/she" style than in "I" style. We can see this exact usage in Paul when he writes in 2 Corinthians 12:1-5:

[30] That does not exclude the replacement of the "Human One" title, within the history of the Jesus-traditioning, by "I," or the reverse: the simple "I" could have given way at times to "Son of Man/Human One."

[31] Cf. Rudolf Bultmann, *Theology of the New Testament*, trans. Kendrick Grobel (New York: Scribners, 1955), 1:29.

> *It is necessary to boast; nothing is to be gained by it, but I will go on to visions and revelations of the Lord [= that came from the Lord]. I know a person in Christ who fourteen years ago was caught up to the third heaven—whether in the body or out of the body I do not know; God knows. And I know that this person—whether in the body or out of the body I do not know; God knows—was caught up to Paradise and heard inexpressible things that no mortal is permitted to utter. On behalf of such a one I will boast, but on my own behalf I will not boast, except of my weaknesses.*

Paul here shifts three times from "I" to "a person,"[32] then shifts back to "I"-form when he speaks of his weaknesses. He uses the third-person form to speak of things he prefers to be reticent about, matters he cannot speak about as one would talk about everyday, visible things. He does not want to boast.

Thus there are situations in which tact and a sense of style demand that one speak in the third person. Jesus also betrays that very tact, discretion, and sense of style when he speaks of the Son of Man and thus of himself in that way. To assume such speech is about two different persons is simply not to acknowledge a stylistic form. Conclusion: Jesus really spoke about the "Son of Man/Human One" and he meant himself. Paul Hoffmann's objection[33] that if Jesus spoke in the third person it would not have been at all clear to his hearers that he meant himself when he said "Son of Man," and therefore he simply could not have been referring to himself, is not persuasive. For example, when Jesus says, "Foxes have holes, and birds of the air have nests; but the Son of Man has nowhere to lay his head" (Luke 9:58), the listeners could very easily conclude that he was talking about himself. Hoffmann's argument is conclusive only if one can first eliminate all the sayings about the *present* working of the Human One as inauthentic or reinterpret them as general sayings about the Human One as such—in the case of Luke 9:58 making the text say, "unlike foxes and birds, a human is an unhoused being."

But why does Jesus use the cryptic expression "Son of Man/Human One" at all? The answer: because here he is referring to a biblical text that was highly suitable for expressing his mission and

[32] Paul actually uses "inclusive language" here, speaking of "a person" [*anthrōpos*] or "such a one." —Trans.

[33] Cf. Paul Hoffmann, art., "Menschensohn II," *LTK* 7 (Freiburg: Herder, 2006), 131.

his understanding of himself. This brings us to our second question: where did Jesus get the expression? Answer: from the seventh chapter of the book of Daniel.[34] There the symbolic figure "Daniel" describes the following night vision:

> *I, Daniel, saw in my vision by night, and behold, the four winds of heaven were stirring up the great sea. And four great beasts came up out of the sea, different from one another. The first was like a lion and had eagles' wings. . . . Another beast appeared, a second one, like a bear. It was raised up on one side; it had three ribs in its mouth between its teeth and was told, "Arise, devour more flesh!" After this, as I watched, another appeared, like a leopard, with four wings of a bird on its back and four heads; and dominion was given to it.*
>
> *After this I saw in the night visions, and behold, a fourth beast, terrible and dreadful to look at, and strong beyond all measure. It had powerful iron teeth and was devouring, breaking in pieces, and stamping what was left with its feet. It was different from all the beasts that preceded it, and it had ten horns. As I was considering the horns, another horn appeared, a little one sprouting up between them, and three of the earlier horns were torn out. And behold: there were eyes like human eyes in this horn, and a mouth speaking arrogantly.*
>
> *As I watched,*
> *thrones were set in place,*
> *and an Ancient One was seated.*
> *His clothing was white as snow,*
> *and his hair like pure wool;*
> *his throne was fiery flames,*
> *and its wheels were burning fire.*
> *A stream of fire issued*
> *and flowed out from before him.*
> *A thousand thousands served him,*
> *and ten thousand times ten thousand stood before him.*
> *The court took its place,*
> *and the books were opened.*
>
> *I continued watching until the [fourth] beast was put to death because of the arrogant words it was speaking. Its cadaver was cast into the fire and destroyed. As for the rest of the beasts, their dominion was taken away. . . .*

[34] The following interpretation of Daniel 7 relies primarily on Norbert Lohfink, "Der Begriff des Gottesreichs vom Alten Testament her gesehen," in his *Studien zur biblischen Theologie*, SBAB 16 (Stuttgart: Katholisches Bibelwerk, 1993), 152–205, at 196–99.

> *As I went on watching in the night visions,*
> *I saw one like a human being*
> *coming with the clouds of heaven.*
> *And he came to the Ancient One*
> *and was presented before him.*
> *To him was given dominion*
> *and glory and kingship,*
> *that all peoples, nations, and languages*
> *should serve him.*
> *His dominion is an everlasting dominion*
> *that shall not pass away,*
> *and his rule shall never fail.* (Dan 7:2-14)

This symbolic text was written in Israel during a time of great crisis of faith and of persecution. It spoke of the threat of Hellenization and thus the destruction of Jewish faith by the Syrian king Antiochus IV, who ruled from 175 to 164 BCE. Therefore the text says: it is night. The great sea spoken of in the night visions is not a body of water that can be geographically located. It is the world ocean, the primeval sea, and thus an image of chaos.

So the four beasts emerge from the chaos, and they themselves represent social chaos. They stand for four world empires, or we could say four societies, each more bestial and evil than the one before it. The lion, for the author of the book of Daniel, was the great power Babylon. The bear was the empire of the Medes, the leopard that of the Persians.

With the fourth beast the author nearly loses control of the imagery, so horrible is it. This is *the* beast itself. It is the world power that was most dangerous to Israel's faith: the Hellenistic empire of the Seleucids, a successor to Alexander's. The ten horns are ten Hellenistic rulers. The last horn, the "little one," is Antiochus IV.

As the arrogance of the last horn reaches its climax, an ancient one appears: this is God. God alone, and not the bestial world empires, is ruler of the world and of history. They have only been assigned the right to rule in a limited and transferred fashion (Dan 7:6, 12). That God is the true sovereign over history is evident in what follows: A heavenly court is assembled to judge all the world empires, but especially the beasts. The sentence is carried out immediately. Then a fifth empire appears before the world court, a fifth society. As previously the symbols were lion, bear, leopard, beast, now the corresponding symbol is the human being. The whole series—lion, bear, leopard, beast, human being—thus represents successive societies. The fifth society is, of course, very carefully dissociated from those that precede it. It is no longer brutal, no longer bestial, but finally a human society. Therefore it is symbolized not by beasts but by a human. All exegetical interpretations that see the Son of Man/ Human One from the outset as a heavenly savior-figure fail to take the collective character of the figure in Daniel 7 seriously. Since the Human One stands at the end of a series of states or societies, it, too, can only be a social reality.

We must see what a sharp distinction the text makes at this point: the fifth society does not arise out of the sea of chaos but comes from the heavens. It comes "with the clouds of heaven" (Dan 7:13). Thus the new, eschatological society comes from above. It cannot be made by human beings. It is God's gift to the world. It is the end of all violent rule.

And yet, even though this ultimate and final empire, this rule without end, comes from above, it does not float above the world. Despite its heavenly origin it is altogether earthly and worldly. It is the longed-for true, eschatological Israel, for in the subsequent interpretation of the vision it is identified intimately with the "holy ones of the Most High." An interpreting angel says to the seer:

> *These four great beasts are four kings who shall arise out of the earth. But the holy ones of the Most High shall receive the kingdom, and possess the kingdom forever—forever and ever. . . . And the kingdom and the dominion and the greatness of the kingdoms under the whole heaven shall be given to the people of the holy ones of the Most High; their kingdom shall be an everlasting kingdom, and all dominions shall serve and obey them.* (Dan 7:17-18, 27)

Thus not only the vision itself but its context makes clear that this is about empires, societies—and the one society represented by the "human being" is Israel. But it is not simply the Israel of the present. It is the hoped-for eschatological Israel. It is a counter-reality over against all social constructions of history thus far, which either relied on brutal violence or could not survive without it.

The Son of Man/Human One is thus a figuring-forth of the true Israel that serves God-Father alone in the then-finally-revealed reign of God. The true Israel and the then-revealed reign of God cannot be separated. It is God's own sovereignty that will then be revealed—in a finite, human society.

But is it certain that Jesus relied on Daniel 7 for the figure of the Human One? In the secret apocalyptic literature of early Judaism the Human One in Daniel 7 was regarded as a majestic figure who would hold judgment in God's name at the end of time and would establish salvation and justice. This is attested by the imagery in the so-called "Book of Parables" in *Ethiopian Enoch* (*EthEn* 37–71) and in 4 Ezra (chap. 13). But 4 Ezra was created only after the destruction of Jerusalem, and there is dispute about when the "Parables" in 1 Enoch were written. They come either from the first century BCE or the first century CE, but it is also possible that these "Parables" have a redaction history behind them, one that extended over a considerable period of time.

Even if those "Parables" already existed in Jesus' time there remains the question whether Jesus knew them or not. It is much more plausible that he drew the symbol of the Human One not from some esoteric sources but from Sacred Scripture itself, for one thing is certain: Jesus had access to the picture of history in Daniel 7; its whole drama was familiar to him. When he spoke of the *coming* of the reign of God, the interpretation of history in Daniel 7 was part of the mix. Still: Jesus also modified that interpretation of history. What was different in his telling of it?

First of all, there was the time scheme! In Daniel 7 the five empires or five societies succeed one another: first Babylon, then the Medes, then the Persians, then the Seleucids—and only when the rule of all the world empires has expired does the true realm, the true God-society, appear. Only then begins the rule of the Human One who is so deeply connected to the reign of God. For Jesus, in contrast, the reign of God is already beginning, in the midst of this history, in the midst of the still-ongoing power of the world empires, represented at that time by the brutal and violent rule of Rome.

But with Jesus there was still more that changed, in contrast to the scheme of Daniel 7: the new society of the reign of God not only begins in the midst of the still-existing epoch of the world empires; it is now indissolubly linked to a single individual. While the Human One in Daniel 7 was still a collective person, Jesus now speaks of himself as the Son of Man. "Son of Man/Human One" is thus no longer a mere symbol of the true eschatological Israel; it is at the same time a mysterious name for Jesus himself. *He* is the Human One; he embodies in himself the new society of the eschatological Israel.

Finally, there is a third modification—and the most significant: it is said of the Human One in Daniel 7, at the end of the vision, that "all peoples, nations, and languages shall serve him." But Jesus has said of himself:

> *The Son of Man came not to be served but to serve, and to give his life a ransom for many.* (Mark 10:45)

On this point Jesus has again surpassed the historical projection of Daniel 7. Jesus' rule is based on his service, his surrender even to death. So Jesus altered the statements made in Daniel 7, but those very changes—palpable especially in the motif of service—show that in speaking of the "Son of Man" he is referring directly to Daniel 7. For what we change is already presupposed, and evidently the very symbol of the "Son of Man" was a welcome expression for what he had to say about himself. Why?

1. As we will see in the next chapter, the concept of the "Messiah" could very easily be misunderstood as political. That was not the case with "Son of Man/Human One." It was not provocative.

2. Already in Daniel 7 this concept was associated with a majesty equal to that of the hoped-for messianic king, if not even surpassing it: "His dominion is an everlasting dominion that shall not pass away" (Dan 7:14).

3. With this concept Jesus could simultaneously express his lowliness, his humility, since the Human One in Daniel 7 is also the end of all societies based on self-exaltation and violence. And a rule that abandons violence can rely only on God; it is defenselessly delivered over to the powers and rulers of history. Thus the symbol of the Human One allows the linking of statements of majesty with those of lowliness.

4. In Daniel 7 the figure of the Human One embodies Israel. But one must say precisely the same about Jesus. He is the representative not only of the reign of God but likewise of the true, eschatological Israel. Thus the idea of the "Son of Man/Human One" expresses something essential about Jesus. That is another reason why he chose this concept, on his own initiative, with his own particular sensitivity to central texts in Sacred Scripture. It is superfluous to see him here

as dependent on notions about a part of a version of the book of Enoch about whose dating we are not even certain.

5. But what is decisive is that what Jesus says about himself thus remains coded. Speaking of the "Son of Man" preserves his reticence. It remains to some extent enigmatic, and it is just what so fascinates Jesus' listeners. They cannot be entirely sure about who this Son of Man really is. We have already noted a number of times how restrained Jesus is when he speaks about himself.

That was a long introduction, but it was necessary if we are really to understand Luke 12:8-9. In his version Matthew replaced the words "Son of Man/Human One" with Jesus' "I" (cf. Matt 10:32, 33), but that was an intervention in the text of the Sayings Source, which spoke here of the "Son of Man." By using such a significant phrase Jesus had avoided speaking of himself literally as a counselor or accuser or even as judge in the presence of God. He speaks, instead, of the Human One, the "Son of Man," but he means himself.

Likewise, the *form* of Luke 12:8-9 speaks in favor of Jesus' authentic speech. Again we are looking at a double saying, so typical of Jesus, which as a whole constitutes an antithetical parallelism. The fact that in the second part the Human One is no longer mentioned as such but is replaced by a passive has no deeper significance; it simply reveals a command of style, either by Luke or in earlier stages of the tradition. A double saying made up of mathematically precise correspondences can be monotonous and boring. So in verse 9b we simply have to insert the words "Son of Man" or "Human One."

What is the significance of the angels in this *logion*? Exegetes have toiled over the question. Are they the heavenly court, or the audience for the judgment? Or are they simply one of the many substitutes for the name of God, which must be avoided? If we take the structure of the text seriously, then there is a correspondence between

> *before human beings*[35]
> and
> *before the angels of God*.

[35] NRSV "others." The Greek is ἔμπροσθεν τῶν ἀνθρώπων (before human beings) and the "Son of Man" is ὁ υἱὸς τοῦ ἀνθρώπου. —Trans.

But since the expression "before human beings" simply means the public at large, confession of Jesus cannot remain something internal; it dare not hide itself from the public. Hence in the first place "angels" can mean nothing but the *heavenly* public. The Human One will acknowledge, openly and unmistakably, before God and the whole heavenly world, those who previously, within history, have publicly acknowledged him. Thus a judgment scene is not excluded.

Nevertheless, this double saying thereby betrays something that was concealed by the concept of the "Son of Man" from those who heard it then and yet was mysteriously open, namely, a claim that would have shocked them: Jesus not only explains Torah like one who is sovereign over it; he not only proclaims the reign of God. He is so profoundly one with God and stands so directly in place of God that those who encounter him have to choose not only in light of the reign of God but also in light of the person of Jesus himself. It is in him, in his person, that each chooses: for or against God.

53. I Am (Mark 14:62)

The titles of majesty that Jesus might have used for himself, and that are vehemently and frequently discussed, include not only the *Human One* but also the *Messiah*, that is, "the *Anointed One*." That idea also has its basis in the Old Testament, where kings were anointed as a sign that they were installed by God. Certainly, from the time when the experiment with the state came to an end—not only due to external attacks by Assyria and Babylon but also through internal decay—no more kings were anointed.[36] Instead, and apparently at a very early time, hopes arose for a royal savior figure who would finally ensure peace, reverence for God, righteousness, sanctification, and help for the poor. Important texts in which those hopes were formulated include especially Psalm 72; Isaiah 9:1-6; 11:1-10; Jeremiah 23:5-6; 30:8-9; 33:14-16; Ezekiel 34:23-24; 37:24-25; Micah 5:1-4; Zechariah 9:9-10—although the title "Messiah" does not appear in any of them.

It is impossible to reconstruct a unilinear history leading to a unified concept of the Messiah, because there was none. There was a

[36] The rulers of the Hasmonean period were no longer anointed.

river of hopes, building especially on the promise to David in 2 Samuel 7:10-16, but those hopes cannot be summarized in a single idea. They were found in many places and had the greatest possible variety of groups behind them. Hence I will refer here simply to the so-called Psalms of Solomon. They were composed in Hebrew in the first century BCE but have survived only in Greek and Syriac translations.[37] The seventeenth psalm begs for the coming of the true eschatological king, and here that king is also called "Messiah." PsSol 17 thus offers us a fairly certain image such as quite a few people in Israel had at the time of Jesus' appearance—especially in Pharisaic circles—of what the work of the Messiah was supposed to be.

At the beginning (and again at the end) this psalm insists that God alone is the true sovereign, the only savior, and royal rule belongs only to God (17:1-3). These opening verses are followed by a look back at history: God chose David to be king over Israel and swore to him and his descendants that his line of succession would never end. The one praying the psalm reminds God explicitly of that oath (17:4); the reference is to 2 Samuel 7:10-16 (cf. Ps 89:3-4). But David's throne was made desolate—by external enemies and by Israel itself (PsSol 17:4-20). After verse 21, then, the psalm prays for the enthronement of the longed-for ruler, the true "Son of David" (17:21), the "LORD's Messiah" (17:32; cf. 18:7), and at the same time it prays for that ruler's future appearance.

This ruler will cleanse the city of Jerusalem from pagan peoples (17:22)—the Gentiles must serve under his yoke (17:30)—and will gather all Israel as a holy people before God (17:26). The tribes will again receive their proper places in the Land (17:28), and no strangers and foreigners will be allowed to dwell in Israel any longer (17:28); this ruler will judge all the tribes so that there can be no injustice among them any more (17:26-27). Then all those in Israel will be holy, so that the pilgrimage of the nations to Zion can begin (17:30-31). Moreover, this eschatological ruler will also destroy all *lawless* nations and will do so with only a word (17:24, 35). In Israel itself all sinners will be

[37] In what follows I will be using the translation and commentary by Svend Holm-Nielsen, *Die Psalmen Salomos*, JSHRZ 4, Poetische Schriften (Gütersloh: Mohn, 1977). [The English translation is based on R. B. Wright, "Psalms of Solomon," 639–70 in James H. Charlesworth, ed., *The Old Testament Pseudepigrapha* 2 (Peabody, MA: Hendrickson, 1983).]

rooted out by the power of this word (17:36) so that all Israel will be holy (17:26, 30, 32). No reliance will be placed on military might, but trust will be given to God alone (17:33-34). The psalm ends with:

> *Blessed are those born in those days*
> *to see the good fortune of Israel,*
> *which God will bring to pass in the assembly of the tribes.*
> *May God dispatch His mercy to Israel,*
> *may He deliver us from the pollution of profane enemies.*
> *The Lord Himself is our king forevermore.* (PsSol 17:44-46)

That or something similar must represent how a good many people in Israel at the time of Jesus must also have imagined the longed-for messianic time. Besides, the Old Testament contained many possibilities for varying the image of the hoped-for savior figure. It is already apparent in PsSol 17 that texts from the whole Hebrew Bible are being used here. This psalm is a positive mosaic of Old Testament texts (cf., e.g., 2 Sam 7:10-16; Pss 2:8; 72:11; 89:3-37; 110:5-6; Isa 11:1-5; 52:1). It is true, however, that people did not always and everywhere imagine the destruction of Israel's enemies as guardedly and abstractly as does PsSol 17:24, 35-36. In the Palestinian Targum on Genesis 49:11 it sounds a little different:[38]

> *How beauteous is the King, the Meshiha who will arise from the house of Jehuda! He hath girded his loins, and descended, and arrayed the battle against his adversaries, Slaying kings with their rulers; neither is there any king or ruler who shall stand before him. The mountains become red with the blood of their slain; his garments, dipped in blood, are like the outpressed juice of grapes.* (Targum Yerushalmi I)[39]

But now, at last, we come to the crucial question: Did Jesus call himself "Messiah" *in his preaching before the crowds*? The answer is clearly "no." Jesus proclaims the reign of God that is now beginning, but *in this phase of his preaching* he does not describe himself as Messiah.

What about the reactions of people in the Gospels showing that Jesus was regarded as the Messiah? In Mark's Gospel (differently

[38] See Hermann L. Strack and Paul Billerbeck, *Kommentar zum Neuen Testament aus Talmud und Midrasch* (see part 4, n. 30 above), 4/2, 877–78.

[39] Source: https://www.sefaria.org/Targum_Jonathan_on_Genesis.49.11.

from Matthew[40]) there is only a single text in which someone from the crowd addresses Jesus as "Messiah." This is in the healing of blind Bartimaeus near Jericho (Mark 10:46-52). When Bartimaeus hears that Jesus is passing by, he cries aloud:

> *Jesus, son of David,*
> *have mercy on me!* (Mark 10:47)

That was a confession of the Messiah, for as we have seen, the Messiah is called "son of David." The cry does probably show that in Israel, alongside the opinion that Jesus was a prophet (Luke 7:16) or even an ancient prophet come again (Mark 8:28), there were also suggestions that he was the expected Messiah. In the story Jesus accepts the appellation and heals the blind man.

On the other hand, at Caesarea Philippi he accepts Peter's calling him Messiah but immediately warns his disciples not to speak of him as such (Mark 8:27-30). At that point he is alone with the disciples. If we take the two texts together—the command to silence in Mark 8:30 and the cry of blind Bartimaeus and his healing—we may conclude, at least as far as the narrative level of Mark's Gospel is concerned, that Jesus does not consider it simply false to call him the Messiah but he does not want the title to be used carelessly and before the right time.

Bartimaeus's cry then acts as a signal to readers of Mark's Gospel that the situation has changed. We can only understand the story in Mark 11:1-11, which follows immediately, as Jesus' messianic entry into the Holy City. In that narrative Jesus deliberately rides into the city on a young donkey; as with the entry of a king he allows branches and clothing to be strewn along the way, and he does not oppose the acclamation of those entering with him: "Blessed is the coming kingdom of our ancestor David!" It is absolutely clear that Zechariah 9:9 is the background for this:

> *Rejoice greatly, O daughter Zion!*
> *Shout aloud, O daughter Jerusalem!*
> *See, your king comes to you;*
> *just and victorious is he,*

[40] Cf. Matt 9:27; 12:23; 15:22; 21:9, 15.

humble and riding on a donkey,
on a colt, the foal of a donkey.

The crucial question, obviously, is how we should evaluate this narrative historically. Had the "Davidic-messianological expectations" of the people only concentrated themselves "in the orbit of Jerusalem"[41] and then been poured out on Jesus? Against his will? Or was the whole thing nothing more than Jesus' arrival in the capital city along with a lot of pilgrims, and was it only Christian legend that stylized and elevated it, after Easter, into a royal entry?

There are no adequate reasons for that skepticism—unless one is convinced from the outset that Jesus could in no way have understood himself as the Messiah. There is not the smallest indication anywhere in the text that he distanced himself from the shouts of the accompanying crowd during his entry.

It seems that by entering on a young donkey Jesus deliberately intended to place a sign. He wanted to come into the city as a humble and unarmed Messiah, as in Zechariah 9:9, and also as one who proclaims the reign of God as in Zechariah 14:9 ("And the Lord will become king over all the earth"). The radical renunciation of all violence that is formulated immediately after Zechariah 9:9, in verse 10 ("I[42] will destroy the chariot from Ephraim and the war-horse from Jerusalem; and the battle bow shall be destroyed, and he shall command peace to the nations") fits precisely within Jesus' self-understanding. He knew Zechariah 9:9-10—as he knew all of Scripture—and he applied this text to himself.

Likewise the temple action that takes place immediately after this event in Matthew's and Luke's versions can only be understood as like the entry into the city: a messianic sign-action. Still, the fully decisive scene takes place before the council. Here Jesus is asked by the high priest himself, the supreme religious authority in Israel, whether he is the Messiah:

Are you the Messiah, the son of the Blessed One? (Mark 14:61)

[41] These terms come from Jürgen Roloff, *Jesus*, 4th ed. (Munich: Beck, 2007), 107.

[42] Thus the Hebrew; the LXX has "he" and is followed by NRSV and NABRE. The AV retained "I." —Trans.

Jesus answers:

> I am;
> and you will see the Son of Man
> seated at the right hand of the Power,
> and coming with the clouds of heaven. (Mark 14:62)

Especially since Rudolf Bultmann, newer exegesis has repeatedly judged not only Peter's confession of Jesus as Messiah but Jesus' own acknowledgment before the council as fictive scenes. All the Gospel texts containing statements about the Messiah are said to be constructions formulated for the purpose of anchoring post-Easter Christology in the history of Jesus himself. But here a clear critique of the critics is in order. It is correct that Jesus did not proclaim himself as Messiah when he first appeared publicly in Galilee. That he was reticent about the title "Messiah" and treated it with the utmost caution is likewise correct. But none of that in any way excludes what Mark's Gospel reports about the acute situation in Jerusalem.

That is to say, there is no avoiding the fact that, after Pilate's sentencing of him, Jesus was mocked by Roman soldiers as "King of the Jews" (Mark 15:16-20) and was then executed under a sign reading "The King of the Jews" (Mark 15:26). That *titulus crucis* must certainly have had a basis in the proceedings before the Roman prefect, and correspondingly in the preliminary investigation and procedure of the council. When Jesus was formally asked by Caiaphas whether he was the Messiah he could not say, "No, I am not." He could not do so even though he treated the title with reserve. He could define the title more precisely, however, and that is just what he did next. Naturally, what happened in that night assembly later became public. The members of the council themselves must have had an interest in justifying their proceeding—to say nothing of the possible presence of a Jesus-sympathizer such as Joseph of Arimathea within the council itself.[43]

In addition, we should note with regard to Caiaphas's question that "Son of the Blessed One" is the same as "Son of God" and fits

[43] That Joseph of Arimathea was a member of the Sanhedrin is favored not only by his being called "a respected member of the council" but also by the fact that he must have been a prominent person to have dared to request an audience with Pilate (Mark 15:43). He must also have been rich, else he would not have been able to afford a rock-hewn tomb near the city wall (Mark 15:46).

smoothly within the long list of Jewish expressions used, out of reverence, to avoid speaking the word "God."[44] When the very next words are about "power" we are looking at another example of such circumlocutions. And calling the Messiah "Son of God" derives ultimately from the messianic interpretation of 2 Samuel 7:14 ("I will be a father to him, and he shall be a son to me"); that is attested by a text among the writings found at Qumran.[45] The high priest thus asks Jesus as unmistakably as possible, supported by two concepts available at that time, whether he is the Messiah. That "official" question was almost necessary, given Jesus' two sign-actions: entry into the city and action in the temple. At the same time Caiaphas is seeking a ground on which to be able to accuse Jesus before the Roman prefect as a revolutionary.

Jesus' answer is utterly clear. He acknowledges his messianic dignity but at the same time interprets it by saying that the council will see him as the Human One seated at God's right hand and coming on the clouds of heaven. We can leave open the question whether in this situation Jesus actually spoke of the "Son of Man," but the simple assertion that he will be "seated at the right hand of God" was a claim to the highest imaginable majesty, for that is more than a place of honor. Here Jesus is citing Psalm 110:1, which "makes Zion's king the 'throne companion' of YHWH. YHWH and the king exercise royal rule together."[46] The fact that this passage from the Psalms played such a highly significant role after Easter (cf. Acts 5:31; Rom 8:34; Eph 1:20; Col 3:1; 1 Pet 3:22, etc.) is not a sign that here a later Christology has been inserted into the proceeding before the high priest. We could, after all, turn the question back on itself and ask why, after Easter, Psalm 110:1 began to play such a central role. Jesus threatens the council with Psalm 110:1, saying he will be their judge. In the critical situation before the highest religious authority in Israel at that time he abandons all reticence and openly affirms his majesty.

[44] "The Blessed [One]" is an abbreviation of the usual formula, "The Holy One, blessed be He."

[45] Cf. Peter Stuhlmacher, *Biblical Theology of the New Testament*, trans. Daniel Bailey (Grand Rapids: Eerdmans, 2018), chap. 9.

[46] As is said of Psalm 110:1 by Erich Zenger in Frank-Lothar Hossfeld and Erich Zenger, *Psalms 3*, trans. Linda M. Maloney, Hermeneia (Minneapolis: Fortress Press, 2011), 148.

Nevertheless, Jesus' strict reserve about statements of messianic sovereignty *up to this moment* was highly significant and must be taken seriously as a theological fact. What was the reason why Jesus dealt so reservedly with the title "Messiah"?

In the first place there were political reasons for his reticence. In the ears of many Jews, but most certainly in those of the Roman occupying forces, the word "Messiah" echoed uprising and resistance to Rome. That, of course, was one-sided: Jewish ideas of the Messiah were richer and more differentiated. The Old Testament itself, in part, paints this ruling figure who is to come in different colors. Still, as multiple and various as the ideas were, in Jesus' time "Messiah" had long since become a dangerous, provocative word. Jesus could not have wished that his gathering of Israel be interpreted even distantly in terms of Zealot uprising. That would not only have falsified his entire message: in all probability his effectiveness would then have been very swiftly brought to a violent end—already in Galilee.

But there are still deeper reasons for Jesus' reserve: the "Anointed One" and "Son of David" in PsSol 17 does without "horse and rider and bow" (17:32); even so, he destroys his enemies in Israel itself and among the nations. The Messiah of the Palestinian Targum produces similar destruction, but in a bloodier form. None of that fits Jesus, who intended neither to destroy hostile nations nor to get rid of his opponents in Israel. For him, nonviolence is fundamental. Jesus never, ever proclaimed that Jerusalem must be "cleansed of the Gentiles." Quite the contrary: in his temple action he drove the merchants from the forecourt in a symbolic sign-action so that the forecourt might be cleansed for the coming of the Gentile nations (Mark 11:17).

Apparently the concept of the Messiah was as unsatisfying an image for him as that of the eschatological prophet in explaining his real mission. It was not only about majesty; it was just as much about lowliness. So he prefers to speak indirectly of who he is. Even the entry into the Holy City was still a rather indirect sign-action, at least as far as Jesus was concerned. He rode into the city on a donkey. Donkeys, notoriously, are stubborn animals and completely unsuitable for battle—so he rode into the Holy City on a donkey. That was certainly an expressive sign, but it was not a public proclamation. It is only before the high priest that Jesus speaks directly—as we have seen, in a situation in which any kind of indirectness would be falsehood. But even there he did not take the initiative. He was asked.

Thus, on the whole, Jesus' reserve with regard to the popular image of the Messiah was maintained. If we look closely we can see that through his absolute nonviolence, his reception of sinners, his openness to the Gentiles, but above all through his free acceptance of persecution and death he gave the idea of the Messiah a new definition. In fact, he partly reversed it. It was only on the basis of that new definition that the earliest community could then call him the Anointed One, the *Christos*.

Part Six

Israel's Crisis

We can dream about what might have happened if Jesus' appearance had transformed all Israel: if everywhere in the villages and cities of the Land the people had welcomed his message of the now-appearing reign of God—if his deeds of power had been recognized as signs of the "new creation"—if he had found more and more disciples—if the Jesus movement had become more and more powerful, not in external strength but in reverence for God and nuptial joy (Mark 2:19)—if the communities of the Pharisees had understood that Jesus wanted what they wanted: a holy Israel, but one dedicated to "justice, mercy, and fidelity" (Matt 23:23) and not to the meticulous fulfillment of more-and-more-subtle purity rituals—if the scribes had perceived Jesus not as one who violated their traditional interpretations (Mark 7:5) but as God's eschatological messenger who opened to them the innermost meaning of Scripture—in short, if the revolution in Israel we love to imagine had succeeded on a broad basis.

Probably Jesus never dreamed that way. He knew that the history of the world proceeds differently: more bitterly, even murderously, because it contains a stubborn resistance to reality, to trust, and to God. Jesus portrayed the way the world's real history develops when he soberly put the parable of the sower before their eyes (Mark 4:3-8): a sower goes forth to sow, and a considerable part of the seed falls on a thin layer of soil over a rocky base and withers; another part grows up but is strangled by thorns and thistles. At any rate, the point of this parable is not hopelessness in the face of the contrary nature of history and the miseries of society but the certainty that God accomplishes miracles: a part of the seed comes to ripeness, and because the shoots have "tillered" or "stocked" themselves,[1] in the end the field brings a superabundant harvest.

[1] For the biological phenomenon of "tillering" or "stocking" that Jesus clearly alludes to here cf. Gerhard Lohfink, *The Forty Parables of Jesus* (see preface, n. 1 above), 67–71.

Jesus must have seen his own work in terms of that model: even the so-called "Galilean spring"[2] began immediately with attacks from scribes who took profound offense at his associations with sinners (Mark 2:13-17). And the attacks continued. It is true that the Gospels speak of admiration for Jesus and of profound faith, but they tell just as much, and amazingly often, of increasing resistance. It is no accident that the *logia* addressed to the Pharisees and scribes are among the harshest and most unpleasant words of Jesus that we know.

Perhaps most persistent among the forms of resistance he encountered was the kind of skepticism that showed its face in Nazareth (Mark 6:1-6), or the dry disbelief that asserted only a sign from heaven could be convincing (Luke 11:29). In each case it represented a profound non-understanding of what really happened through Jesus and what he was truly about. "When you see a cloud rising in the west, or a wind from the south, you know how to interpret it," he tells the crowd. "You can assess the state of the weather very precisely. But you do not recognize what is happening in your midst at this very moment" (cf. Luke 12:54-56).

Through Jesus, Israel had fallen into the most profound crisis in its history. Everything could be fulfilled, but everything could also collapse for good. We are usually not aware of the fundamental character of this situation, but that is the only basis on which to interpret Jesus' anger and the depth of his sorrow. His harsh judgment on places like Chorazin, Bethsaida, or Capernaum (Luke 10:13-15) was not primarily caused by his being personally offended at the lack of success his work found in those places. No, it was about the history of God with God's people, about the people of God, about God's immense gamble on healing the world.

Jesus was no naïve dreamer. He knew that evil exists—either publicly demonstrated in hard opposition or veiled in pious fanaticism, naked desire for sensations, or weary skepticism. But he believed in the miracle God is working. For him the miracle lay in the people

[2] The concept of a "Galilean spring" comes from Theodor Keim, *Geschichte Jesu nach den Ergebnissen heutiger Wissenschaft übersichtlich erzählt* (Zürich: Orell, Füßli, 1873). Keim was referring to an initial phase of Jesus' activity that he poetically described as follows: "Brief is the springtime; Jesus experienced that, too. The young green shoots, the fragrant blossoms, the delight of the people and the students, the joyful walk of Jesus himself were displaced in but a few months by a hot, dry summer and fierce thunderstorms, by slackenings, fights, and flights" (Translation LMM).

who had left everything to follow him, but also in the many silent and faithful sympathizers throughout the Land of Israel. He counted on both groups, and through them he expected—and still expects—the abundant harvest of the reign of God.

54. You Strain out Gnats (Matt 23:24)

In the introduction to this sixth section we spoke about the Pharisees and their meticulous fulfillment of increasingly subtle purity rituals. This chapter concerns one example: many Pharisees considered it an obligation to sieve all liquids through a fine-meshed cloth before drinking them, in order to keep them free of dirt or tiny creatures, especially gnats. For them, that represented more than mere hygiene: it was a purification ritual intended to fulfill a commandment of Torah, namely, Leviticus 11:20-24:

> *All winged insects with four feet are detestable to you. But among the winged insects with four feet you may eat those that have jointed legs above their feet, with which to leap on the ground. . . . But all other winged insects that have four feet are detestable to you. By these you shall become unclean; whoever touches the carcass of any of them shall be unclean until the evening.* (Lev 11:20-24)

"Those that have jointed legs above their feet, with which to leap on the ground" refers to the various kinds of locusts, grasshoppers, and crickets. Those may be eaten; indeed, roasted grasshoppers were a delicacy. But all other winged insects were considered unclean and might not be eaten.

The Torah thus makes a sharp distinction between edible animals and those that are not to be eaten, and obviously that applied not only to small animals but to large ones as well. Such distinctions are by no means uncommon in our own civilization and in many others. None of us, other than participants in survival courses, would eat earthworms. Likewise, in the West (by contrast with some East Asian countries) eating the flesh of cats and dogs is taboo. It should be noted that when the relevant food taboos in the book of Leviticus repeatedly call something "detestable," that does not represent hatred of animals; in the first instance it refers to attitudes that are known to us also—think only of most people's reactions when wasps penetrate their bedrooms or cockroaches appear in their kitchens.

Still, the passages in the Old Testament about "unclean" animals are about more than that. It is not only a question of danger or disgust but represents the establishing and limitation of a sphere that is "holy" and therefore renders one able to participate in the cult. The Land of Israel, and most especially a locus like the temple, must be "holy" in that sense. Moral and customary dimensions are implied and are by no means excluded, but this kind of purity and holiness implies more than mere morality. It also represents a distancing from all pagan uncleanness.

Thus when people in Israel carefully filtered out tiny gnats they found in their wine or water it was not only for hygienic reasons. That kind of hygiene is nothing unusual for us either, and was known in the whole ancient world. Who wants to drink wine with flies in it? But here it was about something more: the purity and holiness of the Land of Israel before God. And that, naturally, was precisely the point of honing and expanding biblical purity rules as the Pharisean scribes did.

Jesus did not fundamentally reject this kind of purity, which—as we have said—by no means excluded *moral* purity, but he dealt freely with it and broke from it when it interfered with or even served as a block against true purity—that is, inner integrity, justice, fidelity, and love. Then his reaction could be not only ironic but even sarcastic, as in the saying we are treating here:

> You strain out gnats
> but swallow camels. (Matt 23:24)

This saying (which comes from Matthew's special material) is one of the shortest and sharpest of Jesus' sayings. Once again it is an antithetical parallelism. Gnats and camels are contrasted—one of the smallest animals and one of the largest. Both were considered impure, for camels were also unclean animals that could not be eaten (Lev 11:4). Certainly the antithesis lies not only in the contrast between *smallest animal* and *largest animal* but also in that between *carefully strain out a gnat* and *swallow a camel (without hesitation)*. The whole saying, in its Greek structure, is a chiasm.

Jesus—apparently addressing Pharisees—says, "You are concerned to fulfill the Torah to the last detail, and for that purpose you have thought out a whole list of interpretive principles, but at the same time you permit things that are much worse." We might add: lovelessness, injustice, mercilessness, exclusion, calumnies.

Here again we have an example of how Jesus could, with the greatest brevity and sharpest irony, expose misshapings of what God intended Torah to be and to accomplish. Certainly he did so not merely to uncover them but to evoke insight. His listeners are supposed to be shocked, and through their shock they should come to understanding.

Obviously we are all the addressees. It is true that cultic purity no longer plays a role in our daily lives, but straining out gnats and swallowing camels continues in many other ways. How, otherwise, can we explain how the (fully justified) protection of animals such as bats, toads, wasps, and wolves is pursued passionately by many groups in our society while in 2022 there are in the United States alone at least 2,500,000 homeless children: about 12 percent of the total number of persons without shelter. They are at best ignored, at worst hunted out of their makeshift "habitats." At the same time, the ongoing destruction of Native American families remains invisible. There could be many other examples of the currency of Matthew 23:24. Jesus' sarcastic saying about gnats and camels touches us all.

55. Woe to You, Lawyers! (Luke 11:52)

As we have seen, the *logion* about gnats and camels was addressed to the Pharisees. It will appear, on the other hand, that the following *logion* addresses the scribes, the specialists in Torah. Certainly Pharisees and scribes did not represent two different worlds. Many scribes were members of the Pharisaic communities. The *logion* we will treat here was found in the Sayings Source (cf. Matt 23:13 // Luke 11:52), but it has proved extremely difficult to reconstruct, as we will see right away. In Luke's version the saying is:

> Woe to you, lawyers!
> For you have taken away the key of knowledge;
> you did not enter yourselves,
> and you hindered those who were entering. (Luke 11:52)

A key, of course, goes with a house that someone can lock and unlock. Here the house is knowledge. "Entering the house of knowledge" is thus a metaphor for "achieving knowledge." But which knowledge?

Of what serves one's salvation (cf. Luke 1:77) or of how the Torah should be correctly interpreted? In any case the formulation is unusual; the word "knowledge" (*gnōsis*) appears in the Gospels in Luke 1:77 and 11:52 and nowhere else. Matthew's text is simpler and easier to understand. There the same saying reads:

Woe to you,
scribes and Pharisees, hypocrites!
For you lock people out of the heavenly reign.
For you do not go in yourselves,
and when others are going in, you stop them.

If we compare the two texts we see that, while this is the same Jesus-saying, the two versions are radically different.

Was this saying originally about the "key of knowledge" or about the "reign of God"? "Key of knowledge" is more difficult than "reign of God," and more difficult texts are often more original than their smooth and accessible parallels since it is possible that they have been made easier to understand.

Moreover, was the saying in its earliest version addressed to lawyers, or to lawyers *and* Pharisees? If the original saying was not about the "reign of God" but instead the "key to knowledge" it was more probably addressed to the lawyers.

And was the scathing "hypocrites!" part of the *logion* from the beginning, or was it added later? Our *logion* is one of a series of seven "woes" in the Sayings Source. Matthew expands six of them with "you hypocrites!" but Luke does not do so even once. Why would Luke have eliminated the word that lays his opponents bare when he uses it elsewhere (cf. Luke 6:42; 12:56; 13:15)? There is thus a good deal in favor of the opinion that the characterization of the Pharisees and lawyers as "hypocrites" was first added by Matthew.

On the other hand, the past tense in Luke does not match the other "woes," which almost exclusively have to be in the present. Here, it seems, Matthew is closer to the original wording. Conclusion: we cannot be really certain about the original wording of our *logion* even in the Sayings Source; still, it seems sensible to use Luke's version as the basis of our study.

I have written at somewhat greater length here in order, once again, to make it very clear that reconstructing the original wording of a

Jesus-saying is not always simple. We must constantly keep in mind that the handing on of Jesus' *logia* was a living and continuing process that tried not only to retain the original but at the same time to place it in the church's present day. Matthew's composition directed against the scribes and Pharisees in particular shows how the communities for which Matthew wrote his Gospel were still involved in disputes and dialogues with the neighboring synagogues.

On the other hand, the *logion* we are considering here shows that such controversies had already begun with Jesus, and even then they were very sharp in their expression. Jesus accuses the lawyers of not doing what, given their profession, they ought to do, namely, open the Sacred Scriptures to the people. They do just the opposite, Jesus says: they do not unlock Scripture for the people; they lock it tight. They do not make *particular mistakes* in interpreting biblical texts but they prevent a right *overall interpretation* of Scripture. They have put aside the key to understanding the Bible, and not only for those who depend on them as their teachers but even for themselves.

But what, now, is the crucial point at which the direction of Sacred Scripture is being misunderstood or even falsified by Jesus' opponents as a whole? Here a look at the parable of the Pharisee and the tax collector (Luke 18:9-14) can help us.

The Pharisee in this parable stands before God as a correct partner. *God* gave the commandments and *he* keeps them to the letter, and even beyond their original wording, since fasting twice a week is no more demanded by Torah than is tithing everything one buys (Luke 18:12).[3] This man knows nothing of the lostness and entanglements of humanity. Above all, he is utterly unaware of his own misery. He sees the hopeless situation of the people of God only in the person of the toll collector who has entered the forecourt of the temple with him. He despises the man because a toll collector does not keep the commandments. He constantly makes himself impure, and he exploits others. Even so, at the end of the parable the toll collector is declared justified and the Pharisee is not, because the toll collector has admitted his lostness, his inability, his guilt, and he has begged God's mercy.

[3] The Pharisees' reasoning was: "If I buy something from someone it might be that he has not tithed his income. Therefore I will tithe even what I buy from him so that I may not participate in his sin." That is a work of supererogation.

What Jesus here presents as a single instance—namely, the undeserved mercy of God—is a fundamental feature of the Old Testament. The Hebrew Bible is not a collection of laws; it is not exhausted by listing its commands and prohibitions, for all the commandments are part of an unheard-of story: that of divine mercy freely given to Israel, which it receives as an unbounded promise and that again and again rescues it from its misery. The basic theme of the Bible is an unending history of liberation. Those who are fixated on commandments and prohibitions cannot see that fundamental theme and so cannot understand the nature of the reign of God. They lack the key to the knowledge of Sacred Scripture. They do not enter into the salvation offered by God and they prevent others, too, from entering.

In the sayings collection of the so-called Gospel of Thomas, discovered at Nag Hammadi in Egypt in 1945,[4] there is a Jesus-*logion* that matches the statement of this one precisely, even though it uses a completely different metaphor:

> *Jesus said: "Woe to you, Pharisees!*
> *You are like a dog lying in the cattle-manger.*
> *It neither eats nor lets the cattle eat."* (GThom 102)

It is not certain that this is an authentic saying of Jesus. Gyula Moravcsik showed, in a pivotal article in 1964, that the "dog in the manger" was a common and well-known slogan throughout the ancient world.[5] It was in popular usage but was also used by educated people to describe those who cannot enjoy something on their own but do not allow others to enjoy it either. In the proverb or comparison the dog has made itself comfortable in a manger and keeps the horse or donkey or cow from eating.

Could it be that Gospel of Thomas 102 rests on a common proverb that was later attributed to Jesus? That is not impossible, but it could

[4] It was known that this gospel supposedly written by the apostle Thomas existed; a number of church fathers mention it. The valuable discovery at Nag Hammadi is a translation of the lost Greek text into Coptic. The origin of the earliest version is usually dated to the mid-second century. The one who collected the sayings was familiar with the Synoptic Gospels.

[5] G. Moravcsik, "'Hund in der Krippe.' Zur Geschichte eines griechischen Sprichworts," *Acta Antiqua Academiae Scientiarum Hungaricae* 12 (1964): 77–86. Cf. also J. B. Bauer, "Echte Jesusworte?" in W. Cornelis van Unnick et al., *Evangelien aus dem Nilsand* (Frankfurt: Heinrich Scheffler, 1960), 108–50.

very well be that Jesus himself used the proverb for his own purposes. At any rate it expresses with amazing precision what our *logion* also means to say with "you do not go in yourselves, and when others are going in you stop them."

Would Jesus speak in much the same way to us exegetes and biblical scholars and, beyond us, to today's theologians? "You neither eat nor let the cattle eat!" I hope not, but at the very least we need to ask ourselves the question every day.

56. For Those Outside, Everything Comes in Riddles (Mark 4:11)

The lawyers are quite convinced that they understand Sacred Scripture. They are certain that they have the "key to knowledge" in their hands. Yet they block the door to a true understanding of Scripture against those entrusted to them, and they also obstruct their own access to it. They themselves have not "entered." That was precisely the point of the *logion* in the preceding chapter. But Jesus has more to say about not understanding.

For example, we have Mark 4:11, a *logion* within the so-called "parables theory" that Mark developed in the wake of the parable of the sower (Mark 4:10-12). He constructs the overall scene as follows: Jesus is on the shore of Lake Gennesaret. A great crowd has gathered. Therefore he gets into a boat and teaches from the water; that yields a better acoustic. Jesus wants them all to understand him, even those in the last rows. Jesus teaches the people "in parables" (Mark 4:2). As an example Mark chooses the parable of the sower, but evidently Jesus told his parables to the people without explaining them. Later, when he is alone with his companions, especially the Twelve, they ask him about the meaning of the parables, and he answers them:

> *To you has been given the secret of the reign of God,*
> *but for those outside, everything comes [only] in parables;*
> *in order that "they may indeed look, but not perceive,*
> *and may indeed listen, but not understand;*
> *so that they may not turn again and be forgiven."* (Mark 4:11-12)

I need not go into detail about the second part of this text. Let me just say, briefly, that it is a shortened quotation of Isaiah 6:9-10, which speaks of the hardening of Israel's heart. Isaiah's preaching leads not to the people's repentance but the contrary: to their hardening. When the Bible speaks in this sense of "hardening" by God it by no means refers to a hardening of innocent people. Rather: people harden themselves, refuse to listen, and thus become guilty. But God also hardens people (more precisely: God allows people to harden themselves), in order to reach a particular goal in history.[6] For example, God hardens Pharaoh's heart so that God can bring Israel out of Egypt.

The quotation from Isaiah is placed with the "parable theory" of Mark's Gospel in order to explain the non-understanding of many in Israel, but primarily Jesus' opponents. Regrettably, as a result this biblical "theology of hardening" was combined with "parable theory," which is a mixing of two very different things. On the basis of that mixing the impression arose that Jesus deliberately avoided explaining his parables to the people in general, or at least did not clarify them in their whole depth; he really explained them only to his disciples (cf. Mark 4:33-34). In that way the disciples became an esoteric circle who had secret knowledge. Still worse: an inevitable result was the impression that Jesus deliberately refused to explain his parables to the people so that they would be hardened and prevented from understanding anything at all.

Clearly that was *not* the sense of the parables. Jesus told a great many of them; they are at the center of his preaching. They interpret the nature of the reign of God. And obviously they are meant to be understood—but *as parables*. That is: they are not explanations in the form of pictures one can forget as soon as one has understood the subject itself and is able to express it "in more precise theological form." That is just what Jesus' parables are *not*. They are not didactic aids to learning. They lead us, in a wondrous way, into the event of the reign of God. They not only unlock it but also involve the hearers in that very event. The mystery of the reign of God remains. The parables most certainly cannot be replaced by abstract theological explanations. It is true that parables have to be interpreted, but at the same time they remain parables and must not be robbed of their clothing—that is, of their images and metaphors.

Jesus shaped and told his parables in masterful fashion. The one about the lost son, for example, is one of the best texts in world literature. Certainly he also interpreted his parables, but he did so as

[6] For the biblical concept of "hardening" cf. Gerhard Lohfink, *Im Ringen um die Vernunft* (see part 3, n. 30 above), 343–44.

one must interpret parables, and he most assuredly did not interpret them only to his disciples, making them an esoteric secret society. Often the interpretation consisted simply of his speaking them in a real situation so that the goal of the parable in question was revealed simply from the circumstances. Then, too, any difference between the people and the disciples was erased.

Where, then, did the "parable theory" we encounter in Mark 4:10-12 come from? The trigger for this misunderstanding seems to lie in the *logion* I am considering in this chapter:

> *To you has been given the secret of the reign of God,*
> *but for those outside, everything comes [only] in parables.*

The crucial point here is "[only] in parables." The Hebrew word for "parable" is *mašal*; Aramaic, *mathla*. But *mašal* and *mathla* refer not only to "parables." They cover every kind of enigmatic speech, even "riddles."[7] If we retranslate the *logion* in that sense its suggested meaning would be:

> To you has been given the secret of the reign of God,
> but for those outside it is all an enigma.

That seems to have been the original meaning of this saying. It has nothing at all to do with Jesus' parables, but we can now understand how it could have been read as a "parable theory." It is all about the term *mašal*. Thus we must commit the radical act of cutting our *logion* out of its current context in Mark 4.[8] With Jesus it had a different *Sitz im Leben*.

Evidently the saying reflects an experience Jesus had to undergo again and again: many people did not understand his preaching. They were longing for the reign of God, but they thought it had to come in power and glory; it had to overthrow everything, drive out all of Israel's enemies, crush everything that was evil. Many people failed to understand Jesus, too. Was he the Messiah? But if he was, everything about him would have to be radically different: he would

[7] A useful overview of examples can be found in Joachim Jeremias, *Parables of Jesus* (part 3, n. 25 above), 16n22.

[8] Literary arguments favor this as well. Cf. Jeremias, *Parables of Jesus*, 13–18.

eliminate his opponents by the mere words of his mouth. We have seen the image of the Messiah presented in the Psalms of Solomon (chap. 53). They expected something like that.

Still, there were not only those who were disappointed by Jesus and did not understand him; there were also those who regarded him as a dangerous charlatan, one who would lead the people astray, someone driven by the devil. Obviously we cannot exclude the possibility that those opponents were also concerned for truth, for the right interpretation of the Scriptures, for the will of God. Evidently Jesus summed up the broad current of non-understanding and misunderstanding that battered him more and more powerfully by saying "for those outside it is all an enigma."

The statement is so remarkable because it assigns no guilt at all. Jesus only says, probably with great sorrow: they do not understand. They cannot incorporate the reign of God into their system. It is all a riddle to them. They remain "outside." They lack the "key of knowledge."

Still, that is only the second clause in the antithetical parallelism into which our saying has been built. Its first clause contrasts non-understanding with its opposite: those to whom the reign of God "is given." It is thus not something they have earned. It has been given them by God (*passivum divinum*), entrusted to them, placed in their hands so they can hand it on to others. Jesus must have spoken this *logion* to his disciples, especially to the group of the Twelve, but he seems to include all those in Israel to whom God has given understanding. "Those outside" are those in Israel who do not understand.

Hence the "secret [*mystērion*] of the reign of God"[9] is not an enigma. It is what God truly wills and what God gives to those who are open to it. It could already be found in Israel's scriptures. Jesus is at work to unlock it once and for all. It is transformation of the world—even those who lack understanding are right about that. But it is a transformation of the world that happens as described in the Sermon on the Mount: through solidarity among the people of God, unconditional forgiveness, love of enemies, nonviolence, purity of heart, absolute trust in the one, true God.

[9] The concept of "mystery" (*mystērion*) appears in the first three Gospels only in Mark 4:11 *parr*. However, we should not conclude from its absence that Mark 4:11 could not have come from Jesus, for *mystērion* plays a central role in Daniel 2, and for Jesus the book of Daniel was extremely important because of the presence there of the concepts of the "reign of God" and the "Human One/Son of Man."

Most profoundly and ultimately, the secret of the reign of God is also the mystery of Jesus himself. But we have often spoken of that, and we will have more to say about it.

57. When You See a Cloud Rising in the West (Luke 12:54-56)

When Jesus argues, he does so with the utmost clarity. Evidently he observed his surroundings very closely and attentively. He argues in terms of rips in clothing and wineskins; he knows how a sheep looks when it has been torn by wolves; he plays on how salt can become tasteless and how children quarrel when playing games;[10] he talks about the foxes' holes, the birds' nests, the speck in the eye, the narrowness of a needle's eye, and the tillering of wheat;[11] he does not fail to notice how invitees at a dinner work their way to the best places;[12] he also knows how important keeping track of the weather is for those who work the land and those who fish the lake. He speaks about the rules of weather in a highly critical saying in Matthew 16:2b-3 that is directed at the Pharisees and Sadducees:

> *When it is evening, you say,*
> *"It will be fair weather, for the sky is glowing red."*
> *And in the morning,*
> *"It will be stormy today, for the sky is murky."*
> *You know how to interpret the appearance of the sky,*
> *but not the signs of the times.*

Important manuscripts lack this Matthean text. There are indications that it is a later insertion. At any rate, there it is—and it is apparently a variant on the version we find in Luke:

> When you see a cloud rising in the west,
> you immediately say, "It is going to rain";
> and so it happens.

[10] Mark 2:21-22; Luke 10:3; 14:34-35; Matt 11:16-17.

[11] Luke 9:58; Matt 7:3; Mark 4:8; 10:25. For the phenomenon of "tillering" in Mark 4:8 cf. Gerhard Lohfink, "Das Gleichnis vom Sämann (Mk 4,3–9)," *BZ* 30 (1986): 36–69; more briefly "The Biology of the Reign of God," in *Between Heaven and Earth: New Explorations of Great Biblical Texts*, trans. Linda M. Maloney (Collegeville, MN: Liturgical Press, 2022), 303–5.

[12] Luke 14:7-11.

> And when [you see] the south wind blowing,
> you say, "It is going to be hot";
> and it happens.
> You hypocrites!
> You know how to interpret the appearance of earth and sky,
> but why do you not know how to interpret this *kairos*? (Luke 12:54-56)

When we compare the two versions we can see right away that they are speaking of quite different weather phenomena: "red sky at night" or "red sky at dawning" in numerous manuscripts of Matthew's Gospel,[13] but a single cloud or a south wind in Luke's. Interpreters have collected significant meteorological observations to explain this. For example: in Israel a single cloud in the west (that is, coming from the sea) could actually be a portent of heavy rain. That precise weather phenomenon is described in 1 Kings 18:41-45. By contrast, in Israel the wind that brings blistering heat comes not from the south but from the east (cf. Gen 41:6; Ezek 17:10). Here it seems that Luke transferred a weather rule from his own location to Israel.

Such investigations make a lot of sense, but in the present context they need be of no further concern to us. We can presume that the weather rules Jesus actually quoted (however they were then handed on) were familiar and easily recognized. Otherwise he would have robbed his own argument of its power.

How does the argument run? Jesus concludes from the heavier to the lighter matter.[14] Those who are competent to assess the heavens and the earth and to predict the weather on that basis must surely be in a position to judge what is right before their eyes. Jesus thus reproaches them for acting stupider than they are. What is happening right now in their midst is the coming of the reign of God, obvious to everyone in the healing of the blind, the lame, and the lepers. Everyone can see it just as one can see a rising cloud and feel the east wind. "You are in the middle of the event," Jesus tells his listeners. "If you want to, you can certainly assess the present *kairos*." The *kairos* is *this time*, given by God who is bringing something absolutely new that is, at the same time, a moment of decision.

[13] This is clearly the source of the mariners' saying: "Red sky at night, sailors' delight; red sky at dawning, sailors take warning." —Trans.

[14] For what follows cf. Michael Wolter, *The Gospel According to Luke* (see part 3, n. 3 above), 2:171–72.

It is surely no accident that precisely in these last decades the expression "signs of the time(s)" (sometimes singular instead of plural) that has been plucked from Matthew 16:2b-3 and that, as we have said, is on an uncertain text-critical footing, is experiencing a boom in the church. The Second Vatican Council had already assigned it a significant place in its constitution *Gaudium et Spes*, where we read:

> *To carry out its task, the Church has always had the duty of scrutinizing* the signs of the times [signa temporum] *and of interpreting them in the light of the Gospel. . . . We must therefore recognize and understand the world in which we live, its expectations, its longings, and its often dramatic characteristics.* (*GS* 4)

If we then look again at Matthew 16:2b-3 it is, of course, easy to see that there the "signs of the times" are directly *contrasted* to the events, rules, and knowledge of the world. For Jesus it is about the "signs" of the inbreaking reign of God—that is, its deeds of power—and the *kairos* in Luke 12:56 is the time given by God for the promises now being fulfilled, which compel people to make a decision. In the conciliar text just cited it is precisely the opposite: there the "signs of the times" are not the Gospel and Jesus' deeds of power but the "expectations and longings" of the world that must be interpreted in light of the gospel.

In the years since *Gaudium et Spes* the "signs of the times" have enjoyed more applications. The expression has been used for everything in society that could stimulate the church to radical change—in fact, for everything in which the world is ahead of the supposedly foot-dragging church in terms of knowledge and implementation.

Since Melchior Cano (1509–1560) there are said to be "places" (*loci theologici*) in the church in and out of which theological knowledge can be derived. These are primarily Sacred Scripture, tradition, the councils, the permanent teaching office, and theology. Beyond those established "theological *loci*," however, Melchior Cano recognized other sources of theological knowledge: history, for example.

There can be no doubt that time, history, and notable developments in society really are sources of knowledge for the church's treasury of faith, which must be grasped ever anew and plumbed more and more deeply. That is evident in the actual development of the church and the unfolding of its theology. Israel itself has borrowed inspiration and even building blocks from other peoples and cultures that stimulated its knowledge of God and its community life. But that was only one side of its road to theological knowledge. The other side is Israel's history, one of constant exodus. It began with Abraham and became the basic fact of the history of the people of God. Again and again Israel had to turn away from the religious practices and social procedures of its environment. Non-accommodation to the "nations" is a crucial and fundamental principle of Torah.

Hence it is cause for reflection when, as is now the case in Germany, the church styles the "signs of the times" almost euphorically as a source of theological knowledge for reform of the church, almost the primary source. In the New Testament, at any rate, the God-given *kairos* is ultimately Jesus himself (Luke 12:54-56), and the "signs of the times" are his deeds of power and the preaching of the reign of God (Matt 16:2-3). Love for Jesus and his words must be the true source of every reform movement within the church.

Consequently, at this point let me offer a small appendix for readers who are interested in correct theological language: In Matthew 16:3 the Greek text speaks not of "signs of the time" but "signs of the times" (*sēmeia tōn kairōn*).[15] The plural was evidently meant to signal that the consequential misreadings of God's signs—that is, God's miracles in history—are not only taking place now against Jesus but have been occurring throughout the whole history of Israel. On the other hand, the original version of the *logion* in Luke 12:56 has *kairos* in the singular, thus referring to what is now present to the eyes of the people of Israel in Jesus and his mighty deeds. Hence the translation "signs of the time" points to the original version of the *logion* in Luke.

Vatican II, in the passage from *Gaudium et Spes* 4 that I have quoted, correctly uses the plural (*signa temporum*), but the official German translation gives it as singular. This represents a basic exegetical mistake, one we can observe in the documents of Vatican II and also in the inflationary use of the expression "signs of the time" that has been observable since then. In the New Testament the *kairos* of Luke 12:56 as well as the "signs of the times" in Matthew 16:3, a later insertion dependent on Luke, are not signals from the world and society but refer to Jesus' miracles and the miracles of God throughout Is-

[15] English translations, from the AV onward, have always used the plural "times" in Matt 16:3, as in the Latin *signa temporum* in *Gaudium et Spes*, but in Luke 12:56 they interpret the parallel phrase καιρὸν τοῦτον not as "signs of the time" but as "signs of *this* time" or "signs of the *present* time." —Trans.

rael's history. It is precisely there, with the experiences of Israel and with what Jesus did and taught, that all church reforms must begin.

58. Not through Observation (Luke 17:20-21)

Luke 17:20 reads: "Once Jesus was asked by the Pharisees when the reign of God was coming, and he answered . . . ." Evidently Luke, the evangelist, arranged this question from the Pharisees himself in order to have a frame for *two* important Jesus-sayings that were part of his special material.[16] The first reads:

> The reign of God is not coming with things that can be observed. (Luke 17:20)

"Observation" (Greek *paratērēsis*) at that time meant careful looking, even testing—for example, by physicians or astrologers. But with that word we already move partly into the extended field of ancient "portents" or "auspices."[17] For people in antiquity portents had a weight we can scarcely imagine any longer. Every unusual and surprising phenomenon in nature and history was regarded as an expression of divine powers. These were signs from the divine world and must absolutely be noted. A sudden bolt of lightning was not a bolt in our sense but far, far more. The same was true of an eclipse of the sun, an earthquake, a surprising bird-call, or an inexplicable sneeze: any of these could be important portents.

Great events that overturned everything were in any case portended by preliminary signs. The people of antiquity were absolutely convinced of that, and consequently they paid careful attention to unusual things, tested them, and sought to classify them. Whole lists of portents foretelling good or evil were produced in the ancient world. It is precisely at this point that *paratērēsis* comes into play. It was a *terminus technicus* for close "observation" of such portents.[18]

[16] Thus in what follows I presume that Luke himself created the narrative frame for 17:20-21. He then placed the two authentic Jesus-sayings in 20b and 21b within that frame and also, borrowing from Mark 13:21, created a bridge in 21a. Obviously that remains a hypothesis.

[17] For this subject cf. *Der kleine Pauly* 4, 1151–53: *Prodigium.*

[18] Cf. A. Rüstow, "*Entos Ymōn Estin.* Zur Deutung von Lukas 17,20-21," *ZNW* 51 (1960): 197–224, at 199.

Naturally there was skepticism about belief in portents, even in antiquity, and all the more so in Israel. Yet in that case, too, there was an expectation of preliminary signs, especially in apocalyptic literature. The book of the prophet Joel describes the portents of the final events as follows. God is speaking:

> *I will show disquieting portents in the heavens and on the earth, blood and fire and columns of smoke.*
> *The sun shall be turned to darkness, and the moon to blood, before the day of the LORD comes, the great and terrible day.* (Joel 2:30-31 [Hebrew 3:3-4])

This is about the "day of the LORD," that is, the day of judgment at the end of time. Similarly, signs predicting the coming of the reign of God must have been expected. But Jesus rejects any kind of "observations" in that regard. So much for the first Jesus-*logion* in our text! Luke continues that first *logion* with a kind of "commentary," referring to Mark 13:21:

> *nor will they say* [about possible portents], *"Look! here* [is one!]*" or "There* [is one!]*"*

The brackets are used to make it clear that "Look, here . . ." does not refer directly to the reign of God but to its portents.[19] Luke then adds a second Jesus-*logion* that has still greater weight than the first, because here not only is the testing of portents of the reign of God declared nonsense but Jesus gives a positive statement about why that is the case:

> For see, the reign of God is in your midst. (Luke 17:21)

That is: there cannot be any more portents of the reign of God *because it is already here*. That character of the reign of God as already having come corresponds altogether to other Jesus-sayings we have encountered. Recall Luke 11:20: "But if it is by the finger of God that I cast out the demons, then the reign of God has come to you." Of course, the crucial question is *in what way* the reign of God is already present.

[19] Cf. Michael Wolter, *The Gospel According to Luke* (see part 3, n. 3 above), 2:301.

What I have translated here as "in your midst"[20] represents Greek *entos hymōn*. Exegetes have long discussed what precisely that can mean.

Martin Luther translated, "The reign of God is within you."[21] That is certainly a possible translation of the Greek. Then the statement would mean: nothing is visible from outside, but the reign of God is already present in the soul, within the believers. As I have said, that translation is one possible meaning of the Greek. But that invisibility is not at all compatible with the way Jesus has spoken about the reign of God. For:

> *The blind receive their sight, the lame walk, the lepers are cleansed, the deaf hear, the dead are raised, the poor have good news brought to them.* (Luke 7:22)

A second possibility: *entos hymōn* could also mean "within your sphere of influence," "in your field of operations," "at your disposal." *Entos* does have that meaning in some passages of Greek classical literature, and it is especially frequent in a great many ancient papyrus documents.[22] But is that really what Jesus meant with this *logion*? Did he actually want to say: "The reign of God is already at your disposal—you simply have to repent"?

Finally, *entos hymōn* can also mean "with you" or "between you" or "among you." That is how the majority of Bibles now translate it. In any case, the statement that God dwells among God's people is good biblical language: compare only Exodus 17:7 or Zephaniah 3:15.

However we decide this question, in any case Jesus wants to say: "The reign of God has already come. It is right here, and so the question about portents for the rule of God completely misses the point. That is taken care of. If you go on asking about portents that is just

[20] NRSV "among you."

[21] Similarly Origen, *De oratione* 15.1: "It is therefore plain that he who prays for the coming of the kingdom of God prays with good reason for rising and fruit bearing and perfecting of God's kingdom within him." Trans. William A. Curtis. https://ccel.org/ccel/origen/prayer/prayer.i.html.

[22] Cf. C. H. Roberts, "The Kingdom of Heaven (Lk XVII.21)," *HTR* 41 (1948): 1–8; Hans Klein, *Das Lukasevangelium*, KEK 1, 3 (Göttingen: Vandenhoeck & Ruprecht, 2006), 570–71, and esp. A. Rüstow, "*Entos Ymōn Estin*" (see n. 18 above), 197–224, at 213–18.

a deflection; in fact, it is a cowardly flight from the real decision you have to make: namely, about your 'yes' or 'no' to me, to my words and my deeds of power."

Thus our *logion* is directed against the same unwillingness to decide that was already the subject of Luke 12:54-56, and so it sheds light on Israel's profound crisis. Hesitating and waiting for portents that can then be tested to see whether they are real portents, and then using them to assess when the reign of God is really coming—all that completely misses the *kairos* in which Israel now stands.

59. No Sign from Heaven (Luke 11:29)

The previous chapter showed that Jesus had apparently been asked about portents for the coming of the reign of God. His saying that it "is not coming with things that can be observed" presumes questions of that sort; it cannot be understood otherwise. But a distinction must be made: people not only asked Jesus about portents. Others—evidently his opponents—demanded of him a "sign from heaven" (Luke 11:16). That is not the same thing. In the understanding of Jesus' contemporaries, "portents" must precede the coming of the reign of God, and they want to prepare for them. The demand for a sign, in contrast, represents a questioning of Jesus' claim to speak and act with divine authority.

In the face of this sovereign claim Jesus' opponents ask for a "sign" to legitimate him. They do not specify more precisely how they imagine that legitimating sign; probably they are thinking of something spectacular, altogether unusual, but in any case brought about by God. Jesus categorically refuses to provide any such authentication. The crucial text reads:

> This generation is an evil generation;
> it demands a sign,
> but no sign will be given to it
> except the sign of Jonah. (Luke 11:29)

Luke derived the wording of this brief and uncompromising *logion* from the Sayings Source, for Matthew presents the same text with some minor deviations (cf. Matt 12:39). Mark has it also, though in a different version:

Why does this generation ask for a sign?
Amen, I tell you,
by no means will a sign be given to this generation. (Mark 8:12)

Which version is probably closest to an original Jesus-saying: that of Mark or that of Luke/the Sayings Source? More probably the Sayings Source, for it is the more difficult version since it speaks of the "sign of Jonah" without explaining what that might be. In Luke/the Sayings Source, however, it is followed by:

For as Jonah became a sign to the people of Nineveh,
so the Son of Man will be to this generation. (Luke 11:30)

Still, that statement is not exactly a clear explanation. Besides, in Luke and before that in the Sayings Source it forges a connection between the mysterious saying in Luke 11:29 and the threat in Luke 11:31-32 about the queen of the South and the Ninevites. Luke 11:30 functions as a link.

Hence the *logion* in Luke 11:29 could originally have been spoken by Jesus without any immediate commentary. It was a puzzle, meant to needle and to make people uneasy. That, certainly, does not exclude the possibility that Jesus explained it to his opponents afterward. It is possible to leave a riddle unexplained—sometimes that is a very effective move—but normally, after a certain pause, one offers the solution. It is thus quite possible that the literary bridge in Luke 11:30 still reflects Jesus' own solution. Still, when Ulrich Luz emphasizes that Luke 11:29 "is not understandable without further explanation"[23] he neglects the breadth of possible uses of language we can observe in Jesus' usage—from statements clear as glass to multiple forms of parabolic speech to riddles; from apparently implacable threat to profoundly sympathetic consolation. Moreover, in almost all cases we have no idea of the concrete situation within which a particular saying was uttered. Quite often it is the situational context that gives the key to understanding a spoken text.

After Easter, certainly, the communities could not hand on the riddles without explaining them, but when they had no explanation it would have been tempting to drop the puzzling "except the sign

[23] Cf. Ulrich Luz, *Matthew 8–20* (see part 3, n. 7 above), 215.

of Jonah." We can easily imagine that Mark (or the tradition before Mark) did exactly that.

The fact that the double saying in Luke 11:31-32 was added to our *logion* in Luke 11:29 shows that the latter goes back directly to Jesus. The earliest church had problems with that *logion*; for them it was certainly a riddle, and a riddle it remains. Luke 11:29, the saying in Matthew 11:12 about the violent taking heaven by force, and the saying about the temple (Mark 14:58) remain among the most difficult and most hotly disputed of Jesus' sayings. What could he have meant by this particular *logion*?

The oldest attempt at interpretation lies in the link already mentioned, in Luke 11:30 ("For just as Jonah became a sign to the people of Nineveh, so the Son of Man will be to this generation"). Here, evidently, the *parousia* of the Human One is being connected to the "sign of Jonah." The apparent meaning is: as Jonah became a sign of judgment for the Ninevites—since he proclaimed God's judgment on Nineveh—so the returning Human One will become a judgment on this generation.

Another, equally ancient, attempt at interpretation is found in Matthew 12:40. Here the interpretation of the "sign of Jonah" takes a completely different course: as Jonah was in the belly of the sea monster three days and three nights and was then rescued by God, so also Jesus will be three days and three nights in the heart of the earth and then will rise from the dead. Here, then, Jesus' resurrection is the "sign of Jonah."

Exegesis has swung back and forth between those two types of interpretation from that day to this. Each has likewise enjoyed the widest range of variations, but ultimately every attempt has aimed at validating one or the other type. What to do? In my opinion there is only one possibility for building a secure path here: we have to ask whether the gospel tradition contains an authentic saying of Jesus about Jonah that can show us what it was about Jonah that really interested Jesus. And there is one; it is the double saying about the queen of the South and the Ninevites, previously cited, that the Sayings Source already attached to the material of Luke 11:29. In that second part it says:

> *The people of Nineveh will rise up at the judgment*
> *with this generation and condemn it,*
> *because they repented at the proclamation of Jonah,*
> *and see, something greater than Jonah is here!* (Luke 11:32)

As we have seen: everything speaks in favor of the idea that this saying comes from Jesus himself. It shows the aspect of Jonah that touched or even fascinated Jesus: it was not his three-day sojourn in the belly of the sea monster but his appearance in the city of Nineveh, his proclamation of judgment, and the Ninevites' repentance. Those who argue that in Judaism at that time no one was interested in Jonah's entry into the city of Nineveh but only in his being rescued from the fish[24] are taking the wrong road from the start. The question is not what it was about the Jonah story that interested Jewish exegetes at that time but what was in the front of Jesus' own mind. That, according to Luke 11:32, was evidently Jonah's proclamation of judgment in Nineveh (and the repentance of the entire city). Thus the theory that urgently recommends itself is that, in pointing to the "sign of Jonah," Jesus is speaking of the preaching of judgment by the prophet Jonah and the penance and repentance of Nineveh.

Interpreters also puzzle about the question of the "sign" at this point. Why talk about the "sign of Jonah"? Then, for example, it may be said that, supposing we presume that this is not about the rescue from the fish but about Jonah's preaching of judgment, that creates a significant difficulty, since preaching or a preacher is not a "sign."[25] Then other exegetes respond that among Israel's prophets there were very free transitions between proclamation of the word and sign-actions. Therefore Jonah's preaching could certainly have been understood as a sign.[26] Other interpreters seek to avoid the same difficulty by saying that here the person of the prophet is itself the sign, and there is good biblical evidence for that: they point to texts such as Isaiah 8:18 or Ezekiel 12:6.[27]

These references to the very complex concept underlying this sign are correct, but there is a much simpler way to explain the expression "*sign* of Jonah." Jesus' opponents, after all, were asking for a divine sign *witnessing to him*. In his riddling words Jesus must have taken up that demand quite firmly and said: "You will not receive a sign

[24] Thus esp. Joachim Jeremias, *TDNT* 3, 409.

[25] Thus, e.g., Josef Schmid, *Das Evangelium nach Lukas*, RNT 3 (Regensburg: Pustet, 1960), 207, or Heinz Schürmann, *Das Lukasevangelium. Zweiter Teil*, HThKNT 3.2 (Freiburg: Herder, 1994), 273.

[26] Cf. Markus Tiwald, *Kommentar zur Logienquelle* (Stuttgart: Kohlhammer, 2019), 108n248. [English: *The Sayings Source: A Commentary on Q*, trans. J. Andrew Doole (Stuttgart: Kohlhammer, 2020), 110.]

[27] Thus, e.g., Karl H. Rengstorf in *TDNT* 7, 233–34.

from God—other than a terrifying sign of judgment like that of Jonah. *That is the sign* you get."

Fundamentally, this is a very simple rhetorical figure, namely "irony." Jesus speaks ironically here. He takes up the opponents' word "sign" and turns it back on them. The divine sign of witness his opponents demand will be a proclamation of judgment.

Here is an example to make the underlying rhetorical figure still clearer: An employee says to the boss, "I really, really need three days off," and the boss responds, "Very good, spend three days in the cellar here and use them to sort out the stacks of files for the digitalization we have been planning so long." Luke 11:29 contains the same figure; the only difference is that Jesus is not an authoritarian and sarcastic employer. He is the deeply concerned eschatological messenger of God who does everything he can to show his opponents how serious the situation is.

The demand for a divine sign is an evasion of the decision that is demanded of them now, at this hour, for the true sign from God is standing before them. The sign is Jesus himself with the authority that speaks itself in every word he says, and it is the healings that Jesus performs before their eyes. To demand a further sign of affirmation can only mean asking for a spectacular, highly visible miracle. Jesus will have none of it. It would contradict the rationality of God's actions in the world, and it would degrade Jesus himself to the status of a magician.

Demanding a kind of demonstration from God is nothing other than asking to be dispensed from believing. Only the devil asks for demonstrations that dispense from faith (cf. Matt 4:1-7; Luke 4:1-4, 9-12). Therefore Jesus brusquely refuses the requested sign and points ironically and in alienating fashion to Jonah's proclamation of judgment. There is your sign!

Could it be that Mark, or his model text, by omitting the reference to Jonah, portrayed Jesus' attitude of refusal more sharply? That would be a misunderstanding of Luke's version, for it is by no means the case that the threatening phrase "except for the sign of Jonah" in Luke 11:29 "relativizes"[28] Jesus' rejection of the demand for a sign. It is not relativized; it is honed.

[28] Thus, e.g., Hans Klein, *Lukasevangelium* (see n. 22 above), 418.

60. Whoever Does Not Gather with Me (Luke 11:23)

The circumstances surrounding the tradition of the *logion* that now follows are far simpler than those in the preceding chapter. Luke 11:23 and the parallel in Matthew 12:30 have exactly the same wording and certainly come from the Sayings Source. Both the strict form[29] and the sharpness of the diction speak in favor of an authentic word of Jesus:

> Whoever is not with me is against me,
> and whoever does not gather with me scatters. (Luke 11:23)

Moreover, in Matthew 23:37 // Luke 13:34 ("How often have I desired to gather your children") we have another Jesus-saying that contains the key word "gather." Add the first petition of the Our Father, which Jesus evidently regarded as the most urgent plea in the prayer he gave his disciples since it has first place. "Hallowed be your Name" (Matt 6:9 // Luke 11:2), against the background of Ezekiel 36:19-28, has a specific meaning, its content clearly defined: it is about the eschatological gathering and restoration of the people of God. That is *the* way in which the name of God is hallowed.[30] Thus everything favors the authenticity of Luke 11:23—which, in addition, fits precisely within the conflicts we are speaking of in this part of the book as "Israel's crisis."[31]

Jesus did not invent the idea of the "gathering of Israel." In this case he could refer to a broad biblical witness,[32] for the gathering of

[29] Each of the two lines is an antithetical parallelism, and the two lines themselves, in relation to one another, constitute a parallelism. Those who think that "scatter" in the second line is an escalation of "against me" in the first line can speak of a "climactic parallelism."

[30] For a detailed discussion see Gerhard Lohfink, *Jesus of Nazareth* (see part 4, n. 36 above), 64–66.

[31] The saying in Mark 9:40 (// Luke 9:50) seems to contradict Luke 11:23, which reads "whoever is not against us is for us." But the apparent contradiction is resolved as soon as we note that Mark 9:40 and, correspondingly, Luke 9:50 are addressed to the disciples, while Luke 11:23 is for the public. There can be no vague neutrality toward Jesus, but the disciples are called to show generosity toward their apparent competitors.

[32] For more on the concept of the "gathering of Israel" see Gerhard Lohfink, *Does God Need the Church? Toward a Theology of the People of God*, trans. Linda M. Maloney (Collegeville, MN: Liturgical Press, 1999), 51–60. Oddly enough, this central concept of biblical theology is not listed in the great theological lexicons such as *LTK* or *TRE*.

the scattered people of God had been one of the basic principles of Israel's theology since the exile. Deuteronomy 30:1-4 reads:

> *And when all these words have come upon you, the blessings and the curses that I have set before you, if you take them to heart among all the nations where the* Lord *your God has* **scattered** *you, and when you return to the* Lord *your God, you and your children, and you listen to his voice with all your heart and with all your soul, just as I am commanding you today, then the* Lord *your God will restore your fortunes and have compassion on you and turn to you,* **gathering** *you from all the peoples among whom the* Lord *your God has* **scattered** *you. Even if some of you are dispersed to the end of the heavens, from there the Lord your God will* **gather** *you, and from there will bring you back.*

We can see from this text that the idea of the "gathering of the people of God" presupposes that they are "scattered" among the nations. Above all, however, we can observe that the paired concepts of "gathering/scattering" in Luke 11:23 are good biblical language. The "gathering from where they have been scattered," that is, from the Diaspora, plays a major role especially among the prophets, and it always bears great theological weight. "Gathering" thereby becomes a soteriological *terminus technicus*, that is, a fixed concept designating the bringing of salvation.[33] "Gathering" Israel is then very often parallel to "delivering," "rescuing," "healing," and "redeeming" Israel.[34] In this way the concept acquires a certain autonomous significance as a term for the coming of salvation, even though "gathering from the Diaspora" continues to be part of the idea.

The purpose of the gathering is a renewed dwelling in the Land. Certainly the gathering of the people of God means more than simply a physical bringing-together; it always signifies as well that the people achieves an inner unity (Ezek 37:21-22). The division between the Northern and Southern Kingdoms will be healed by the gathering of God's people (Isa 11:12-13). The rivalry between tribes will come to an end. Gathering from the exile is thus not only a return to the Land but also the overcoming of the fatal divisions within the people of God.

[33] Cf. Peter Mommer, קבץ, *qbs*, *TDOT* 12, 486–91, at 490–91.

[34] Cf. 1 Chr 16:35; Pss 106:45-47; 147:2-3; Isa 43:3-5; Jer 31:10-11; Zeph 3:17-19; Zech 10:8-10.

In the last decades before Christ the gathering of Israel increasingly became a central statement regarding Israel's salvation, comparable to the rescue from Egypt, which is Israel's primal confession. God will lead Israel out from among the nations "with a mighty hand and an outstretched arm," as once they were led out of Egypt (Ezek 20:34). In this way the return, the being-led-back from the Diaspora, became more and more clearly a fundamental statement about God, God's essence, and God's action. That appears from the relative-clause construction in Isaiah 56:8:

Thus says the L*ORD* *God,*
who gathers the dispersed of Israel.

The concept of gathering now represents the *eschatological* uniting and rescuing of Israel, and it is always God who gathers the people.[35] The concept of gathering does not appear in the messianic texts of the Hebrew Bible.[36] Even later, in the Jewish Eighteen Benedictions (*Shemoneh Esreh*) the eschatological gathering of Israel is attributed not to the Messiah, but to God.[37]

First and foremost, we must keep all that in mind. Only then can we see what an enormous claim Jesus is making when he says that it is he himself who is now gathering Israel. He thus attributes to

[35] Cf. Neh 1:9; Pss 106:47; 107:3; 147:2; Isa 11:12; 40:11; 43:5-6; 54:7; 56:8; Jer 23:3; 29:14; 31:8; 32:37; Bar 4:37; Ezek 11:17; 20:34, 41; 28:25; 34:13; 36:24; 37:21; 39:27-28; Mic 2:12; 4:6; Zeph 3:19-20; Zech 10:10.

[36] The eschatological gathering of Israel is a matter for God, and God alone. That is especially clear in Isaiah 11, where the messianic reign is announced. Verses 1-10 speak of the working of the "shoot from the stump of Jesse"; then, in vv. 11-12, the theme of the eschatological gathering of Israel appears, and precisely at that point the subject is once again God's self.

[37] The only exception to the rule seems to be PsSol 17:26, which says of the Messiah: "He shall gather in a holy people." But that unmistakably refers to the regular judicial assemblies and to gatherings for worship, not to the eschatological gathering of Israel: cf. PsSol 10:7; 16:16, 43-44. Another exception could be Apoc. Ab. 31:2 (1). Here Paul Rießler, *Altjüdisches Schrifttum außerhalb der Bibel* (Freiburg: Kerle, 1928), translates "then he [the Messiah] calls my despised people out of all nations." Belkis Philonenko-Sayar and Marc Philonenko, *Die Apokalypse Abrahams*, JSHRZ 5.5 (Gütersloh: Gütersloher Verlagshaus, 2019), translate: "and [that one] will summon my people who have been subjected by the heathen." Thus the translation is uncertain here; moreover, the Apocalypse of Abraham was written, at the earliest, near the end of the first century CE.

himself, quite as a matter of course, an action that in the Old Testament is reserved to God alone. People in Israel may "gather together," but they cannot "gather" the people of God.

Here again we have a witness to that indirect or implicit Christology that is more telling and more thrilling than all the Christology in titles of majesty. Jesus sees himself as the one who, in God's stead, brings Israel home, liberates it, saves and redeems it. We can understand that in the face of such language the people were astonished (Mark 1:22) and Jesus' opponents were enraged. The scribes, at least, must have understood what such language meant, because the linkage between key concepts played a significant role in their interpretation of Scripture. Luke 11:23 was a set of fighting words that permitted no further neutrality. It was necessary to make a decision about Jesus just as once in Shechem, after the crossing of the Jordan, the people had to decide about God (Josh 24:15): for or against.

61. But You Were Not Willing (Luke 13:34-35)

Again within the following speech-unit Jesus speaks about the eschatological gathering of Israel—now, however, not in hostile words but in a series that amounts to a statement of guilt, announcement of punishment, and profound lament. Again the *logia* come from the Sayings Source; they are attested by Luke 13:34-35 and Matthew 23:37-38. I have chosen Luke's version:[38]

> Jerusalem, Jerusalem, you who kill the prophets
> and stone those who are sent to you!
> How often have I wanted to gather your children together
> as a hen gathers her chicks[39] under her wings,
> but you were not willing!
> See, your house is left *to you*. (Luke 13:34-35)

[38] The Sayings Source adds at the end of this *logion*: "But I say to you, you will see me no more until [the day] comes when you say: Blessed is the one who comes in the name of the Lord." Since I am uncertain whether this sentence is part of the original Jesus *logion* I will not treat it here.

[39] Thus NIV. The Greek text here has *nossia* = the nest or the "brood," the chicks growing there. The author notes that the German word for "brood" has become a term of abuse, so he has substituted "chicks."—Trans.

The city of Jerusalem is addressed directly—as, for example, in Lamentations 2:13, 18. A double address is uncommon in Greco-Roman literature, but it is frequently used in the biblical context.[40] This "Jerusalem, Jerusalem" is an urgent and serious beginning, but it becomes all the more urgent as, right away, a fixed biblical tradition is brought forward: that of the violent fate of the prophets (cf. 1 Kgs 19:10; 2 Chr 36:15; Neh 9:26; Jer 2:30, etcetera).

Still, this line of lament so familiar to the audience is followed immediately by a very personal cry from Jesus. He uses an image that is found nowhere else in the Bible:[41] that of a hen who calls her chicks and tucks them under her wings. Commentaries regularly refer here to familiar biblical texts in which God extends sheltering wings like an eagle (cf. especially Deut 32:11; Ruth 2:12; Pss 17:8; 36:7; 63:7; Isa 31:5). Michael Wolter has rightly pointed out, however, that we have a different image here: biologists distinguish, as regards birds and their young, between "nest-stayers" and "nest-leavers." The nest-stayers remain longer in the nest and are sheltered and fed by their parents there. The nest-leavers, in contrast, are scarcely out of the egg before they begin to explore their surroundings. The mother bird (Jesus is clearly speaking of the hen here) has to constantly call them back under her wings. This is a different image from that of the eagle, which spreads its wings so that there may be protection "in the shadow of its wings." Only the image of a bird that calls its nest-fleeing young together fits the concept of "gathering."[42] As we have said: this image does not appear elsewhere in the Bible. It is another example of the precision and attentiveness with which Jesus observed his world.

[40] Cf. Gen 22:1 (LXX); 22:11; 31:11 (LXX/A); 46:2; Exod 3:4; 1 Sam 3:4, 6 (LXX); 1 Kgs 13:2; Isa 29:1; Matt 7:21; 23:37; 25:11; Luke 8:24; 10:41; 22:31; Acts 9:4; 22:7; 26:14. For instances in Jewish literature see Gerhard Lohfink, "Eine alttestamentliche Darstellungsform für Gotteserscheinungen in den Damaskusberichten (Apg 9; 22; 26)," *BZ* 9 (1965): 246–57, at 205.

[41] The closest possible match is Ps 36:7: "How precious is your steadfast love, O God! All people may take refuge in the shadow of your wings." For this verse see Norbert Lohfink, *In the Shadow of Your Wings: New Readings of Great Texts from the Bible*, trans. Linda M. Maloney (Collegeville, MN: Liturgical Press, 2003), 98–110. Still, the crucial difference between that verse and Luke 13:34 is that the former lacks the call of the mother bird and so the keyword "gather." On the other hand, the psalm does speak of the light of righteousness, which causes humanity to flee to Zion, to shelter under God's protection.

[42] Cf. Michael Wolter, *The Gospel According to Luke* (see part 3, n. 3 above), 2:205.

"How often have I desired to gather your children together" in Jesus' lament has led to unending discussions. Had Jesus, as John's Gospel suggests, attended the Passover feast in Jerusalem for at least three years and appeared there publicly (cf. John 2:13; 6:4; 11:55), so that he could say "how often"? Or must we remain with the Synoptics' chronology, in which the mature Jesus appears in the capital city only once—at his last Passover? The best answer is, as ever: in our *logion* Jerusalem represents the whole of Israel. The capital city stands for the whole Land.[43] Jesus has tried again and again to gather the people of God—but in vain!—in vain at least as far as the officialdom is concerned.

Hence the bitter lament: "but you were not willing." But it is not only lament; it is a pronouncement of guilt, and Jesus does not stop there. He immediately announces the punishment: "See, your house is left *to you*."[44] That could mean that God is leaving the temple, in which case "your house" would be nothing other than the temple. God would abandon the place where the divine presence had once taken up residence, and as soon as God has left the temple it is no longer "God's house" but only "your house." That is by no means an aberrant interpretation: the book of Ezekiel paints a picture of how the "glory of the LORD" leaves the temple and thus abandons Israel (Ezek 10:18-19; 11:22-23)—but also speaks of how, one day, it returns (Ezek 43:1-9).

Still, the word "house" in Semitic languages is open to many meanings. It can mean not only a building but also the family, the dynasty, the community, or the state. Jesus could thus also have wanted to say that God is abandoning Israel to itself. That interpretation of Luke 13:35a is possible on the basis of the Old Testament, and it even seems apropos here since Psalm 81:11-12 says:

> *My people* **did not listen** *to my voice;*
> **Israel did not want me.**
> *So I* **gave them over** *to their stubborn hearts,*
> *so that they might follow their own plans.*

[43] There is, however, another reason why Jerusalem is named here as representative of the whole of Israel: Jerusalem was the seat of the council, and there Jesus' real opponents resided.

[44] Here Matthew inserted an interpretive expansion of the text he found in the Sayings Source: "See, your house is left to you, *desolate*."

This passage from the Psalms brings us close to our speech-unit with its comparison to the mother hen who summons her children with her voice. Animals listen to such voices. Israel, in contrast, has *not listened* to Jesus' *voice*. So Jesus must say, as God does in Psalm 81:12, "But you *did not want me*."[45] And as in the psalm ("So I *gave them over* to their stubborn hearts"), so now "Your house is *given over* [= left] to you."

On the one hand that is complete freedom as God gives it. God accepts no forced relationships, not even between God and creatures. Human beings may choose their own way and abandon the way of God, but that means being left to themselves and subjected to their own plans—with all the bleak desolation that follows. Precisely for Israel that is the most fearful thing that can be imagined. "Your house is left to you" = "You may go your own way" = "We have nothing more to do with each other" is the worst sentence of punishment Jesus could ever speak.

Thus at the end of the interpretation of Luke 13:34-35 the question remains: What is this? Is it still speech that warns, that means to frighten and to lead beyond fear to repentance? Or does it say, "You were not willing," with all the consequences that follow? We will pose the same question again in the next chapter.

62. Woe to You, Chorazin! (Luke 10:13-15)

Jesus could not have spoken the double saying we are dealing with in this chapter just *sometime or other*. It fits only at the end of his activity in Galilee. Jesus is getting ready to leave; whether he is already preparing to go to Jerusalem for the Passover feast, we do not know. In any case he is looking back over his work in Galilee. He names three places where he evidently taught and healed most often: Chorazin, Bethsaida, and Capernaum. The doublet comes to us from the Sayings Source and Luke 10:13-15 repeats it rather precisely in the form it had there.[46] Matthew expanded the second part of the saying

[45] In Israel's prophetic literature the keyword "listen" (in the negative) is often combined with the verb "will/want [God]" in the sense that Israel does not want God. See the instances in Hossfeld and Zenger, *Psalms 2* (see part 3, n. 4 above), 325n14.

[46] I am referring for the reconstruction of Q 10:13-15 to Marius Reiser, *Jesus and Judgment* (see part 5, n. 14 above), 223–24.

and accommodated its form to that of the first part (Matt 11:20-24). Here I am following Luke's version:

> Woe to you, Chorazin! Woe to you, Bethsaida!
> For if the deeds of power done in you
> had been done in Tyre and Sidon,
> they would have done penance long ago, sitting in sackcloth and ashes.
> But at the judgment
> it will be more tolerable for Tyre and Sidon than for you.
> And you, Capernaum, will you be exalted to heaven?
> You will be brought down to Hades [the realm of the dead, Sheol].
> (Luke 10:13-15)

Beatitudes and their direct opposites, "woes," were common in antiquity and were very popular. They were typical especially of the Near East and the biblical world. The Old Testament contains no fewer than forty-five beatitudes and some fifty woes.[47] That both these speech-forms were so common in the world of the time must be connected with the fact that in those days speech was thought to be much more powerful than it is now.

Therefore it is unimaginable that Jesus muttered the "woes" given here under his breath or spoke them only in the company of his disciples. Not only the second-person address ("Woe to you, Chorazin!" "And you, Capernaum!") demands a public forum. The judicial sentence at the end of each of the two sayings must also be given publicly. In this double saying Jesus is speaking as a judge.

Before a judge can condemn, the guilt of the accused must be established. That, too, happens here. Jesus accuses three places, apparently as representative for all of Galilee. Or are Capernaum, Bethsaida, and Chorazin singled out? In any case Jesus must have been more active in those three places than elsewhere. That is clear in the case of Capernaum; it seems that Jesus occasionally made a stop there in Peter's house (Mark 2:1). Likewise, a number of miracles are set in Capernaum (Matt 8:5-13; 17:24-27; Mark 1:21-34; 2:1-12). For Bethsaida we have only the story of the healing of a blind man in Mark 8:22-26. As regards Chorazin we know nothing at all. The place is not

[47] Cf. Marius Reiser, *Sprache und literarische Formen des Neuen Testaments. Eine Einführung*, UTB 2197 (Paderborn: Schöningh, 2001), 158–59.

named anywhere in the Bible apart from Luke 10:13 and its parallel in Matthew 11:21. The Gospels are not biographies of Jesus in today's sense; they follow the model of ancient biography in shedding light only on the crucial points.

As judge, Jesus must pronounce judgment: the three privileged places *as a whole* did not repent at his preaching. There is no debate about the repentance of individuals. This is about more: *community* in repentance and *communion* in believing the one who is now announcing the presence of the reign of God. Without such community there cannot be what Jesus means by the reign of God, and he cannot find such a new communion of life in those three places. Hence the sentence: "Woe to you!"

This condemnation is made still sharper by a comparison: Tyre and Sidon, seen in the Old Testament as the very prototypes of pagan cities, condemned because of their wealth and pride (cf. Isa 23; Jer 47:4; Ezek 26–28; Joel 4:4-8; Zech 9:2-4), would have long since performed penance "in sackcloth and ashes" in light of Jesus' preaching. That reference to Tyre and Sidon must have been an utter outrage to pious Jews, since Jesus' judgment says that the places in Israel that have not repented even in the face of his preaching and despite his saving and healing works will be worse off at the judgment than the most despicable of pagan cities.

A brief aside on "sackcloth and ashes": in the view of ancient peoples sorrow and penance could not be only a matter of the heart. They had to be expressed visibly and drastically—in a horribly itchy garment of goat or camel hair, often worn even at night; in refusal to eat and drink; in ashes on the hair and on the mat where one slept (Jonah 3:5-6 LXX).

The second part of the double saying has a sharp point that goes beyond the charges in the first part: Jesus plays on the mocking poem in Isaiah 14:4-21 aimed at a Near Eastern imperial figure. It would have been all the more powerful if it had circulated in the lifetime of the king in question[48] since its form is that of a threnody, a lament of the nations over his death. In reality it is biting satire and rejoicing

[48] Scholars argue over which emperor is represented by the figure in Isa 14:4-21—Sargon, Ashur-uballit II, Nebuchadrezzar, Nabonidus, Alexander the Great—or whether this is simply the personification of a merciless world power. Even if the satire is based on a historical king, the figure has repeatedly appeared anew.

over the fact that they are finally rid of him. At the center of this parody the arrogant magnate boasts that he is rising above the heavens and setting his throne there, higher than the stars. He wants to be like God, but he is mightily disappointed: he is thrown down to the utmost depths; his bed is now maggots and his coverlet is worms (Isa 14:11-15). Out of this song, which would still have been sung in Jesus' time because people continued having to deal with occupiers and emperors, Jesus quotes just two short phrases (Isa 14:13, 11) in order to uncover the self-deception of the people of Capernaum.

Readers of Matthew's and Luke's Gospels are reminded of another saying in which Jesus reveals the terrible self-deception of many who had seen and heard him. On the day of judgment they will defend themselves by saying: "'But we ate and drank with you, and you taught in our streets.' Yet he will retort, 'I tell you, I do not know where you come from'" (Luke 13:26-27; cp. Matt 7:22-23).

Jesus could have commented in the same or a similar way on the double saying in Luke 10: on the day of judgment many people from Capernaum will appeal to their acquaintance and daily encounters with him. But they drew no consequences from any of it.

The way Jesus speaks here is horrifying. Was it intended to change people; did he still hope to provoke them to repentance? Or was it all a definitive condemnation and a judgment in advance?

63. Shut Out of the Eschatological Banquet (Luke 13:28-29)

We end this sixth part with the exegetically most difficult and theologically thorniest of all the *logia* about "Israel's crisis." In Matthew it reads:

> *Many will come from the rising and the setting*[49]
> *and will recline at a meal with Abraham and Isaac and Jacob*
> *in the royal realm*[50] *of heaven,*
> *But the heirs of the realm*[51] *will be thrown into the outermost darkness,*
> *where there will be weeping and gnashing of teeth.* (Matt 8:11-12)

[49] I.e., "east" and "west" —Trans.

[50] βασιλείᾳ.

[51] Ὁι υἱοὶ τῆς βασιλείας (lit.: sons of the βασιλείᾳ).

Matthew positioned this clearly-structured antithetical parallelism[52] within the story of the centurion at Capernaum (8:5-13). The centurion is a Gentile. He asks Jesus to help his sick servant. Jesus is amazed at his unshakeable trust and says, "Amen, I tell you, in no one in Israel have I found such faith" (8:10). Then follows the saying that is our subject here.

It is clear from the context that by the "many" who come from east and west Matthew means the Gentiles, and with the "heirs of the realm" he means the Jews. But who precisely? The whole of Israel? or only the present generation? Against "all Israel" is the fact that Abraham, Isaac, and Jacob remain present at the eschatological meal, and yet Matthew makes no distinction among the "heirs of the realm." He could have said: "but many heirs of the realm will be expelled" (or, more correctly: "will have no access to the banquet of the end time"). But he does not write that way. Certainly we have to admit that such distinctions do not fit the categorical style of the speech, but in any case it is clear that in Matthew the *logion* as a whole is based on the model of the "pilgrimage of the nations" (chap. 37).

However, this scheme is now reversed. In the Old Testament promise of the pilgrimage of the nations the Gentiles come to Zion to obtain a share in the blessing that rests on Israel. That is not only a glorification of the true God; it also restores the honor of Israel that has so often been besmirched. It is true that in Matthew 8:11-12 the Gentiles come to Zion, but it seems as if they come there *to take the place of Israel*, and Israel—at least the present Israel—is expelled. Israel is not only excluded from the end-time meal but is separated forever from its holy ancestors, since the grouping of Abraham, Isaac, and Jacob in the Old Testament always represents the oath God swore to Israel—that it would forever possess the Land (= the promised inheritance; cf. Genesis 50:24; Deuteronomy 1:8; 34:4, and frequently elsewhere). Only by keeping all that before our eyes can we see how dreadful this Matthean text is.

And what about Luke? In that Gospel the corresponding *logion* is not built into the story of the centurion at Capernaum but stands instead within a discourse that is parable and warning in one. The parable is the one about the closed door (Luke 13:22-30). To accommodate

[52] The antithesis consists in (a) the contrast between "coming" and "being thrown out" and (b) the juxtaposition of "many" = Gentiles / "heirs of the kingdom" = Jews.

the saying to the parable Luke reversed the two parts of the antithetical parallelism, intending in that way to achieve a better link to the parable discourse. Therefore he also accepted a rather violent change whereby those excluded "see" those reclining at the meal and know themselves as those who have been expelled. They thus become spectators to the eschatological meal, howling and gnashing their teeth:

> *There will be weeping and gnashing of teeth*
> *when you see Abraham and Isaac and Jacob and all the prophets in the reign of God, and you yourselves thrown out.*
>
> *Then people will come from rising and setting, from north and south,*
> *and will recline at table in the reign of God.* (Luke 13:28-29)

To anticipate the crucial point: in this version of Jesus' words it is altogether clear that it is not the whole of historical Israel that is to be expelled, but only this generation. That is clear from the presence not only of "all the prophets," a group extending to John the Baptizer, but also of those addressed as "you." But that is only a glance ahead!

In comparison with the Matthean version, Luke has some small differences that are certainly attributable to Luke himself: the expansion "all the prophets" just mentioned, the addition of "from north and south" (Luke wanted to name all four points of the compass), and then, as indicated, there are the greater differences, namely, the reversal of the two parts of the saying and the motif of "seeing." Those were the changes Luke made. If we consider also the striking deviations from the Matthean version (the absence of the "many" and the "heirs of the realm") as well as the fact that Matthew must have added the expression about the "outer darkness,"[53] the version in the Sayings Source that was available to both evangelists can be reconstructed as follows:

> They will come from the rising and the setting
> and recline with Abraham, Isaac, and Jacob at the meal in the reign of God.
> But you will be cast out
> where there will be weeping and gnashing of teeth.

[53] Matthew is fond of the expressions "outer darkness" (Matt 22:13; 25:30) and "weeping and gnashing of teeth" (Matt 13:42, 50; 22:13; 24:51; 25:30).

By way of exception I must once again make a hypothetically reconstructed text the basis for interpretation; otherwise there would be no way to deal with the differences between the Matthean and the Lukan versions, for it is only through reconstruction of the version in the Sayings Source that we can clearly see how profound those differences are. The following reasons support the reconstruction offered here:

- Matthew speaks of "many" who will come from the rising and setting (of the sun). That is a deliberate reference to the text of Isaiah 2:1-5, the famous picture of the pilgrimage of the nations. That passage speaks twice of the "many nations" who come to Zion to hear the teaching of the LORD and to renounce violence. There are reasons to think that it was Matthew who first introduced the biblical promise of the pilgrimage of the Gentile nations to Zion into his version of the *logion*.

- One such reason is that the word "many" is absent from Luke's version, and this fact leads necessarily to the question: is he speaking—and is the version in the Sayings Source speaking—about the pilgrimage of the nations to Zion at all? The doubt grows that much stronger when we take a closer look at the statement "they will come from the rising and the setting." There is no mention of the compass points anywhere in the numerous Hebrew Bible texts about the pilgrimage of the nations, but that information is typical of sayings about the "gathering" by God of the exiles of Israel in the Diaspora at the inbreaking of the time of salvation.[54] Then God will gather Israel, scattered among the nations, from the east and from the west, from the north and from the south, and lead it back into its Land. For the gathering of Israel *from all points of the compass* cf. Psalm 107:2-3; Isaiah 11:12; 43:5-6; 49:12; Jeremiah 31:8; Baruch 4:37; 5:5; PsSol 11:2-3.

If this observation by newer exegetes[55] is correct, it has enormous consequences: then our *logion* is not about Gentiles taking Israel's

[54] The motif-complex of the "eschatological gathering of Israel" is especially indicated by the use of *sōzomenoi* in v. 23. Likewise, in the LXX "coming" (*hēxousin*) describes both the eschatological "coming" of the nations and the gathering of Israel. Cf. Michael Wolter, *The Gospel According to Luke* (see part 3, n. 3 above), 2:199, 204.

[55] Cf. esp. Wolter, *Luke* 2:204; also Markus Tiwald, *The Sayings Source* (see n. 26 above), 144–45.

place but about the Israel gathered by God for the festal meal of the end time, joining with Abraham, Isaac, and Jacob (Isa 25:6-8), while those from the homeland who have heard Jesus and seen his miracles will be thrown out and remain forever outside. This interpretation fits extremely well in the context within which our *logion* stands in Luke's Gospel. There Jesus speaks, beginning at verse 25, to listeners of his own generation who boast of having known him well but for whom his message has no consequences. "You will be thrown out" refers clearly, then, to the now-living generation of Israel or, perhaps more precisely, to the listeners who stand before him and reject him. The *logion* would have had the same context in the Sayings Source.[56] A comparable situation would fit Jesus as well.

We may assume that the version in the Sayings Source was largely identical to an authentic word of Jesus. There is really nothing that speaks against it. And in this book we have already become acquainted with a number of sayings that point in the same direction, especially the double *logion* about the queen of the South and the Ninevites (chap. 50) and the woes over the three cities (chap. 62).

There have been many things in part 6 that had to be dealt with at greater length and with more redaction-critical questions than was normal elsewhere in this book. That is because in the course of church history the words of Jesus we have considered here have again and again been brought to bear against Judaism. As early as the second century the great theologian Irenaeus of Lyons, so influential in later centuries as well, wrote that the church had *taken the place* of the chosen people (*Adv. Haer*. 4.36.2). Thus was proclaimed the salvation-historical rejection and disinheriting of Israel.

Irenaeus was not even the first representative of this Christian anti-Judaism. There were similar utterances before and contemporary with him. Thus far the discussion was entirely on the theological level, but as soon as the church of the martyrs became the "church of the empire" that theology would reveal its consequences. Beginning with the year 380, Jewish synagogues were repeatedly destroyed

[56] Cf. Paul Hoffmann and Christoph Heil, *Die Spruchquelle Q. Studienausgabe, Griechisch und Deutsch* (Darmstadt: Wissenschaftliche Buchgesellschaft, 2002), 90–93.

and their destruction was condoned and even instigated, at least in part, by priests and bishops. Bishop Ambrose of Milan played a sad role in all that.

Since then it has happened again and again, and more and more frequently, that Jewish fellow-citizens have been isolated, persecuted, driven out, or killed. One-sided or false interpretations of the Gospels have been among the reasons for that history of horror. Only Auschwitz finally opened the church's eyes to what had been happening for so many centuries—and compelled it to read the texts of the New Testament in a new light, but above all with greater care.

Consequently, let us first look again at the *logion* in Matthew 8:11-12. Does it say that Israel has forfeited its election and is forever excluded from salvation? The question must, of course, be asked on two levels: first as regards the historical Jesus and second for the evangelist Matthew. For the present I will stay with Matthew's Gospel.

Here there is another text similar to Matthew 8:11-12, namely, the Matthean version of the parable of the violent vineyard workers (Matt 21:33-46). As early as Irenaeus this text played an important role in a theology of Israel's rejection. In Mark's version of the parable Jesus says that the owner of the vineyard will come "and destroy the tenants and give the vineyard *to others*" (Mark 12:9). Matthew took that statement from his source text, expanded it, and sharpened it. Now, in his version, it reads:

> *Therefore I tell you, the reign of God will be taken away from you and given to a people that produces the expected fruits.* (Matt 21:43, alt.)

The affinity of this text with Matthew 8:12 (where the "heirs of the realm" will be thrown into the outer darkness) is obvious. The metaphorical circumstances are different, but the statement points in the same direction; in fact, the text in Matthew 21 is more clearly aimed at the "disinheriting of Israel." It says directly that the reign of God will be given to another "people." So is Matthew 21:43 a confirmation and amplification of what Matthew was already hinting at in 8:12?

Yes and no! The statement is stronger but at the same time more precise, because here the context makes clear who are the addressees of this judicial decree: not all of Israel, not even this whole generation, but only Israel's current leaders. In fact, the whole speech in Matthew 21:23-46 is addressed to the chief priests, the elders of the people, and the Pharisees (cf. Matt 21:23). The end of the discourse makes this utterly clear:

> *When the chief priests and the Pharisees heard his parables, they realized that he was speaking about them. They would have liked to arrest him, but they feared the people, because they all regarded him as a prophet.* (Matt 21:45-46)

Clearly, for Matthew (and for his Markan model as well) the parable of the violent tenants was not addressed to the people, and therefore it also does not speak about Israel and its rejection; rather, it is about the people's leaders. *They* are threatened with judgment. The reign of God will be taken away from *them*. Should we not, then, presume the distinction made here for Matthew 8:11-12 as well?

We have to admit that when Matthew 21:43 says that God's realm will be given to another "people" the suspicion necessarily arises that it may not be referring only to the people's leaders but to all of Israel. Then the leaders would be representative of the whole nation. And Matthew's passion account contains that nightmarish text that has embedded itself so deeply in Christian consciousness: Pilate says, "I am innocent of this man's blood; see to it yourselves," and "the people as a whole" answer:

> *His blood be on us and on our children!* (Matt 27:25)

In other words: "we take responsibility for his death." What is crucial here is the solemn theological expression "the people as a whole," which Matthew inserted into Mark's passion account. Mark spoke only of a shouting "crowd." "The people as a whole" in Matthew's insertion means more.

It is understandable that the later theology of the disinheritance of Israel developed out of this line of Matthean thinking (Matt 8:11-12 → 21:43 → 27:25). Even if it were true that Matthew really saw things differently, he certainly wrote words that were easily misunderstood. So didn't Irenaeus and a long tradition of interpretation have some justification for appealing to Matthew to support their theory of the "disinheritance of Israel"?

Let us, for the moment, assume the worst: that the author of the Gospel of Matthew really wanted to express a theology of disinheritance. In that case, obviously his voice is not the *only* one we should listen to, since there is a different one as well, namely, that of Paul in Romans 9–11, speaking about whether Israel has been expelled from the history of salvation or whether its election by God is irreversible. And here the voice of the letter to the Romans is weightier than all the other voices in the New Testament because Paul posed the question explicitly, fundamentally, and at great length.

In other words: in seeking a theological answer about God's enduring faithfulness to God's people or, conversely, a possible rejection of Israel, the whole of the New Testament and, above all, Romans 9–11 (especially 11:29) must be heard. More than that: the Jewish scriptures have to be listened to as well, because the question whether God can reject this people and seek another is treated at length in the Hebrew Bible (especially in Exod 32:7-14). That is to say that the whole question can only be answered "canonically," which means including the whole of Sacred Scripture. That is obvious in principle, but unfortunately it is too often forgotten—and that always happens when Scripture is regarded not as a single book but as a collection of individual books that have nothing to do with each other.

That was all about Matthew's Gospel and our focus-text, Matthew 8:11-12. Ultimately I am not concerned with Matthew's theology but rather with the words of Jesus himself, and here again the question arises: are there sayings of the historical Jesus that speak of a rejection or disinheritance of all Israel because, in its decisive hour, Israel did not listen to him?

If we review the words of Jesus spoken of in this book thus far we can, of course, think of many sayings in which Jesus interprets Torah, with a theretofore unheard-of authority, in terms of its center and innermost purpose and goal. But obviously that has nothing to do with a disinheritance of Israel. Jesus is not creating a "new people" but the contrary: he is bringing the Torah, and with it the people of Abraham, to their perfection and supreme dignity.

As *logia* that might be truly relevant for this question we may think of chapters 50 and 54–63, that is, primarily the words of Jesus treated in this section on "Israel's Crisis." If we look at those *logia* more closely, chapters 54 and 55 stand out right away. They are clearly addressed solely to the group of the Pharisees (Matt 23:24) or that of the scribes/experts in the Law (Luke 11:52). The woes Jesus utters in these *logia* warn the people against the Pharisees and scribes, or else they warn those groups themselves about what they are doing.

It is different when Jesus addresses all his hearers or his Jewish contemporaries—for example, with expressions like "this house." That does not refer to all Israel but only to "this generation." When, in Luke 11:23, Jesus says, "whoever does not gather with me scatters," the reference is obviously to his Jewish contemporaries, the generation now living. They are indirectly threatened with judgment: Luke 11:31-32 speaks directly about "this generation." At the final judgment the queen of the South and the people of Nineveh will rise from their places and stand forth as witnesses against Israel.

This series also includes Luke 11:29. We may recall that it is about signs of authenticity. Those who demand them are probably leading persons from Jerusalem—Sadducees, scholars of the Law, perhaps also Pharisees—but Jesus speaks in general terms of "this generation": "This generation is an evil generation: it asks for a sign, but no sign will be given to it except the sign of Jonah." As we have seen, the sign of Jonah is the threat of judgment and the repentance of the Ninevites. That, and nothing else, is what this generation is receiving in place of the sign they are asking for. So here again it is about then-present-day Israel and not Israel as a whole.

The series also includes Mark 4:11; Luke 12:54-56; and Luke 17:20-21, because here again it is about people in Israel who are face to face with Jesus. Besides, in the three texts just named no one is threatened with punishment. Jesus only states, deeply sorrowing, that they do not grasp the *kairos* and are unable to decide.

More difficult is Luke 13:28-29. Those who are directly acquainted with Jesus, hear his preaching, see his mighty works, but remain completely uncommitted are told: "You have no share in the reign of God. You will look from afar, seeing how from all directions scattered Israel is gathering around the patriarchs for the banquet of the end time, but you will be thrown out into the darkness." That is terrifying—yet it is clear that there can be no question here of a rejection and disinheritance of Israel as a whole. It seems probable that what is meant is that many of Jesus' contemporaries will be excluded from the joy of the reign of God.

Luke 10:13-15, the words spoken to Chorazin, Bethsaida, and Capernaum, also indisputably include words of judgment. It will be more bearable for the Gentile cities of Tyre and Sidon at the judgment than for those three places. Capernaum is even told that it will be thrown into the underworld. Is that just about these particular towns, or do they represent all Galilee? And is that not a condemnation at the final judgment? Even if that is so, there is not the most distant possibility that this saying is about the rejection and disinheritance of Israel. It is still about the generation Jesus himself encountered.

There remains only the Jesus saying that seems most threatening to Israel: Luke 13:34-35. It is addressed to Jerusalem, which kills the prophets and stones those sent to it. Probably the whole of Israel is represented by its chief city in this *logion*, and it is not just about the present generation since it refers to the long history of the murdering of prophets. But still more serious is the fact that, as we saw, Psalm 81:11-12 is the background. There God abandons Israel, which does not "listen to God's voice" and (like a young woman who rejects her suitor), simply "does not want" her lover. It is left to its own will and the stubbornness of its heart, "to follow its own counsels." If there are any of Jesus' authentic words that could speak about the rejection of Israel it would be these.

Still, here at the latest we must ask again: even if this interpretation of Luke 13:34-35 is correct, what kind of *speech* is this? Is it "information" about Israel's fate, about its punishment by God and, ultimately, about the end of its election and calling? Or is it not a very different kind of speech, one we have described previously and that appears in the Bible over and over again, especially among the prophets: speech that is meant to shock, and with that shock to bring about change and lead to repentance? We have to keep that in mind. To the very end Jesus desired to win over his own people, not to judge them.

I admit that there is still uncertainty—but Jesus himself eliminated that uncertainty when, at his last meal with his disciples, in anticipation of his death, he surrendered his life for the sake of his people Israel—symbolically represented by the Twelve who were present with him—so that the history of election that began with Abraham should not end with his death but might continue. The last part of this book will be about that.

Part Seven

In View of Death

The following part 7 collects a last group of Jesus-sayings in which Jesus views his death through the greatest variety of images. These are really words "in view of death." We will not look at the so-called passion predictions, however; those are aware in detail of how Jesus' life ended. The most extreme of them is Mark 10:33-34, where Jesus tells the Twelve:

> *See, we are going up to Jerusalem, and the Son of Man will be handed over to the chief priests and the scribes. They will condemn him to death and will hand him over to the Gentiles. These will mock him, and spit upon him, and flog him, and kill him. And after three days he will rise again.*

This text is rightly regarded as *vaticinium ex eventu*, a prophecy based on knowledge of an event that has already happened. That is very clear from the relatively large number of details that follow the course of Mark's passion narrative quite closely: arrest, judgment before the Sanhedrin, condemnation, handing over to the Romans, ridicule, scourging, execution, resurrection on the third day.

Could Jesus have predicted what was going to happen to him with such precision? Would not such foreknowledge directly contradict his human reality? It belongs to the nature of human beings—even one completely holy and unblemished—that life remains a venture into darkness. The truth that Jesus is fully united with the will of God, indeed is "God's son," precisely *cannot* mean that he saw his life spread out before him like a map. Jesus, like all of us, had to dare to live in the mystery of God. Anyone who denies him that venture is in danger of denying Jesus' true humanity.

Certainly that does not mean that Jesus traveled with his disciples to his last Passover in Jerusalem naively and unsuspecting. It would be a serious historical error to deny him, in principle, all the *logia* he spoke in expectation of his death. The fate of the Baptizer alone, and most certainly the increasingly sharp attacks of his opponents, must have shown him what was awaiting him. Besides, the *logia* we will consider here differ greatly in form and imagery from one another.

64. With a Baptism Must I Be Baptized (Luke 12:49-50)

It is possible that the following *logion* comes from the Sayings Source, in which case Matthew deliberately omitted it.[1] That is not definite. The text could come from Luke's special material. Once again we are faced with a double saying. It reads:

> I came to cast fire on the earth,
> and how I wish it were already kindled!
> I have a baptism with which I must be baptized,
> and what stress I am under until it is completed! (Luke 12:49-50)

The two parts of the saying match very smoothly. They not only establish an antithetical parallelism contrasting fire and water; there are also correspondences between "wish" and "be under stress" as expressions of the speaker's inner feelings and between "be kindled" and "be completed" as future events. The parallelism is still clearer in the Greek text, where "fire" and "baptism" (= water) stand at the beginning of each part.

Not a few exegetes believe that Luke took the first saying from tradition and that it could come from Jesus, but that the second was carefully composed by Luke to match the structure of the first.[2] For that purpose he is said to have used a saying from Mark 10:38-39, where Jesus tells the two sons of Zebedee who want to be enthroned in privileged places next to him in the coming reign of God:

> *You do not know what you are asking.*
> *Can you drink the cup that I drink,*
> *or be baptized with the baptism that I am baptized with?*

The interpreters who think Luke is the author of the second saying then often add that even apart from the existing material in Mark 10:38-39 there are two of Luke's favorite words here ("stress" and "completed"), pointing to the third evangelist. Let us consider this

[1] We can imagine a number of reasons: one would be that Matthew had to limit his material; at twenty-eight chapters his Gospel is, in any case, the longest, and there were clear restrictions on the length of any ancient book.

[2] Cf., e.g., Hans Klein, *Lukasevangelium* (see part 6, n. 22 above), 466: "v. 50 is a Lukan construction based on Mark 10:38."

stylistic argument! We should be aware of the limitations of word statistics; after all, an author can certainly apply her own style to a tradition, but it still remains tradition. Matthew and Luke have reworked their Markan model in myriad places and imposed stylistic changes, but the fact of their editing does not show that they did not have Mark as their source. And as regards the supposed reliance on Mark 10:38-39, could it not also be the case that Luke is not dependent on Mark here but that both the words supposedly spoken to the sons of Zebedee in Mark's version and the second part of our double saying are ultimately drawn from the same source—namely, Jesus himself?

So let us not get involved in reconstructions that are by no means compelling, but instead simply try to understand Luke 12:49-50 from the start as a unified composition that could certainly be located at the end of Jesus' work in Galilee. The following interpretation will seek to show that this is possible.

Jesus says of himself that he has come "to bring [or: cast] fire." One meaning of *pyr ballein* (= cast fire) is "lay a fire"—certainly intending also to enkindle larger objects. In the *Iliad* we can read how the defenders of Troy try to set fire to the Greeks' ships, and the identical expression is used: *pyr ballein* (Homer, *Iliad* 13.628–29). Much later and in a different context we may think of the Roman catapults that shot heavy, burning logs over the walls of a besieged city.

But what does Jesus want to set on fire? Not the whole world; no, he wants to set fire to *Israel*. Obviously that has to be understood in a metaphorical sense, but even so we encounter here, as in many other *logia*, the demanding language of Jesus. On the literary level of Luke's Gospel the translation of *gē* as "earth" is, of course, correct. Luke is probably thinking already of the later mission to the Gentiles. Jesus, on the other hand, can only have meant the "Land"—the land of Israel (cf. chap. 51).

What, then, does Jesus mean by "fire"? Some interpreters think of the tongues of fire at Pentecost, but that could only apply to Luke's work. A greater number regard the fire as a symbol for the judgment of the end time.[3] Joachim Jeremias even speaks of the "consummation

[3] Cf. Friedrich Lang (*TDNT* 6, 944) on this passage: "Jesus will bring a judgment of fire on the earth in which He Himself will be implicated. The meaning of πῦρ here is controlled by the basic sense of the eschatological judgment of fire, but the judgment is present in and with Jesus."

of the world."[4] But the motif of a world in flames belongs to apocalyptic, and Jesus is not speaking here as an apocalypticist like, for example, the author of the third and fourth books of the Sibylline Oracles.[5]

The reference to judgment is better, since in the Jewish scriptures the metaphor of "fire" often stands for judgment. But that concept, too, could very easily be misunderstood here—for example, in the sense of the fiery judgment John the Baptizer had announced (Luke 3:9, 16-17). The Baptizer *threatened* Israel with that judgment, thus driving people to baptism and repentance. With Jesus, in contrast, the threat of judgment is not found at the beginning; instead, he speaks of the Good News that the reign of God is near. So if he "has come" and "wishes" that his fire may be kindled everywhere in Israel and encompass the whole land, that fire must primarily mean something positive.

That is quite possible with the metaphor of "fire." It is not only we today who speak of the "fire of enthusiasm." The disciples at Emmaus say after eating with the Risen One: "Were not our hearts burning within us while he was talking to us on the road and opening the meaning of the scriptures to us?" (Luke 24:32). The fire that Jesus wants to kindle everywhere is the fire of undivided commitment, the excitement, the *passion* for the reign of God. Certainly that by no means excludes discernment, decision, separation, and struggle—including conflicts that run through whole families. Those are, indeed, drastically described just after this, in Luke 12:51-53. Jesus wants to bring all of Israel into passionate movement—toward the reign of God. In that sense he wants to cover the land with "fire."

That is how he began. That is how he appeared. He also found disciples, and many people ran after him. There may even be an undertone in this first sentence indicating that the initial sparks are already glowing, but the fire has scarcely begun to extend throughout the whole land. It has not yet burst into flame. On the contrary: there is a threat that it will be extinguished. Hence Jesus' longing cry: "How I wish it were already kindled!" That is: "How I wish that it was already burning [everywhere in Israel]!"

[4] Joachim Jeremias, *New Testament Theology* (see part 1, n. 8 above), 102.

[5] For the "world on fire" cf. esp. Sib. Or. 3.83–92; 4.173–87.

Then follows the second part of the double saying. As often happens with antithetical parallelisms, it brings the goal and climax of the series. Jesus must have recognized that the gathering of Israel into the reign of God, which he regarded as his true goal, would follow no straight path and most assuredly no smooth one. So, as he *himself* wanted to kindle fire in the Land, so must he *himself* now follow a path that runs in an irritatingly different direction: he must pass through a dreadful baptism, that is, a destructive flood. We could also understand the parallelism in the sense of "indeed . . . but":

> *Truly, I have come to cast fire everywhere in the Land . . .*
> *but now I must pass through a flood . . .*

Here the water is not the saving element that protects from the fire of judgment, as it was for the Baptizer; these are the "wild and raging waters" as, for example, in Psalms 124:4-5 and 69:14-15. Fire and water played a crucial role in the Baptizer's preaching also, and Jesus takes the concepts of "fire" and "baptism" from him, but he gives the fire and the (baptismal) water a different meaning. The fire is no longer simply the fire of judgment but also the fire of zeal—and the water, in turn, is not rescue but destruction.

At some point Jesus must have recognized that if he was to reach Israel at its depth and transform it for the reign of God he must no longer only preach and gather people; instead, he must pass through death. This "baptism," as he calls it, is unavoidably before him—and he wishes he had already endured it. Still, the concrete form his death will take remains for him in this moment still undetermined. That, too, favors the authenticity of the double saying.

Likewise in favor of its authenticity is that the first part of the double saying only attains its intended goal through the second part, and the second part presupposes the first. The two parts are firmly linked not only by rhetorical elements but also by what they say. It is superfluous and unnecessary to try to separate them with literary surgery! In this double saying Jesus himself speaks to us. He speaks of the only way in which the grain of wheat can bear fruit, and with that he exposes the essence of Christian existence. Decades later Paul would develop it in his baptismal theology (Rom 6:1-14). But what is perhaps most disturbing about this text is that in it we may perceive and sympathize with how Jesus himself was led on a path of knowledge and recognition.

65. On the Third Day I Will Be Finished (Luke 13:31-32)

"I have a baptism with which I must be baptized, and what stress I am under until it is completed!" (Luke 12:50). This Jesus-saying, which occupied us in the previous chapter, points to a kind of *intermediate phase* within Jesus' public mission: probably he is not yet on the road to his last Passover in Jerusalem, but the so-called "Galilean spring"[6] is over.

This interim phase contains another Jesus-saying, namely, Luke 13:32, which is tightly linked to an extremely unusual encounter without which it cannot be understood at all. The encounter is only briefly noted; it is a kind of introduction to the Jesus-saying that follows. So we are again looking at a formally correct apophthegm:

> At that very hour some Pharisees came and said to him, "Get away from here! Herod wants to kill you!" But he answered them: "Go and tell that fox: 'Look, I am casting out demons and performing cures today and tomorrow—and on the third day I will be finished.' "[7] (Luke 13:31-32)[8]

This text must reflect a real event—if only because of the simple fact that Jesus calls his ruler, Herod Antipas (who is the subject here), a "fox." Likewise in favor of its genuineness are the clear-sightedness, inner freedom, and authority of the speaker. How should we picture the background of the event?

Evidently Jesus is somewhere within Herod Antipas's district—probably in Galilee, less likely in Perea. We can scarcely suppose that Herod really means to get rid of Jesus; it is more probable that he wants him out of his territory. Having someone within his jurisdiction

[6] For the phrase "Galilean spring" see part 6, n. 2 above.

[7] NRSV: "I finish my work." Again the AV comes closest to the author's interpretation: "I will be perfected." —Trans.

[8] In v. 33 the apophthegm takes a further step: "Yet today, tomorrow, and the next day I must be on my way, because it is impossible for a prophet to be killed outside of Jerusalem." This is possibly a link forged by Luke himself to the threat against Jerusalem that follows in 13:34-35; that is certainly favored by the fact that it contains a variation on the preceding sentence. Moreover, the variant contains the *schema* of the "journey" that Luke develops so thoroughly, and the Jerusalem theme is also formulated in Lukan terms. On this cf. esp. Michael Wolter, *The Gospel According to Luke* (see part 3, n. 3 above), 2:204–5.

who is gathering crowds around him could create difficulties; after all, Herod Antipas had to keep an eye on Rome at all times. Rome was very much opposed to popular movements; they could too easily expand into uprisings. Hence it is quite possible that Herod made use of some Pharisees to whisper a death threat in Jesus' ear. That certainly does not mean that these Pharisees were "sent" to Jesus by Herod. Crafty politicians use more refined methods: they leak information to people they know will certainly pass it on to the right place.

If things played out that way we may of course ask whether the Pharisees saw through Herod's ploy. The text leaves all that open. But for the moment we can suppose that it happened that way. Then Jesus likewise understood the game. He tells the unofficial "embassy" that Herod is, after all, a "fox," which in ancient opinion meant he was cunning and sly but completely powerless and insignificant. We should also not overlook the fact that in the ancient world foxes could be thought of as smelly beasts.

Still, Jesus only uses the colorful word "fox" in his dialogue with the Pharisees. It is not part of his message to Herod himself; he has something different to say to him. It is so brief and clearly structured that any messenger could remember it. It also contains a wordplay—at least in Greek. Note the echo between *apoteleō* (accomplish, perform) and *teleioumai* (from *teleioō*, complete, fulfill, perfect).

> Listen, I am casting out demons
> and performing cures today and tomorrow—
> and on the third day I will be finished.

In essence this message tells the tetrarch: "I am not the least bit interested in what you are trying to pull off. I will go my own way, do what I must do, and what I am doing is aimed at a clear goal. But I will take no orders from *you*; I obey only God." This message speaks both authority and complete surrender to the will of God. Jesus follows the path his heavenly Father has designated for him.

At this hour Jesus is still in the dark about where that path will lead. He has to follow it step by step. In no way should we interpret "on the third day" (= the day after tomorrow; very soon) as referring to Jesus' resurrection. Today's Christian readers may have it in the back of their minds; Luke would also have understood it that way. But in this book we are trying to appreciate sayings as words of the historical Jesus, and the series "today, tomorrow, and on the third day" simply refers to a particular space of time that is no longer very extensive but that has to run its course before he reaches his goal.

Only when we have a clear idea of the direction of Jesus' message to Herod can we go a step farther. The Greek word *teleioō*, here translated "finish" or "fulfill" or "perfect," can mean "complete something" when it is used in the active or middle voice, but here it is probably passive and can describe the end of a life. And probably it is a *passivum divinum*. In that case Jesus is saying: "My life will be fulfilled by God." Then Jesus is very probably speaking indirectly about his life's ending—in veiled, oblique language—but evidently with clear knowledge of the danger to his life and the nearness of his death.

66. Fear Not, Little Flock! (Luke 12:32)

Luke 12:32 is a truly delicious piece of Jesus-tradition, preserved for us only by Luke. There is no serious reason to think it could not come from Jesus—unless one is convinced beforehand that Jesus simply could not have said anything that even *remotely* refers to the church. In this saying also, Jesus is thinking of his death—and, beyond it, is laying the cornerstone for the church as the eschatological Israel. But let us take a closer look:

> Fear not, little flock,
> for it is your Father's good pleasure
> to give you dominion [*basileia*]! (Luke 12:32)[9]

In Luke's Gospel this saying is directed at the disciples (cf. Luke 12:22), and it must have been so addressed by Jesus himself, but we have to be more precise. The addressees are called a "flock," and so they must be those to whom Jesus had said "I am sending you out like lambs into the midst of wolves." That saying (Matt 10:16 // Luke 10:3) is part of the tradition-complex of the mission discourse. Hence in the *logion* we are considering here Jesus was most probably operating within the same metaphorical field he had used in that other saying when he was sending the Twelve on mission. And thus we have good reason to believe that the original addressees of Luke 12:32

[9] NRSV *et al*. "the kingdom."

are the Twelve—that is, those whom Jesus had sent as a broadly visible demonstration of his will to gather all of Israel.

Another Jesus-saying confirms that it is the Twelve who are the addressees of Luke 12:32. In Matthew 19:28 // Luke 22:30 the twelve disciples are told: "You will judge the twelve tribes of Israel." That magisterial office of judging evidently presumes the authority spoken of in Luke 12:32, and so we may assume that the "little flock" in this *logion* also refers to none other than the Twelve.

They are a "little" flock, tiny in comparison to all of Israel (which is often referred to in the Jewish scriptures as "God's flock").[10] When Jesus adopts that designation for Israel here and applies it to the Twelve it certainly has ecclesial relevance since it means that here the Twelve are addressed as *Israel*.

Jesus tells this Israel-in-miniature: "Fear not!" That, too, is altogether based on the theology of the Hebrew Bible. The formula is not simply about soothing the fear of those addressed. It is the beginning of proclamations of salvation. Very often it introduces a divine promise that brings new things and changes the situation in Israel (cf. Gen 26:24; Isa 41:10-14; 43:5; Jer 46:27).

This new thing is introduced with a solemn formula: "it is your Father's good pleasure. . . ." The expression "your Father" is striking, and it is characteristic of Jesus.[11] But above all we should note that this "your Father" is part of the discourse from the Sayings Source in which Jesus tells his disciples that they need not worry any longer because now their Father in heaven is caring for them (Matt 6:32 // Luke 12:30). Once again, then, there is reference to the dangerous and exposed situation of the disciples. What is crucial is "good pleasure." The background lies in Hebrew concepts (probably *rāṣāh* above all), that can only be translated in the sense of it has "pleased" your Father; it is God's joy, pleasure, will, decision. And what does this joyful decision consist of? It is to "give" the *basileia*, that is, "rule," "authority," to the twelve disciples Jesus has chosen. That is the central statement of this *logion*. It is the starting point for everything, and now we must ask in detail what it means. Has God already decided, but not yet carried out the decision? Or is the transfer, the entrusting

[10] See the extended discussion by Joachim Jeremias, "ποίμνη, ποίμνιον," *TDNT* 6, 499–502.

[11] On this see Gerd Theissen and Annette Merz, *The Historical Jesus* (see part 4, n. 39 above), 526–27.

of the *basileia* happening now, in this moment, when Jesus speaks the *logion* in question?[12] In discussing the matter of the "Human One" I already pointed to Daniel 7, where we read:

> *To him* [the Human One] *was given dominion and glory and* **sovereignty**, *that all peoples, nations, and languages should serve him. His dominion is an everlasting dominion that shall not pass away, and his sovereignty shall never be destroyed.* (Dan 7:14)

This realm introduced in Daniel 7 with the symbol of the "Human One" (= "Son of Man") and that stands in sharp contrast to the beastly kingdoms previously described is the true, eschatological Israel, since in the interpretation of the vision that then follows it is equated with "the holy ones of the Most High" (cf. Dan 7:17-18, 27).

When Jesus says in our *logion* that the tiny flock of the Twelve will be "given *dominion*" he is evidently referring to Daniel 7:14. What was said then is happening now. The core of eschatological Israel was already established with the choice of the Twelve (Mark 3:14). Now, before his death, Jesus hands over the dominion to the twelve disciples—as God had handed it over to him.

By worldly measure it is all ridiculous. These twelve lambs, constantly threatened by wolves, are not Israel, and Israel is not the world. Most certainly Israel does not hold sway over the world. But for Jesus these twelve disciples are a real symbol and source of growth for eschatological Israel—and for him Israel alone is the hope of the world. In God's strategy it is anything but ridiculous; it is about a fundamental structure of the biblical message.

Since there has been repeated reference to "dominion" and our text clearly speaks of "dominion" (*basileia*) that is to be handed over to this

[12] There is a clear answer to this question on the *redactional level* of Luke's Gospel: At Luke 22:29—that is, within the great Last Supper discourse—Jesus says, "I confer on you, just as my Father has conferred on me, a royal rule [*basileia*]." For Luke, then, 12:32 is proclamation and promise; 22:29 is discharge and fulfillment. Luke 22:29 has a performative character: it really should be translated "hereby I confer on you . . ." If we ask about the historical Jesus, of course, the question arises whether Luke 22:29 is an authentic saying of Jesus. It is almost certain that v. 28 was formulated by Luke himself and he could have shaped v. 29 on the basis of 12:32. Consequently I have decided to leave open the question of the authenticity of Luke 22:29 and to interpret Luke 12:32 in isolation.

tiny flock we need to remind ourselves once again that Jesus adopted the promise of Daniel 7 for his image of eschatological Israel—and he adopted it also for himself, because he understood himself to be the embodiment of eschatological Israel. He said publicly that he himself was the "Human One." But one central aspect of the text of Daniel 7 he did *not* adopt, namely, the part that says that "all peoples, nations, and languages" must serve the Human One.

Precisely at this point Jesus, as we have seen, distinguished himself from the figure in Daniel 7: "The Son of Man came not to be served but to serve" (Mark 10:45). And he demands the same of the Twelve and, beyond them, of all his disciples (Mark 10:43-44). The eschatological Israel, then, must not dominate; it must be pure service, a selfless "being-for-others." The church, as the beginning of the eschatological Israel, dare not understand itself in any other way, and it must not live in any other way. If it does so nevertheless, if it relies on paternalism, power, and rule by force, it is no longer the recipient of "the Father's good pleasure."

One final note: Jesus says "It has pleased your Father to give you dominion." When he promises the Twelve in such a solemn form "what has pleased the Father" and what he himself has represented during his life, he can only have done so in expectation of his death. We do not know exactly when, but it must have been "in the face of death."

And still a final note: in Catholicism Matthew 16:18-19 plays an enormous role regarding the foundation of the church. Rightly so! But why do Luke 12:32; 22:29[13] not have the same weight as Matthew 16:18-19? If they did, the church would be reminded every day that it is not built on power but on its own powerlessness and its selfless service—and that all the goodness that is in it comes from God alone.

67. Judges Over the Twelve Tribes of Israel (Matt 19:28)

The story of the man whom Jesus called to discipleship and who went away sorrowful because, on account of his wealth, he did not want to follow Jesus (Mark 10:17-22), as well as the subsequent dialogue between Jesus and his disciples (Mark 10:23-31), was expanded by Matthew, who added the following *logion*:

[13] Cf. n. 12 above. The question of the authenticity of Luke 22:29 is completely irrelevant to the issue of its authority for the church's belief.

Amen, I tell you, at the renewal of all things, when the Son of Man is seated on the throne of his glory, you who have followed me will also sit on twelve thrones and judge the twelve tribes of Israel. (Matt 19:28)

That saying has a parallel in Luke's Gospel (cf. Luke 22:28-30), in a very different place: namely, within Jesus' discussions with his disciples after the Last Supper. The word may come from the Sayings Source; in fact, it could be that the whole Sayings Source ended with this very *logion*. But however that may be, the text that both Matthew and Luke used as their model would probably have read:[14]

You who have followed me
will sit on twelve thrones
and judge the twelve tribes of Israel.

There is no reason to think this is not an authentic saying of Jesus. He must have spoken it to the group of the Twelve as a promise and, apparently, also as a consolation and encouragement for what would happen to this "little flock." It is obvious that he could have done so only "in the face of death," clearly aware that the time of his mission was coming to an end.

However, this saying is extremely off-putting for us today. Can it really be a consolation or an encouragement to be able to judge others? And as Christians, do we dare to do it at all? Didn't Jesus himself tell us: "Judge not, so that you may not be judged" (Matt 7:1)?

In order to find an entry point to Matthew 19:28 we should first note the following: In Israel at that time the idea that the pious and faithful among the people of God would one day join God in judging the world was certainly not unknown.[15] Paul took it as a matter of course. In his opinion the "saints," that is, the members of Christian communities, would judge the world with Christ, the world's judge, in their midst. Since members of the Corinthian community sued one another before pagan judges, Paul wrote to them:

Do you not know that the saints will judge the world? And if the world is to be judged by you, are you [*yourselves*] *incompetent to try even trivial cases?* (1 Cor 6:2)

[14] For the tradition criticism here let me refer to Marius Reiser, *Jesus and Judgment* (see part 5, n. 14 above), 258–62.

[15] Cf., e.g., Wis 3:8; 1 En. 38:5; 91:12; 95:3.

The author of Revelation speaks of the martyrs' reigning together with Christ. They are to be seated on thrones and will be given authority to judge (Rev 20:4). The crucial question, however, is: *in what way*, according to the Bible, will this "judging-with" by those who believe in the true God take place in that eschatological future? Much could be said about that; I will restrict myself to just a few texts. In the great Final Hallel of the Psalter (Pss 146–50) we find the following passage:

> *Let the faithful rejoice in triumph;*
> *let them be joyful on their beds.*[16]
> *Let the praises of God be in their throat*
> [as] *a two-edged sword in their hand;*
> *to wreak vengeance on the nations*
> *and correction*[17] *on the peoples;*
> *to bind their kings in chains*
> *and their nobles with links of iron;*
> *To inflict on them the judgment decreed;*
> *this is glory for all his faithful people.*
> *Hallelujah!* (Ps 149:5-9)

This text presumes that the oppressed and the poor (v. 4) who are the "true Israel," will judge the foreign peoples. At first glance they seem to do it in the way the apocalyptic literature imagined "co-judging" at that time: in the final reckoning God's opponents and Israel's enemies will be slain at the hands of the devout. In 1 Enoch it sounds this way:

> *Woe to you who love the deeds of unrighteousness:*
> *wherefore do ye hope for good hap unto yourselves?*
> *Know that ye shall be delivered into the hands of the righteous,*
> *and they shall cut off your necks*
> *and slay you, and have no mercy upon you.* (1 En. 98.12, R. H. Charles trans.)

[16] The meaning of "beds" here is disputed. They could be carpets—prayer rugs or the kind used for sleeping—but they could also be shelves in tombs; then the resurrection would have preceded. See Norbert Lohfink, *Lobgesänge der Armen. Studien zum Magnificat, den Hodajot von Qumran, und einigen späten Psalmen*, SBS 143 (Stuttgart: Katholisches Bibelwerk, 1990), 123.

[17] For this translation see Norbert Lohfink, *Lobgesänge der Armen* (see n. 16 above), 123.

Such a picture is certainly unthinkable for the Psalms. There God is implored to take vengeance, but one does not take vengeance into one's own hand. Above all it is important to note that "vengeance" in Psalm 149 and many other places in the Old Testament does not mean "revenge" (as it is too often translated) but accounting for all past injustices. The word used here in parallel to "vengeance" is "correction." Thus it is a matter of the restoration and establishment of right and justice.

We should also notice that no universal bloodbath is ordered here. It is not that whole nations will be destroyed, as one might initially interpret verse 7. Instead, their "kings" and "nobles" are to be taken prisoner, as verse 8 details more clearly.[18] This is to say that the judgment is focused on the real agents of evil in the world: the oppressors, the exploiters, the persecutors, and those who have been the ministers of injustice—but not the collectivity of whole nations.

There is even an exegetical stance that reads Psalm 149 to say that here the exercise of judgment by the oppressed and disowned is identical with their praise of God.[19] That is: insofar as the oppressed have praised God despite their profound misery and have never ceased their praise in spite of all persecution it is *they* who will judge the oppressors. At the Last Judgment this fidelity that gives witness will be revealed—and in that very way the persecuted will be a judgment on their persecutors.

The crux of this interpretation is verse 6b. The introductory *waw* (= and) is read as *waw explicativum*. Then praise of God *is* a two-edged sword in the hands of the poor. There is much to be said for this interpretation. It would show that at a crucial point—namely, at the end of the Psalter that is prayed again and again—the Hebrew Bible by no means presents the co-judging by the devout in a theologically primitive, resentment-laden way.

But even if that interpretation were inaccurate, it is true in any case that Psalm 149 shows that the great, eschatological praise of the Psal-

[18] Probably the infinitives in v. 8 are *explanatory* of those in v. 7. Then judgment would be carried out on the nations in that their powerful would be seized and executed.

[19] For this stance on the interpretation see esp. Erich Zenger, *Psalmen. Auslegungen 1. Mit meinem Gott überspringe ich Mauern* (Freiburg: Herder, 2011), 53–60, as well as Zenger's essay in Hossfeld and Zenger, *Psalms 3* (see part 5, n. 46 above), 641–53.

ter in its five final Hallel-Psalms cannot sound forth unless at the same time the endless suffering endured by Israel's poor and oppressed throughout history is uncovered—and that involves a co-judging by those very ones who have been poor and deprived.

Obviously Jesus' saying "do not judge, so that you may not be judged" is true as well. Still, we dare not ignore the dialectic of the fact that the same Jesus who said those words also ordered his disciples to shake from their feet the dust of every settlement in Israel that has not accepted their proclamation of the reign of God (Luke 10:10-11). Thus because of their refusal the places in question have become subject to judgment. The sign-action of shaking off dust is to mean: "We, the proclaimers, are guiltless and do not want to be involved in the judgment that now threatens you." Thus basically the Twelve are already performing sign-actions that promise salvation or judgment by their very proclamation of the reign of God. Hence it rightly follows that they will participate in the final judgment.[20]

Let me end with a final note or, better, an expansion of what I have said about Psalm 149—precisely because for today's Christians the biblical statement about co-judging has become so alien, if not positively suspect. What does dogmatic theology say about the theme of "judgment" in the tractate on eschatology? Among many other things it holds that judgment in the theological sense does *not* mean that there will be an investigation at the highest levels, after which others *will adjudge a person's salvation or damnation.*

Judgment means, rather, that in our encounter with the indescribable love of God we will for the first time recognize the full power of what we have done to other people, by action or inaction. The suffering we have caused for others will then become our own. The misery that criminal wielders of power have imposed on the innocent will become their own misery because now the truth of history and the situation of their victims stand revealed before their eyes, no longer to be concealed. But at the same time the happiness we have given others through the power of God will become our own happiness. That is how judgment happens, and in no other way. God does not need to sit in judgment on us. We will become a judgment to

[20] Marius Reiser has rightly pointed this out: *Jesus and Judgment* (see part 5, n. 14 above), 248–49.

ourselves. We will be our own magistrates. Current dogmatic theology rightly describes the Last Judgment as a "self-judgment."[21]

Thinking further along that line, we see that the "judgment" exercised by the people of God with its saints, including especially the twelve disciples, is nothing other than a witness to the faith and love of this very people of God. The witness of the faithful has been carried out in history—and on the last day it surrounds the one Witness, Jesus Christ, in whom the entire reality of witnessing to the true God found its goal and ultimate reality. The judgment exercised by the faithful thus consists of the witness of their lives. In that sense it is indeed true that their praise of God, the summit of their believing existence, will be a judgment on others.

But in the absence of that witnessing existence the people of God must judge itself. To the extent that it has been indifferent, divided, and unbelieving, the people of God will be judged even by righteous pagans and those willing to repent. Jesus also spoke about that, as we know, when he threatened that the queen of the South and the people of Nineveh would be a judgment on this generation in Israel (Luke 11:31-32).

And let me add another closing remark on these considerations about "self-judgment": obviously what has been said in this chapter is also relevant to the question of the role of the Jewish people in salvation history. If it is the case that the authors of the Sayings Source placed the disciples seated on twelve thrones at the end of their collection of *logia*, did they mean to say that now Israel has been judged guilty and stripped of its election?[22] After everything that we have seen and reflected upon, such a theology (if the Sayings Source ever advocated it) is unacceptable. We must deal with the concept of "judgment" in a more nuanced fashion. It is not always a condemnation to punishment and most certainly not always a judgment that ends

[21] See, more fully, Gerhard Lohfink, *Is This All There Is? On Resurrection and Eternal Life*, trans. Linda M. Maloney (Collegeville, MN: Liturgical Press, 2017), part 4.

[22] "The Logion Q 22,30, with the announcement of judgment over all Israel, marks an end-point. It means saying farewell to Israel." Thus Paul Hoffmann, "Herrscher in oder Richter über Israel? Mt 19,28/Lk 22,28-30 in der synoptischen Überlieferung," in *Ja und nein. Christliche Theologie im Angesicht Israels. FS zum 70. Geburtstag von Wolfgang Schrage*, ed. Klaus Wengst and Gerhard Sass (Neukirchen-Vluyn: Neukirchener Verlag, 1998), 253–64, at 264.

with destruction. In fact, in the Psalms of Solomon (PsSol 17:26) "judging" is the same as "ruling."

In addition, we must not overlook the dialectics of history: considering the course of past centuries it seems that all Christians who have been guilty of anti-Judaism must pass through a dreadful self-judgment—in that they will have to recognize and experience, to the depths of their existence, what they have done to their Jewish sisters and brothers. In that sense the Jews will also be *our* judges. We today dare no longer speak about Matthew 19:28 without saying that with the utmost clarity.

68. Ransom for Many (Mark 10:45)

The story in Mark 10:35-45 begins with a plea for official positions in the reign of God. When it comes, the two sons of Zebedee want to sit at Jesus' right and left; that is, they want the top places. The story of their petition develops into a discourse about ruling and serving in which Jesus speaks first to the sons of Zebedee and then to the other ten. The Jesus saying to be considered here comes at the end of the discourse:

> The Son of Man came not to be served but to serve,
> and to give his life a ransom for many. (Mark 10:45)

Matthew took the *logion* from Mark, word for word, and also retained the structure of the whole section (Matt 20:20-28). Luke placed the corresponding discourse, in a different form, in the room where the Last Supper took place and eliminated the sons of Zebedee's petition together with the *logion* in Mark 10:45. The reason for its removal remains obscure.[23] First let us ask: what, exactly, does the saying mean?

We have already seen that Jesus took the idea of the Human One directly from Daniel 7 and applied it to himself, while at the same time changing it. In Daniel 7 the "Human One" means the true Israel that, in contrast to all previous societies—who are compared to voracious animals—no longer relies on its own power but receives from

[23] Probably for Luke the preceding "words of institution" in the Last Supper room were sufficient to indicate the salvific significance of Jesus' death.

God alone everything that it is. "All peoples, nations, and languages" (Dan 7:14, 27) must serve that Israel.

Jesus links the idea of the "Human One" with himself because with him and the appointment of the Twelve that true eschatological Israel is already beginning. But that changes the concept of the "Human One." The service of the nations to the people of God becomes the service of the people of God to the nations—because Jesus has *not* come to be served but to serve. Precisely this *intervention* in the world of ideas in Daniel 7 reveals Jesus' independent *reference* to Daniel 7.

Now, in the same sovereign manner, Jesus also uses Isaiah 40–55 (so-called Deutero-Isaiah). In those chapters the "Servant of God" plays a crucial role. The Servant of God is also a figure of Israel there—more precisely, a figure of Israel exiled to Babylon.[24] Isaiah 52:13–53:12 says of this Servant, cut off from Zion and profoundly degraded, that with his humiliation, displacement, and suffering he bore "the sins of many" (Isa 53:12e) as representative substitute.[25] The keyword "many," which appears no fewer than four times in Isaiah 52:13–53:12, appears now in our *logion* as well.

Beyond that, there is still another connection to Isaiah 52:13–53:12, namely, "give his life" (Isa 53:12). Evidently Jesus has entered into the figure of the "Human One" of Daniel 7 and also that of the Servant of God in the book of Isaiah.

Still, if "give his life" and "many" were the only threads connecting Mark 10:45 and Isaiah 40–55 the link between our *logion* and the Isaiah passage would be uncertain. But there is another keyword in Mark 10:45 that indicates the connection. It is that of "ransom," which points directly to Isaiah 43:3. We must read the context of Isaiah 43:3 also if we are to understand what "ransom" means there:

But now thus says the L*ORD*,
the one who created you, O Jacob,
the one who formed you, O Israel:
Do not fear, for I have **redeemed** *you;*
I have called you by name,
you are mine!

[24] Of course, the idea of the "servant of God" is open also to those who remained near Zion. We cannot speak of a complete and precise separation.

[25] German "Stellvertretung," lit. "taking the place of," is difficult to render exactly in a single English word. "Representative substitution" comes fairly close. —Trans.

When you pass through the waters I am with you;
and through the rivers, they shall not carry you away;
when you walk through fire you shall not be burned,
no flame shall consume you.
For I, the Lord, am your God,
I, the Holy One of Israel, am your **Savior**.
I give Egypt as your **ransom**,
Ethiopia and Seba in exchange for you.
Because you are precious and worthy in my sight,
I give whole lands in return for you,
whole peoples in exchange for your life.
Do not fear, for I am with you!
I bring your offspring from the east,
and from the west I gather you;
I say to the north, "Give them up!"
and to the south, "Do not withhold!"
Bring my sons home from far away
and my daughters from the end of the earth!
For everyone who is called by my name,
I created, formed, and made for my glory. (Isa 43:1-7)

This word of God announces liberation and homecoming for the part of Israel that was deported to Babylon, but certainly the scenery at the end of the passage also speaks to those from all Israel who do not live in the "Land Between the Rivers" but somewhere else in the Diaspora. They return to Zion from everywhere. Those deported to Babylon will travel to Jerusalem on a road laid solely for them (Isa 40:3-4; 43:19) and nothing will disturb them—neither water nor fire (that is, neither unapproachable terrain with raging rivers nor burning heat)—for it is *God* who is their liberator (Isa 43:3).

However: those exiled to the Land Between the Rivers are under the control of the king of Babylon. They belong to him; they have become his property. And here one of the most thrilling images of the Bible comes into play: *God buys their freedom*. God pays the king a ransom for this poor, mistreated Israel because in reality it is "God's" people and must belong forever to God alone (Isa 43:1). But it is not simply because it must belong to God alone; the reason is far greater: God "loves" Israel (Isa 43:4).

But how does that ransoming take place, concretely? The "ransom" paid to the king of Babylon consists of fruitful, rich lands—namely, the huge region extending up the Nile as far as Nubia. In fact, after conquering Babylon the Persian emperor Cyrus I released the deportees, and in 525 Cambyses II (ca. 558–522 BCE) took possession of Egypt. But we need not concern ourselves here with this historical level and all the questions that might arise. The crucial point is the series of soteriological concepts used in Isaiah 43:1-7: those of "redemption" (43:1), "saving" (43:3b), and above all "ransom" (43:3c). What was Jesus thinking when he said—alluding to Isaiah 43:3 and so, of course, to its context—that he has come *to give his life as ransom for many*?

Initial observation: If the retrieval from Babylon had its price, then most certainly so did a new life for Israel in Jesus' time. Releasing Israel from its stasis and self-enclosure in view of the now-arriving reign of God cost something—and in fact, a shocking amount. The image of the ransom is made concrete by the surrender of the rich lands along the Nile, which even then were the breadbasket of the Mediterranean world. The very image signals a high price. The ransom is Jesus' life. Add to this, however, that the concept of "ransom" in the Old Testament was derived from legal language. It could represent a payment as substitute for a forfeited life—for example, when a bull, because of its owner's carelessness, has killed someone. According to law the owner of the beast must be slain, but can purchase reprieve by paying a ransom (Exod 21:29-30). We have to keep the legal background of the concept in the *logion* in mind as well: with his own life Jesus redeems the forfeited life of the "many." But for whose benefit is the high price to be paid?

That brings us to a second observation: Immediately after the keyword "ransom" in Jesus' saying stands the inconspicuous word "for," a word that also played a crucial role in Isaiah 43:3-4. Jesus gives his life "for (= on behalf of) many." And who are the "many?" In Isaiah 43 the "for" clearly refers to Israel; in Isaiah 52–53 it is plainly for the nations.[26] In Mark 10:45 it remains open. We may suppose that for

[26] Cf. Isa 52:14, 15; 53:11, 12. Obviously this reference assumes that the "servant of God" in Deutero-Isaiah and especially in the so-called Servant Songs represents Israel and not a prophetic or royal individual. There are serious reasons for this. See Norbert Lohfink, "'Israel' in Jes 49,3," in *Wort, Lied und Gottesspruch. FS für Joseph Ziegler*, ed. Josef Schreiner, FB 2 (Würzburg: Echter, 1972), 217–29; also Gerhard Lohfink and

Jesus also it refers to Israel but also beyond Israel to the nations. In any case what we have here is a representative action, something done on behalf of someone else.[27] Jesus gives his life on behalf of Israel, "for" Israel—and according to numerous Old Testament texts Israel is representative "for" the nations.[28]

A third observation: When God, in Isaiah 43:3-4, gives whole lands and peoples for Israel's life, God gives what belongs to God. After all, God created not only Israel. When Jesus gives his own life for Israel just as *God* gives whole nations for Israel, then here again, as in many of his other sayings, he is acting in place of God (cf. chaps. 16, 18, 30, 48, 50, 52, and 66).

I think that, with all this, it is clear that in Mark 10:45 Jesus takes up not only the concept of "ransom" but, together with it, a whole fabric of biblical theology: for example, the self-surrender of the Servant of God in Isaiah 53 and the service of Israel on behalf of the nations in Isaiah 2. Such interweavings are already the basis of the biblical texts. Uncovering these kinds of connections and intersections corresponds exactly to the creative way in which Jesus applies his Bible.

It is hard to understand why a significant number of biblical scholars, in Germany at least, have denied and continue to deny that Jesus spoke the words found in Mark 10:45. One reason is probably an understanding of Jesus' preaching of the reign of God that is too one-sided and superficial.[29] A typical argument[30] is that Jesus preached a Father who is willing to forgive unconditionally. It is said

---

Ludwig Weimer, *Maria—nicht ohne Israel. Eine neue Sicht der Lehre von der Unbefleckten Empfängnis* (Freiburg: Herder, 2008), 223–30.

[27] Thus correctly Peter Stuhlmacher, *Biblical Theology of the New Testament* 1 (see part 5, n. 45 above), chap. 10. He speaks of "substitution of existence."

[28] Cf. esp. Isa 42:6; 49:6, but also a text like Gen 12:2-3.

[29] Another reason, of course, is the argument that "I have come" could only have been formulated on the lips of later community theologians from a post-Easter standpoint. It remains a mystery to me why Jesus himself, facing the threat of death, could not also have composed it.

[30] Especially noteworthy examples for such theses are offered by Peter Fiedler, "Sünde und Vergebung im Christentum," *Concilium* 10 (1974): 568–71; idem, *Jesus und die Sünder*, BBET 3 (Frankfurt: Peter Lang, 1976), 277–81; Werner Zager, "Die theologische Problematik des Sühnetodes Jesu. Exegetische und dogmatische Perspektiven," in idem, *Jesus und die frühchristliche Verkündigung. Historische Rückfragen nach den Anfängen* (Neukirchen-Vluyn: Neukirchener Verlag, 1999), 35–61.

that for that loving Father one day to have ceased being so generous and suddenly insisting on things like ransom, representative suffering, and atonement simply does not match Jesus' message and praxis. Jesus' welcoming of sinners to table companionship had nothing to do with a substitute suffering, certainly not an atoning death; it was purely a consequence of the now-revealed reign of God.

But such arguments vitiate the essence of Jesus' preaching. From the very beginning the proclamation of the reign of God signified a radical "for"—namely, "for" the poor and helpless who followed Jesus, "for" Israel, "for" the world. That is evident not only in Jesus' healings of the sick but in his own life. When he demands of his disciples that they abandon everything, not only their parents, their families, their houses and fields, but even their own "I," that is simply a reflection of what he demands of himself. His life, from the beginning of his public mission, was shaped by this "for others." The disciples he gathered around him learned from him to forgive, to be reconciled with one another, to care for one another, to serve, to ignore themselves and turn their eyes to the people of God. Take away all that and the proclamation of the reign of God would have been an empty façade. Surrender of one's own self was a "given" from the beginning of Jesus' work. When then, one day, he spoke of offering his life "for many" the ground was already long since laid. What was new was only the increasingly tense situation and the theological interpretation with which that intensification had to be answered.

After all, what would happen if this absolute "for" the others encountered indifference—or resistance—or even a desire to destroy it? What would happen if the whole of Israel were to reject Jesus' message about the reign of God? Would not Israel's existence then cease to have meaning; would it not squander salvation for itself and the nations and push God's action in choosing Israel *ad absurdum*? Therefore Jesus, and Israel, in the moment when precisely that outcome threatens, have arrived at an entirely new situation—and that new situation calls for a new interpretation.

The argument that previously Jesus has never spoken of his blood or of substitution and atonement misses the point. It assumes that the existence of individuals and that of whole peoples are ahistorical. Above all: it presumes that God's revelations are ahistorical "information" about God's self. But that is altogether unbiblical. *Jesus, in a new situation of escalating mercilessness, interprets the very death that threatens him as the ultimate and definitive saving decree of God*. He does so by using concepts prepared for him by his Bible, above all Isaiah 40–55. He at first does so tentatively, as in the texts we have considered previously. He then does it with finality and in a deeply moving fashion at his last meal.

69. The Words at the Last Supper (Mark 14:22-24)

The words of administration that Jesus speaks at the Last Supper are firmly embedded in sign-actions, and those actions in turn are located in the sequence of the Jewish Passover meal.[31] For that reason I must discuss the context of the Lord's words more fully in this chapter[32] than in others—and in this case that applies to the meal itself. There are two lines of tradition for the Last Supper account: Mark 14:22-24 // Matthew 26:26-28 and 1 Corinthians 11:23-25 // Luke 22:15-20. I have chosen Mark 14:22-24 as our basic text:[33]

> During the meal he took bread, and said the blessing.
> Then he broke [the bread] and gave it to them, saying: "Take! This is my body."
>
> And he took a cup, said the prayer of thanksgiving, gave it [the cup] to them, and all of them drank from it. And he said to them, "This is my blood, [the blood] of the covenant, which is poured out for many."

[31] Was Jesus' last supper a Passover meal? Despite the essential work of Joachim Jeremias (*The Eucharistic Words of Jesus*, trans. Norman Perrin [New York: Scribner, 1966]), this continues to be disputed. It is not possible to review the whole discussion within the framework of this book. In my opinion the reasons for thinking it was a Passover supper are by far the strongest. There are clear theological reasons why the author of the Fourth Gospel describes the meal in a way that virtually excludes its being held on the Passover night. For a brief, balanced description of important indicators favoring the framework of a Passover meal cf. Martin Hengel and A. M. Schwemer, *Jesus and Judaism* (see part 1, n. 4 above), 615–20.

[32] In this chapter I am making use of Gerhard Lohfink, *Does God Need the Church?* (see part 6, n. 32 above), 190–200. The text has been shortened and edited for use here.

[33] Again, I cannot go into the reasons for preferring the Markan version here; it would break the limits of the book and draw us away from our goal. Let me refer to the discussions of the question in Rudolf Pesch, *Markusevangelium* 2 (see part 3, n. 16 above), 354–77. For parts of the interpretation of the Last Supper event and the words of institution I am following not only Pesch but also Peter Stuhlmacher, *Biblical Theology* 1 (see n. 27 above), chap. 10.

Jesus knows what awaits him. His messianic entry into the city (chap. 53) would certainly have aroused animosity among his opponents. His speech in the temple, but above all his actions there, then led the high priests and scribes to decide to get rid of him (Mark 11:18; 14:1-2). They regarded Jesus as someone who was *leading the people astray*.[34] He must have known about it. He had to expect to die.

Knowing that, he celebrated the Passover supper with his own, and he did so, as prescribed, within the city of Jerusalem. It was his last time together with those he had chosen, and his last opportunity to give his death a universal interpretation—one that places this death among the other saving deeds of God, but above all in the context of his proclamation of the reign of God. The sequence of the Passover meal was especially opportune for that purpose because this meal in particular had long contained special gestures, instructions, and interpretive words.[35]

In this book we have often considered Jesus' prophetic sign-actions, clustering especially around the sending of the Twelve. Such sign-actions are not only "illustrations" but establish new reality. The very appointment of the Twelve (Mark 3:14) was one such sign-action. Jesus saw the beginning of eschatological Israel in his choosing them and sending them out—corresponding to the reign of God now coming to pass. In exactly the same way, Jesus' healing miracles and expulsions of demons were not merely benefits for the sick; they were signs of the reign of God now being realized. The summit and climax of all these signs came at his last meal. Therefore it would be completely false to say that the bread and wine of the Eucharist are *only* visualizations, *only* symbols, *only* signs. That would be an utterly one-sided and watered-down concept of "sign." Signs, even in normal, everyday life, and especially in interactions between persons,

[34] For the concept of the "deceiver" or "impostor" cf. Matt 27:63; John 7:12, 47; Justin, *Dial.* 69.7; 108.2. For the historical problem see August Strobel, *Die Stunde der Wahrheit. Untersuchungen zum Strafverfahren gegen Jesus*, WUNT 21 (Tübingen: Mohr Siebeck, 1980), 81–92.

[35] There were the bitter herbs, the unleavened bread, the lamb, the first (*Kiddush*) cup, the second (*Haggada*) cup, the third cup (the cup of blessing), and the fourth (*Hallel*) cup. The meal made present the exodus from Egypt and looked forward in hope for the Messiah. An ancient Aramaic interpretive word over the unleavened bread said: "See, *this is the bread* of affliction that our ancestors had to eat when they came out of Egypt."

often signify much more. They not only illustrate or indicate something; they can create a new reality.

Mark depicts what is special about this Passover meal thus: Jesus does not celebrate it with his natural family, in accordance with the Jewish Passover ritual. He celebrates with his new family, and not with a random group of disciples who came together more or less accidentally, but—as Mark explicitly says—with the Twelve (Mark 14:17). It is true that this last meal had the family intimacy that belongs to the *Pascha*, and yet the very choice of participants points emphatically to Israel or, more precisely, to the eschatological gathering and new creation of Israel that Jesus began with the establishment of the Twelve.

During the meal Jesus takes bread, speaks the thanksgiving over it, breaks it into pieces, and gives it to the Twelve. That is the prescribed ritual. It is the table prayer before the meal itself, after the appetizers have been eaten and the presider has recalled the exodus from Egypt. Mark says nothing about the appetizers, the Passover liturgy, or any other elements of the meal. The tradition he is following presumes that everyone is familiar with all of that. Mark and his tradition speak only of what is special, what is unique about this last meal of Jesus[36]—including the fact that Jesus interprets the broken bread with the words "this is my body."

"Body" here must not be misunderstood in the Western sense as the opposite of "soul." "Body" means the person, the whole human being. Jesus is saying: "I myself am this bread, with my whole history and my life. My life will be broken like this bread. I give it to you so that you may have a share in me."

Hence this sign-action by Jesus is a prophecy of his death. Jesus announces his death in the sign of the broken bread, but at the same time it is more than a prophecy of death: Jesus gives the Twelve a share in his existence, which is now surrendered to death. Evidently his death has a depth dimension in which the Twelve, and therefore Israel, must have a share. What that consists of, Mark—in contrast to the Pauline-Lukan strand of tradition about the Last Supper—says nothing at this point.

[36] For the course of the Passover meal cf. Joachim Jeremias, *The Eucharistic Words of Jesus* (see n. 31 above), 84–88.

Without saying so, the Markan tradition assumes that the main course of the meal followed immediately after the table prayer and the words of interpretation over the bread: the lamb with bitter herbs, bread, and the fruit mixture called *ḥaroseth*. At the end of the main course the one presiding at the meal took the third cup, the "cup of blessing," and spoke another prayer of thanksgiving over it. Here Mark takes up the account again because now, once more, something special happens: Jesus also makes the sharing and drinking of the blessing-cup a sign-action. After speaking the thanksgiving he interprets this third cup as follows: "This is my blood, [the blood] of the covenant, which will be poured out for many."

The ideas here are highly compressed—almost too much so for us today—but we should not blame the ancient text for that. For Jewish ears at that time a few central keywords, often just one, sufficed to recall a broader biblical context. What is Mark's text saying?

First: Jesus points again to his imminent death. He interprets the cup of red wine as his blood that will soon be shed. "Shedding blood" means "killing." Jesus will be killed. But here again he is not only prophesying his death. The text does not speak simply of Jesus' blood but of his "blood of the covenant," and that is an allusion to the events in Exodus 24:4-11, which tells of God's making the covenant with Israel at the foot of Sinai. There Moses builds an altar and twelve stone pillars, sprinkles the altar with the blood of sacrifices, reads the covenant to the twelve tribes, and then sprinkles the people with the blood also, saying:

> *This is the blood of the covenant*
> *that the* LORD *thus makes with you in accordance with all these words.*
> (Exod 24:8)

After that, Moses and the elders of Israel are allowed to share a meal on the mountain with God, who, as the crucial partner to the covenant, is symbolized by the altar; the other partner is the people. That is why both the altar and the people are sprinkled with sacrificial blood. The contractual document is read aloud. The making of the covenant is celebrated with the meal that then follows.

It is crucial for the later interpretation of Exodus 24:8, 11 that three motifs are linked together here: God's covenant with Israel, the blood with which the covenant is sealed, and the meal. In Jewish traditional interpretation at the time of Jesus the sprinkled blood was understood as the means of *atonement* for Israel's sins.[37] Against that background Jesus' words over the cup of blessing in Mark 14:24 can only mean that Jesus' life is being surrendered to death. His blood that then flows out is not shed for nothing: it is the "blood of the covenant"; that is, it renews and completes the covenant God once made with Israel at Sinai and that is now broken through the rejection and killing of Jesus. This eschatological renewal of the covenant, which is at the same time a new creation and new founding of Israel, takes place through the blood of Jesus, which frees Israel from its guilt and atones for it. It is thus quite correct that the Pauline-Lukan Last Supper tradition speaks here of the new (= renewed) covenant (1 Cor 11:25; Luke 22:20).

If we take this background seriously, then the "many" of which the words over the cup in Mark's version speak can in the first place only be Israel. Jesus interprets his violent death as dying for Israel, an atoning surrender of his life for the life of the people of God. This reference to Israel should be clear from the very fact that Jesus gives the cup of blessing to the Twelve, his chosen representatives of the people of the Twelve Tribes. But the reference to Israel is equally clear because of the mention of the covenant at Sinai. That covenant was made with Israel, and when it is renewed it must again be with Israel. The "many" thus primarily are the people of the Twelve Tribes.

Still, we cannot stop with that statement. We have already seen (chap. 68) that reference to the "many" comes from Isaiah 52:13–53:12. The servant of God suffers in place of the many, and in that text from Isaiah in which "many" is a *leitmotif* the "many" are clearly the pagan peoples.[38] Thus, along with Israel, the nations are also in view. That is not a problem, for in the theology of the Old Testament, as we have seen, Israel is representative of all nations. It is not chosen for its own sake but for the sake of the world.

Thus we may summarize the basic statement of the Last Supper tradition as offered by Mark this way: *Jesus, during the ritual of the*

[37] Targum Onqelos says at Exod 24:8: "Moses took the blood and sprinkled it on the altar in order to make atonement for the people, and he said: 'See, this is the blood of the covenant that the LORD has made with you in accordance with all these words.'" Targum Yerushalmi I is similar.

[38] Isaiah 52:15 shows that the "many" in the fourth Servant Song are the "nations."

Passover meal, interprets the broken bread and the red wine in terms of his imminent death. And by giving the bread and wine to the twelve disciples he gives them, and thereby Israel, a share in the power of his death, the death that is at the same time interpreted as atonement for Israel's guilt and a renewal of the Sinai covenant. But beyond eschatological Israel, this new and definitively given salvation is extended to the many peoples of the world.

What Jesus says here and, very soon after, redeems with his death is anything but innocuous. The Last Supper tradition—whether that of Mark or of Paul—presupposes that Jesus, in his death, *becomes the place* of eschatological atonement for Israel. But that means it is no longer the temple that is the legitimate place of atonement; it is Jesus himself with his surrender of his life even to death. The table around which Jesus gathers with his disciples now definitively becomes the center of Israel. There are no truly credible reasons to make historical subtractions from Mark's Last Supper account, certainly not to call it into question in principle. The same is true, of course, for the Pauline line of tradition.

We already saw in the preceding chapter that relatively many exegetes regard the *logia* in which Jesus gives a theological significance to his own death as nonauthentic. Redemption, substitution, sacrifice, and above all atonement are ideas used by the post-Easter communities to come to terms with Jesus' horrible execution on the cross.

Surely, literary-critical or tradition-critical observations are scarcely the real reasons why such positions are repeatedly advocated. The decision happens beforehand—even before historical criticism is applied. Rudolf Bultmann once made that clear, with his typical candor, when he wrote in his famous essay "New Testament and Mythology":

> How can my guilt be atoned for by the death of someone guiltless (assuming one may even speak of such)? What primitive concepts of guilt and righteousness lie behind any such notion? And what primitive concepts of God? If what is said about Christ's atoning death is to be understood in terms of the idea of sacrifice, what kind of primitive mythology is it according to which a divine being who has become [a human being][39]

[39] German: *Mensch*. —Trans.

> atones with his blood for the sins of humanity? Or if it is to be understood in legal terms, so that in the transactions between God and human beings God's demands are satisfied by the death of Christ![40]

We can sense from this text how much harm has been inflicted, even in the heads of educated scholars, by superficial and profoundly unbiblical ideas of "satisfaction" in the history of Christian piety. By "satisfaction" I mean the idea that *God's wrath at human sin must be placated by deeds of satisfaction*!

Rudolf Bultmann's words, however, reveal still more: the human being who lives in the wake of the European Enlightenment can no longer associate concepts such as substitution and atonement with the autonomy they have so laboriously acquired. So they refuse to link those ideas with Jesus. But is "representative atonement" really impossible to reconcile with enlightened reason? Representation/substitution and atonement can only be scurrilous mythological ideas when the experience of the people of God has been lost. For life within the people of God, representation and atonement—rightly understood, of course—are, in fact, elementary. They do not detract from the dignity and independence of a person. But let us look more closely!

First, substitution: Israel's existence always depended on individuals who believed *with their whole being*. That the scarlet thread of revelation (that is, the history of divine enlightenment) did not break was due to Abraham, Moses, Elijah, Amos, and Isaiah; to King Josiah, John the Baptizer, and many others. Still others could share in their faith and so come to faith themselves. It is not a word game to say of Abraham that whoever he blesses will be blessed and that through him all generations on earth will receive blessing (Gen 12:3). Jesus, in becoming a representative on behalf of the many, is not an exotic exception but the high point and final culmination of a long history of representation in Israel. It is only by way of representation that faith can be handed on at all.

Substitution or representation in this context never means dispensing others from their own faith and repentance; it should make both

[40] Rudolf Bultmann, "New Testament and Mythology," in his *New Testament and Mythology and Other Basic Writings*, ed. and trans. Schubert M. Ogden (Philadelphia: Fortress Press, 1984), 7.

possible. True substitution does not incapacitate; it desires nothing more than that the other may be free to act. It happens when one person takes the place of another—not to "replace" the other but to enable that other to take possession of her or his own space.[41]

Every human being in her or his natural existence depends on countless substitutes. Where would we be without our mothers, fathers, teachers? By their efforts they have enabled us, slowly and arduously, to become independent. And how could we get along without administrators, intermediaries, politicians, merchants, technicians, and all the specialists we need just to be able to live?

When I drive my car across a high bridge I trust those who calculated its capabilities and those who built it. They did it "for me." I myself could never have built the bridge. The engineers, architects, and builders are substitutes for all those who use the bridge as a matter of course.

Likewise the people of God is a network of substitutions, but a much more closely woven one—and precisely because without free, responsible action it simply could not exist. What applies to individuals is even more valid for the life of faith: human beings depend on help. Left alone, they would shrivel. The sentence abstracted from Kant's *Critique of Practical Reason*,[42] "You can because you should," is highly questionable. Against the background of Jewish-Christian tradition it would have to be: "You can, if you will accept help."[43]

[41] Cf. the comprehensive and informative work of Karl-Heinz Menke, *Stellvertretung. Schlüsselbegriff christlichen Lebens und theologische Grundkategorie* (Einsiedeln: Johannes Verlag, 1991), 17. At this point he refers to Dorothee Sölle, *Stellvertretung. Ein Kapitel Theologie nach dem "Tode Gottes"* (Stuttgart: Kreuz Verlag, 1982). [English: *Christ the Representative: An Essay in Theology after the "Death of God"* (London: SCM, 1997).]

[42] Cf. Immanuel Kant, *The Critique of Practical Reason* (Chicago: Encyclopaedia Britannica, 1952), 302: "He [Author's note: = one who in a difficult situation must decide according to conscience] judges, therefore, that he can do a certain thing because he is conscious that he ought, and he recognizes that he is free—a fact which but for the moral law he would never have known." Apparently the dictum "you can because you should" was later abstracted from this sentence. At any rate, in 1942 Walter Schmidkunz edited a collection of quotations from Kant in the series *Münchner Lesebogen*, no. 11, under the title *I. Kant, Du kannst, denn du sollst. Vom Ethos der Pflicht* (Munich: Münchner Buchverlag). The formula in the title does not appear among the quotations. I am grateful to P. Giovanni Sala, SJ, of Munich, for this information.

[43] I owe this formulation to Dr. Dr. habil. Ludwig Weimer.

The supposedly "autonomous" person, who thinks she or he needs no help and no substitutes, of course has them anyway: for example, the media, who all too often think for us, shape us according to their own models and thereby disempower us without our noticing it. A person always has substitutes, most certainly in the era of the new digital media. The only question is: which?

Second, atonement: The revulsion of people today at the idea of atonement or satisfaction is, in fact, much stronger than their attitudes toward substitution, even though atonement is nothing more than substitution carried to its ultimate consequence. But we can only understand what "atonement" or "satisfaction" means if we look at the difference between atonement in the Old Testament sense and what it means in the world of the religions.

In the realm of mere religion atonement is primarily a human deed by which one attempts to appease one's gods for one's own failings. One gives up something especially dear and precious in order to propitiate the deity or the powers that have influence over one's life. The initiative comes from the human side and its purpose is to attain security. People have developed the most varied cultic mechanisms in order to secure their existence.

Israel was familiar with all those mechanisms but had seen through them and reconsidered them in light of its experience of God. Basically, it turned them on their heads, because in Israel all atonement comes from God. It is divine initiative. Atonement is a new enabling of life, given by God. Satisfaction is the gift of living in the presence of the holy God—close to God—in spite of one's own unholiness and constant, repeated sinning. Achieving satisfaction does *not* mean pacifying God or putting God in a forgiving mood; it means letting ourselves be snatched by God from a death we deserve.[44] Israel knew that human beings cannot work off their guilt and that both atonement and forgiveness come from God. Atonement, like covenant and the forgiveness of sins, is a gift one can only receive.

Certainly that still does not answer the truly burning question. What I have just said was only a first, fundamental step. The biblical concept of atonement is much more complex. That is, we have to ask further:

[44] Cf. Hartmut Gese, "The Atonement," in his *Essays on Biblical Theology,* trans. Keith Crim (Eugene, OR: Wipf & Stock, 2018), 93–116, at 99.

If everything comes from God's initiative, why is there need for atonement? If God has brought about atonement just as God forgives, why is simple forgiving not enough? Why cannot God simply say: your guilt is remitted, everything is forgiven and forgotten, it's all okay?

The answer can only be: Because then reality would be concealed; the burden of sin and its consequences would not be taken seriously. It is not all okay. Sin does not dissolve into the air, even when it is forgiven. Sin always has consequences. It blights something within ourselves and something in the world around us. It always has a social and historical dimension. Every sin sinks into human society, corrupts a part of the world, and creates a harmful environment—and such environments can form a network. Even if God has forgiven all sin and guilt, the *consequences* of sin are not erased. What Adolf Hitler set in motion was by no means banished from the world with his suicide in the Führerbunker on 30 April 1945—even if he regretted it (although his "Political Testament" to the German people reveals that regret played no part in his nature). The fearful consequences of National Socialism are poisoning society even today, and they are at the root of repeated new eruptions of evil in the world.

Thus the effects of human guilt have to be dealt with, and that, too, is something people cannot do for themselves any more than they can absolve themselves. Genuine working off of guilt is only possible on a basis that God must establish. God did that in creating the people of God, and through Jesus it was renewed and perfected.

There is a text from Dag Hammarskjøld, second secretary general of the United Nations, who was killed in a plane crash near Katanga on 17 September 1961 as he was attempting to end the civil war in the Congo, that can help us better understand the connections we have been describing. It is in Hammarskjøld's diary, published after his death under the title *Markings*.[45] It reads:

> Easter 1960. Forgiveness breaks the chain of causality because he who "forgives" you—out of love—takes upon himself the consequences of what *you* have done. Forgiveness, therefore, always entails a sacrifice. The price you pay for your own liberation through another's sacrifice is that you in turn must be willing to liberate in the same way, irrespective of the consequences to yourself.

[45] Dag Hammarskjøld, *Markings*, trans. Leif Sjöberg and W. H. Auden, with an introduction by W. H. Auden (New York: Knopf, 1964), 197.

This clear-sighted text, confirmed by Dag Hammarskjøld's own life and death, sheds light on what is at stake when we speak of representative atonement: love forgives. But it cannot forgive the consequences of sin because they have long since put their brand on history. The chain of causality initiated by the sin continues on its own. If love is really love, then, it not only forgives but assumes responsibility for the consequences of what the other has done. And that costs something. It cannot be done without sacrifice.

And it can only succeed when many work to heal the consequences of others' sins. Dag Hammarskjøld points to that when he says that one's own liberation obligates one to give oneself for the liberation of others. Thus begins a new chain of causality, one that works against the chain created by sin.

When the New Testament tradition speaks of Jesus' atoning death it means that through his death—a death entirely *for others*, self-emptying to the utmost, *agapē* in the most radical sense—he has broken through the web of evil in the world and created a new basis on which it is possible to work off the consequences of sin.

Thus Jesus' death does not effect a magical redemption that is conveyed to those in need of redemption in a mysterious and arcane way. That Jesus died for our sins does not mean that we ourselves need no longer die to sin. His death is not a substitutionary action; it is the catalyst and enabling of a process of liberation that continues. But the social basis on which it continues is the eschatological people of God. It began with the creation of the Twelve, but it was only with Jesus' self-surrender for the sake of Israel, even to death, that the new chain of causality was forged and redemption and liberation are bestowed on the world once and for all. The Fourth Evangelist says it in a penetrating image:

> *Standing near the cross of Jesus were his mother, and his mother's sister, Mary the wife of Clopas, and Mary Magdalene. When Jesus saw his mother and the disciple whom he loved standing beside her, he said to his mother, "Woman, here is your son!" Then he said to the disciple, "Here is your mother!" And from that hour the disciple took her into his own home.* (John 19:25-27)

The scene may certainly have been intended to legitimate the Beloved Disciple as a witness to the tradition, but there is something more fundamental here as well: Jesus founds a "new family," that is, the basis on which people who in fact have nothing whatsoever to do with one another can join together in unconditional solidarity. It is the place where true reconciliation with God and one another is possible. But people cannot create this new possibility for themselves. It has to come from the cross. It had to be instituted by the death of Jesus, and Jesus' death must remain a living thing in the form of being-made-present in the newly instituted togetherness.

The basic model for this event was already laid down in the Old Testament: forgiveness of sins and a place of reconciliation were given *by God*: in spatial terms with the temple and the mercy seat on the ark (Exod 25:17) and in temporal terms on the great Day of Atonement (Lev 16:29-34). But Israel must enter into this "space" and "time" with its readiness for repentance, for reconciliation, for responsive love. In this way the "consequences of sin"—the webs of evil and guilt that arise out of sin—are worked off. The "basic model" for God's liberating and saving action was thus already given in the Old Testament. But now Jesus himself stood in place of the temple, and in place of the many days of atonement there is the one day on which he gave himself for the many.

We need to remember that in Jesus' death his message about the *basileia* attained its utmost depth. When, at the Last Supper, he interpreted his approaching death as a representative atonement, he did not withdraw his previous proclamation of God's mercy; instead, he was actually laying the ground for the social reality of that mercy. God is not content simply to forgive; in the death of Jesus God gives the place in which not only sin but also its consequences can be removed.

Still, in view of Jesus' previous preaching his death reveals something else as well: it shows in the clearest possible light the hidden and lowly form of the reign of God. That reign will not come without persecution and sacrifice; indeed, it will not come without daily dying.

What had always echoed in Jesus' preaching comes fully into the light through his death: the *basileia* demands letting-happen and self-surrender; it cannot come without pure receptivity, and the reception is always also a suffering. The reign of God comes precisely where Jesus himself can do no more: when he hands himself over and surrenders himself for God's reality.

Thus the idea of the reign of God undergoes an ultimate clarification and intensification through Jesus' death. It will no longer be possible to speak of that concept without speaking at the same time of the death of Jesus. That changes nothing about the overflowing fullness of the reign of God as we have spoken about it in previous chapters, but that fullness comes only in and through a daily dying.

Does that take back everything said in this book about the all-transforming power of the reign of God? We used words like "cataclysm," "revolution," and "changing the world." No, none of that is undone! It is all still true. But the world-change that God is effecting in the midst of history does not happen as a drama on an open stage. It happens God's way—as a tiny amount of sourdough transforms a great quantity of flour (Luke 13:20-21). It is likewise true of the reign of God: a growing thing makes no noise. The coming of the reign of God happens quietly, unflappably, and doggedly. It happens everywhere when people believe in Jesus Christ, hope for everything from him, let go of themselves and follow him.

70. Toward the Eschatological Feast (Mark 14:25)

The Passover celebration was, from the beginning, a *retrospect* on Israel's rescue from Egypt (Exod 12:1-14; Deut 16:1-8). So the Passover meal was a memorial meal—"memorial" being understood, of course, as an ever-new making-present. But in Jesus' time the festival celebration also included a *prospect* of the coming of the Messiah, for it ended with a psalm sequence (Mark 14:26) concluding with Psalm 118,[46] which was interpreted messianically, especially in verse 26:

> *Blessed is the one who comes in the name of the* Lord*!*

Thus the Passover night had also become a celebration that made present the redemption that was to come. That also helps us to understand why Jesus would have laid out the interpretation of his death during the celebration of *this* night above all.

Thus the theme of the "Messiah" was certainly present at that evening meal: the joy that Messiah would come soon, the hope for liberation. Jesus, however, did not use the word "Messiah" at this celebration. Evidently here still, as previously, he was reticent about using that inadequate title of dignity for himself. Even in the words of institution he speaks only indirectly of his authority. Obviously it

[46] For an extended discussion see Joachim Jeremias, *The Eucharistic Words of Jesus* (see n. 31 above), 257–60.

was present. Ultimately he defines his imminent death as the restoration and renewal of the covenant that God once made with Israel at Sinai. That is immense in itself; nevertheless, here again everything remains indirect and veiled. That is the case even in the single saying in which, at this last meal, Jesus looks directly to the future:[47]

> Amen, I tell you:
> I will never again drink of the fruit of the vine until that day
> when I drink it new in the reign of God. (Mark 14:25)

It has, in fact, been said that Jesus appears in these words "as the master of table and host in the future kingdom."[48] But nothing of that can be seen. Here again Jesus puts himself completely in the background. What he says is, first of all, a prophecy of his death, yet, just like the words of institution, this so-called "eschatological prospect" also goes far beyond a mere prophecy of death. It speaks Jesus' imperturbable confidence *that he will take part in the feast in the coming reign of God.*

Certainly what Jesus says is more than a hope, more than an anxious expectation. The festive meal in the coming reign of God will take place. No one can prevent God from bringing that reign into being. Still, there appears in this word of the Lord as in so many others what I have pointed to again and again: the reign of God has already come in Jesus' preaching and deeds of power; it happened in everything he did and taught. But its pure and unclouded visibility is still in the future. As in the Our Father ("your kingdom come"), so also here Jesus speaks of the "perfected form" of the reign of God. That is still to come.

[47] The logion in Mark 14:25 follows immediately after the words of institution over the wine. Matthew took the *logion* almost word for word from Mark, and its positioning as well (Matt 26:29). In Luke, however, the *logion* is in another place and in a rather extensively altered wording, namely, *before the words of institution*. Instead of "until that day when I drink it new in the reign of God," Luke writes: "until the reign of God comes" (Luke 22:18). There it is the conclusion to Luke 22:14-17, a text hotly discussed by exegetes. I will pass over all the tradition- and literary-critical questions associated with Luke 22:14-17—including the question whether Mark 14:25 or Luke 22:18 has the more original version. The content-variations between the two versions are insignificant. I consider Mark 14:25 more concrete and therefore earlier.

[48] Martin Hengel and Anna Maria Schwemer, *Jesus and Judaism* (see part 1, n. 4 above), 619.

And as on previous occasions Jesus speaks here also of that perfected form in the image of a meal. Compare only Luke 13:29 // Matthew 8:11 and Luke 22:30. It is true that Jesus was always sparing in his description of the coming reign of God. He did not project any sentimental images; instead, he preferred to begin to anticipate what is to come in the reality of now and today. He only allowed himself, on a very few occasions, to use the image of the meal, and as our *logion* shows he even shrank the meal to the act of drinking wine. Thus the image he uses here for the coming meal in the reign of God is one filled with abundant life.

In Mark's and Matthew's accounts our *logion* comes immediately after the words of institution, directly following the words that are the basis of the Christian eucharistic celebration. Every Eucharist thus acquires an unstoppable dynamic impetus toward the future. This is clear, moreover, not only in Mark and Matthew but also in the words of Paul when he adds to his own Last Supper tradition: "for as often as you eat the bread and drink the cup, you proclaim the Lord's death *until he comes*" (1 Cor 11:26). The agenda for the Eucharist in the *Didachē* reveals the same openness toward the return of Christ; it ends with *Marana tha* ("come, Lord Jesus!"); cf. also 1 Corinthians 16:22; Revelation 22:20. Since the introduction of the new *Missale Romanum* of 1970 the eucharistic celebration in the Roman Catholic Church has at last returned to the custom of clearly proclaiming the eschatological dynamic that was already present in Mark 14:25:

> We proclaim your death, O Lord,
> and profess your resurrection
> until you come in glory.

I began this book with the question: what were the first words Jesus spoke in "direct discourse" in the individual Gospels? In Mark they were:

> The time is fulfilled, and the reign of God has come near;
> [therefore:] repent, and believe in [this] gospel! (Mark 1:15)

Now, at the end of this book, we may similarly ask: what were the last words Jesus spoke before his death? In Mark and Matthew they are:

> My God, my God,
> why have you forsaken me? (Mark 15:34 // Matt 27:46)

Those words are an elemental cry for help—and they are quite often interpreted as an expression of despair. Thus Rudolf Bultmann, after a meager listing of the supposedly certain facts of Jesus' life, concludes by speaking also of Jesus' death and writes:

> How or whether Jesus made sense of them, this we cannot know. We must not conceal the possibility that he broke down completely.[49]

Bultmann was certainly not demeaning Jesus. His remarks are only for the purpose of undergirding his basic thesis: that one may approach Jesus not through historical arguments but solely through the *kerygma*. The present book does not concede that there is an unbridgeable gap between history and *kerygma*. It cannot end without saying a clear "no" to this and similar interpretations of Jesus' last words. Jesus did not end his life in despair. The quoted "My God, my God" is the beginning of Psalm 22. Evidently Jesus recited that psalm, in a voice others could hear, as his dying prayer. In those days no one prayed silently; prayer was spoken aloud.

And Jesus did not speak only the beginning of Psalm 22 but the whole of it, for one of those standing near the cross said "he is calling for Elijah" (Mark 15:35). That was nothing but a misunderstanding or a mocking parody of *eli attā* from the middle of the psalm (Ps 22:11). *Eli attā* means "You are my God" and is thus an affirmation of trust and assent, but it could be misunderstood as *Elijjā tā*, "Elijah, come!" Elijah was appealed to as one who helps those in mortal danger. Misunderstanding or mockery? We can leave that question open.

But if Jesus prayed the whole psalm he also spoke its final words. The whole psalm presumes a *todah*, a temple worship service with a

[49] Rudolf Bultmann, "Das Verhältnis der urchristlichen Christusbotschaft zum historischen Jesus," SHAW.PH 3 (1960): 11–12. Translation LMM. Cf. Bultmann, *History of the Synoptic Tradition*, 273.

thanksgiving offering. In such a (private) service the one praying first described to friends and relatives the mortal danger that had been faced and then praised God who had granted rescue from it. That last part, in Psalm 22, sounds like this:

> *You have rescued me.*
> *I will declare your name to my brethren;*
> *in the midst of the congregation I will praise you:*
> *Praise the* L*ORD*, *you that fear him!*
> *stand in awe of him, O offspring of Israel;*
> *all you of Jacob's line, give glory!*
> *For he does not despise nor abhor the poor in their poverty;*
> *neither does he hide his face from them;*
> *but when they cry to him he hears them. . . .*
> *The poor shall eat and be satisfied,*
> *and those who seek the* L*ORD shall praise him:*
> *"May your heart live for ever!"*
> *All the ends of the earth shall remember and turn to the* L*ORD;*
> *and all the families of the nations shall bow before him.*
> *For* **dominion** *belongs to the* L*ORD;*
> *he rules over the nations.*
> *[All the mighty on earth—they* **eat and bow down in worship***];*[50]
> *all who go down to the dust fall before him.* (Ps 22:21-24, 26-29, BCP alt.)

Jesus died in that assurance. When he spoke Psalm 22 as his dying prayer—certainly faltering and struggling for breath—he was able, in the end, even to repeat the two key concepts from our *logion* in Mark 14:25: the reign of God and the festive banquet of the nations.

[50] Heb. (conjecturally) "All the fat ones have eaten." —Trans.

Closing Reflections

In nearly every one of the seventy chapters of this book the question had to be asked: what was the original wording of the Jesus-saying now under discussion? After all, many of these *logia* come to us in the four Gospels in different versions. Often we even had to seek the probable wording of a *logion* in a totally hypothetical text—that is, in the so-called Sayings Source. In every case it appeared that the evangelists quite often made changes to the Jesus-sayings they were looking at—or the change might have happened in the process of tradition before them. All that made the interpretation exciting but also sometimes difficult.

That may have disappointed some readers. Does theology, or Christian faith, really have to grapple with such questions? Can't we just interpret the text as we have it? Can't we trust it in faith? Is there really any need for this tedious discernment, questioning, and reconstruction?

In essence the answer is easy. If Jesus were nothing but a myth—a fictional figure "who never was but always is,"[1] thus never really existed but is timelessly present as an interpretation of the world and human existence and offers a variety of meanings—then we would not need any historical inquiries. We could simply interpret the world in light of that mythical truth and be comforted. Historical criticism would be meaningless; it would actually destroy the myth.

[1] This famous quotation is from the Neoplatonist Sallust, from his writing "On the Gods and the World" (chap. 4). The exact quotation is: "Now these things [that the myths of the gods tell] never happened, but always are." Sallust was a close friend of the emperor Julian "the Apostate" (331–363 CE). In opposition to the attacks of Christian theologians on the Greek myths of the gods he interprets those sometimes offensive stories as statements about the eternal divine in the world and how to attain to it.

And if Jesus, together with what he did and experienced, were a fairytale figure something similar would apply: we would listen as the fairytale was told, be shocked at the brutality of the wicked and delighted at the cleverness and charm of the principal figures, but above all we would be glad that, in the end, the outcome was bad for the wicked and happy for the good. We would not need to care about how the fairytale came to be, who first told it, and who gave it its final form. All that matters in a fairytale is that it has an inner truth, is properly structured, and is well told.

It is quite different with Jesus. He is neither a fairytale nor a myth. The church's dogmatic theology says of him that he is "truly human," and the Prologue to John's Gospel says that in him "the *logos* of God was made flesh" (John 1:14). "Flesh"—that is, here is someone with body, soul, and spirit, someone who belongs fully to the world, who has a particular time, a particular history, a particular nation. Concretely: Jesus was a Jew, lived in first-century Palestine, and grew up within the lower middle class—very probably in a deeply believing Jewish family. Thus, because he is truly human, he was also subject to real history with all its uncertainties, imponderables, irregularities, and surprises.

Obviously all that is likewise true of the words he spoke. They have not been preserved for us shining and untouched; they share in the rips and wounds of human communication: for example, being misunderstood by people who hear them; the concrete circumstances in which a particular saying was uttered not being recorded; texts being located in new, totally altered situations and thereby deprived of their original meaning; even that a person's important statements are simply lost. In short: even the words of Jesus have been and are exposed to all the dangers to which human language is subject.

For me it is a small miracle that, in spite of that difficult background, the words of Jesus open a whole world to those who examine them with historical-critical methods. There are many more than seventy sayings to be found. Seventy *logia* are a selection, a prescribed limit. There are many more. And that is unusual. We have received a great many books from antiquity, many of them written by important authors and with highly significant content. But here we are faced with something entirely different: a considerable number of "sayings" of a single person that were at first transmitted altogether by word of mouth and at the same time are authentic. In that respect alone Jesus' words are a phenomenon.

It is true that in Greek and Roman antiquity, in the ancient Near East, and especially in the Hebrew Bible and Jewish literature there are a great many collections of sayings, but in part these collected "sentences" are not genuine "sayings." Quite often they are statements derived from literary works—for example, Menander's *Comedies*—and therefore they are *written* compositions. Or they may be proverbs of altogether unknown origin that were subsequently attached to a familiar name. The prime example in the Jewish scriptures is Solomon.

The closest cousins to Jesus' sayings are the words of the Hebrew prophets—not only as regards their linguistic and theological profile but also in the mode of their transmission: first oral tradition, then written. Certainly we cannot exclude the possibility that prophets cooperated with scribes or that they themselves wrote down the words they received. (Isaiah 30:8 speaks of such an action.) We know of nothing like that in Jesus' case.

What is decisive, however, is that as regards both the *form* and the *content* of his sayings Jesus is far superior to the precepts of wisdom and popular advice for living in most of the ancient sayings collections. The unusually high number of striking, well-honed, and vivid sayings we have from Jesus speak a completely different theological language than the often trivial proverbs in most ancient collections of sayings; moreover, they offer us a sharply drawn picture of Jesus himself, so that we really can know what he wanted and who he was. Even if we apply only some of the *logia* we have from him, how they gleam with the message about God, and in what a perfect form! And all that in spite of the circumstances of ancient tradition we just spoke about!

The image of Jesus that is given even through his *logia* need not be summarized again in these closing remarks. It is enough to forget all the interpretation and simply read Jesus' words again and let them soak in. Perhaps then the reader can even understand why, with a few exceptions, I have not used *reconstructed* texts as a basis, but almost always have kept to those in the Gospels themselves. That was meant to make clear that the true, genuine Jesus is the Jesus of the Gospels, the one in whom the church believes. I cannot and may not believe in a historical reconstruction but only in the living Christ of the Gospels—that is, of the church that proclaims him.

Why is that so? Because we can only vaguely grasp the nature and thus also the mystery of a human being. That applies to every person without exception, even a child who is still not a fully-formed human being but already gazes at us with shining eyes. It is true of our mothers and fathers. Often it is only after their death that we understand what they really have been for us. It is true even of one's spouse. What a joy it is that spouses remain a mystery to one another, each a person one can only encounter in trust and love! It must be all the more so with Jesus Christ. Ultimately he can only be experienced through intimations—that is, in our experience of those who have followed him in the confidence of faith, which means in the believing experience of the church.

That is the fundamental presupposition of this book, and on that basis it should be clear that there can be no yawning gulf between the church's faith in Christ and sober historical reconstruction. The two need and enhance each other. Faith needs historical critique, because Christian faith is a radically rational belief. It wants nothing to do with speculations, pipedreams, and ideologies. But historical criticism requires the faith of the church so that it may not fall victim to private prejudices or prior judgments based on ideology.

Now having arrived nearly at the end of this book, I must issue another warning. "Jesus' most important words"—not only are many *logia* missing, but so are all of Jesus' parables and the multiple texts that tell of his mighty deeds. We have to keep that in mind. "Sayings" or "*logia*" are characterized by a shapely and sharply honed form. The content often matches the form. They are meant to disturb, to urge, to tear off the masks behind which we hide ourselves. We have observed that rigorous character in many of Jesus' sayings—but it is not the whole Jesus. Above all his parables, such as the ones about the lost son (Luke 15:11-32) or the lost drachma (Luke 15:8-10), show us a very different Jesus, one who pursues the lost with mercy and an abundance of joy.

Every author who writes a book is aware that not everything is predetermined. Things develop: some fade, others emerge more and more clearly—a lot must be shortened while other aspects prove more and more important. In this book there are three things that came ever more powerfully to the fore and that have surprised even me the most.

The first is the current actuality of Jesus. We live in a time when violence is increasing: the power of worse and worse weapons that at the same time are more and more refined; the arrogance of people-despising, shameless dictators (as I am writing this the Russian President Vladimir Putin has attacked Ukraine); even in Western democracies there are sharper and sharper contrasts and oppositions between hostile groups that are no longer willing to compromise; and waves of hatred, disinformation, calumny, and destruction of reputations are swelling in the new social media (but not only there). Jesus stands firmly and absolutely against violence, against any kind of lust for power, against every untruth. Everything, then, depends on whether world society will follow him, imitating his fundamental stance, or not. More precisely: everything depends on whether the church will follow him with renewed obedience, because only in that way can the world follow him.

The second thing that emerged for me more and more clearly is the unexampled decisiveness with which Jesus distanced himself from everything "normal" in society.

- It is normal to be in solidarity with one's friends and to despise one's enemies or to hurt them when possible. Jesus demands that his followers love even their enemies (Matt 5:44).
- It is normal to hit back when someone attacks us. Jesus demands that his followers—notice: his followers, not the state—turn the other cheek (Matt 5:39).
- It is normal for us to form a critical opinion about everyone we encounter and to spread it whenever the occasion arises. Jesus asks his followers: "Why do you see the speck in your neighbor's eye . . . ?" (Matt 7:3-5).
- It is normal to secure a good place everywhere and on all occasions, one that matches our self-image and shows *who* we are. Jesus tells us to "go and sit down at the lowest place" (Luke 14:10).

What Jesus demands are behaviors that are simply not normal—and not only are they not normal: we say they are out of touch with everyday life and are impractical, basically impossible; and not only are they impossible, they would debase a person.

What Jesus calls for is, in fact, humanly impossible (Mark 10:27). It is even profoundly shocking—especially for a society in which "self-determination" is the most sacred thing and "self-surrender" in the sense of Mark 8:34 is a joke. Still, the behaviors he asks of us are not eternal precepts of wisdom. They are directly connected to the coming of the reign of God. That approaching realm changes everything. It means upheaval. It makes possible what is impossible because it is pure grace (Mark 4:26-29). It creates a new way of being together *in contrast* to the familiar, the ordinary, what is always usual. And this new being-together, this new community, has a clearly defined place: the people of God, the eschatological Israel, the church.

Israel has always fought for this contrast. The Different, the New, the Overturning of all things had already begun when God called Abraham and his family out of his land, away from his relatives and the household of his father and mother, to a land that for the moment was pure promise (Gen 12:1-3). The revolution continued as God called Israel out of Egypt so that it might not conform itself to the structures of a "theocracy." So it continued. Again and again individuals or small groups in Israel rose up and, without regard for themselves, sought the social will of their God and, when necessary, distanced themselves from the religious and political practices of their surroundings. The pinnacle of that ever-renewed awakening was Jesus. He was the goal and at the same time the end point of a long journey within Israel.

If the church wants to follow Jesus today it cannot avoid being a *contrast* to many things in today's society.[2] A church that wants only to be dialogical, communicative, discursive, evolutionary, without boundaries, practicing partnership, tolerant of everything, but above all "compatible" with everything around it and thereby ignores its own roots will destroy itself. It is true that the church must test everything in the world and hold to what is good (1 Thess 5:21), but first and above all it must seek what Jesus commanded it and strive to live it within its own ranks. "To be like other nations" was one of

[2] For the debate on "church as contrast-society" cf. Gerhard Lohfink, *Wie hat Jesus Gemeinde gewollt? Kirche im Kontrast*, rev. ed. (Stuttgart: Katholisches Bibelwerk, 2015), 172–88, 219–27.

Israel's oldest temptations (1 Sam 8:20). It is still a fundamental hazard to the church as well.

But now, at last, for the third thing that has impressed me ever more strongly as I sought to understand Jesus' words. That is Jesus' majestic dignity, underlying every word he spoke. Recall just one example from chapter 60: in the last centuries before Christ the promise of the "gathering of Israel from throughout the Diaspora" increasingly became a central description of salvation, comparable to the rescue from Egypt that is Israel's primal credo. As once out of Egypt, so again will God lead this people, God's people, out from among the nations "with a mighty hand and an outstretched arm" (Ezek 20:34) and gather it once more. In this way the eschatological "gathering" of the people of God becomes ever more clearly a fundamental statement about God, God's will to save and sanctify God's people—even independently of a summoning from throughout the Diaspora (Isa 56:8). When Jesus dares to say that it is he who gathers Israel (Luke 11:23; 13:34), within the statement lies a colossal claim; Jesus thus, quite as a matter of course, attributes to himself a deed that in the Old Testament and early Judaism was reserved for God alone.

When the church confesses that Jesus is not only truly human but also truly God, that means he is the perfect image of God, God's definitive word, God's never-to-be-revoked deed of salvation for this world. That is certainly not a shining robe that the church later hung on Jesus; it rests on the majestic claim that revealed itself, modestly, discreetly, and yet clearly, in every one of the seventy sayings of Jesus we have spoken of in this book.

To the God of Jesus Christ, who has told us everything in Jesus, who has spoken God's whole reality in him, be praise and honor forever. Amen.

Acknowledgments

First of all I thank my brother Norbert. He read the entire book and suggested a whole series of improvements. Incidentally, we are often mistaken for one another: I receive missives meant for him and vice versa. It is really quite simple: he is the older of the two of us and therefore chose the Old Testament as his *métier*; I, as the younger, got the New Testament. The younger thanks the elder with all his heart.

Another important helper in the composition of this book was my friend Marius Reiser, formerly professor of New Testament in Mainz. There is probably not a single place in this book where serious exegetical choices had to be made that was not the subject of a telephone discussion between the two of us. I remember those conversations, in which I learned a lot, with the greatest pleasure.

As so often, at this point I again thank my reliable helper Hans Pachner, who collected important written resources for me; then Raphael Jaklitsch and Gerd Block, my IT specialists who were much more reliable than my computer, which is overdue for retirement; and also Dr. Bruno Steimer of Herder, who supported this book, like so many others, with his abilities and untiring readiness to help.

Obviously fond greetings go also to Francesa Bressan in Freiburg, in the Foreign Rights division at Herder. Every year I am grateful for her competence and attentiveness as new translations of my books appear. *Di nuovo mille grazie, Francesca*!

Thanks are also due once again to the Rev. Dr. Linda M. Maloney, who has translated this book into English so clearly and reliably, as she has so many others. The same hearty thanks to Hans Christoffersen, editorial director at Liturgical Press, for his continued interest and fruitful cooperation.

This time Elisabeth Hagmaier read and corrected my manuscript. She has the eye of a teacher who doesn't miss much, and she is as precise in her corrections as she is in performing with a string quartet. I thank her most sincerely for the time she devoted to this book alongside her professional duties.

And now, finally, to all those who have accompanied me through the last thirty-five years in faith and in brotherly and sisterly community. Without that I could not truly have understood many things in Sacred Scripture. God's blessing on you all!

Gerhard Lohfink

Works Cited

Albertz, Rainer. "Hintergrund und Bedeutung des Elterngebots im Dekalog." *ZAW* 90 (1978): 348–74.

Austin, John L. *How to Do Things with Words.* Cambridge: Harvard University Press, 1962.

Bauer, J. B. "Echte Jesusworte?" in W. Cornelis van Unnick et al., *Evangelien aus dem Nilsand*, 108–50. Frankfurt: Heinrich Scheffler, 1960.

Betz, Hans Dieter. *The Sermon on the Mount*. Hermeneia. Minneapolis: Fortress Press, 1995.

Beutler, Johannes. "Ihr seid das Salz des Landes (Mt 5,13)." In *Nach den Anfängen fragen. FS Gerhard Dautzenberg*, edited by Cornelius P. Mayer, Karlheinz Müller, and Gerhard Schmalenberg, 85–94. GSTR 8. Gießen: Selbstverlag des Fachbereichs, 1994.

Blinzler, Josef. "Εἰσὶν εὐνοῦχοι." *ZNW* 48 (1957): 254–70.

Blundell, Mary Whitlock. *Helping Friends and Harming Enemies: A Study in Sophocles and Greek Ethics.* Cambridge: Cambridge University Press, 1989.

Bösen, Willibald. *Galiläa als Lebensraum und Wirkungsfeld Jesu. Eine zeitgeschichtliche und theologische Untersuchung.* Freiburg: Herder, 1985.

Bosold, Iris. *Pazifismus und prophetische Provokation. Das Grußverbot Lk 10,4b und sein historischer Kontext*. SBS 90. Stuttgart: Katholisches Bibelwerk, 1978.

Braulik, Georg. "Der blinde Fleck—das Gebot, den Fremden zu lieben. Zur sozialethischen Forderung von Deuteronomium 10,10." In *Menschenrechte und Gerechtigkeit als bleibende Aufgaben. Beiträge aus Religion, Theologie, Ethik, Recht und Wirtschaft. FS für Ingeborg Gabriel*, edited by Irene Klissenbauer, et al., 41–63. Göttingen: Vandenhoeck & Ruprecht, 2020.

Bultmann, Rudolf. *Theology of the New Testament*. Vol. 1. Translated by Kendrick Grobel. New York: Scribners, 1955.

———. "Das Verhältnis der urchristlichen Christusbotschaft zum historischen Jesus." SHAW.PH 3 (1960): 11–12.

———. *The History of the Synoptic Tradition*. Translated by John Marsh. New York: Harper & Row, 1963.

———. "New Testament and Mythology." In *New Testament and Mythology and Other Basic Writings*, edited and translated by Schubert M. Ogden. Philadelphia: Fortress Press, 1984.

Conzelmann, Hans. *An Outline of the Theology of the New Testament*. Translated by John Bowden. NTL. London: SCM, 1969.

Crüsemann, Frank. *The Torah: Theology and History of Old Testament Law*. Translated by Allen W. Mahnke. Minneapolis: Fortress Press, 1996.

Fiedler, Peter. "Sünde und Vergebung im Christentum." *Concilium* 10 (1974): 568–71.

———. *Jesus und die Sünder*. BBET 3. Frankfurt: Peter Lang, 1976.

Fiensy, David A., and James Riley Strange, eds. *Galilee in the Late Second Temple and Mishnaic Periods*. 2 vols. Minneapolis: Fortress Press, 2015.

Fritzsche, Carl Friedrich August. *Evangelium Matthaei*. Leipzig: Fleischer, 1826.

Fuchs, Ernst. *Studies of the Historical Jesus*. Translated by Andrew Scobie. London: SCM, 1964.

Gass, Erasmus. "'Heilige sollt ihr werden. Denn heilig bin ich, JHWH, euer Gott.' Gott, Mensch, und Nächster in Lev 19,11-18." In *Menschliches Handeln und Sprechen im Horizont Gottes. Aufsätze zur biblischen Theologie*, 288–323. FAT 100. Tübingen: Mohr Siebeck, 2015.

Gese, Hartmut. "The Atonement." In *Essays on Biblical Theology*, translated by Keith Crim, 93–116. Eugene, OR: Wipf & Stock, 2018.

Gnilka, Joachim. *Das Matthäusevangelium* 1. HThKNT 1.1. Freiburg: Herder, 1986.

———. *Das Matthäusevangelium* 2. HThKNT 1.2. Freiburg: Herder, 1988.

Hammarskjøld, Dag. *Markings*. Translated by Leif Sjöberg and W. H. Auden, with an introduction by W. H. Auden. New York: Knopf, 1964.

Hengel, Martin. *War Jesus Revolutionär?* CwH 110. Stuttgart: Calwer Verlag, 1970. [English: *Was Jesus a Revolutionist?* Translated by William Klassen. Philadelphia: Fortress Press, 1971.]

———. "Jesus und die Tora." *TBei* 9 (1978): 152–72.

———. *Nachfolge und Charisma. Jesus und die Evangelien* series. Kleine Schriften 5. Edited by Claus-Jürgen Thornton. WUNT 21. Tübingen: Mohr Siebeck, 2007.

Hengel, Martin, and Anna Maria Schwemer. *Jesus and Judaism*. Translated by Wayne Coppins. Waco, TX: Baylor University Press, 2019.

Hesiod. *Works and Days* 353–54. Translated by Christopher Kelk. https://www.poetryintranslation.com.

Hoffmann, Paul. "Herrscher in oder Richter über Israel? Mt 19,28/Lk 22,28-30 in der synoptischen Überlieferung." In *Ja und nein. Christliche Theologie im Angesicht Israels. FS zum 70. Geburtstag von Wolfgang Schrage*, edited by Klaus Wengst and Gerhard Sass, 253–64. Neukirchen-Vluyn: Neukirchener Verlag, 1998.

———. "Menschensohn II." *LTK* 7. Freiburg: Herder, 2006.

Hoffmann, Paul, and Christoph Heil. *Die Spruchquelle Q. Studienausgabe, Griechisch und Deutsch*. Darmstadt: Wissenschaftliche Buchgesellschaft, 2002.

Holm-Nielsen, Svend. *Die Psalmen Salomos*. JSHRZ 4. Poetische Schriften. Gütersloh: Mohn, 1977. [English translation in this book based on Wright, R. B. "Psalms of Solomon." In *The Old Testament Pseudepigrapha* 2, edited by James H. Charlesworth, 639–70. Peabody, MA: Hendrickson, 1983.]

Hossfeld, Frank-Lothar, and Erich Zenger. *Psalms 2*. Translated by Linda M. Maloney. Hermeneia. Minneapolis: Fortress Press, 2005.

———. *Psalms 3*. Translated by Linda M. Maloney. Hermeneia. Minneapolis: Fortress Press, 2011.

Jeremias, Joachim. *The Parables of Jesus*. Translated by S. H. Hooke. New York: Scribners, 1955.

———. *The Eucharistic Words of Jesus*. Translated by Norman Perrin. New York: Scribner, 1966.

———. *New Testament Theology: The Proclamation of Jesus*. Translated by John Bowden. New York: Scribner, 1971.

Kant, Immanuel. *The Critique of Practical Reason*. Chicago: Encyclopaedia Britannica, 1952.

Keim, Theodor. *Geschichte Jesu nach den Ergebnissen heutiger Wissenschaft übersichtlich erzählt*. Zürich: Orell, Füßli, 1873.

Klein, Hans. *Das Lukasevangelium*. KEK 1, 3. Göttingen: Vandenhoeck & Ruprecht, 2006.

Lang, Bernhard. "Grußverbot oder Besuchsverbot? Eine sozialgeschichtliche Deutung von Lk 10:4b." *BZ* 26 (1982): 75–79.

Lohfink, Gerhard. "Eine alttestamentliche Darstellungsform für Gotteserscheinungen in den Damaskusberichten (Apg 9; 22; 26)." *BZ* 9 (1965): 246–57.

———. "Das Gleichnis vom Sämann (Mk 4,3–9)." *BZ* 30 (1986): 36–69.

———. *Wem gilt die Bergpredigt? Beiträge zu einer christlichen Ethik*. Freiburg: Herder, 1988.

———. *Does God Need the Church? Toward a Theology of the People of God*. Translated by Linda M. Maloney. Collegeville, MN: Liturgical Press, 1999.

———. *Jesus of Nazareth: What He Wanted, Who He Was*. Translated by Linda M. Maloney. Collegeville, MN: Liturgical Press, 2012.

———. *No Irrelevant Jesus: On Jesus and the Church Today*. Translated by Linda M. Maloney. Collegeville, MN: Liturgical Press, 2014.

———. *Wie hat Jesus Gemeinde gewollt? Kirche im Kontrast*. Rev. ed. Stuttgart: Katholisches Bibelwerk, 2015.

———. *Im Ringen um die Vernunft. Reden über Israel, die Kirche und die Europäische Aufklärung*. Freiburg: Herder, 2016.

———. *Is This All There Is? On Resurrection and Eternal Life*. Translated by Linda M. Maloney. Collegeville, MN: Liturgical Press, 2017.

———. *The Forty Parables of Jesus*. Translated by Linda M. Maloney. Collegeville, MN: Liturgical Press, 2021.

———. *Between Heaven and Earth: New Explorations of Great Biblical Texts*. Translated by Linda M. Maloney. Collegeville, MN: Liturgical Press, 2022.

Lohfink, Gerhard, and Ludwig Weimer. *Maria—nicht ohne Israel. Eine neue Sicht der Lehre von der Unbefleckten Empfängnis*. Freiburg: Herder, 2008.

Lohfink, Norbert. "'Israel' in Jes 49,3." In *Wort, Lied und Gottesspruch. FS für Joseph Ziegler*, edited by Josef Schreiner, 217–29. FB 2. Würzburg: Echter, 1972.

———. *Great Themes from the Old Testament*. Translated by Ronald Walls. Chicago: Franciscan Herald Press, 1981.

———. *Lobgesänge der Armen. Studien zum Magnificat, den Hodajot von Qumran, und einigen späten Psalmen*. SBS 143. Stuttgart: Katholisches Bibelwerk, 1990.

———. *Studien zur biblischen Theologie*. SBAB 16. Stuttgart: Katholisches Bibelwerk, 1993.

———. *In the Shadow of Your Wings: New Readings of Great Texts from the Bible*. Translated by Linda M. Maloney. Collegeville, MN: Liturgical Press, 2003.

Luz, Ulrich. *Matthew 1–7: A Commentary*. Translated by Wilhelm C. Linss. Minneapolis: Augsburg, 1989.

———. *Matthew 8–20*. Translated by James E. Crouch. Hermeneia. Minneapolis: Fortress Press, 2001.

Menke, Karl-Heinz. *Stellvertretung. Schlüsselbegriff christlichen Lebens und theologische Grundkategorie*. Einsiedeln: Johannes Verlag, 1991.

Moravcsik, G. "'Hund in der Krippe.' Zur Geschichte eines griechischen Sprichworts." *Acta Antiqua Academiae Scientiarum Hungaricae* 12 (1964): 77–86.

Origen. *De oratione* 15.1. Translated by William A. Curtis. https://ccel.org/ccel/origen/prayer/prayer.i.html.

Pesch, Rudolf. *Freie Treue. Die Christen und die Ehescheidung*. Freiburg: Herder, 1971.

———. *Das Markusevangelium* 2. HThKNT 2. Freiburg: Herder, 1977.

Philonenko-Sayar, Belkis, and Marc Philonenko. *Die Apokalypse Abrahams*. JSHRZ 5.5. Gütersloh: Gütersloher Verlagshaus, 2019.

Ratzinger, Joseph. *Called to Communion: Understanding the Church Today*. San Francisco: Ignatius Press, 1996.

Reiser, Marius. *Jesus and Judgment: The Eschatological Proclamation in Its Jewish Context*. Translated by Linda M. Maloney. Minneapolis: Fortress Press, 1997.

———. "Numismatik und Neues Testament." *Bib* 81 (2000): 457–88.

———. "Love of Enemies in the Context of Antiquity." *NTS* 47 (2001): 411–27.

———. *Sprache und literarische Formen des Neuen Testaments. Eine Einführung*. UTB 2197. Paderborn: Schöningh, 2001.

———. *Der unbequeme Jesus*. BTS 122. Neukirchen-Vluyn: Neukirchener Verlag, 2011.

———. "Ethik und Anthropologie in der Spruchweisheit Jesu." *TTZ* 126 (2017): 58–82.

———. "Jesus und das Geld." *SNTSU.A* 43 (2018): 187–201.

———. "Die Neugestaltung von Ehe und Familie im frühen Christentum." *TBei* 52 (2021): 109–20.

Rießler, Paul. *Altjüdisches Schrifttum außerhalb der Bibel.* Freiburg: Kerle, 1928.

Roberts, C. H. "The Kingdom of Heaven (Lk XVII.21)." *HTR* 41 (1948): 1–8.

Roloff, Jürgen. *Jesus*. 4th ed. Munich: Beck, 2007.

Rüstow, A. "*Entos Ymōn Estin*. Zur Deutung von Lukas 17,20-21." *ZNW* 51 (1960): 197–224.

Schmid, Josef. *Das Evangelium nach Markus*. RNT 2. 3rd ed. Regensburg: Pustet, 1954. [English: *The Gospel According to Mark*. Translated by Kevin Condon. Staten Island, NY: Alba House, 1968.]

———. *Das Evangelium nach Lukas*. RNT 3. Regensburg: Pustet, 1960.

Schmidkunz, Walter, ed. *I. Kant, Du kannst, denn du sollst. Vom Ethos der Pflicht. Münchner Lesebogen* series, no. 11. Munich: Münchner Buchverlag, 1942.

Schmithals, Walter. *Das Evangelium nach Markus 2. Kapitel 9,2–16,18*. ÖTK 2/2. Gütersloh: Gütersloher Verlagshaus Mohn, 1979.

Schniewind, Julius. *Das Evangelium nach Markus*. NTD 1. Göttingen: Vandenhoeck & Ruprecht, 1963.

———. *Das Evangelium nach Matthäus*. NTD 2. Göttingen: Vandenhoeck & Ruprecht, 1964.

Schockenhoff, Eberhard. *Kein Ende der Gewalt? Friedensethik für eine globalisierte Welt*. Freiburg: Herder, 2018.

Schramm, Tim, and Kathrin Löwenstein. *Unmoralische Helden. Anstößige Gleichnisse Jesu*. Göttingen: Vandenhoeck & Ruprecht, 1986.

Schürmann, Heinz. *Das Lukasevangelium. Erster Teil*. HThKNT 3.1. Freiburg: Herder, 1969.

———. *Das Lukasevangelium. Zweiter Teil*. HThKNT 3.2. Freiburg: Herder, 1994.

Sölle, Dorothee. *Stellvertretung. Ein Kapitel Theologie nach dem "Tode Gottes."* Stuttgart: Kreuz Verlag, 1982. [English: *Christ the Representative: An Essay in Theology after the "Death of God."* London: SCM, 1997.]

Stier, Fridolin. *Das Neue Testament.* Munich: Kösel; Düsseldorf: Patmos, 1989.

Strack, Hermann L., and Paul Billerbeck. *Kommentar zum Neuen Testament aus Talmud und Midrasch.* 9th ed. Munich: Beck, 1997.

Strobel, August. *Die Stunde der Wahrheit. Untersuchungen zum Strafverfahren gegen Jesus.* WUNT 21. Tübingen: Mohr Siebeck, 1980.

Stuhlmacher, Peter. *Der Brief an Philemon.* EKK 18. 2nd ed. Düsseldorf: Benziger; Neukirchen-Vluyn: Neukirchener Verlag, 1981.

———. *Biblical Theology of the New Testament.* Translated by Daniel Bailey. Grand Rapids: Eerdmans, 2018.

Theissen, Gerd. *The Gospels in Context: Social and Political History in the Synoptic Tradition.* Translated by Linda M. Maloney. Minneapolis: Fortress Press, 1998.

———. *The Religion of the Earliest Churches: Creating a Symbolic World.* Translated by John Bowden. Minneapolis: Fortress Press, 1999.

Theissen, Gerd, and Annette Merz. *The Historical Jesus: A Comprehensive Guide.* Translated by John Bowden. Minneapolis: Fortress Press, 1998.

Thesiger, Wilfred. *Arabian Sands.* London: Penguin, 1991.

Tiwald, Markus. *Kommentar zur Logienquelle.* Stuttgart: Kohlhammer, 2019. [English: *The Sayings Source: A Commentary on Q.* Translated by J. Andrew Doole. Stuttgart: Kohlhammer, 2020.]

Wolter, Michael. *Das Lukasevangelium.* Tübingen: Mohr Siebeck, 2008. [English: *The Gospel According to Luke.* 2 vols. Translated by Wayne Coppins and Christoph Heilig. Waco, TX: Baylor University Press, 2016.]

Zager, Werner. "Die theologische Problematik des Sühnetodes Jesu. Exegetische und dogmatische Perspektiven." In *Jesus und die frühchristliche Verkündigung. Historische Rückfragen nach den Anfängen*, 35–61. Neukirchen-Vluyn: Neukirchener Verlag, 1999.

Zenger, Erich. *Psalmen. Auslegungen 1. Mit meinem Gott überspringe ich Mauern.* Freiburg: Herder, 2011.

Index of Important Topics

There are passages in this book to which I want to call special attention because they are not printed as excursuses. Their page numbers are given in boldface in this index. The other numbers refer to important themes that recur throughout the book.

Index of Scriptural Passages

Numbers in boldface indicate passages that are the subject of a whole chapter.

Liturgical Table

With the aid of the following table the reader can see where the majority of the words of Jesus discussed in this book appear in the Sunday calendar of the Roman Catholic Church (Years A, B, and C). Corresponding occurrences in the *Revised Common Lectionary* are given in brackets. The liturgy for weekdays is not included. The numbers in the right-hand column refer to the individual chapters.

A	3 Advent [RCL Epiphany 3B]	2, 4
A	Ordinary Time 5 [RCL 18]	27
A	Ordinary Time 6 [RCL 1A]	30, 31, 32, 33, 35
A	Ordinary Time 7 [RCL 2A]	36
A	Ordinary Time 8 [RCL 3A]	42, 47
A	Ordinary Time 12	52
A	Ordinary Time 13 [RCL 9C, 18C, 8A]	16, 25, 29
A	Ordinary Time 15 [RCL 15C]	56
A	Ordinary Time 29	45
A	Ordinary Time 31 [RCL 26A]	23
B	Lent 1 [RCL Lent 1B]	1
B	Palm Sunday 5 [RCL Palm Sunday B]	53
B	Ordinary Time 7 [RCL 2B]	48
B	Ordinary Time 8 [RCL 3B]	8, 9
B	Ordinary Time 15	12
B	Ordinary Time 22 [RCL 17B]	44
B	Ordinary Time 24 [RCL Lent 2B; 19B]	26
B	Ordinary Time 26 [RCL 21B]	28, 34
B	Ordinary Time 27 RCL 22B]	46
B	Ordinary Time 28 [RCL 23B]	22, 43
B	Ordinary Time 29 [RCL 24B]	24, 68
B	Corpus Christi [RCL Palm Sunday B]	69, 70

C	Passion Gospel for Palm Sunday	67
C	Ordinary Time 6 [RCL 1C; All Saints]	7
C	Ordinary Time 7 [RCL 2C]	37, 40
C	Ordinary Time 8	41
C	Ordinary Time 9	49
C	Ordinary Time 13 [RCL 8C]	17, 18, 19
C	Ordinary Time 14 [RCL 9C]	6, 11, 12, 13, 14
C	Ordinary Time 15	3
C	Ordinary Time 17	15, 39
C	Ordinary Time 19 [RCL 14C]	66
C	Ordinary Time 20 [RCL 7A, 15C]	51, 64
C	Ordinary Time 23 [RCL 18C]	21
C	Corpus Christi [RCL Palm Sunday B]	69